SPAIN
1001 Sights

An Archaeological
and Historical Guide

SPAIN
1001 Sights

An Archaeological and Historical Guide

James M. Anderson

UNIVERSITY OF CALGARY PRESS
ROBERT HALE • LONDON

© 1991 James M. Anderson. All rights reserved
First published in Canada 1991 and Great Britain 1992

University of Calgary Press　　　　Robert Hale Limited
2500 University Drive N.W.　　　　 Clerkenwell House
Calgary, Alberta, Canada T2N 1N4　Clerkenwell Green
　　　　　　　　　　　　　　　　　London EC1R OHT

Canadian Cataloguing in Publication Data
Anderson, James M. (James Maxwell), 1933-
　Spain, 1001 sights

　Includes bibliographical references and index.

　ISBN 0-919813-93-3 (University of Calgary Press)
　ISBN 0-7090-4850-5 (Robert Hale Limited)

　1. Spain—Description and travel—1981-
—Guide-books. 2. Spain—Antiquities—Guide-books.
3. Excavations (Archaeology)—Spain—Guide-books.
4. Spain—History. I. Title.
DP14.A52 1991　　　914.6′04′83　　　C91-091703-5

Printed in Canada

This book has been published with the help of a grant from
the Alberta Foundation for the Literary Arts.

∞ This book is printed on acid-free paper.

Dedicated to

Virginia Anderson and Louise Lea

CONTENTS

Acknowledgements xi

Maps xiii

Preface xv

Introduction xix

Geography xxi

Part One: Background

1. Prehistory

Paleolithic period 3
Hispanic cave cultures: general distribution and chronology 4
Mesolithic or Middle Stone Age 5
Neolithic, Megalithic and Bronze Age Cultures 6
    Origins and cultural characteristics. 6
    Megalithic structures 7
    Chalcolithic period 7
    Bronze Age 8

2. Iron Age: Celts and Celtiberians

Early migrations 11
Distribution of Hispano-Celtic peoples 12
Cultural characteristics: economy 12
The Celtic legacy 14

3. The Iberians

Distribution of indigenous Iberian tribes 15
Cultural features, art and architecture 15
Necropoli and sanctuaries 16
Written documentation 17
Iberian and Basque 18
Tartessians 18
Intrusive cultures: Phoenicians, Carthaginians and Greeks 19
    Historical context 19
    Punic art 19
    Greek influence 20
Demise of the Iberian culture 21

4. Roman Spain

Military history 23
Economic factors 25
Architecture 25

Theatres, amphitheatres and circuses 26
Baths 26
Temples 27
Triumphal arches 27
Villas 27
Communications 28
Cities and towns 29
Aqueducts 30
Necropoli and funerary monuments 30
Decline of Roman Spain 31
The Roman legacy 31

5. Paleo-Christian and Early Christian Periods

Introduction and spread of Christianity 33
Art and architecture 34
Necropoli and sarcophogi 35
Mosaics 36
Germanic Spain 36
Visigothic migrations 37
Art and architecture 38
Visigothic legacy 39
Asturian churches and architecture 39
Rupestrian sanctuaries 40

6. Moslem Conquest

Military and political events 43
The Caliphate of Córdoba 44
The Taifas 45
The Almoravides and Almohades 45
Nasrid Granada 45
The Moslem legacy 46
Mozarabe architecture 46
Mudéjar architecture 48

7. Hispano-Jewish Communities 51

Part Two: Sights and Sites

Sources of Information, Conventions 58
Andalucía 59
Almería 60
Cádiz 65
Córdoba 70
Granada 75
Huelva 80
Jaén 84
Málaga 94

Sevilla 105
Gibraltar 111

Aragón 113
Huesca 114
Teruel 117
Zaragoza 125

Asturias 131
Oviedo 131

Cantabria 141
Santander 142

Castilla - La Mancha 149
Albacete 150
Ciudad Real 154
Cuenca 158
Guadalajara 162
Toledo 167

Castilla y León 175
Avila 176
Burgos 181
León 188
Palencia 193
Salamanca 197
Segovia 202
Soria 204
Valladolid 210
Zamora 212

Cataluña 215
Barcelona 216
Gerona 223
Lérida 230
Tarragona 234

Extremadura 239
Badajoz 240
Cáceres 245

Galicia 251
Coruña, La 252
Lugo 255
Orense 260
Pontevedra 264

Madrid, Comunidad de 269

Murcia 273

Navarra, Comunidad de 279

País Vasco 287
    Alava 288
    Guipúzcoa 295
    Viscaya 298

Rioja, La 301
    Logroño 301

Valenciana, Comunidad 307
    Alicante 308
    Castellón de la Plana 312
    Valencia 318

Suggested Routes 327

Glossary 339

Bibliography 345

Index of towns and villages 351

ACKNOWLEDGEMENTS

For assistance in Spain:

Dr. Blech of the German Institute of Archaeology, Madrid
Dimas Fernández-Galiano Ruiz, Director Museo Provincial, Guadalajara
Francisco Martínez Cabrera, Arqueólogo Municipal of Liria, Valencia
Marcelino Sanchez Ruiz, Director Escuela Taller de Ubeda, Jaén
Manuel Santonja Gómez, Director, Museo Arqueológico de Salamanca

Maribel and Fernando López, Alcalá de Henares, Madrid
Antonio Stolle Alvarez, Sacerdote, Wamba, Valladolid
Guillermo Moleno, Alcalá de Henares, Madrid
Sr y Sñra Javier Leguina, Villa de Cáparra, Cáceres
D. Manuel Cabello Janeiro, Ubrique, Cádiz
Fermín Ropero Jurado, Villanueva de Algaides, Málaga
Jordi Camats Farré, Tornabous, Lérida
Rudolf Langen, Málaga
Lazaro López Gil, La Rioja
Francisco Javier Lozano Martínez, Hellín, Albacete
Bartolomé Solek Cano, Alcalde de Antas, Almería
Rafael Martínez Cadórniga, and Abraham Martínez Ordóñez,
Villamartín de la Abadia, León.
Sr y Sñra Domingo García Aparicio, Mengibar, Jaén
José Faubel Lis, Alguacil Municipal, Liria, Valencia
Enrique Grandal Alvarez, Orense
Peter de Haven Biddle, Estepona, Málaga
Bill Mongar, Puerta Duquesa
Manuel Rodríguez Botía, Mula, Murcia
Sr y Sñra Agustín Moriche, Ciudad Rodrigo

Thanks are also due to the many hundreds of others who guided me along
the way.

Also for assistance and hospitality:

In Canada

Marie and Stanley Tumpach
Ginny and Jim Cathcart
Elaine Sorensen and Munroe MacPhee
Drs. Carol and Joel Prager
Dr. and Mrs. Tim Travers

In England

Nancy and Len Bowley
David Corre and Lisa Hamilton
Jill and Paul Killinger
Audrey and Bill Hall
June and Jeremy Ryan-Bell
Jack Bruce
Mary Ayton
Adrienne and Rex Wilkinson

In France

Françoise and Lucien Labedade
Dr. and Mme. Jean Larroque

In Germany

Dr. and Mrs. Jurgen Untermann, Köln

In U.S.A.

Anne and Gordon Anderson

Special thanks are due to my Research Assistant, Sheridan Anderson. Her unflagging enthusiasm from start to finish in dealing meticulously with a large assortment of facts, a myriad of details, and countless and sometimes strenuous visits to sites and archives, helped make this work possible.

Gratefully acknowledged here are the photographs provided by Siwan Anderson. All photographs and illustrations are copyright by the author.

The author also wishes to express his gratitude to the University of Calgary Press, and especially to Linda Cameron, Director, John King, Production Coordinator, Windsor Viney, Editor, and Brian Moorman, Cartographer.

MAPS

Regions of Spain 1
Provinces of Spain 2
General Distribution of Ancient Peoples in Spain 20
Andalucía 59
Aragón 113
Asturias 131
Cantabria 141
Castilla - La Mancha 149
Castilla y León 175
Cataluña 215
Extremadura 239
Galicia 251
Madrid, Comunidad de 269
Murcia 273
Navarra, Comunidad de 279
País Vasco 287
Rioja, La 301
Valenciana, Comunidad 307

PREFACE

Throughout the million or so years that the Hispanic peninsula has been inhabited, numerous cultures have come and gone, some identified only by vestigial traces of human remains and artifacts, others by monumental structures of enduring stone. From early Paleolithic cave dwellings, to megalithic burial tombs, fortified Iberian towns, the introduction of writing by Phoenicians and Greeks, the highly skilled engineering projects of the Romans, the appearance of Christianity and the subjugation of much of the peninsula by Germanic tribes, the kaleidoscopic array of cultural changes is, in this guidebook, here placed in perspective. The influences that shaped the Hispanic landscape appear to have been primarily of European and eastern Mediterranean provenance, although North Africa also played a part which reached its zenith in a later day when the peninsula was absorbed into the Moslem world.

This historical and archaeological guidebook to Spain introduces the reader and traveller to the very foundations of the modern state from the earliest period down to the Moslem conquest in the year A.D. 711. The historical perspective is given tangible substance by the identification and location of archaeological sites which relate to the periods in question. It is hoped that this book can be fruitfully employed as a field manual for travellers inclined to see all they can of the country, and as a handy reference for those who cannot visit the sites but who wish to know more of what Spain has to offer than can be found in the usual guide books.

Of the thousands of sites found in mainland Spain, some are exceedingly well preserved while others have all but disappeared. Those that are not protected by city, provincial or state authority are still subject to be lost through urban and holiday development. Even the sites that are protected may be ravaged by selfish hands. During the period of antiquity and the Middle Ages, people seeking treasure and the easy money that such treasures might bring on the open market tore the ancient cemeteries asunder, pillaged the tombs, smashed walls and monuments for anything of interest that might fetch a profit.

In the past, when all visible and easily accessible sites had been plundered, a period of neglect set in. The broken remains of great edifices (the Alhambra is a good example), dolmens, villas, necropoli, and castros were abandoned to the elements. The stones that were left were then often re-used to build nearby houses, churches and towns, or broken up and ejected from the fields to facilitate ploughing. Only monuments of utilitarian value such as important bridges, roads and aqueducts survived. Even priceless and beautiful prehistoric cave paintings have not been immune to irreplaceable loss. Often the precious painted figures have been obliterated by years of smoke from shepherds' fires, chiselled from the rock by souvenir hunters, doused with water to enhance their image on photographs, or defaced by graffiti.

Happily, in the latter half of the twentieth century a new official climate prevails. The damage done in previous times is being repaired by restoration projects all over the country whenever the money can be found, and ancient sites are beginning to almost resemble some of their old splendour. Similarly, many new excavations are in the planning stage awaiting the appropriate financing.

xv

But now a new threat has made itself felt in the form of the modern-day tomb robber with a metal detector which, in the hands of the present barbarian, is usurping the domain of the archaeologist and, as before, the precious artifacts are being torn from the ground and sold in the market place. The despoiler of historical sites does his clandestine work under cover of darkness or in remote, unguarded places.

There is still a great deal to see and enjoy in Spain, however, and new sites are being uncovered every year. On the other hand, some of the excavated sites are again covered over after the removal of artifacts, to preserve them from vandals and weather or, as may be the case, in order to construct a hotel or amusement park over them.

In this sense, this book can never be complete, nor entirely up to date. The unpredictable discovery of a Roman villa by a road-building crew, a sudden archaeological boardroom decision to excavate a site due to the proposed construction of a football stadium where previous surface finds were found (*excavación de urgencia*), or the drying up of funds to maintain a minor site entailing its re-covering, all make a definitive statement impossible.

For the inquisitive traveller there is frequently the problem of lack of directions. Information is often available concerning the approximate location of local sites and inquiries can be made, of course, in various places (see page 58), but most sites are not signposted, and those that are often present an initial indication on a highway, then leave the explorer to guess which way to go in a bewildering network of farm roads, paths, or open country.

Archaeological maps pinpoint sites in terms of degrees and minutes, but even if one is an experienced navigator they still fail to say if anything remains to be seen at a site. Often it is on a farm where the plough has turned up an artifact or two, or if anything remains on location it has been re-covered and lies under a field sown with wheat. To discover all this is time consuming and frustrating.

The purpose of this book is to assist the traveller in ascertaining what sites, and sights, lie along the route, their degree of accessibilty, what conditions may be expected, and how to find them. Their *raison d'être* is given when relevant. In some cases permission to enter is mandatory and must be obtained from local authorities, thus still entailing a visit to the Ayuntamiento, and often a guide is required. Many sites are fenced, but there are few of these that do not have holes in the wire big enough to step through. This never seems to invite trouble unless one is carrying a metal detector. At one large, unfenced site in the province of Granada the guardian of the ancient burial ground collected thousands of bottle caps from the local bars and strew them around the grounds to frustrate clandestine metal detecting operations. At another site in the province of Lérida a local gentleman saw me peering through the fence at the remains of an Iberian town, opened the padlocked gate by lifting it off the rusted-out hinges, and cordially invited me to enter.

For many, visiting sites is much more exhilarating than going to a museum where the sterile contents are cut off in time and place from the cultures that created them. Items may be of easy access, but there is no passion, no spirit, no haunting wind carressing the columns of a temple where a man or woman stood two thousand years ago praying to the gods. Museums never transport one back by emotive experience. Items neatly arranged and labelled under glass just do not seem to have that power. But almost every city and town in the country has a museum of some description for the deposit of local artifacts as well as sufficient descriptions of their holdings. This book is not a guide to museums and their contents, but rather a report on one great museum—Spain.

Of the fifty thousand or more sites in the country (there are over fourteen hundred in the relatively small province of Lugo, ca. 750 in Salamanca, etc.) only a small percentage offer something visible, palpable and interesting to the non-specialist since money for maintenance, vigilance, reconstruction and new discoveries is still pitifully inadequate.

As Spain is undergoing extensive highway development programs, the road directions given may not always be as accurate as one would like, and there may be better ways to approach a site than the directions presented; but it is hoped that enough information is given for the reader to identify the location of the place of interest and arrive with a minimum amount of delay.

There is a rule of thumb that can often be applied: if you know that the sought-after site is near but cannot quite pinpoint it, go to the hermitage that you may well see nearby or on the hill above you. It will probably be abandoned, but that is usually where the site is located. Churches were constructed in the midst of numerous ancient monuments to demonstrate the superiority of Christianity and to exorcise the pagan spirits that may inhabit the spot. Useful also for the builders was a good supply of already-cut stone.

Almost every tourist book on Spain devotes ample attention to the most spectacular attractions such as the Roman aqueduct at Segovia, the Arab Mosque of Córdoba and the Alhambra in Granada. While these are of great interest, they are not treated extensively here. Instead, the traveller is directed to the often "underdiscovered" sights not found in any detail, if at all, in guide books.

The time surveyed here begins with the first appearance of human cultures in Spain and terminates with the last of the major external forces that helped shape the cultural make-up of the country—that is, the Moslem communities of the Middle Ages. Some further comments are incorporated, however, concerning their continuing legacy in the form of Mudéjar architectual decoration. Similarly, Jewish society, distinct and separate, continued as a mostly intellectual force down to the closing decade of the fifteenth century, and its most important remains are mentioned up to that period.

Major influences after the tenth and eleventh centuries emanated from Europe and were responsible for the thousands of Romanesque churches, Gothic and Renaissance architecture, and other innovations that tended to remake Spain in the image of Europe. In this guide, the reader will find discussed those historical forces whose influences helped make Spain distinct from the rest of the Continent.

INTRODUCTION

Like many other nations, modern Spain was moulded by diverse events in which foreign cultural elements fused with those of autochthonous societies to establish a unique civilization. By the time of the reconquest of the Moslem territories by Christian forces, Spanish conventions were firmly established and no new great events came to disturb the balance. The character of the nation was formed.

The cultural forces that shaped Spain recede in time to the Paleolithic period of singular cave paintings in the Franco-Cantabrian area (already different from Europe and Africa where such early manifestations of cave paintings are unknown), and evolved with the aid of external stimuli through the mostly imported Neolithic, Bronze and Iron Ages.

Indigenous Iberians, Basques, Tartessians, and the little-known Asturians and Cantabrians, perhaps descendents of Bronze Age societies (there is no firm evidence that they were otherwise), were clearly influenced and modified by contact with Celts, Phoenicians, Greeks and later Carthaginians and Romans. The last laid the foundations for a new society conceived in the image of Rome. Except for the Basques, the other peoples faded from the scene as separate and unique social or political entities.

The most profound imported ideology was that of Christianity which made its appeareance on the Hispanic peninsula in the first century A.D. and rapidly strengthened, never relaxing its firm grip on the population. Through physical conquest and the offering of social benefits, Romans unified the disparate cultural substructure of the Hispanic tribes; through spiritual seduction offering desired psychological values, Christians gave them a specific and collective set of principles.

Of no great cultural impact, the Germanic tribes, who at first rendered asunder the already disintegrating Roman Empire, settled down to live in reasonable harmony with the Hispano-Romans. The Visigoths helped organize the religious administration of the country after their conversion from Arianism.

The appearance in A.D. 711 of a Moslem army, and the subsequent conquest of all but the northern fringe of the Iberian peninsula and the Pyrenean high country, interjected a religious and cultural wedge into Hispanic society which had a profound effect on the future of the country. This last great thrust of an alien intrusive element resulted in a Hispano-Roman-Visigothic-Semitic society and a nation of distinctive and salient features unparalleled in Europe.

To piece together the multiple cultural facets that shaped the Hispanic peninsula, it is necessary to put into perspective the relative chronology of events and try to anchor them in time by cultural periods. Such periods cannot in any real sense be isolated from the whole, of course, and simply form a historical continuum, but for convenience terms such as Neolithic, Chalcolithic, Bronze Age, and so on, are employed.

Leaving aside the technical aspects of radio-carbon and other kinds of scientific dating, one of the most important aspects of ancient cultures was its pottery, whose types, associated with a culture in a given time-frame and place, can be used to date other cultures where it appears, and thus connections

xix

between cultures can be established. Ceramic material is abundant and (unlike metal objects) almost indestructible. Paleolithic man, hunter and gatherer, did not produce pottery. Its appearance is generally associated with the Neolithic period, when people settled down to a domestic life of animal and crop raising. There are, to be sure, scores of different styles of pottery found in Spain—some produced locally, some imported from places such as Greece and Italy. One of the most common, which is related to certain periods or cultural phases, is that bearing simple shapes and generally decoratively impressed by the serrated edge of the sea shell (Latin *cardium*) to make marks in the clay. The pottery, called Impressed Ware, or in Spanish, *cardiales*, is associated with the first Neolithic farmers of about 5000 to 3500 B.C. It is believed to have come from the Eastern Mediterranean. Another is the Bell Beakers, Spanish *campaniforme*, pottery (from *campana*, "bell" and *forme*, "form") associated with the Chalcolithic period and widespread over Europe. It takes its name from the inverted bell-like configuration of the vessels usually made without handles and often decorated with bands or geometrical designs. A third type is called Terra Sigillata, a distinctive red ware with a bright, glossy surface, either plain or decorated, produced in the first three centuries A.D. Its name derives from the stamp by which the potter frequently added his name to the product.

Other manifestations of early cultures may be in the form of inscriptions. In Spain the ancient Iberians, a cultural and ethnic—but apparently not a political—composite of tribes, left numerous inscriptions whose differences in the use of writing (vocabulary, signs, and direction of writing) help to determine geographical groupings even though the documents have not been deciphered. Celtiberians employing either the Iberian or Roman writing systems also left written documentation which can be read and which illuminates certain facets of their culture. Punic and Greek written matter, and certainly Roman inscriptions and documentation often clearly mark an event.

Of special importance are the architectural monuments the ancient cultures left behind, as these constitute the sights about which this book is concerned. Towns, dwellings, walls, fortificatons, arches, portals, cisterns, temples, caves, bridges, roads, aqueducts, cemeteries, and more—where to find them and why they are there, are the subject matter here.

The first part of this book discusses the major historical phases in the history of the Iberian peninsula. The second part is divided into sections corresponding to the fifteen major regions of Spain (Andalucía, Aragón, etc.), which in turn are sudivided into their various provinces—e.g., Almería, Cádiz, Córdoba, Granada—and these into the city, town or hamlet where, or near where, the site under discussion is found. Under each province, besides the best known places, additional sites are given at the end of the section.

Generally, the reader is guided to the place of interest by reference to the capital city of the province as the starting point. Note that the name of the provincial capital is the same as the province with the following exceptions: Alava: Vitoria; Guipúzcoa: San Sebastián; Vizcaya: Bilbao; Navarra: Pamplona, all in the Basque country. In a few cases, the region and the province constitute the same geographical area, e.g., Asturias/Oviedo, Cantabria/Santander, Murcia/Murcia, Navarra/Navarra, La Rioja/Logroño.

Geography

The Iberian peninsula is roughly pentagonal in shape and is, in large part, high and dry, crisscrossed by mountain formations. In a rather general way, three parallel mountain ranges traverse the country from east to west. The Pyrenees and Cantabrians form a great chain across the north, while in the centre, the Guadarramas, along with the Sierras de Gredos and Gata, rise up to respectable heights. Across the southern Mediterranean coastal areas stretches the complex Baetic Cordillera including the majestic Sierra Nevada.

The most prominent morphological feature is the central meseta which ranges in height from between six hundred and one thousand metres. The country as a whole has an average elevation of approximately six hundred metres, with the highest point in the southern Sierra Nevada reaching 3,478 m. Spain is the second most elevated and mountainous country in Europe after Switzerland.

Extending over about two-fifths of the country, the meseta encompasses primarily Castilla y León and Castilla - La Mancha along with Extremadura. It is cut in two by the Guadarrama mountains and their westward extensions. To the north it is confined by the Cantabrian mountains, while to the east it is bounded by the Iberian mountains and the Ebro depression in Aragón. To the south it is bordered by the Sierra Morena in Andalucía.

The peninsula tilts toward the west, and except for the river Ebro which flows from the west to east near the foothills of the Pyrenees, other major rivers—from north to south the Miño, Duero, Tajo, Guadiana, and Guadalquivir—flow from east to west and empty into the Atlantic ocean. The coastal fringes and the lines of the river valleys, especially that of the fertile Guadalquivir, were the areas that most readily attracted early settlers and set the course of invading armies.

The peninsula's long shoreline is washed by the Atlantic ocean to the north and west, and by the Mediterreanean in the south and east.

Spain occupies about four-fifths of the nearly six hundred thousand square kilometres of the Iberian land mass; the remainder is given over to its western neighbour, Portugal.

PART ONE
BACKGROUND

Regions of Spain

Provinces of Spain

1. PREHISTORY

Paleolithic period

The remains of Lower Paleolithic or Early Stone Age man, his primitive tools and camp fires, have been found in several places on the Hispanic peninsula. At Venta Micena, near the town of Orce in the province of Granada, one such site, recently discovered, consisted of a large quantity of animal bones, including elephant and rhinoceros, dating back to the beginning of the period. Another such find was made near Torralba in the province of Soria in 1961, where excavations yielded the remains of fires, stone hand axes and scrapers made by elephant hunters about three hundred thousand years ago. Near Atapuerca, in the province of Burgos, paleontological studies and excavations have uncovered human bones dating back a quarter of a million years.

The Middle Paleolithic is represented by the presence of Neanderthal man, who entered the peninsula through Pyrenean passes and whose flint tools, camp fires and animal bones from roasted meals are found in caves from Bañolas (in the province of Gerona) to Gibraltar.

From the Upper Paleolithic and the appearance of Homo sapiens beginning around forty thousand years ago, there is ample evidence of man's residence in Spain from Navarra to Asturias, especially during the later part of the period. Humans also seem to have entered Spain through the Pyrenees. Numerous caves and rock shelters contain evidence of human presence in the form of skeletons, refined flint, ivory and bone tools and decorated ceremonial objects, bonfires and the usual culinary remains.

The Paleolithic or Old Stone Age in the north of Spain has been subcategorized into three general periods beginning with the appearance of man several million years ago. Each period saw a little refinement or improvement in the use of stone and bone tools and weapons.

Paleolithic	Years ago		
Lower		–	100,000
Middle	100,000	–	35,000
Upper	35,000	–	10,000

Nothing tells us more about these prehistoric people than their art, however, and there is little that prepares the modern visitor for one of those caves exhibiting Paleolithic paintings. The very nature of the drawings, their age and artistic excellence is often awe-inspiring. Only a small part of these exquisite endeavours is well preserved, and this also is fading away, slowly decaying as it comes into contact with modern civilization.

Hispanic cave cultures:
general distribution and chronology

Two cultural groups of early inhabitants of Spain are clearly in evidence: that of the older northern region in which Paleolithic populations carefully painted or engraved representations of the animals they hunted in select places in their caves, and that of the Mediterranean coasts where artistic endeavours were later and very different.

The Cantabrian coast of northern Spain constitutes an important region for the study of Paleolithic art. The chain of mountains running across the north contains many caves, most of which were inhabited in prehistoric times, and there is a string of painted caves along the coastal fringe from Santimamiñe, near Bilbao, to Candamo, near Oviedo.

Caves were inhabited by peoples arriving on the peninsula from Europe perhaps as early as about thirty-five thousand years ago. It should be kept in mind, however, that most dates in the realm of cave dwellings are estimates and, as such, are often controversial. The earliest known fossilized remains of man in Spain are much older than cave artifacts and drawings—the latter in great part attributed to the Magdalenian culture of the Late Upper Paleolithic period, or about fourteen or fifteen thousand years ago.

The study of prehistoric cave art is rather recent, dating back only to the early nineteenth century. It still took the scholarly world another fifty years to absorb the fact that Stone Age man was capable of such works of art and beauty. Perhaps the most difficult idea to comprehend was that these exquisite and naturalistic paintings and engravings long preceded the earliest art from Mesopotamia, Egypt, China, India and Greece. Even as late as 1880, when Sanz de Sautuola published his important findings of Paleolithic cave art (some thirteen thousand or more years old, discovered by his daughter in the now world-famous cave of Altamira near Santillana del Mar in the province of Santander—the so-called Sistine Chapel of rupestrian art), his work met with scepticism and hostility.

The most important areas in Spain for Paleolithic cave paintings are in the provinces of Asturias and Santander. Here, within relatively short distances, some of the finest çave art in the world is readily available for examination.

The decoration of caves in Paleolithic times appears only to occur in Europe, with the greatest concentration in northern Spain and southwestern France, where they were perhaps done by the same people. Rupestrian art in other parts of the world, such as in Africa or North America, is much later.

In caves that contain carbon material it has been possible to establish fairly precise dates of occupation, although that does not necessarily conform to the period of the paintings, since many caves were inhabited over periods of thousands of years. Only when, as was sometimes the case, pictures were superimposed over others does a relative chronology emerge.

Not only do many of the northern Spanish caves display naturalistic paintings and engravings of animals—some long extinct from the region, such as bison or elephants—and occasionally a person, but signs and abstract symbols were often recorded. These may take the form of tectiforms, claviforms, puntiforms, meanders, and geometrical patterns whose significance is now of a transcendental nature.

Prominently featured in some of the caves are human hand imprints on the walls, which seem to be nearly universal in cave art and perhaps one of the earliest forms represented. The hand was either dipped in dye and flattened directly against the wall of the cave, or pigment was blown from the mouth or a hollow reed or bone with the hand on the wall to present a silhouette. The pigment itself was generally composed of vegetable dyes, often mixed with blood.

Cave art, which began in the Franco-Cantabrian area and had been practiced for millenia, began to decline as the artists seemed to lose their skills and motivation. A different kind of rock art began to make its appearance in the eastern part of the Hispanic peninsula, where the paintings were not placed deep inside dark shadowy caves and executed by the flickering light of a fire, but were located under shallow rock shelters and exposed to the fresh air and sunlight. Here, unlike the paintings of the northern caves, the human figure takes on the role of protagonist.

Mesolithic or Middle Stone Age

The Mesolithic, the period of transition between the Paleolithic and Neolithic, is characterized not only by the persistence of the old hunting and gathering way of life, but also by some changes in the development of flint industries in which microliths became abundant. The flintworkers specialized in the making of smaller implements such as arrow heads, for the bow had come into use by this time, and was employed in the hunting of small animals and birds. This period coincided with the withdrawal of the Pleistocene ice sheets as well as the big game animals such as mammoths, and came to an end with the introduction of farming and stock-rearing in the Neolithic.

During this phase, Mesolithic man also turned to more reliance on food from the sea and learned how to make boats for the undertaking. In Spain, the period encompasses the span of time between about ten thousand years ago (or a little earlier) down to the beginnings of the Neolithic phase. During this period the cave art of the Levantine style developed along the eastern Mediterranean coasts of the country and extended well inland.

Among the Mediterranean coastal ranges, the paintings which still exist are often in shallow hollows, with the maximum number in the provinces of Castellón de la Plana, Valencia and Teruel. Unlike the northern caves—with their drawings generally of large animals, especially those man hunted—those of the Levante also display figures of men and women engaged in activities as diverse as hunting, dancing, making war and gathering honey. They employed the bow and arrow, wore short skirts or trousers, and sometimes headgear, and appear in stylized, or at times abstract, representations. The scenes are usually filled with action.

Educated estimates place the beginning of the Levantine rock art soon after about eight thousand years ago. The art persisted down into Neolithic and later times, ceasing altogether as late as the first millennium B.C. It displays several phases: simple linear and geometrical forms, followed by flat painted large animals such as bulls. In time bulls became less evident and deer more prominent, being sometimes painted over earlier representations of the bulls; this may have been due to a change in cult. Static human figures also begin to appear in this phase. Later, human and animal depictions became more stylized, showing daily living and warfare in graceful, flowing movement. From about 2000 B.C., the art work declined again into static forms, with some reference to agricultural products.

The colour used by the native artists was generally red. As elsewhere conservation problems have arisen when the shelters and caves have been used and visited by contempory man. Many of the drawings have been defaced or have disappeared except for vague outlines. Under such circumstances questionable interpretations arise. It is not clear, for example, whether some of the scenes depict domestic dogs or, in some cases, riding horses, the latter would help date a painting to some time after 1500 B.C., when horses were introduced into the western Mediterranean area. There is at least one picture of a horseman at El Cingle de la Mola Remigia in the Gasulla gorge, Castellón de la Plana, wearing a crested helmet which places him neatly in the Bronze Age.

Many of the sites are in difficult terrain and may entail strenuous hiking and climbing over broken ground. Because of their remoteness, new sites are still being found. Those given in the following pages are either particularly interesting and in good condition, or are reasonably accessible.

Neolithic, Megalithic and Bronze Age cultures

Origins and cultural characteristics

Although the so-called Neolithic revolution had begun in the Near East several thousand years before, infiltrations onto the Hispanic peninsula initiating a new way of life, the New Stone Age, can be dated back to about 5000 B.C. The newcomers lived in caves or huts made of branches, raised livestock, and engaged in rudimentary farming with stone hoes and sharpened sticks. These farming people of the Early Neolithic period appear to have arrived in Spain in small groups, perhaps from the Danubean River Basin, by following the coasts of the Mediterranean. Carbon-14 dating of cultivated grains of wheat and barley found in the Cova de l'Or in Alicante date back to around 4500 B.C.

During the following centuries further colonists arrived to settle in Cataluña and Valencia and, in a more decisive manner, in Almería, whence they spread knowledge of Neolithic agriculture throughout the region. The period, lasting to about 3000 B.C., was characterized by the transformation from hunting and gathering to settled agricultural and animal-raising societies, by flint mining, by the use of polished stone tools, by the use of pottery, and by garments made of cloth. The remote regions of the centre and north of the peninsula, where the Mesolithic way of life continued much longer, remained less influenced by the new developments.

Neolithic sites with visible remains are few. The culture, especially in its initial phases, is known primarily from occupied cave sites, remnants of necropoli and Impressed Ware—the pottery of the early Neolithic farmers that spread around the western Mediterranean including the coasts of Spain.

Megalithic structures

The Greek word *megalith* means "great stone," and is normally used for any structure in Europe built of large stones—usually set upright—and dating between about 5000 to 500 B.C.

Generally associated with the late Neolithic period or early Bronze Age in Spain are megalithic collective graves of various kinds that were used for the burial of the clan or family over a period of several generations.

The commonest megalithic monument is the dolmen, a burial chamber constructed of upright stones with one or several cap stones laid across it to form the roof. Dolmens can be found in Spain and Portugal, and around the coasts of Europe. Remains of human burials have been discovered in many of them. Some dolmens have passage-way entrances, others do not. They were often covered by a mound which has, in many instances, disappeared. Some are rather simple in structure with a single chamber, others have multiple burial chambers connected by passages. Some are "passage graves" consisting of a slab-covered corridor of upright stones. There were many variations. Some of the tombs had portholes cut into them for reasons still unknown (to allow spirits to escape? to pass in food? to add more bones without moving a large piece of stone?). Some had symbols etched into the stone.

Whether or not the idea of megalithic structures in Spain was imported or an in situ development, is unclear. These structures are to be found on the Iberian Peninsula in almost all the provinces with the most spectacular in the south.

Cist graves—box-shaped burial structures made of stone slabs set on edge and placed below ground or on the surface and covered over by a protective barrow—appeared during the Late Neolithic period and continued in use into the Bronze Age. To this type belong various groups of graves in Cataluña and the Basque region.

During the Neolithic and into the Bronze Age, caves and rock-cut chambers continued to be used for burial purposes. Corresponding to the Neolithic period were the caves of La Mujer at Alhama de Granada, Murciélagos at Albuñol, Granada, Lóbrega in the province of Logroño and a few others in Cataluña; there is now nothing left to see of the burial practices, only the sites themselves.

The Iberian peninsula lacks aligned megalithic monuments (such as Stonehenge, Avebury, or those found in Brittany) and there are few menhirs, i.e., single standing and usually unadorned stones. The largest concentration of menhirs is in the Basque country where, unlike other regions of the peninsula, numerous stone circles are to be found. Both were placed in certain spots, it might be suppposed, to commemorate an event or mark hallowed ground.

Chalcolithic period

From the Greek *chalco* "copper" plus *lithic* "stone", this term is sometimes employed to show the continued use of stone artifacts along with the use of copper. The period is also referred to as the Copper Age. Spanish terms for this period are Eneolítico (Eneolithic)—from Latin *aeneus*—or Calcolítico.

There may have been no period when copper was the primary material for tools and weapons, since stone continued to be used along with copper and bronze artifacts appeared while stone was still in use.

During this period of transition, in the second half of the tnird millenium B.C., decorated ceramics known as Bell Beakers were produced. They spread throughout Europe but their Spanish origins are controversial. Copper Age settlements in Spain are characterized by the use of this pottery, generally found in funerary contexts, and by stone and copper artifacts.

Transitional between Neolithic and Bronze in the use of both copper and stone tools is the ancient town of Los Millares in the province of Almería, situated in one of the richest mining areas of Spain and dating back to about the middle of the third millenium B.C. Eastern Mediterranean influences are evident in the ruins, but these influences may have been due to either migrations or cultural diffusion; the process of acquisition is unclear.

Bronze Age

The introduction of metallurgy into the Hispanic peninsula substantially altered the social make-up of the Neolithic settlements and transformed the peninsular demography as the rise of urban life attracted people from the country. Social classes developed, presumably on the basis of relative skills in the new industries. Regions endowed with abundant metal deposits became centres of attraction, especially the valley of the Guadalquivir, Almería, Granada, certain areas of Portugal, and the northwest where deposits of tin were plentiful.

About 1700 B.C. the civilization of El Argar appeared with advanced metallurgical techniques involving the mixture of copper and tin to make bronze. According to some investigators this settlement, in northeast Almería, owed its origins to immigration from the Eastern Mediterranean, although others prefer to see it as the result of local evolution of the Los Millares Culture. The houses and walls of the town are little preserved, but interments were discovered within the enclosure. The site seems to have contained about six hundred inhabitants in the urban area.

El Argar influence spread throughout the region, spawning numerous settlements with similar metallurgical characteristics, and new sites are still being uncovered today.

The Age of Bronze in Spain chronologically covers the period from around 2000 B.C. to around 700 B.C. and is usually divided into three phases:

Bronze Age	Date B.C.
Early	2000 — 1500
Middle	1500 — 1200
Final	1200 — 700

Little is known about the cultures of the Early Bronze period. The settlements were generally situated on easily defensible hills, although some caves were still in use. The dwellings tended to be square with rounded corners and made from branches or, in some cases, adobe and roofed with vegetable matter. From the presence of artifacts such as stone mills or grinders and hoes, along with animal bones in the villages, the people appear to have been agriculturalists concerned mostly with wheat, sheep and goats. Their diet seems to have been supplemented by hunting, fishing and the collection of wild fruit. Moulds and forges indicate metallurgical activity but many implements were still of stone. There is generally little or nothing left of these early sites after the artifacts have been removed.

The Middle Bronze period shows an increasing number of agricultural settlements and increasing contacts between them. In this phase also the influence of the El Argar culture became widespread, including the adoption of the Argarian funeral practices in which the dead were individually buried in fossae within the confines of the village and with modest personal items. The settlements remained on hill tops with walls protecting the more vulnerable slopes, although in some places, as on the plains, they might occupy only a small mound. In such places a strong fortified tower in the centre and up to six metres in height backed up the front line of several concentric defensive walls. Dwellings might be of wood or adobe, and roofs of branches and clay. Different regions produced different structures depending on the terrain and availabilty of materials. In some places houses were distributed in a haphazard fashion with no trace of urban order. The people of the period were farmers as well as miners and metallurgists.

The Bronze Age, like those before it, is an obscure period, and many inferences must be made from the archaeological finds concerning the methods and manner of cultural features. The people of the Middle Bronze period practised an economy much like those of the earlier period but with greater elaboration and advances in agriculture and the working of metal.

Not unlike the earlier phases, the final phase of the Bronze Age carried on the same traditions but with more specialization and technical advances in metallurgy (arms, alloys, moulds), more elaborate hierarchical relationships within society, and with an inceasing number of settlements with more intense commercial interaction locally and further afield.

For further reading concerning the Late Neolithic and Chalcolithic periods, see *The Bell Beaker Cultures of Spain and Portugal* by R.J. Harrison, Peabody Museum of Archaeology and Ethnology, Cambridge, Mass. (1977).

A comprehensive study of drawings and general locations is given in *Rock Art of the Spanish Levant* by Antonio Beltrán, Cambridge (1982). Also, *El Primer Arte Valenciano II* by J. Aparicio Perez et al., Valencia (1982), and *Prehistoric Europe* by Philip Van Doren Stern, New York (1969).

For an introduction to the rupestrian paintings of the Paleolithic period, see *The Caves of France and Northern Spain* by A. and G. Sieveking, London (1962). A general view of Paleolithic Spain is found in *Fossil Man in Spain* by H. Obermaier, New Haven (1924).

2. IRON AGE: CELTS and CELTIBERIANS

Early migrations

In the initial phases of the first millennium B.C. a major change in the cultural and linguistic panorama occurred which affected large areas of the Hispanic peninsula, especially in the central and northern regions. New types of settlements and burial rites, along with metallic and ceramic elements appeared, similar to those found in western Europe but unknown in Spain until that time. These innovations were due to migrations of Indo-European peoples (Celts or pre-Celtic populations) to the peninsula. Establishing themselves primarily in Cataluña, these early immigrants incinerated their dead and buried the ashes in urns in a defined area of level ground. Consequently this culture, which appears to have reached its apogee between about 900 and 600 B.C., is referred to as the Urn Field Culture. The disappearance of this cultural entity, which appears to have migrated from central Europe down the Rhône River Valley and across southern France into Spain, was perhaps due to its absorption into the local Iberian populations.

About the same time, other Indo-Europeans—probably Celts—penetrated the peninsula through the western Pyrenees and established what is now one of the earliest known settlements of its type near Cortes de Navarra.

From about 500 B.C. down to Roman times, identifiable Celtic tribes entered the Hispanic peninsula through various Pyrenean mountain passes and, deterred from the Mediterranean coastal regions (presumably by the Iberians) fanned out over the central meseta, making their way as far as the Atlantic seaboards of Spain and Portugal. This new population has been identified from reports of contemporary Roman and Greek historiographers (mostly in connection with their resistance to Roman hegemony), from archaeological remains, and from inscriptional material. Some Celtic towns have been discovered from their ruins, while others are known from coin inscriptions and from statements of ancient writers, but with sites still unidentified. From the beginning of the Roman conquest of the peninsula, Roman authors spoke of Celtiberians, a name that in its widest applications seems to refer to all the Celtic tribes who inhabited the interior areas of the central meseta. As a generic term it should, perhaps, be restricted to the settlements along the Middle Ebro where there is clear evidence of Iberian and Celtic cultural mixture, although even here the predominant characteristic of the towns was Celtic.

Iron working was introduced into the Hispanic peninsula—where iron was at first restricted in use and treated almost as a precious metal—from Europe, presumably by Celtic peoples, early in the eighth century B.C. The period, Edad de Hierro, is categorized generally as Iron Age I and Iron Age II, the former down to the fifth century B.C., the latter from then on. The first period is characterized by a prolongation of the cultural and economic features imported from central Europe as seen, for example, in the change of funeral rites. Inhumation was common among the Bronze Age villages of Spain before the arrival of Indo-Europeans. The methods of burial of the people of the First Iron Age employed the rite of incineration, and although the traditional inhumation was sometimes used it was, apparently, reserved for the privileged classes. The second phase witnessed the increased usage of iron and the emergence of the Celtiberian cultures at least in those regions in which Celtic and Iberian identities to some extent merged.

Distribution of Hispano-Celtic peoples

The Celtiberians were a conglomeration of tribes such as the Lusones, Bellos, Tittos, Arevacos and Pelendones, among others mentioned by ancient authors. They were first mentioned by Polybius and Livy in the third century B.C. From the Roman point of view, theirs was a region of uncompromising harshness in both soil and climate but nevertheless rather well populated. The most numerous of these Celtic peoples were the Arevacos, an agricultural tribe who were situated on the slopes of the upper Duero River and inhabited such towns as Numancia, Agreda and Sigüenza. Celtic tribes were also well spread out over the central and northern regions of Spain; for example, the Vacceos occupied the land around Burgos, Palencia and Valladolid. Their neighbours to the southeast were the Arevacos; to the southwest in Avila, Cáceres, Salamanca and Zamora were the Vetones, and so on.

The eastern area of the meseta which is today Castilla - La Mancha, was populated by a nucleus of Carpetanians and Celtiberians surrounded by others on the periphery, such as Lusitanians, Vacceos and Oretanians. The Carpetanians occupied large zones of Toledo, Madrid, Guadalajara, Ciudad Real and Albacete, while the Celtiberians controlled the mountainous regions of Guadalajara, Soria, Zaragoza, Teruel and Cuenca.

Cultural characteristics: economy

The Hispanic Celts seemed to have been a fairly uniform people in religion, language and basic customs. Politically, they were organized into groups or clans which the Romans called *gentilitates*. They were agricultural people and warriors who paid homage to natural objects (the sun, moon, forests, springs, mountains and rivers), who cremated their dead, and developed the social practice in times of peace of the *hospitium*, that is, a form of hospitality often embodied in small artifacts signifying the belief that strangers were sent by the gods and thus welcome. Indicative of this was the first-century tablet or tessera of hospitality (a bronze plaque) found near Luzaga in Guadalajara, fifteen by sixteen centimetres with holes through it to fix it on the wall, and written in the

Celtic language using the Iberian writing system. It seems to offer hospitality from one tribe to another.

Their religious rites were replete with magic, but like many agricultural societies with emphasis on nature worship, they built few temples in tribute to their deities. On the contrary, they paid homage to them in open fields and clearings in forests—these were the sanctuaries. In Spain, as among Celts in general, the oak tree was a particular symbol of veneration.

The Celts of the central regions appear to have been rather bellicose, responding to threats from neighbours and with territories expanding or contracting depending on the outcome of a battle or war. The common practice was to incinerate the dead and bury them with precious personal objects, but those fallen in battle achieved a higher honour and were left on the field to the vultures and other birds who, it was said by a Roman author, would carry their souls to heaven.

Celtic necropoli in Celtiberia constituted avenues of oblong stones set vertically in the ground about one to one and a half metres apart above each urn; they were without social class distinction. Sometimes the ashes of the dead were placed in a hole in the ground with possessions, but without an urn. Sometimes a cemetery shows a type of grave in which the urn was protected by a structure of sandstone blocks set around and over the hole, a practice that seems to have been influenced by Iberian customs.

Villages were generally placed on strategic hills and walled, the houses constructed rectangularly with adobe walls on stone foundations; around the walls were benches. The floors were simply pounded earth and the roofs foliage and vegetable matter. Houses were placed against their neighbours and streets arose haphazardly; there seems to have been no urban planning. In some localities of the Carpetanians, natural or artificial caves were employed as dwellings.

Walled villages and towns sometimes displayed defensive towers, heavily defended gates and even fields bristling with vertical stones to inhibit the use of cavalry in an attack. They were independent enclaves even within the framework of their own tribes and readily fought among themselves, a custom which facilitated the Roman conquest. Nevertheless, according to the Romans themselves the Celtiberians were robust, indomitably proud, brave and fiercely independent, and preferred death to the surrender of their arms. They fought the Romans by tactics strange to the enemy—guerrilla warfare—and employed for the purpose small round shields, javelins, darts, bows and arrows, swords, double-bladed axes and daggers. They braided their hair and let it hang over the neck for further protection. They attacked on the run and sometimes two on a horse. The fine quality Celtiberian double-edged sword was in great demand and even adopted by the Roman army.

Celtic sculptures, almost life size, depicting warriors carrying small circular shields, are known from the region, but generally asssociated with the Celts are the rough, zoomorphic sculptures characteristic of the western meseta. This is the area of the Culture of the Verracos, which shepherds supposedly placed in the fields as divine protectors of the flock. This curious manifestation of Celtic art appeared during the second phase of the Iron Age. While the near life-size granite representations of bulls (or pigs, according to some scholars) do not display much detail, they do have a certain vital quality; they were placed throughout the territory of the Vettones. They have seldom been found in situ, but three, discovered at Las Cogatas in the province of Avila, were situated outside the walls of the settlement beside the road that led into the second enclosure, which appears to have been used for farm animals.

Verracos, often several, have been found at about thirty-six places in the province of Avila alone, and some were produced after the Roman conquest, judging from one with a funerary inscription dedicated to the gods, engraved on its flank in Latin, discovered in 1975 on a farm at Martiherrero.

Celtic cultures of the northwest are known primarily from habitation sites or settlements called castros which are found throughout Galicia, in western Asturias and northern Portugal. Castros were fortified enclosures utilizing the natural defence of the terrain and surrounded by walls, moats or both.

Some castros consisted of one enclosure, some two, and a few had even three more-or-less concentric configurations. The dwellings located in such enclosures generally appear to have been randomly placed, although in some cases streets existed between them.

The houses themselves were circular in design, although rectangular structures do occur, perhaps due to Roman influence. They are generally three to five metres in diameter. The walls were usually stone and the roofs of straw or branches and conical in shape, although some consisted of two slopes supported by interior posts. Their height was generally about four metres. Stone-walled structures were relatively late, however, and earlier houses were often constructed from wood, mud, or even foliage. In some cases artistic designs in the form of spirals or other patterns decorated the door jambs.

The Celts imposed themselves on the earlier Bronze Age inhabitants of the meseta, dispersed in small nuclei and seemingly practised a precarious economy of subsistence. This state of affairs continued as the Celtic tribes fused with the autochthonous peoples. The eastern section of the meseta became fairly densely populated by Celts in pre-Roman times. The economic base was generally pastoral—mostly sheep raising—but there were also agricultural products such as cereals, especially wheat, and some rice. Iron tools and weapons were employed and metallurgy was one of the important occupations.

The Celtic legacy

Archaeological testimony of the Hispano-Celtic peoples is found in the form of graves, pottery, weapons, villages and towns, and also in place names ending in -briga, "fortress," such as Mirobriga, in the province of Badajoz and in -dunum, "hill," such as Berdún in the province of Aragón. The Celtic peoples who dwelt in the eastern region of the peninsula, that is, the Celtiberians, learned to write from the Iberians and Romans with whom they were in contact and they have left a number of inscriptions in the Celtic language employing either the Iberian or Latin alphabet.

Less tangible than the physical remains of settlements and artifacts are the anthropological and cultural characteristics of northern Spaniards, who often display northern European features such as red hair and blue eyes and in whose superstitions, legends, and even music Celtic influences are evident.

For further reading see *Historia de España. Introducción:Primeras Culturas e Hispania Romana,* Vol. I, by M. Tuñón de Lara et al., Barcelona (1980), Chapters V and X.

3. THE IBERIANS

Distribution of indigenous Iberian tribes

Occupying much of the Mediterranean coasts from southern France west of the Rhône River to southern Spain during the latter half of the first millennium B.C. were a people of unknown provenance and affiliations referred to as Iberians. They may have been simply a continuation of the Neolithic and early Bronze Age people that previously inhabited the peninsular coastal regions. Our knowledge of the distribution of these ancient people is derived from the archaeological evidence and from statements of contemporary Roman and Greek authors. Iberian inscriptions with differences in orthography, the lexicon, and writing styles indicate a southern and a northern grouping, the former dwelling in Andalucía (primarily in the eastern section) and in Murcia, while the latter occupied the coastal lands, for some distance inland (Albacete, Jaén, Lérida and Teruel), and northward to beyond the Pyrenean Mountains. The inhabitants of the Mediterranean littoral of Spain (today Andalucía, Murcia, Valencia and Cataluña), in contact with Greeks and Phoenicians, reached a high level of culture that flourished in the fourth and third centuries B.C.

Cultural features, art and architecture

Iberian culture can be uniquely defined by its painted pottery (often depicting battle scenes, animals, plants, dancing, and the playing of musical instruments), by votive offerings found in Iberian sanctuaries usually in the form of statuettes, by walled cities—generally on hilltops, with remains of walls, towers, houses and cisterns—and by the numerous inscriptions they left behind on lead plaques, stone, pottery and coins. Seemingly united in language and culture with some variations, the Iberians appear to have been politically heterogeneous, with their territory consisting of independent settlements, some of which are still preserved in general outlines. Iberian culture was in part influenced by the Greeks and perhaps less so by the Phoenicians and Carthaginians, as evidenced in their sculpture and their methods of writing.

One of the most artistic pieces of Iberian sculpture is the bust of a woman, measuring a little more than one half metre in height, known universally as La Dama de Elche, a work of the fifth century B.C. by a sculptor who was clearly familiar with Greek works of art. Found in 1897 at El Cerro de la Alcudia near Elche in the province of Alicante, the famous lady now reposes in the Archaeological Museum of Madrid.

Seemingly related to the cult of the dead were the figures in the form of bulls with human male heads, sphinxes with human female heads, snakes, birds, and so on. From Cerro de los Santos (Murcia) came over one hundred, many of them sculpted in stone; from Despeñaperros (Jaén) and Castellar de Santisteban (Jaén) came some five thousand figurines in bronze, generally about eight to ten centimetres high, while La Serreta (Alicante) has yielded many earthenware figures.

Figurines were often produced by moulding wax into the desired form, covering it with clay, opening a hole in the covering top and bottom, pouring molten bronze into the top hole while allowing the wax to drain out the bottom; removing the clay left the bronze figure. Warriors with lances and shields, on foot or on horseback, women shrouded in elegant shawls, small statues of suppliants with offerings (a dove, coin, a loaf of bread) in the palm of their hands, and so on, were made in this way. Many hundreds of these figurines are in the National Archaeological Museum of Madrid.

The sphinxes with human female heads of Montealegre (Albacete), Salobral (Alicante) and Santo Tomé (Jaén) can be related artistically to similar archaic Greek forms.

From decorated pottery, meticulously painted, much of it from Liria in the province of Valencia, we learn something about Iberian living with regard to warfare and weapons, dancing, musical instruments, horses, hunting and fishing, for all of which they seemed to have had a fondness. Clearly depicted as well are male and female manner of attire.

The protective walls encompassing Iberian habitation sites (sometimes the only thing that remains) are of great interest. They represent one of the oldest methods of construction, the cyclopean wall, which contained large blocks of stone weighing up to ten tons laid flat. The blocks were wedged together by means of small stones lodged in the cracks, which were then filled with earth. Cyclopean masonry is still to be seen in the walls of the Nea Polis of Emporión, at Ullastret (Gerona), at Despeñaperros—in part of the southern wall—and at Ibros in Jaén. At Tarragona the lower part of the wall around the old part of the city serving as the base for the Roman wall may be of Iberian construction. The line of the Iberian wall was sometimes broken by the appearance of a square or round tower, as at Ullastret.

The houses of Iberian towns sometimes had several rooms, some with benches attached to the walls. Iberian remains at Azaila in the province of Teruel contain wide, stone-paved streets with sidewalks, rectangular houses with stone and adobe walls, and wooden post-supported roofs. Roman influence is evident in the layout of the city.

Necropoli and sanctuaries

The Iberians practised incineration of the dead, perhaps learned from the Celts, and the ashes were placed in clay vessels of generally local production, but sometimes in imported Greek containers or stone urns. The funeral urn or vessel was then buried in a simple grave or sometimes in subterranean caverns or mausolea, and sometimes along with personal possessions of the deceased. Cemeteries appear to have been placed well away from the corresponding towns and those of some Iberian habitation centres have not been found. In other cases the cemeteries are known but not the town. One of the most notable stone-constructed necropoli where something still remains to contemplate is that of Toya in the province of Jaén.

In contact with Greeks and Phoenicians, Iberians produced beautiful works in ceramics and sculpture in the fifth to third centuries B.C. Much of this work proceeded from sanctuaries where it was offered as ex votos or tokens of worship. Some of the most important sanctuaries were at Despeñaperros, Castellar de Santisteban, Cerro de los Santos, La Serreta (mentioned above), Cigarralejo de Mula (Murcia)—where the figurines suggest that the local divinity presided over the protection of horses—and Llano de la Consolación (Albacete). In all of these cases, however, there is little left in situ.

The sanctuaries were sacred places in caves or on mountain tops, but no clearly defined Iberian temples are known. Most of the sculptures that adorn museums and private collections come from these and other places consecrated by these ancient people. The offerings and ex votos, besides statuettes of human beings, often consisted of parts thereof, representing an infected or damaged arm, leg, hand or eye. Figurines of domestic animals were also offered, seemingly to placate the gods and alleviate some livestock disease or ailment.

Written documentation

Iberian documentation was usually inscribed in a semi-syllabic derivative of the Graeco-Phoenician script for most of whose individual signs phonetic values are known. The meaning of the words and the over-all sense of the documentation, however, remains undeciphered. In a few cases the Iberians used a Greek alphabet to write their own language.

Documentary remains from the Levante and northeastern regions of the peninsula are the most numerous, spanning at least five centuries, with inscriptions from Ampurias (Greek Emporión) dating back to the fifth century B.C., from the fourth century at Ullastret, and coin legends from the end of the third century. Lead pressed into thin sheets was a common material for inscriptions throughout the Mediterranean basin and inscribed lead plaques were used in Iberian territory from the fourth century B.C. and became more numerous in subsequent centuries.

Besides these, the Iberians produced rupestrian inscriptions often relating to funerary stelae and ceramic inscriptions in the form of potters' marks, graffiti, or longer texts which often appear to relate to the scenes depicted on the vessel in question. An important group of Iberian ceramics comes from Liria in the province of Valencia whose pottery, like that of other regions, is in the style of its Greek precursors.

Inscriptions incised on gravestones and cippi reflect Roman influence and are especially prevalent from Ampurias, Tarragona and Sagunto, all focal points of Roman interest. Most of these inscriptions seem to belong to the first and second centuries B.C.

Iberian coins were minted in a number of localities, ranging from Obulco in Andalucía to Ampurias in Cataluña. The coins, inscribed with place names or personal names, were issued in silver, bronze or copper.

Iberian and Basque

As is generally known, the Basque language has no substantiated antecedents and is the only living western European language that is not of Indo-European origin. It has no established relationshps with any other language. The ancient Iberian tongue, perceived only through inscriptional material, also has no identifiable progenitors. The two languages have a number of words in common, however, especially among surnames. Both cultures existed in adjacent and perhaps overlapping areas of the Hispanic peninsula north of the Ebro River in Aragón, and this linguistic relationship could have been due to borrowing words and names from one culture to the other. On the other hand, there could be a more deep-seated linguistic and cultural relationship that dates back to a common ancestor—the problem is far from solved. There is a school of thought that perceives linguistic affinities between Basque and the languages of the Caucasus (or their common ancestor) but this also has proved elusive. (See section on Sites, País Vasco).

Tartessians

In the opposite corner of the peninsula from the Basques, the southwest including western Andalucía and southern Portugal, were the Tartessians with whom the Phoenicians came into contact at an early period. The name of the kingdom (or, perhaps, the capital city), Tartessus, is taken from Greek and figured in ancient Greek legends. The apparently equivalent Hebrew word, Tarshish, that is mentioned numerous times in the Old Testament, may have been the same place. From Tarshish during Solomon's reign, (973–933 B.C.) came ships bringing gold and silver, ivory, apes and peacocks. Greeks competed with Phoenicians for the wealth of Tartessus, but after their defeat in the naval battle of Alalia off Corsica in 535 B.C., they pulled back from the extreme western Mediterranean and allowed the Phoenicians to control the lucrative commerce in precious metals and the sought-after tin. The Semites closed the straits between the Pillars of Hercules, jealously guarded their trading routes, and between about 520 and 505 B.C. it seems they destroyed Tartessus.

Funeral inscriptions in an undeciphered language found in western Andalucía and southern Portugal (the Algarve and Alemtejo), and treasures and weapons dug from the ground and dredged from the sea seem to support the contention of classical writers concerning the existence of Tartessus. Except for the artifacts—jewels and tombstones in museums throughout the region—the Tartessian civilization, like others before and since, appears to have vanished from the earth.

Intrusive cultures: Phoenicians, Carthaginians and Greeks

Phoenician and Carthaginian remains in situ on the Iberian peninsula are not plentiful. While it is clear that Phoenician sailors and merchants made contact with the coasts of Spain as early as the eighth century B.C. or before, their settlements were small and geared to commercial enterprises, especially in fish-curing industries and the exploitation of metals. Of particular interest were gold, silver and tin, all in short supply in the east—the tin was required to make bronze armaments.

Historical context

After Nebuchadnezzar destroyed Tyre in 573 B.C., the mandate for the exploration and exploitation of the western Mediterranean passed to the Phoenician colony of Carthage near present-day Tunis. The Carthaginians capitalized on the natural wealth of Spain through small and relatively unimportant *factorías* and trading stations. Not until a short time before the Second Punic War did they seriously attempt to colonize and rule the country. Their hegemony in Spain was to be short-lived, however—to the victorious Romans went the spoils.

Phoenician and Punic remains (the two are not easily distinguished) come primarily from the city of Cádiz, ancient Gadir, and its necropolis at Punta de la Vaca, from the necropolis of Ebysos on the island of Ibiza, from Villaricos in the province of Almería and a few other places. The artifacts taken from these sites date between the sixth and first centuries B.C.

Recently discovered are a series of small Phoenician sites or *factorías*, the best known of which are situated along the southern coast a little east of Málaga. Some further discoveries have also been made around the city of Huelva. They date back to the seventh or eighth centuries B.C., and many do not appear to have survived beyond the sixth or fifth centuries B.C.

Punic art

A spectacular treasure of Punic origins was uncovered by workmen at Aliseda in the Province of Cáceres in 1920 and dated to the sixth century B.C. The golden hoard contained exquisite filigree earrings, necklaces, a heavy bracelet, a diadem with filigree rosettes set with turquoise, a golden girdle, an amethyst scarab, rings, a bronze mirror, glass objects and a Carthaginian silver pitcher. The treasure appears to have been buried during the third century B.C. when the Carthaginian Empire collapsed before the encroachments of the Romans. From the various Punic cemeteries have been recovered numerous artifacts ranging from jewels and painted ostrich eggs to little clay figures, bronze bracelets, necklaces, and ceramics. Some of the oldest finds come from the Punic necropolis at Carmona, where little ivory plaques, remains of chests, combs and so on were engraved in a style of the eighth or seventh centuries B.C.

Greek influence

Most archaeological traces of Greek culture in Spain are found in fragments of pottery, some sculpture and weapons and, after about 470 B.C., silver coins. Quantities of pottery have been found in the vicinity of Huelva and fall within the period of about 800 to 550 B.C. A Corinthian helmet, discovered in 1938 near Jerez de la Frontera, appears to date back to about 630 B.C. Bronze sculptures of Greek origin found in Spain were generally produced some time after 600 B.C. and the numerous vases or drinking cups usually date from the fifth to third centuries B.C.

The first appearance of Greeks on the Iberian peninsula was more or less contemporary with that of the Phoenicians. Later, continuing their westward exploration and colonization from southern Italy, the Greeks founded the city of Massalia (Marseilles) at the mouth of the Rhône River about 600 B.C. and moved down into Spain to establish Emporión about fifty years later.

Phoenician and Punic interests dominated in the south of Spain, while Greek activities were mainly confined to the northern Mediterranean coastal regions, principally those of Cataluña, where the only proven Greek urban site has been found at Emporión. It may be noted here that classical authors mention Greek sites along the eastern coasts such as Hemeroscopeion near Denia (Alicante), at Akra Leuke, now Tosal de Manises (Alicante), at Abdera and Adra

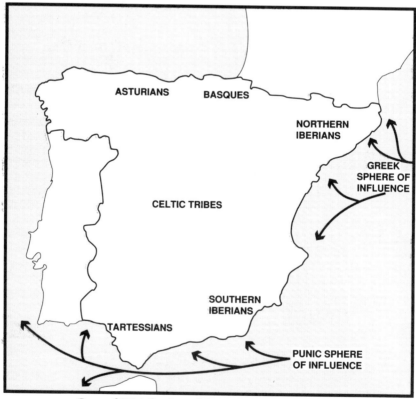

General Distribution of Ancient Peoples in Spain

(Almería), and Mainake, a little east of Málaga. Greek pottery found in these regions also suggests settlements or at least trading stations. With regard to the priority of interests in the south of Spain, the preponderance of evidence suggests Phoenician control over the area. The use of a Greek alphabet among Iberian peoples of the region around Alcoy (Alicante), however, indicates that Greek influence did radiate southward.

Demise of the Iberian culture

The Iberian legacy has been bountiful but somewhat unrevealing for an assessment of its origins and diffusion.

The subjugation of the Iberian peninsula by foreign interests began with the extension of Carthaginian control from their foothold at Cádiz. Under Hamilcar Barca the southwest was secured, and upon his death in about 228 B.C. his son-in-law, Hasdrubal, continued the expansionist policy and founded a new port at Mastia (Cartagena). With the assassination of Hasdrubal, Carthaginian power fell into the hands of Hannibal, who persisted in the suppression of the Hispanic tribes. Hannibal's defeat at the hands of the Romans ushered in a new period of foreign hegemony on the Hispanic peninsula. Unlike the bellicose Celts of the central and northern regions, and the indomitable Basques of the western Pyrenees, the autochthonous people of the Mediterranean coastal areas, the Iberians, seem to have submitted more easily to the prevailing circumstances and moved into the prosperous Roman towns, abandoning their hilltop villages in favour of more comfortable and secure living. The transformation was relentless, and the local cultures and languages disappeared in the course of a few generations. If the indigenous peoples of Mediterranean Spain survived much after the time of Augustus there is no record of them, and their cultural influence on later generations is at best obscure and unportentous.

Iberian sites are found north of the Pyrenees in southern France at Mailhac, Ensérune and Montlures (to mention a few), but the vast majority of Iberian towns, sanctuaries and cemeteries were located in Spain. Often there is little or virtually nothing to see. The sites discussed in the following pages are those that display clearly visible remains; the Iberian name of these sites is often unknown.

For further reading on the subject of the Ancient Iberians and their relationships with other cultures see *Ancient Languages of the Hispanic Peninsula* by J. M. Anderson, Lanham, MD (1988). For Iberian art and culture see *The Ancient Spaniards* by G. Nicolini, Farnborough (1973, first published in French as *Les Ibères*) and *Arte Ibérico en España* by A. García y Bellido, Madrid (1979).

For Iberians in their cultural setting see *The Iberians* by A. Arribas, London (1964), and *Spain at the Dawn of History* by R. J. Harrison, London (1988). Harrison examines Phoenician, Punic and Greek aspects of ancient Spain as well as Iberian.

Dealing exclusively with the Greeks is *The Greeks in Spain* by R. Carpenter, (1925, reprinted Bryn Mawr, 1971).

4. ROMAN SPAIN

Military history

During the First Punic War between Rome and Carthage (264–241 B.C.) which began in a dispute over Sicily, Rome won the island and in the following years took over Corsica and Sardinia. As Rome grew more and more belligerent, General Hamilcar Barca was charged by the Carthaginian Senate to renew activities on the Iberian peninsula. Landing an army at Gadir (Cádiz) in 237 B.C., he set about building an Iberian empire from which to recruit manpower and exploit natural wealth.

After the death of Hamilcar by drowning, his son Hannibal eventually assumed authority, continued the policy of conquest, and in the year 219 B.C. began the long siege of Sagunto, a town favourably disposed toward Rome. This action initiated the Second Punic War between the cities of Carthage and Rome, one of the titanic struggles of history. Hannibal's army marched north, crossed the Alps and descended into Italy. In response to this audacious move, the Romans sent an army to Spain under the command of Gnaeus Scipio. They disembarked at Emporión on the Bay of Rosas (today San Martín de Ampurias) in August of the year 218 B.C. Shortly thereafter, the Iberian town of Tarragona fell to the Roman legions, who converted it into permanent winter quarters and a base of operations for the Ebro River region.

In 216 B.C. the Roman army crossed the river and in the following year seized Sagunto. With the help of local insurrections against Carthage, the legions entered the mining town of Cazlona and wintered as far south as Osuna. However, Carthaginian reinforcements from Africa pushed the Romans back across the Ebro. In 210 B.C., with the decline of Hannibal's fortunes in Italy, the Roman Senate despatched new armies to Spain which, in 209 B.C., captured Cartagena, the Carthaginian arsenal. With a victory at Bailén, Scipio forced entry into the Guadalquivir valley, and soon after the Carthaginian defeat at Alcalá del Río in 207 B.C. decided the fate of the peninsula. Thereafter all that was left to the victorious Romans was the mopping up.

The next year Cádiz, the last Carthaginian stronghold, fell, and the mighty legions became masters of the southern portion of the peninsula as Punic power in this part of the world ceased. The Second Punic War ended in 201 B.C. on the plains of Zama near Carthage, and triumphant Rome turned her attention toward Spain with a view to further conquest. This was only the beginning. Far from subdued, the peninsula was partitioned in 197 B.C. into two military divisions: Hispania Citerior and Hispania Ulterior, the latter including what is today most of Andalucía.

The Hispanic peninsula was also at times a battleground among Roman factions. Q. Sertorius, governor of Citerior who had opposed Sulla in the Roman class war, set up an independent government in Spain. He founded a Roman school at Huesca and even a Senate along the lines of the Roman legislative body. In 75 B.C. Pompey marched into the Ebro valley and founded Pamplona while Sertorius' declining influence culminated in his assassination. Spain was also a grim battleground in the Roman civil wars, as the struggle between Caesar and Pompey attests.

In 49 B.C. Caesar won a bloodless victory over Pompey's generals at Lérida on the banks of the river Segre, and later, in 45 B.C., he again defeated the armies of the Pompeians in a series of bloody battles in Andalucía, the final blow delivered at Munda, near Montilla, in the province of Córdoba.

Campaigning in Spain was not only a war against enemy resistance— which in the north took on desperate proportions, to the extent that Roman troops under Agrippa mutinied rather than fight the intractable Celts—but also a constant battle against cold, heat, rain, floods, precipitous terrain, lack of supplies, and hunger.

The Roman conquest of the Iberian peninsula took place in three general phases: by around 200 B.C. Rome had conquered and dominated the Mediter-ranean coasts from the Pyrenees to Andalucía—nearly all the territory of the ancient Iberians. In a second assault the high, central meseta was subjugated. During the protracted period in which the Romans attempted to subdue the disunited Celtic hinterland, two native folk-heroes rose to meet the crisis: a shepherd from the Serra da Estrela, Viriathus, at the head of a rugged band of shepherd-warriors, harassed the legions in southern Spain for eight years before his wily foe arranged Viriathus' assassination in 139 B.C. The second was Retogenes, who emerged as leader of the small town of Numantia (Spanish Numancia) on the Duero river near present-day Soria. He held the Roman armies at bay for fourteen years until Scipio Aemilianus, with overwhelming forces, brought the town to its knees in 133 B.C. after a sixteen-month siege. There were few spoils for the victorious army, however, since the starving Numantians preferred suicide to capture. The last endeavour of conquest resulted in the Cantabrian War from 29 to 19 B.C. and finally in the complete subjugation of the northwest. Over this protracted period various generations of the indigenous Hispanic populations gradually abandoned their traditions and adopted the Roman way of life.

The sons of chiefs received training in Latin and administration at spe-cially founded schools, Roman townships were created and veteran colonies were erected, for example at Itálica, founded in 206 B.C, at Carteia on the Bay of Algeciras, founded in 171 B.C., and at Córdoba, which was established as a colony in 152 B.C. Intermarriage was encouraged, and various inducements such as reduction in tribute, land grants and more efficient justice encouraged natives to live peacefully in municipalities. With Augustus, coveted Roman citizenship was awarded to those who aided the Romans, but native traditions in the north continued up to and beyond the demise of the Roman Empire.

Roman penetrations into the Basque regions were small and offered no particular inducement to the populations in these areas to modify their cultural heritage. Eventually, however, over most of the peninsula the Roman way was so thoroughly adopted and the fusion of the peoples so complete that Roman emperors born in Spain would rule over the Empire. The conquest of Spain by the Latin language was as successful as the ultimate triumph of the legions, and the native languages, with the exception of Basque, disappeared.

Economic factors

With sufficient capital and slave labour the Romans were in a position to exploit the mineral wealth of the Iberian peninsula. Gold from Galicia and León in the northwest, silver from the Sierra Morena, iron from Toledo, copper from the region of the Río Tinto, lead from Cartagena and mercury from Almadén all contributed to the growing wealth of the Roman upper classes. While mining appears to have been a lucrative business for some, the work underground was far from appealing. At El Centenillo near Cástulo (Linares) in the Andalucian province of Jaén, vertical wood-lined mine shafts, about a metre in diameter and which descended over two hundred metres into the earth have been found. Horizontal galleries too low for a man to stand upright ran off from them for about a kilometre. Here, branded and fettered slaves worked day and night on their hands and knees, placing the ore in esparto-grass baskets worn around their necks.

There was money to be made also in agriculture, in the production of olives and oil and from wine, a commodity introduced by the Greeks. Cereals, too, were cultivated, and Hispania became the granary of Rome and the wealthiest province in the Empire. Also lucrative were three kinds of plants: flax for linen, esparto grass for sandals and chairs, and cotton. These products nourished a considerable textile industry.

The province of Lusitania was less urbanized than southern Spain but Mérida (Emerita Augusta), its capital, had become one of the great cities of the Roman peninsula, with its primary wealth drawn from the irrigable valleys of the Guadiana and Tajo rivers and from the stock raising of the Alemtejo, famous for its horses. The valley of the Ebro river in Cataluña formed a similar area of intense rural exploitation and these regions were exceeded in importance only by Tarragona, a military and administrative capital.

Livestock investments in the form of sheep and pigs were not overlooked, and through the fish industry, Spain supplied Rome and the Empire with seafood. Salted fish, oysters and garum (a fish sauce appreciated all over the ancient world) made more than a few entrepreneurs happy. The Roman merchants came, invested, grew wealthy and constructed magnificent villas.

Architecture

The great period of Roman building in Spain occurred in the first and second centuries A.D. and especially during the reigns of the Spanish-born emperors Trajan (A.D. 98–117) and Hadrian (A.D. 117–138) with the construction of roads, bridges, aqueducts, forums, baths, monuments, temples, walls, houses, tombs, triumphal arches, circuses and theatres. By preference, the materials employed were generally stone and marble, but bricks and sometimes adobe were also used. The exteriors of their buildings were dressed up with marble and stucco and the insides decorated with pictures, tiled floors and often mosaics—the latter were on rare occasions applied to the walls. Baked mud was sometimes employed in the construction of canals and water pipes, although lead pipes were also used.

For spectacular events the Romans built arenas, for dramatic representatons they constructed the theatre, for mock battles and bloody combats the amphitheatre, for chariot or horse races they leveled the ground for the circus. The vast arenas at Itálica and Mérida were among the largest in the Roman world.

Theatres, amphitheatres and circuses

Roman theatres are well represented in Spain. They may be seen in numerous places, although the finest are those of Clunia, Sagunto, Segóbriga, Itálica and Mérida. The last, built in the year 18 B.C. was, without doubt, unsurpassed on the peninsula and perhaps in the entire Roman Empire. Most were constructed in the Greek style, that is, where possible, taking advantage of a natural declivity of the terrain to establish the seating arrangement. They were built in the shape of a half circle with a raised stage, the orchestra space and the *cavea* or seating area. Their survival was often due to the fact that they were constructed on hillsides that later generations did not covet for new buildings.

Amphitheatres were numerous. Those of Mérida and Itálica are the best preserved. The one at Itálica uses the natural configuration of two hills to form its flanks. The amphitheatre—or as the name indicates, the "double theatre"—was not actually round but elliptical, with seats all around and the arena in the centre. In some cases galleries were constructed under the arena to facilitate the housing and movements of men and beasts, for in the amphitheatre the gladiatorial bouts were held.

Of the Roman circuses little remains since their large, flat surfaces were ideal for the construction of other, later buildings, but there are traces of circuses at Tarragona, Mérida, Toledo, Sagunto, Calahorra, and a few other places.

Baths

Thermal baths not only fulfilled a hygienic and medicinal function in Roman life but they were also places for reunions and entertainment. Some were public and found generally on the outskirts of towns, while others were private, located in country houses or villas. There were many such baths in Spain but few remain today. Itálica had two, Mérida three (two on the outskirts of town), their remains can also be found at Caldas de Malavella, in the province of Gerona, Caldas de Montbuy, Barcelona, Baños de Montemayor, Cáceres, and at Manilva in the province of Málaga, but the most notable remains are those of Baños de Alange, Badajoz, where two circular rooms with baths, 11.3 m in diameter and covered by vaulted ceilings (open in the centre for light) are still in use. The circular pool is five metres in diameter. As in the original construction, water is brought in through lead pipes.

The public bath was a popular institution during all stages of Roman history and was indulged by every level of society. When the Visigoths took charge of Spanish affairs they destroyed or neglected the baths in the belief that they encouraged softness and effeminacy. The Arabs, with the contrary view, revived the tradition and bathing again became fashionable. Both Moslems and Jews used water in their religious ablutions such as the washing of the dead to cleanse them of sins. As the Christian reconquest of the peninsula proceeded, the Medieval Castillian soldiers despised the practice of washing in any form, which they associated with the immoral heretics. Spanish monks considered physical uncleanliness the proof of moral purity and the true faith. After the reconquest, sinful Arabic baths were abolished. In this social context it is a wonder that any of the structures survived at all.

Temples

The Roman temple was an adaptation of the Greek prototype. The platform on which the pillars stood was raised and access was by a flight of stairs in the front. The inner core contained the altar. Various type of pillars were employed in the construction, such as the fluted Doric column or the more slender Ionic pillar, but the most popular seems to have been the Corinthian type with carved decorations of acanthus leaves on the capitals. Of the once numerous temples, few have survived.

At Tarragona and Barcelona some remnants of temples can be seen, with even more complete ones at Vich in the province of Barcelona and at Emporión, Gerona. Some slight vestiges of temples are found at Denia in the province of Alicante, Sagunto, and Segóbriga. In the south, remains of temples can be seen at Itálica, Bolonia, in Cádiz, and Zalamea de la Serena, province of Badajoz, where the tower of the church was constructed on the remains of a Roman temple. At Mérida, at least five temples were erected but only one survives in a fair state of preservation. In the province of Cáceres another Roman temple is preserved at the Alcántara bridge.

Temple remains of a despised religion in a new Christian order were the targets of fanatics, and their despoiling was inevitable. Temples were also often situated in the middle of towns where they received little sympathy from city planners when rebuilding projects took place.

Triumphal arches

Triumphal arches honouring a specific person, such as that erected by Pompey in the Pyrenees at the end of the Sertorian wars, have largely disappeared. Others, serving as entrances to cities (for example, Trajan's arch in Mérida), have persisted. The bridge at Martorell in the province of Barcelona has two arches, one at each end. The bridge at Alcántara in the province of Cáceres has a Roman arch in the middle. Some arches marked territorial limits and are found along old Roman roads: the arch of Bara near Tarragona delimited the boundaries of the two Iberian tribes, the Cosetanos and Ilergetes and stands 12.28m high. Along the same route, the Vía Augusta, between Tortosa and Sagunto in the province of Castellón stands the arch of Cabanes. In Medinaceli, Soria, a beautiful arch is preserved and among the ruins of ancient Caparra, in the province of Cáceres, stands another, rather unique, four-sided arch which appears to have been erected at the crossroads of the town's two main streets.

Villas

The floor plans of Roman houses can be clearly noted at Itálica, Bolonia, Mérida, and Numancia, as well as at villas in diverse places such as Cuevas de Soria and Villa Fortunati near Fraga in the province of Huesca. While villas may be of interest to the traveller—with their various styles, heating and drainage systems, baths, kitchens and rooms—those with mosaics are perhaps the most enlightening. The patterns and decorations give some idea about the artistic temperament, cultural level and wealth of the owner. The employment of a skilled mosaicist probably did not come inexpensively. Two sets of splendid extant mosaics are in the province of Palencia.

At Bolonia, an industrial site, as well as other places, may be seen the vats which were designed for the preparation of garum, the *escabeche* of the ancient world. There are literary references to this sauce dating back to the fifth century B.C. and up until the eighth century A.D. It seems to have been invented by the Greeks. That they were on to a good thing is clear from its popularity. Punic and Roman men of commerce soon learned the trade, but not everyone was fully appreciative of it. Pliny stated that it was the putrefaction of the intestines of fish, and Seneca called it food contrary to nature. Nevertheless, it was produced in large quantities and shipped to the far corners of the Roman Empire. One of the best garum sites today is at Almuñécar in Granada.

Garum seems to have been produced as follows: the viscera of large fish, mixed with smaller fish such as anchovies, was salted and left to dry in the sun for several months, but was frequently stirred. From the drying mass was extracted the remaining liquid which was the garum. The manufacture of this product stimulated other industries, such as the production of amphorae, to contain and ship the delicacy.

Communications

During the first weeks of conquest of any given area the Romans began to build roads. They constructed them in generally a straight line or with wide curves in spite of topographical obstacles. The process accompanied the rise of new towns and the refurbishing of conquered ones. Augustus had two thousand kilometres of roads built in Spain, and they were built to last. For major highways foundations were laid well below ground and no fewer than four layers of stone were added to complete the job.

A major source of knowledge about Roman roads is the Itinerary of Antonius which has been attributed to the Emperor Caracalla but edited anomonyously around the year A.D. 280. The four vases of Vicarello (Tuscany) are inscribed with the itinerary from ancient Gades (that is, Cádiz), to Aguae Apollinares, or today Baños de Vicarello. They provide a list of towns and road stations between Italy and Cádiz. Information about highways that have disappeared also comes from military milestones, now mostly in museums but a few still in situ along the ancient roads, for example, at Puente Bibey in Orense.

The principal highway on the peninsula was the Via Herculea (or Augusta) that ran along the coast from the Pyrenees past Emporión all the way to Cartagena. In the time of Augustus it was extended to Granada, then on to Córdoba, Sevilla, and Cádiz. Later it followed the coast more closely, passing through Almería and Málaga to Cádiz. Many roads branched off into the interior, especially to mining centres and to the major towns.

Another especially important road was that of the Via de la Plata from Astorga to Mérida through Zamora, Salamanca and Cáceres, over which the legions headed north and the gold from the northern mines came south.

The road between Toledo and Mérida, and one from Zaragoza to Toledo and Zaragoza to Astorga, were of no small consequence in Roman control of the peninsula. Later, from the eighth century A.D. onward, pilgrims from Europe en route to the shrine at Santiago de Compostela used the old Roman road that passed through Pamplona (from the Roncesvalles pass), Burgos, León and Lugo.

The Via del Duero, from Zaragoza to Zamora, had great military usefulness, as troops could rapidly be deployed along it to fend off incursions of the Cantabrian and Asturian tribes. At Zamora it linked up with the Via de la Plata.

The construction of the network of roads, generally five metres in width, along with numerous bridges over the rivers went on for centuries. The best and longest extant example of a Roman road is at Puerto del Pico in Avila.

The Roman bridges that supplemented the road network were many, and while some have been destroyed—a few blown up as late as the Spanish civil war of 1936—many others remain today. Fine examples of large bridges are at Alcántara, Salamanca, Córdoba, and Mérida.

The Puente de Alcántara along the highway leading northwest from Cáceres is, perhaps, one of the finest specimens in the entire Roman Empire. Generally, Roman architects set the stone dry (as in this case) but sometimes they used mortar made from lime.

A prominent feature of the Roman bridge is the rounded arch (Spanish *medio punto*); if an obviously old bridge has pointed arches it was either built in the Middle Ages or is a rebuilt Roman bridge. Unfortunately, rounded arches were also a trademark of the Romanesque period and it is not easy or sometimes even possible to tell a Roman bridge from a Romanesque one.

By and large, hundreds of Roman bridges, many with facelifts, have survived either because they were useful and repaired when required or because they were not in the way of agricultural or industrial enterprises.

Cities and towns

Cities were laid out in conjunction with a north-south and east-west line the intersection of which served as the site of the forum, and the rest of the streets ran parallel to these. Some cities in Spain were of Roman foundation, such as Itálica and Mérida, but many others were older Iberian or Celtic towns that became Romanized—voluntarily or otherwise.

The centre of Roman urban life revolved around the forum, a rectangular enclosure surrounded by porticos and columns and containing merchants' shops. Originally the market, the forum evolved into the centre of political, economic and religious activity of the city with the attendant temples, *curias* or tribunals and relevant buildings for the administration of justice. Almost nothing remains in Spain of the forums of the various towns, but the tradition has continued in the modern Spanish *plaza mayor* or central square.

The Romans fortified their cities with walls and towers and while not a great deal remains of these in Spain, enough are there for us to appreciate their importance and manner of construction. According to Julius Caesar, the strongest city in Baetica (now Andalucía) was the hilltop town of Carmona, where the visitor may still see two vaulted entrances and a length of wall with projections of squared, hewn stone. Still visible in Barcelona are two towers of hewn stone and stretches of Roman wall with Medieval and modern constructions backing onto it. Parts of Roman walls may also be seen at Zaragoza, Mérida, Cáceres, Coria, Tarragona, Gerona and Emporión. The most complete Roman wall, over two kilometres long, is at Lugo in Galicia. By the middle of the third century A.D., the construction of massive walls around towns like León, Lugo and Barcelona indicates the threat of barbarian invasions soon to come.

The Romans also constructed ports at their coastal cities, but nothing of these remain. Similarly, lighthouses that dotted the coasts have all disappeared with the exception of the Torre de Hércules in La Coruña, an impressive structure in antiquity and sheathed in the eighteenth century.

Aqueducts

The Romans supplied towns with water through the construction of aqueducts, of which they were prolific builders, and their remains may be seen in all quarters of the peninsula. The best are located at Segovia, Tarragona and Mérida, in that order. The specimen at Segovia where, with only minor repairs, the aqueduct has supplied water to the town up until recent times, was built in the first century out of hewn granite blocks mounted without mortar.

Besides water supply from often distant sources, there was usually a reservoir, such as that at Mérida. The system provided the important function of water distribution. At the end of a course, water flowed into a chamber with three containers, the centre one being lower than the other two so that it received water only from the overflow of the the the others. From the central container water was supplied to the public fountains, circus and amphitheatre. In times of drought these were the sites deprived of water, while private residences and public baths, receiving their water from the flanking tanks, maintained their supply.

Necropoli and funerary monuments

The Romans practised both incineration and inhumation of the dead, but after the second century A.D. the former prevailed. An urn, generally of clay, was placed in a simple hole in the ground. In some cases the hole was paved with flagstones and an ornamental monument placed over the grave. Sometimes mausolea were constructed or caves were used in collective family burials. Often the Romans placed their dead along the sides of the roads near the cities, and at times they were grouped together in true graveyards. Not many Hispanic graveyards from Roman times are known and those that are have not all been excavated. Two notable explored and studied necropoli are located at Carmona and Bolonia. That of Carmona, which was used from Republican to Imperial times, occupies a square kilometre and contains hundreds of tombs, many of which are in subterranean vaults. Most are cremation urns in decorated crypts. The burial ground at Bolonia contains over one thousand tombs, most of which were marked by a small monument. Of the mausolea, few remain standing.

A mausoleum in the form of a tower (the so-called Torre de los Escipiones), beside the Via Augusta five kilometres north of Tarragona, is of squared stone blocks with two statues, probably of slaves, in Iberian dress. In the province of Gerona four such funerary towers exist: Vilablareix, Acuaviva, Lloret de Mar and Emporión (of the last only the base remains). Mausolea in the form of temples are found at Villajoyosa in the province of Alicante, Fabara and Sádaba in Zaragoza, and Sagunto.

A typical tombstone inscription, in this case from Segóbriga in the province of Cuenca, reads:

EVTYCHIA
ANN L
PIA IN SVIS
H S E S T T L

The inscription translates as follows:

Eutiquia,
fifty years old
loved by hers
here lies. May the earth be light upon you.

The name appears to have been Greek. The lady, perhaps a slave. (Note the abbreviations in the last line: *HIC SITA EST SIT TIBI TERRA LEVIS.*)

Decline of Roman Spain

Roman military activity in Spain had not only to contend with indigenous uprisings and rebellions but also with foreign assaults. In the second century A.D. Roman legions and Hispanic auxiliaries thwarted Moorish incursions from Mauritania, and in the third century bands of Germanic Franks and Suevi ravaged the country and laid waste to city, town and villa. By the fifth century, the Roman Empire lay prostrate before the Germanic hordes that poured across the northern frontiers. The towns in Spain ceased to be centres of justice and culture, and became instead citadels of officialdom and privilege.

As the Imperial demands for men and money grew more urgent, troops were withdrawn from Spain and peasants pressed into service. The state snuffed out the municipal institutions, and the remaining peasants, who were nearly slaves, were forbidden to leave the land they worked. As the towns declined, landowners bought up and ruled over huge tracts of land (*latifundia*) and commanded private armies of their own. There was little justice or protection. The idea of the Roman Empire, of law and order, of security and stability (at least for the free man) was now a myth. Salvation could not be expected from Rome and like the slaves, many of whom had already cast their lot with the new religion, more and more of the oppressed urban society looked for solace in the bosom of the Christian church.

The Roman legacy

Physical remains of the Roman Empire can be seen everywhere in Spain, from the monumental aqueduct at Segovia to the smallest fragments of paving stones seen here and there along the Via de la Plata. But perhaps even more lasting than these durable engineering works was the cultural legacy. The southern and Mediterranean coastal cities of Spain constituted nurseries where the Gospel took root and began to blossom in the first century A.D. In the hinterland and the north, pagan practices were still very much alive in the fourth century when the Church was transformed into a bulwark of the ideas of authority and universality that Rome had previously imposed. As it ceased to be semi-clandestine and anti-imperialistic and became the ally of secular power, Christianity brought to these areas a Romanizing influence. Only the Basque remained impervious for a little longer.

During the Golden Age of Roman Hispania, from the first to the third centuries A.D., much of the population was incorporated culturally into the Roman sphere under the auspices of Roman educators, administrators, merchants, soldiers, and technicians. The Empire was not only ruled by emperors born in Spain, but philosophers and poets such as Seneca, Martial and Lucan were of Hispanic origin. Roman conquest also brought stability and order to the bellicose Hispanic tribes. The nineteenth century archaeological discovery of the *Lex Ursonis*, the charter of Urso (modern Osuna), first century copies of the 44 B.C. originals inscribed on bronze tablets, clearly demonstrates the benefits of Roman law. Now in the National Archaeological Museum of Madrid, the documents record the rights and privileges of the members of the colony, ranging from the equal-time clause for prosecutor and defendant in trials to guarantees of citizens' rights to water. Also mentioned are holidays, collection of fines, and even expulsion from city council on moral grounds. Osuna had been the centre of Pompeian resistance to Julius Caesar in the Civil War, and in 44 B.C. Mark Antony sent a contingent of plebeians and freedmen from Rome to establish the colony. The charter was thus for the well-being of the Romans, but the local Iberians also benefited.

Perhaps the most salient cultural legacy of the Romans to the Hispanic peoples was their language. Latin, the *lingua franca* of the Empire, quickly found adherents among those who aspired to the benefits of Rome, and it gradually replaced all the peninsular languages with the exception of Basque. Local linguistic circumstances have led to different varieties of speech in different regions of Spain, but the present-day languages and dialects of Galician-Portuguese in the northwest, Castillian in the centre, Andalucian in the south, Catalán and Aragonese in the northeast are all a continuation of the ancient language of Rome.

For further reading see *Roman Spain* by S. J. Keay, Berkeley, California (1988) and *Roman Spain* by F. J. Wiseman, London (1956). Wiseman's book is an introduction to the Roman antiquities of Spain and Portugal and more suited to the beginner in Hispanic studies of the period.

5. PALEO-CHRISTIAN AND EARLY CHRISTIAN PERIODS

Introduction and spread of Christianity

During the period of the Late Roman Empire various religions vied for authority. Roman deities and emperor-worship existed alongside Christian beliefs and practices, while in the north of Spain Celtic gods persisted up to the end of the fifth century. Pagan practices in Spain had all but disappeared by the sixth century with, perhaps, exceptions in the Basque country, and left only vestigial traces in the remote areas of the north. This is the period designated here as Paleo-Christian.

Unauthenticated tradition associates Saint Paul and Saint James with the earliest teachings of Christianity on the Iberian Peninsula. While this is uncertain, it is clear that the new religion reached Spain in the first century A.D. and already under Nero (A.D. 54–68) there were several Christian martyrs.

Christian converts refused to compromise their beliefs by praying to the traditional Roman gods or to pay homage to the emperor. Roman authorities found this attitude divisive when the country was engaged in civil strife or separatist movements, and persecutions continued. Their action only served to unite the Christians more closely.

During the second century, numerous Christian communities arose which suffered cruel repression and there were many martyrs at the hands of the authorities. The Spanish propensity toward martyrdom exceeded that of all other countries.

By 250 there were substantial Christian followings at Mérida, Astorga, León and elsewhere, linked to those in Carthage and Rome by a network of bishoprics served by a hierarchy of priests and deacons all under the authority of the Pope. Nevertheless, in 259 Bishop Fructuosus of Tarragona and his deacons Augurius and Eulogius were burnt to death in the amphitheatre for refusing to recant their beliefs.

Among the early church councils that met to decide and legislate religious matters, three were held in Spain. The first took place at Iliberris (modern Elvira) near Granada in 305, and was attended by bishops representing all the regions of Spain. It condemned pagan beliefs and dealt with such topics as celibacy among the clergy and prohibition of marriage with non-Christians.

The political authorities had under the Emperors Diocletian (284–305) and

Galerius (305–310) begun major persecutions, however. Saint Felix was martyred at Gerona, Saint Cucufatus at Barcelona, and Saints Justa and Rufina were sentenced to death at Sevilla, the latter for desecrating a pagan procession. One of the most famous martyrdoms was that of Santa Eulalia, killed at Mérida during the reign of Diocletian. Her church at Mérida was constructed in the fourth century, by which time Christian congregations were thriving.

A new era of toleration was introduced in 312 when the Emperor Constantine himself converted to the new religion and assumed a prominent role in church affairs. His religious advisor was Bishop Ossius of Córdoba. From this time on, church power grew rapidly not only in religious affairs but also in secular concerns.

The Spaniard Theodosius, the last emperor to rule the entire Roman world (392–95), made Christianity the official religion and the Church gradually became an instrument of state policy in which compulsory orthodoxy formed the basis of political unity. The Second Council at Zaragoza in 380 was in part concerned with condemnation and persecution of heretics; the Third, at Toledo in 400, discussed and pronounced on matters of orthodoxy and rejected the threatening rival religious practices of Arianism.

Hispano-Roman Christianity was vigorous, evangelical and intolerant, but cracks appeared in the ranks. The Bishop of Avila, Priscillian (some say he was from Galicia) preached a heretical version of the faith and gained a wide following. Not recognized by the Pope, he was eventually executed by Emperor Magnus Maximus (383–388) in 385. On the other hand, he was considered a martyr in Galicia and was the focus of a popular religious movement, Priscillianism, which persisted into the sixth century.

Art and architecture

Before the edict of Milan in 313 the Christian cult was practised in secret, sometimes in cemeteries—inviolate under Roman law—and often in private houses. Corpses were interred in caves or crypts. Primitive Christian art in these first three centuries of persecution revolved around symbolic signs of doves, fish, sheep, anchors and representations of the cross, among others. Sometimes pagan themes were employed in a symbolic manner such as Orpheus attracting the wild animals with his music, an allusion to the efficacy of the divine word. These artistic religious manifestations were in the form of parables.

After the Edict of Constantine, the *labarum* became the official sign of Christianity and practitioners were allowed to construct places of worship. The period of Paleo-Christian art (and extant remains discussed here) was initiated in the first century A.D. and reached its apogee in the fifth century under Visigothic rule. By the sixth century new forms of Christian art replaced the old.

The number of monasteries grew rapidly in Spain from the sixth century onward. Some were located near the larger cities such as Toledo, Zaragoza, Tarragona, Sevilla and Mérida, while others were situated in the country. Some of their names are known, such as San Félix and Agaliense at Toledo, but often they remain anonymous. The most famous were Asanio in the province of Huesca, founded in 506 by the Italian San Victorian; el Servitano at Játiva in the province of Valencia, founded in 550 by Donato who came from North Africa with seventy monks; Santa Engracia near Zaragoza; San Román de Hornija in Zamora; and Samos in Galicia.

As the Roman Empire grew weak and ineffectual, the Church came to stand for order amidst anarchy, for ethical values amidst corruption. It also played an increasingly larger role in administration of municipal affairs and judicial procedures. In short, it fell heir to the Roman Empire, with a mandate for civic, social and religious responsibilities.

The Early Christian basilicas adopted the manner of the Roman judicial basilicas: a rectangular room with a semi-circular apse at the end. In the judicial buildings this served the tribunal; for the Christians, the rituals of the cult. The Christians situated the apse at the east end of the building and the narthex or atrium on the west side; such is the basilica discovered at Emporión. The existence of niches in the north wall leads one to suspect that the area was used as either a *columbarium* or as a baptistry, in which the niches were employed for the clothes of the catechumen.

In the Roman-Christian necropolis of Tarragona the remains of what appears to have been a basilica of the fifth century have been found, with three naves, a transept, a semicircular apse and mosaic floors. The remnants of a fourth-century Paleo-Christian basilica are located near Malpica del Tajo in the province of Toledo.

There are remnants of fifth-century baptistries at Gabia la Grande, (Granada) and at Centelles (Tarragona) and San Miguel at Tarrasa in the province of Barcelona.

Necropoli and sarcophagi

There is nothing to indicate that the early Christians in Spain used massive catacombs in which to bury their dead as they did in Rome, but they did employ for such purposes caves and crypts. Paleo-Christian cemeteries are found in all parts of the peninsula, but many have been renovated so often that there is little left to indicate their original purpose. The crypt of Santa Engracia at Zaragoza, for example, shows no sign of such early use except for the sarcophagi deposited within. Cemeteries were organized in the open air as well as within and around the basilicas. In Emporión the burials took on diverse forms: graves covered over with little tiles as in the Roman style, amphorae used as coffins, and, in the case of lofty personages, stone sarcophagi. Elsewhere in the peninsula are coffins of marble, wood or lead covered over with mosaics and grave inscriptions in which the sign of the cross has taken the place of the initials D.M. (Diis Manibus).

Important Paleo-Christian necropoli are found at Mérida and Itálica, but the most notable is that of Tarragona, discovered in 1923. Situated in the lower part of the city on the banks of the river Francolí, more than one thousand graves have so far been found, along with sepulcral constructons and the basilica. Some have epitaphs of mosaics, or are painted over the stucco as are the necropoli of North Africa. Here also are family mausolea, some of which are subterranean crypts. Some are of solid stone and three or four metres deep with steps leading down. Two are quadrangular, measuring seven metres along the side, with the interior constructed on a cruciform plan. The graves are under the floor.

Of the over one hundred sarcophagi of the Paleo-Christian period, fewer than fifty are decorated or sculpted. The plain coffins or those with a simple decoration in relief in either marble or other stone appear to have been made in Spain, while those decorated with elaborate scenes of figures similar to those of Rome and Provence appear to have been imported from Italy or Gaul, where industries for such artistic work existed. Few are prior to the time of Constantine. Coffins with simply a name or a symbol, such as a fishing scene or pastoral motif, may be earlier, but those sculptured with biblical scenes are post-Constantine of the fourth, fifth or sixth centuries. The plain coffins, the most economical, are from all periods.

Some Paleo-Christian sarcophagi (that is, those found in Christian cemeteries) have pagan motifs, apparently due to the fact that already-sculpted stone from other sources was used.

Mosaics

Paganism was still strong in the late fourth century despite Christian fervour, as may be seen from the style of the mosaics in use at the time.

Mosaic coverings or tiled floors show no difference between Christian and pagan techniques, but only in the figures and symbols employed. Christian symbols were the two-handled chalice and, it seems, the swastika, as found in the so-called Casa-Basílica of Mérida and elsewhere. The mosaics of the Hispano-Roman complex at Centcelles in Tarragona display many scenes from the Old and New Testaments.

It was the custom in Spain, as in North Africa, to decorate the lids of coffins and tombstones with mosaics. The tombstone would often carry the epitaph, some symbol or figure, and perhaps some purely decorative devices. The best are to found in the cemetery at Tarragona.

Germanic Spain

On 31 December 406 the Germanic Suevi, in company with non-Germanic Alans, crossed the Rhine River and entered Gaul. In the year 409 they were joined by the Vandals and crossed the Pyrenees into Spain. The Suevi and one group of Vandals settled in Galicia, the Alans in Lusitania (modern Portugal), and the remaining Vandals in ancient Baetica or Andalucía. In 416 the Vandals in the south and the Alans were attacked and destroyed by another Germanic nomadic tribe, the Visigoths (or West Goths) who were acting in the interests of Rome. Vandals who had settled in Galicia were then permitted to move southward and reside in Andalucía, taking the place of their defeated kinsmen. In 429 they crossed the straits and settled in North Africa where they survived for nearly a century. The Vandals left no lasting monuments in Spain and their passing is noted in only a few place-names, such as the word "Andalucía," adopted from Arabic. Traces of the Alans are also few and found only in place names such as Puerta del Alano at Huesca and Villalán (Villa-Alan) at Valladolid.

Most of the Hispano-Roman cities and towns, such as Toledo, Zaragoza, Mérida, Sevilla and Córdoba, survived the disasters of the barbarian invasions, but others perished in the onslaught leaving only ruins as, for example, at Itálica and Clunia. Some towns disappeared without a trace.

The kingdom of the Suevi survived in northwest Spain for a century and a half before it succumbed to the Visigoths. Their sojourn in northwestern Spain has left hardly a trace.

Visigothic migrations

Having migrated from their Baltic homeland, the Visigoths first appeared along the lower Danube, defending the frontiers on behalf of Rome, at the end of the fourth century. Restless, nomadic, and powerful, they eventually invaded Italy, sacked Rome in 410, and later moved on to Gaul where they established an independent kingdom with their capital at Toulouse. In 415 they moved into Spain and, on the side of Rome, defeated the alien tribes established there before retiring again to Gaul. By 476 they had wrested control of the peninsula from other Germanic peoples and a bankrupt Roman administration. In 507, defeated by the Franks, the Visigoths withdrew permanently to Spain, establishing a centre first at Barcelona and later their capital at Toledo.

The demographic situation in Spain was as follows: the Suevi occupied the northwest, Roman nobles held extensive lands in the centre and south, and along the southern coasts the Byzantines had restored the rule of the Empire in 554. The Basques remained independent in their highlands. Of these groups, the first three were eventually subdued by the Visigoths: the kingdom of the Suevi was completely obliterated while the rout of the Byzantines was not complete until the early part of the seventh century. Under Visigothic rule Spain became politically, if not socially, united.

The Roman way of life had continued throughout the fifth and sixth centuries, but during this period many Roman buildings fell into disuse and decay. Churches and episcopal palaces proliferated, often at the expense of the Roman structures and graveyards, whose stones were quarried for the new construction, a process that continued until recently.

During this period towns such as Clunia in Burgos, Tiermes in Soria and Complutum at Alcalá de Henares in the province of Madrid were all but abandoned. Many great villas continued to flourish in the hands of aristocratic Hispano-Romans, although in some cases Visigothic nobles confiscated much of the good land. From the sixth century onwards churches often became the focal point for estate centres. The decline of towns prompted the owners of the villas to care for the physical and spiritual requirements of their dependents. One such estate church may be seen at Villa Fortunati near Fraga in the province of Huesca.

By the sixth century Barcelona had taken on new importance as a royal and commercial centre and developed a major ecclesiastical complex. A church has been discovered in the old Roman town beneath the city near the Cathedral. It can still be seen with its fine, coloured wall paintings. Remains of early churches have also been found at Segóbriga in the province of Cuenca, Játiva in Valencia and Emporión in Gerona among other places.

In the latter part of the sixth century the Visigothic king Leovigild chose Toledo as the royal capital, which it remained until the Arab invasion of 711. It seems that by preference the majority of the Visigothic population settled north of the Tajo river, in the upper meseta, where many of their cemeteries have been found.

As a ruling caste, the Visigoths at first maintained a kind of apartheid between themselves and the Hispano-Roman population. They were also devoutly Arian, but renounced this doctrine for Catholicism in 589. The unification of Spain under Visigothic suzerainty and the establishment of a monarchy brought the peninsula out of its earlier status as simply a province of Rome. Coupled with Hispano-Roman Catholicism, which set the tone for society, the unifying force of the crown and the adhesive power of the church have withstood the severe centrifugal pressures toward fragmentation that continue up to the present day.

The fusion of the two peoples, Germanic and Hispano-Roman, also took place in the realm of jurisprudence, where the law codes of both nations were amalgamated and recast in one, drafted in Latin, and promulgated around 654 as the *Liber Judiciorum*. Translated in the thirteenth century into Castilian it became known as the *Fuero Juzgo*.

Art and architecture

Before the close of the sixth century, there is little in the way of Visigothic structures to be found in northern Spain. In the south, architectural remains show clear Byzantine influence corresponding to the political state of affairs from 554 when imperial forces summoned by Athanagild, the Visigothic king at the time, arrived and remained until 624. In the seventh century a series of churches was constructed in various parts of the country. Notable features of Visigothic construction and decoration revolve around the type of ashlar masonry, the horseshoe arch, the Maltese cross, spirals, stars and the cable border. One of the most interesting Visigothic churches is that of San Juan de Baños de Cerrato in Palencia. The most typical one is perhaps that of Santa Comba de Bande in the province of Orense, of which San Pedro de la Mata in Toledo seems to be a replica.

In architecture, the Visigoths incorporated ideas they had learned from Byzantium and from the Romans in Italy and Spain.

Visigothic Church of Santa Cruz (restored).
Cangas de Onis, Asturias

Visigothic legacy

The Visigothic kingdom was irretrievably swept away in the year 711 by invaders from Africa, but for many of the conquered, the distant vision during the centuries of reconquest was the establishment of a neo-Visigothic kingdom in Spain. During the Middle Ages, the written words of the Visigothic Saint Isidore, Bishop of Sevilla (d. 636) on history, philosophy, theology and language were studied throughout Europe. The idea of the Visigothic society lingered right up to the nineteenth century, when Spanish-American revolutionaries in the New World stirred their compatriots to action not against the Spaniards of the mother country, but against the Goths.

The Visigoths largely appear to have abandoned their Germanic speech in favour of Latin by the seventh century; consequently, their linguistic impact on Hispano-Latin speech of the period was not of any great importance. There are a few vocabulary items and a few place names, surnames, and baptismal names, such as Fernando, Ramiro, Alfonso and Elvira, derived from Visigothic times.

While the Visigoths were responsible for the destruction of cities and towns that resisted them, they also founded new ones such as Recópolis and Vitoria, perhaps originally military sites. Little is left of Visigothic civil architecture in the cities, but there are some slight remains at Mérida, Toledo and Córdoba. Military construction (walls and towers) followed the usual Roman lines.

Asturian churches and architecture

With the Arab conquest, the centres of Hispanic Christendom in the south and east fell under Moslem control, and although a certain amount of tolerance was practised on the part of the invaders, the Mozarabic church, cut off from the main currents of Christianity, became fossilized and sank into decadence as the more progressive participants emigrated to the Christian principalities of the north.

The Asturian church did not recognize the ecclesiastical leadership of the Metropolitan of Toledo living under Moslem overlordship, and doctrinal antagonism between Asturian and Mozarabe Catholicism emerged by the end of the eighth century. The Metropolitan of Toledo was excommunicated by papal authority in 794 for adhering to outmoded views, and under Alfonso II the Asturian monarchy created a separate ecclesiastical system independent of Toledo.

In the eighth century the northern Christians began, in an area only about fifty by seventy kilometres, to erect a group of pre-Romanesque type buildings of unusual interest, in which they developed their own styles in art and architecture. Asturian churches show fundamental differences from other churches in Spain in ground plan and decoration. Stylistically they continued the Visigothic traditions but in a seemingly more rustic manner. The earliest of these are the Cámera Santa (now part of the Cathedral of Oviedo) and San Julián de los Prados (or Santullano) both constructed for Alfonso II. He also had a large palace in Oviedo constructed, and remains of its baths and drains have been found.

From the reign of Ramiro I there remain San Miguel de Lillo and Santa María de Naranco, just outside Oviedo; the latter was erected as a palace on the slopes of Monte Naranco overlooking Oviedo, but later was used as a church. This palace is the most remarkable example in Europe of ninth-century civil architecture. Other Asturian buildings are Santa Cristina de Lena, San Salvador de Valdediós and San Salvador de Priesca.

Rulers of Asturias-León

Pelayo	718–737	García I	911–914
Fafila	737–739	Ordoño II	914–924
Alfonso I	739–757	Fruela II	924–925
Fruela I	757–768	Sancho Ordoñez	925–929
Aurelio	768–774	Alfonso IV	929–931
Silo	774–783	Ramiro II	931–951
Mauregato	783–788	Ordoño III	951–956
Vermudo I	788–791	Sancho I	956–966
Alfonso II	791–842	Ramiro III	966–985
Ramiro I	842–850	Vermudo II	985–999
Ordoño I	850–866	Alfonso V	999–1028
Alfonso III	866–911	Vermudo III	1028–1037

There is a great contrast between the opulent Al-Andalus and, say, the Great Mosque at Córdoba, and the poor northern Christian communities with their rock-hewn or rustic churches. The lamp of learning flickered on nevertheless in the impoverished and illiterate north in the monasteries, whose cenobitic life was invigorated by Mozarabes immigrating from the Moslem south, bringing their precious manuscripts with them.

The Christian north was a society of warriors and monks. Almost all cultural activity was confined to the monasteries, which built up important libraries, and copyists distributed the religious manuscripts from one to another.

During the ninth and tenth centuries the Asturo-Leonese church grew in authority and wealth; this contrasted with the steady decline of the Mozarabe church in the south. A major aspect of the northern religious expansion was the development of the cult of Santiago (Saint James), whose shrine at Santiago de Compostela in Galicia provided the main nexus with western Europe. By the tenth century, the pilgrims' route across northern Spain to the shrine became one of the most heavily travelled in the west. The thousands of pilgrims along it provided the stimulus for the development of many towns and sanctuaries in the north and were a major force in the Europeanization and modernization of the peasants.

When the capital was moved south from Oviedo to León it became more accessible to foreign influences, and the importation of French Romanesque styles stifled the Asturian architectual forms.

Rupestrian sanctuaries

Besides the thousands of natural caves in Spain used as dwellings down through the millennia there are many more that have been hewn from the rock by the patient labour of poor hands. Many were religious sanctuaries and conform to the Hispano-Visigothic style of construction, for example, in the use of horseshoe arches. Some appear to date back to the seventh century.

They are often found off the main routes of travel, in inconspicuous places, where they were constructed, no doubt, by Mozarabes fleeing Moslem authority. In the province of Alava, for example, there are many man-made caves designed for religious purposes, as there are in the provinces of Logroño, Burgos and Santander. Some caves were also used as dwellings, burial chambers, and for farm animals (as many still are).

Rock-cut churches fell into disuse in the twelfth and thirteenth centuries when the Romanesque churches began to flourish throughout the region.

For further reading, see *Visigothic Spain* edited by E. James, Oxford (1980) and *The Goths in Spain* by F. A. Thompson, Oxford (1969).

6. MOSLEM CONQUEST

Military and political events

The Arabs were one of the beneficiaries of the decline of the Roman Empire. Under the banners of Islam they erupted out of the Arabian deserts and drove across the face of North Africa, converting the local Berber tribes and snuffing out the seven hundred years of Roman and Byzantine culture, leaving only ruins in the sand. In the fateful year of 711, a Berber army, with Arab officers and under the command of General Tarik, Governor of Tangiers, crossed the straits and landed in Spain. They routed the opposing Visigothic army and in the space of few years overran the country. Using the excellent Roman roads, they moved rapidly as far as Zaragoza and Barcelona and made incursions into France. Only in the extreme north, in Galicia and the Cantabrian regions, did they fail to penetrate in force.

The Moslem invaders were in almost continuous dissension, and bitter quarrels broke out among them over power and spoils. New settlers were discriminated against by older ones, Arabs disputed among themselves and with Berbers, both quarreled with Hispano-Romans, and town-dwellers antagonized rural settlers at the same time as they defended their newly-won territories from encroachments by the incipient Christian states to the north. In Damascus, discord among the ruling families, the Ommiads and the Abbasids—claimants to power as the descendents of the Prophet—aggravated the situation in Spain.

In 756, the independent Emirate of Al-Andalus came into existence when prince Abd al-Rahman I, an Ommiad exiled by the victorious Abbasids, arrived in Spain. The social composition of Moslem Spain was made up of Arabs from the East, Berber tribesmen from North Africa, the conquered Christians or Mozarabes ("almost Arabs") and the Muladís or renegades, that is, Spaniards who had converted to Islam. This divisive mixture of groups with different backgrounds and interests, coupled with Mozarabe contacts with the hostile Christians of the north and old rivalries among the Arab ruling families, often led to dangerous conspiracies and bloodshed.

In 801, Charlemagne's troops occupied parts of Cataluña while the Christians of northern Spain made inroads into the Moslem territories. In 844 the Vikings managed to sail up the Guadalquivir River and sack Sevilla. Scarcely had the Viking menace passed than the Moslem clan of the Fatimids began their westward expansion across North Africa causing serious concern to the ruling Ommiads of Spain.

In spite of intermittent wars among themselves, and with the Christian populations in the north of the country, the Arabs established the most enlightened state in all of Europe at the time. The mixture of Arabs and Berbers were known as Moors to the Christians, but it was the Arabs who had inherited the great learning of the Greek classical world, much of which was stored in the city of Alexandria, and brought it to Spain where translators rendered the texts into Arabic, building up a body of knowledge—unparalleled in Europe—concerning astronomy, geometry, botany, medicine and agriculture.

The Caliphate of Córdoba

Throughout the ninth century the threatening Fatimids—a Moslem dynasty claiming descent from Fatima, a daughter of Mohammed the Prophet—and the Christian kingdoms of the north—which were aroused with the desire to reconquer lost territory from the Infidel—were making the Emirate of Córdoba more and more insecure. Dependence on the far-away, oriental Islamic world, with unreliable lines of communication, was no longer a guarantee of security; a separate western Caliphate was a solution to the problem.

Abd-al-Rahman III founded an independent state in 929 and at the same time initiated a policy of reconciliation with the Muladís and Mozarabes. His reign and those of his descendants made this century a period of relative peace and cultural splendour without precedent.

Rulers of Al-Andalus

Abd-al-Rahman I	756–788	al-Hakam II	961–976
Hisham I	788–796	Hisham II	976–1009
al-Hakam I	796–822	al-Mansur	ca. 976–1002
Abd-al-Rahman II	822–852	Abdul-Malik	1002–1008
Mohammad I	852–886	Taifa Kings	1009–1090
al-Mundhir	886–888	Almoravide Empire	1090–1147
Abdallah	888–912	Almohade Empire	1147–1212
Abd-al-Rahman III	912–961	Nasrid Granada	–1492

The Cordoban state reached the height of its power in the middle of the tenth century under Abd-al-Rahman III. His successor ruled for fifteen years and left his twelve-year-old son, Hisham II, as heir. But the government was soon dominated by the Hispano-Arab al-Mansur, The Victorious. Undefeated in battle with the Christian forces of the north, attacking, sacking and burning as far away as Santiago de Compostela, he was the scourge of the Christian communities. His death came in the year 1002, after raising the Caliphate to the pinnacle of its military power, but his son, who obtained the same military power from the impotent Hisham, did not long endure. The dictatorship dissolved into petty kingdoms vying with one another for power.

The Taifas

With the disintegration of the Caliphate, descendants of the Muladís, Berbers and even freed slaves found themselves in a position to seize power in various localities and establish their own petty states or Taifas. Many of these small states, unable to stand alone, became vassals of the Christian kingdoms in ever-changing political and military alignments as the reconquest continued southward. Even the Cid, whose historical image is that of the Great Terror of the Moslems, offered his services to the Taifa king of Zaragoza and ruled for a time in Islamic Valencia.

This fragmentation, of course, facilitated further Christian inroads into the Moslem-held south. When the city of Toledo fell into Christian hands in 1085 the Hispano-Moslems, realizing the encroaching danger, solicited aid from North Africa. The Almoravides answered the call. A puritanical sect among the Tuareg tribes of the western Sahara, they believed in literal obedience to the Koran. Evangelistic, fanatical and militant, they took over Morocco by about 1084. They shunned money and expected to achieve salvation by death in battle. A few months later they came, saw, and defeated Christian forces at the battle of Zalaca near Badajoz and returned to North Africa. Apparently, what they saw, they liked, and three years later they returned, this time with a desire to remain.

The Almoravides and Almohades

The small and weak kingdoms of Islamic Spain fell prey to the invasion of the Almoravides. Córdoba, Sevilla, Granada, Badajoz, and even Valencia and Zaragoza succumbed with little resistance, and Al-Andalus became just another province of this sect whose capital was located at Marrakech. In time the religious fanaticism of these fierce warriors of the desert, diluted by the refined and sensuous culture of the conquered, abated, and the process repeated itself.

Seeking to restore the original values of the faith, the Almohades arose in the Atlas mountains and declared a Holy War, a *jihad*, on the Almoravides. They conquered most of Morocco and invaded Spain in 1150, again to help the petty Taifa chieftans against the Christians. Intolerant and fanatical, they alienated Moslems and Jews alike and effectively ended Arab-Jewish cooperation in Andalucía (see Chapter 7 below).

With the arrival of the Almohades the Moslem capital was temporarily shifted to Sevilla, where the Giralda with its pink, trellis-like brickwork, similar to patterns in Marrakech and Rabat, still stands as a monument to their presence. Internal bickering again soon dissolved their empire into petty kingdoms as before.

With the great defeat suffered by the Moslems at Navas de Tolosa in Jaén and the fall of Sevilla to Christian forces in 1248, Spain of the Prophet became concentrated in the kingdom of Granada.

Nasrid Granada

Confined to what are now the provinces of Almería, Málaga and Granada, Moslem towns and villages fell one by one to the Christian forces under the Catholic monarchs, Isabel and Fernando. Isolated from the centres of Islam,

Nasrid Granada, this vassal state of Castilla, the last of the Taifas, survived for a time through diplomacy and the inability of the forces arrayed against it to repopulate the areas already conquered. The religiously intransigent Isabel, however, with her sights set on a unified Catholic Spain, personally spearheaded the final assault on this last refuge of the Moslems. On the first day of the year 1492, Boabdil, the last Moslem king, surrendered the city of Granada and his precious Alhambra, and went into exile.

The Moslem legacy

The Moslem legacy is most visible in the southern part of the country, where Arabic influence was strongest and is most clearly seen in the architectural monuments left behind, such as the palace of the Alhambra at Granada and the great mosque and royal city of Medina Azahara in Córdoba. The Moslems did not develop the arts of painting and sculpture, but they were renowned for jewelry and mosaics, ceramics and textiles. Arabs introduced the practice of encrusting iron with gold and silver, *damacene*, which is still in use in Spain, and their glazed tiles, *azulejos*, in various colours, possessed a lustre which has never been equalled. Silks and woolens were often decorated with raised gold embroidery, *recamado*, and gold adornment was also used on leather. In the area of agriculture, Arab-inspired irrigation systems are still in use in some places. Architectural decorations such as walls covered with lace-like traceries and vividly coloured plaster were also introduced by the Moslems.

The style of Moslem architecture at Córdoba seems to have been patterned on buildings in Syria, while that of the Alhambra in Granada is more in accordance with that of the Maghreb, that is, Tunisia, Algeria and Morocco. (The Arabs seem to have adopted the horseshoe arch from the Visigoths in Spain and modified it by making it pointed.)

Córdoba became the capital of the western Moslem world and rivalled Bagdad and Constantinople in monumental splendour. It became the largest town in Europe, after Constantinople, with a population estimated at beween five hundred thousand and one million.

With the decline of the Caliphate and the rise of the Taifa kingdoms a good deal of building occurred. In particular, protective city walls, usually of *double enceinte* with square or polygonal towers, were constructed with stone, brick, or cement embedded with pebbles and with a distinctive Moorish type of crenellation. Surviving parts of these fortifications may be seen at Córdoba, Sevilla, Almería, Jaén, Ronda and Málaga, among other places.

Mozarabe architecture

For over a century after the Moslem invasion of Spain, the Christians of the south were allowed to maintain their religion, to elect bishops, and to construct churches. Many dressed like Moslems, learned Arabic and adopted the customs of the invader. Of the buildings erected by these Mozarabes in the south, only two seem to have survived, at least in part: Santa María de Melque (near San Martín de Montalbán, southwest of Toledo, largely ruined) and Bobastro (north of Alora in the province of Málaga, hardly more than a pile of stones). Other examples of this style are the work of refugees who fled from Córdoba, Toledo or Sevilla, during periods of persecution in the ninth and tenth centuries, to Aragón, Galicia, León and Asturias.

Early examples of this style of architecture are churches found in the territory of Asturias and León during the reigns of Alfonso III, El Magno, and his successors García I and Ramiro II.

While varying greatly in type, nearly all the churches include features borrowed directly from the Mezquita at Córdoba and include the Moslem horseshoe arch in both construction and decoration. Windows and doorways are framed in the typical rectangular style, and wooden roofs are often supported on corbels or eaves decorated with stars and helices.

These churches are uniquely Spanish and display an architecture reflected in a society more geared to war than to artistic refinement, to improvisation rather than a distilling of styles. Often they were situated in defensive positions against Moslem attacks and have survived to the present day, albeit somewhat disfigured by subsequent refurbishings. They are churches of individual character unlike the more uniform pre-Romanesque buildings of Asturias. They appear to have been constructed in a kind of symbiosis of two architectural currents—that of the Visigoths, inheritance of the north, and that of the Ommiad Dynasty of Córdoba.

They also varied in floor plan: sometimes they were in the form of the Latin basilica with three naves and one or more apses, while others were of the Byzantine type with one nave, apse and cross with added lateral sections in the Asturian tradition.

There are about fifty Mozarabe buildings in Spain, including such interesting churches as San Cebrián de Mazote (Valladolid) and Santa María de Lebeña (Asturias). San Miguel de Escalada of about 913, approximately thirty kilometres east of León, combines Christian and Moslem influences. Its design reflects Visigothic influences as revived and handed down by Asturian churches of the ninth century. One of the best preserved is Santa María de Wamba in the province of Valladolid. The most exceptional today is perhaps San Baudelio de Berlanga in the province of Soria.

Some of the interesting churches of Mozarabic construction are:

Name	Province
San Miguel de Olérdola	Barcelona
San Quirce de Pedret	Barcelona
San Juan de la Peña	Huesca
Santo Tomás de las Ollas	León
San Miguel de Escalada	León
Santiago de Peñalba	León
San Millán de la Cogolla	Logroño
San Miguel de Celanova	Orense
Santa María de Lebeña	Santander
San Baudelio de Berlanga	Soria
Santa María de Melque	Toledo
San Cebrián de Mazote	Valladolid
Santa María de Wamba	Valladolid

Not a good deal is known about civil art and architecture in the latter centuries of the first millenium A.D., but buildings such as those mentioned above demonstrate the vigorous role played by Mozarabes in the construction and diffusion of ecclesiastical styles into the north of the country.

Mudéjar architecture

Between the twelfth and fourteenth centuries Christian forces had recovered most of the peninsula from the Moslems, but the latter continued to live in *aljamas* or ghettos, and while not allowed to build or maintain mosques these Mudéjares (Moslems living under Christian domination; the word means "submissive") continued their art and architectural forms in the employ of the victors, competing on an ever-decreasing scale with influences emanating from Europe. Mudéjar decoration of lace-like canopies were even used on Christian tombs. The style flourished primarily in the fourteenth and fifteenth centuries and the chief materials were brick, plaster, ceramics and wood. The plaster decoration, the wooden-coffered ceilings and lattice work—elements of Moslem tradition—were also employed among the Jewish communities of Spain. The result was generally pleasing yet inexpensive designs, unique to the Hispanic peninsula and one of the non-European influences that helped shape the artistic personality of Spain.

During the course of the reconquest, Christian kings had seized Moslem palaces at Huesca, Lérida, Toledo, Valencia and Zaragoza and preferred them generally to Romanesque or Gothic style dwellings. Pedro I rebuilt an earlier palace at Sevilla in imitation of the Alhambra. This Alcázar, a fine specimen of Mudéjar style art of which, unfortunately, little remains, was built on the site of the former royal palace of the Almohades. The present building is dated around 1349-1368, but was enlarged by the Catholic monarchs and suffered some ill-conceived alterations during the reign of Carlos I. Much of the building was restored in the nineteenth century.

Throughout the fourteenth century it was the habit of nobles to decorate palaces in Moslem style brick- and plaster-work even in the far north of the country. In the south, Mudéjar decoration in stucco remained relatively pure until it mingled with Renaissance styles, as seen in the House of Pilate in Sevilla. To the north, Mudéjar blended with Gothic in many areas and may be seen, for example, in the brick cloister at Guadalupe in the province of Cáceres.

In the region of Aragón one finds a curious use of Moslem style in which belfries were often detached, like minarets, from the buildings they served. The earlier examples of the thirteenth century may be viewed at Teruel, where they are square in shape and the wall surfaces patterned in brick and decorated with coloured tiles. The fourteenth and fifteenth century towers were generally octagonal, and survive at Alarcón, Ateca, Calatayud, Daroca, Tarazona and elsewhere.

One of the most important aspects of Mudéjar work found in all parts of Spain was ceiling construction. While of many shapes, from flat surfaces to domes, the designs on them were made from tiny pieces of wood to form interlacing geometrical patterns which were then painted or gilded, yielding a rich and sumptuous effect.

This legacy of the Arabs persisted down to the sixteenth century, and is more pronounced in some places than others. In the Jalón valley in the vicinity of Calatayud, for example, there are numerous towers (some leaning precariously) and churches in Mudéjar style. Some of the best Mudéjar towers are the Torreón de la Zuda in Zaragoza and the Torre de San Martín in Teruel. Other examples (out of hundreds) are found in the north where Moslem influences were never very strong, such as Castillo de Coca in the province of Segovia, the convent of Santa Clara in Tordesillas, Valladolid, and the monastery of Las Huelgas in Burgos. Not surprisingly, Toledo has numerous Mudéjar-style buildings. The Puerta del Sol is a fine example of the Toledan Mudéjar style of the fourteenth century. On the left, along the Calle del Arrabal, is the church of Santiago del Arrabal, the largest Mudéjar church in the city.

For further reading see *The Moors in Spain and Portugal* by J. Read, London (1974), *Historia de la España musulmana* by A. González, Palencia, Barcelona (1945), *Moorish Culture in Spain* by T. Burckhardt, London (1972), *A History of Islamic Spain* by W. M. Watt, Edinburgh (1967), and *The Spaniards: An Introduction to their History* by Américo Castro, Berkeley (1971).

7. HISPANO-JEWISH COMMUNITIES

It has been said that a lesser Hebrew prophet, Abdias, made mention of a place of exile called Sefarad, but it is not clear if this referred to the Iberian peninsula, as it is not possible at present even to be sure of a pre-Christian Jewish community in Spain—that is, Jews who may have arrived with the Phoenicians or Greeks. Documentary evidence on a sepulchral tablet from Andalucía places them there in the third century A.D., however, and they eventually claimed Sefarad (Spain and Portugal) as their land.

A century later, in 314, the Christian Council held in Iliberis, Granada inaugurated a history of discrimination against the Spanish Jews which grew worse as the country united in the Christian faith under the Visigoths.

In both Christian and Moslem territory (the latter after the Arabic invasion in A.D. 711), Jews lived in separate communities referred to by the Arabs as *aljamas*. In Aragón they were designated "calls" (from Hebrew *kahal*, "the community"). In the north, where Jewish quarters were few, they were called *juderías*. Each community had its own synagogue and the large ones were subdivided into smaller quarters or *thoras*. Each quarter possessed a synagogue which was the symbol and place of reunion, education, prayer and law.

Of the numerous synagogues that once existed in Spain, only three are still well preserved: two in Toledo—Sinagoga del Tránsito and Santa María la Blanca—and one in Córdoba. The latter was built by Isaac Mejeb in 1314–15 according to an inscription found inside. It measured only about seven by six metres and was presumably not one of the grand category. A Bull by Innocent IV, promulgated in 1250, ordered the destruction of a Cordoban synagogue—probably the primary one—under construction, whose remains can perhaps still be seen in a house on the Plaza de las Bulas almost opposite the small one.

An idea of the number of synagogues may be gleaned from the records. The aljama of Calatayud boasted seven, that of Valladolid, eight, and the judería of a large town such as Sevilla contained no fewer than twenty-three for the community of six to seven thousand families. Ecclesiastical authorities went to great lengths to prevent Jewish houses of worship from exceeding neighbouring churches in size or height, or to be beautified in any significant manner. The king's license was required to build a new synagogue, as well as the permission of the local bishop. Money in the right places helped pave the way for such constructions, but any infringement of the strict design of the building could incite violence and the destruction of the temple.

While the Catholic monarchs, Isabel and Fernando, first showed themselves to be sympathetic to the Jews, they signed their expulsion papers in 1492 without, it seems, much compunction. It has been calculated that between one hundred fifty thousand and four hundred thousand Jews were forced to leave Spain, where their ancestors had lived for centuries. They had to leave behind their money, gold and goods and their houses were sold at a fraction of their value.

Centuries earlier, persecuted by the Visigoths, the Jews must have had few misgivings about a change in dynasty as Arabic forces from North Africa emerged from the desert to consolidate Andalucía. They participated in the Renaissance of Córdoba as men of great knowledge in medicine, astronomy, agriculture, philosophy and theology at the time when Moslem culture and learning were the shining light of Medieval Europe. They were also excellent weavers, tailors, dyers, gold- and silversmiths, bankers and tax collectors. Some were farmers.

The Golden Age of Córdoba in the ninth century continued into the tenth and eleventh centuries in cities such as Toledo, Zaragoza, Granada and Sevilla, but by the end of the eleventh century things had begun to change, as the Islamic Almohades from Morocco ushered in a period of intolerance, a holy war against both Christian and Jew. (Prior to this, battles between Christians and Arabs were often halted from Friday to Sunday in respect for each others' religious beliefs—including the sabbath of the Jews, who fought sometimes on one side, sometimes on the other.) Andalucian Jews fled the onslaught for the distant cities of Cataluña and the north.

Perhaps one of the greatest periods of mutual respect between Jew, Christian and Moslem was in thirteenth century Toledo, where a school of translation, often rendering the eastern classics into Spanish, flourished, bringing the cultures together. These efforts were constantly undermined, however, by the mendicant religious orders and the inflammatory preachings of the Dominican monks, resentful, one can only suspect, of the opulence of the Jews, many of whom were public officials, judges, doctors and interpreters. Under the circumstances, tensions often ran high and tragedy was never far away.

At the beginning of the fourteenth century persecutions became frequent and violent. In 1293 a court in Valladolid prohibited all Jews from owning land and homes. The calls of Valencia and Barcelona were prohibited from engaging in commerce and public posts were no longer open to Jews. The black plague of 1348 decimated some Jewish quarters and Christian authorities, interpreting this as divine judgement, helped in the name of the Almighty to massacre those Jews they could lay hands on. The end of the century saw a deluge of fanatacism and destruction unleashed on the Sephardim.

The kings of Spain had often relied on the Jewish community in matters of finance and administration, at the same time demanding and depending on exhorbitant taxes from their aljamas. Nonetheless, royal judges were generally Hebrews. Ordinary Christians, and much of the hierarchy of the Church, resented the power and authority of these non-Christians, and the kings did little to assuage the anger of the masses against the Jews. They themselves, no doubt, harboured a kind of love-hate relationship with these often astute and divisive Sephardics.

When the Archdeacon of Ecija, himself a descendent of converted Jews, unleashed his impetuous followers on the aljama in Sevilla, the sacking and burning which included the destruction of the synagogues soon spread. Almost all Jewish quarters in cities across the country suffered a similar fate. Many Jews converted to the dominant faith in order to escape with their lives, but many of the converted continued to practise their own beliefs in secret, although always apprehensive of informers' reports to the Christian authorities. At the same time the kings of Spain continued to pretend friendship to exploit the talents of these beleaguered people.

As the reconquest of Spain crept onward, compressing the Moslems into the kingdom of Granada, Isabel and Fernando allowed exiled Hebrews of Al-Andalus to repopulate the towns acquired from the Moslems. Jews from the southern aljamas settled on the Castillian plateau and some even began farming communities in León. When the Pope issued a proclamation declaring that Jews could not exercise any kind of jurisdiction over any Christian, the Catholic monarchs did little to carry it out but did nothing to oppose it. They used the Jews to the end, borrowing their money for the war but delaying any action against them until the reconquest was completed on 1 January 1492. Then expulsion orders were issued and the Inquisition given wide-ranging powers to thwart any perceived back-sliding among those who stayed in the country and converted. Integration into Christian society slowly took place, and important people such as Santa Teresa of Avila, Luis Vives, and Fray Luis de León were reputed to have been descendents of converted Jews.

Jewish contributions to Medieval Hispanic society were in intellectual and practical forms rather than in architectural innovation, art (with some exceptions), and lasting monuments. The reasons are perhaps obvious. Jews of the time, as an often-persecuted minority group, were more concerned with diverting attention rather than drawing it to themselves. It was enough to walk the streets in plain, coarse robes—at times clearly labelled with a Jewish insignia—where any finery would attract the enmity of their Christian neighbours.

Their aljamas looked much like those areas of the Medieval Christians or Moslems. In decoration they leaned toward the Arabic fashions. In fact, without the use of historical documents it is often not possible to tell the difference between Moslem and Jewish quarters. The synagogues reflected the same contrast beween ornamental refinement and inexpensive materials as the churches constructed at the same time by Moslem masons in the Mudéjar style. Arches often were of the horseshoe design.

In this sense, then, there was nothing particularly Jewish about the outward styles of buildings, but only in their use. Jewish baths, for example, which were generally adjacent to the synagogue for liturgical purposes and used by the Sephardic population of a community, were identical to Arab baths and are sometimes considered as such today.

Throughout the Middle Ages, juderías existed in most of the major cities and in many of the smaller towns. Most of them disappeared, expropriated by the local Christians after the decree of expulsion in 1492, but some, at least in their general outward characteristics, have survived and may be visited today.

Sometimes Spanish history books ignore the Jewish presence. After the expulsion of those who refused to go through the pretense of conversion, Jews' houses were confiscated, their temples turned into churches and their graves desecrated. Some relics of their past have, however, escaped obliteration.

There are many towns all over Spain where synagogues have been converted into churches, and Jewish quarters (mostly erased) have been identified from written records. There is generally nothing left of interest, except perhaps for the specialist in Sephardic history. Some further comments on Jewish sites with something to see—albeit sometimes very little—are presented in the notes below.

Town	Province	Sight
Agramunt	Lérida	plaque, Hebrew inscription
Agreda	Soria	judería
Aguilar de Campóo[1]	Palencia	Hebrew plaque
Barcelona[2]	Barcelona	inscription
Berlanga de Duero	Soria	judería, well preserved
Bembibre[3]	León	synagogue
Besalú	Gerona	baths
Chelva[4]	Valencia	judería
Córdoba[5]	Córdoba	judería and synagogue
Gerona[6]	Gerona	judería
Hervás[7]	Cáceres	judería
Oña[8]	Burgos	judería and possible synagogue
Ribadavia[9]	Orense	judería
Sádaba	Zaragoza	synagogue?
Sagunto[10]	Valencia	judería
Sevilla[11]	Sevilla	judería
Sigüenza[12]	Guadalajara	judería
Soria[13]	Soria	tombstones
Tarragona[14]	Tarragona	Hebrew inscription
Toledo[15]	Toledo	judería, synagogues
Tudela[16]	Navarra	judería and plaque
Trujillo[17]	Cáceres	stone tablet
Zamora	Zamora	Hebrew inscriptions
Zaragoza	Zaragoza	baths

¹*The only remains of the judería is a plaque in Hebrew which appears above the Reinosa gate.*

²*Few remains of the Sephardic community have survived. The Jewish quarter was spread out between the Generalitat Palace and the Cathedral. The Carrer del Call (Calle or Street of the Judería) and the Hebrew stone inscription in a wall on the Calle Marlet would have been the area of greatest concentration of the Hebrew community. Nearby Montjuich (Mount of the Jews) was once a Sephardic cemetery. Some of the stones are in the Archaeological Museum of Barcelona.*

³*The parish church was once the synagogue of a town probably mostly composed of Jews in the Middle Ages. Unlike other synagogues crammed into the crowded juderías with little room to build, this one stood in an open and preferential place in relation to the town. Only the church remains.*

⁴*The judería extended along the eastern section of the old town. A gateway marks the limits of the quarter.*

⁵*The Jewish quarter was situated near the wall beside the Puerta de Almodóvar Gate. Passing through the Puerta a right turn leads into the Calle de Maimonides and to number 18, the remains of a Synagogue of 1315 in Mudéjar style. The maze of flower-bedecked, narrow, winding streets of the Barrio de la Judería present one of the best pictures of a Sephardic community of Medieval times one might find today. In the heart of the quarter is a statue of Maimonides, the famous Jewish philosopher and scholar.*

⁶*The call or judería is one of the most interesting in the country. Here is one of the rare monuments of Hebrew civil architecture. The Isaac el Cec or Isaac the Blind Centre is an old Medieval mansion, now restored, which houses an exhibition hall and a place of study of subjects relating to Sephardic matters.*

⁷*An attractive village in the Sierra de Gredos, a little off the road from Salamanca to Plasencia and situated among olive groves and cherry orchards. It retains a well-preserved Jewish Quarter and a Hebrew plaque commemorating the site. Narrow twisting streets, some without issue, make up this evocative Judería.*

⁸*There is a judería on the left just inside the main gate of the town. One of the houses with overhanging balcony on Barruso street may have been the synagogue.*

⁹*Well-defined and preserved judería above the river, with commemorative plaque, containing original Medieval houses with balconies and porticos and later ones of the same design.*

¹⁰*Fairly well-preserved Jewish quarter and Medieval doorway, signposted on the upper edge of town toward the Roman theatre.*

¹¹*The old Jewish quarter in Sevilla is known as the Barrio de Santa Cruz. With narrow streets, cool plazas and white houses lavishly decorated with pots of flowers and wrought-iron window grills, the district has a pronounced Andalucian appearance and is a good example of Sephardic urban living. The synagogue in the vicinity was in use until 1391 and rebuilt as a Baroque church, Santa María la Blanca, in 1659.*

¹²*Easily locatable Jewish section on the slope just below the castle. The Puerta de Hierro (Iron Gate) has been preserved.*

[13]*Located in San Juan de Duero, an old house of the Knights Hospitallers.*

[14]*Near the cathedral in the lane of the Escribanias, number 6, is a Hebrew inscription built into the front. There are also sepulchral tablets preserved in the cathedral and the Provincial Archaeologial Museum.*

[15]*Between the eleventh and thirteenth centuries the city was the capital of Hispanic Judaism. It had two Jewish quarters which made up a large part of the southern half of the city. Two out of about ten synagoques in existence in the fourteenth century remain. Most were destroyed in the rampages of 1391. Santa María la Blanca was founded in about 1180 and rebuilt after a fire in 1250. It was taken over by the Christians in 1405. Used as a barracks in 1791–1798 and later as a carpenter's shop, it has now been restored. Next door are the baths which appear to have been part of the Synagogue. Nearby is the Sinagoga del Tránsito on the Paseo del Tránsito, built in Arabic style in 1366 for Samuel Levi, Treasurer of Pedro I. Levi was subsequently executed by the king and his wealth seized. After the expulsion of the Jews in 1492, Queen Isabel presented the building to the Order of Calatrava and it was dedicated first to Saint Benedict and later to the Death of the Virgin (hence El Tránsito). Restoration of the building after decades of neglect is now fairly complete. There is a Hebrew inscription in praise of God, of Don Pedro and of Levi, and several fourteenth-century Jewish tombstones. Part of the building houses a small Sephardic Museum and Library and displays a map of Jewish communities in Spain prior to their expulsion.*

[16]*Extensive and well-known judería located in the sector between the Cathedral and the river Queiles where it flows into the Ebro.*

[17]*A stone tablet is preserved here bearing a Hebrew inscription and which is used as the lintel of a doorway in Las Tiendas street.*

There were, of course, hundreds more Sephardic communities in Spain but most have disappeared without a trace.

For further reading see *The Jews in Spain* by A. Neuman, New York (1942), *The Spaniards: An Introduction to their History* by Américo Castro, Berkeley (1971), *A History of the Jews* by A. L. Sachar, New York (1960).

PART TWO

SITES AND SIGHTS

Sources of Information, Conventions

In seeking local information concerning the whereabouts and condition of ancient historical sites, there are a number of places one may turn to for assistance.

1. Spanish tourist office. Located in major cities and towns.

2. Ayuntamiento or Casa Consistorial (City Hall). Usually helpful and some have a resident archaeologist. It is sometimes necessary to go here since the Alcalde (Mayor) generally has the keys to locked sites.

3. Archaeological Museum. Found in most cities and many towns, always helpful. Ask for El Director (the Director or Curator).

4. Archivo Histórico Provincial. (Provincial Historical Archives). Found in capital cities. All information on sites in the province is contained here.

5. Taller Arqueológico. (Archaeological Workshop) Often found in the larger towns, sometimes at the Ayuntamiento, the workshop carries out local excavations. There is always a resident archaeologist and a number of helpful students.

6. Casa de la Cultura or Delegación de Cultura. (House of Culture). Found in most towns of any size and always helpful. It is often part of the local library.

There is no shortage of maps on Spain but the MOPU map put out by the Ministerio de Obras Públicas y Urbanismo under the title *España, Mapa Oficial de Carreteras (Offical Road Map)* is the most detailed and well-suited for finding remote hamlets not always found in other sources. Michelin maps are also good, especially those of specific regions, but note that there are sometimes discrepancies among the numbers pertaining to secondary roads.

All sites that fall under the jurisdiction of the Ministery of Culture are closed on Mondays.

In this guide, place names are given in Spanish in the form they are found on most maps; generally a name in the local language (Catalán and Gallego) does not differ radically from the Spanish one. Sometimes it is only a matter of a vowel, for example Spanish "Gerona," Catalán "Girona," or sometimes a consonant such as Spanish "Vich," Catalán "Vic." When place names have no obvious similarities, as in Spanish "San Sebastián" and Basque "Donastia" for the same city, or Spanish "Vitoria" and Basque "Gasteiz," both names are given.

Technical terms are here kept to a minumum, but in keeping with the road signs and indicators within a site which describe sections of it, as well as the places and objects one might wish to ask for such as the *Ayuntamiento* (City Hall) or *ruinas romanas* (Roman ruins), useful terms are glossed at the end of the book.

A final word about local names. When the visitor requests information about a site from villagers, whether it is a Roman mausoleum or rupestrian paintings, it will often have some kind of Moorish connotation in the mind of the person asked. For example, there are many caves in Spain referred to as Cueva de los Moros or "Cave of the Moors" even though they may have had nothing at all to do with the Moors. This is the usual word to denote the Islamic domination of the peninsula: Moors were actually Berbers, many from Mauritania (hence the name), who came to Spain, first as soldiers under the command of Arab officers. All were Moslems, and the Arabs and Berbers together acquired the label "Moors." The predominant cultural influence of Islamic times in Spain was Arabic in most aspects of culture, however, and the terms most often employed in the following pages to describe a relevant locale are "Arabic" or "Moslem."

ANDALUCIA

The southernmost region of the peninsula consists of eight provinces: Almería, Cádiz, Córdoba, Granada, Huelva, Jaén, Málaga and Sevilla. Always a fertile area, it was known to Neanderthal man, whose presence has been documented, with the most important sites at Gibraltar. The region was populated by Paleolithic people first living in caves, such as the Cueva de Nerja in the province of Málaga, and later in perishable wooden huts of the Neolithic and Chalcolithic periods whose remains have not survived the passage of time. Enduring, however, are their stone-built tombs at Antequera in the same province, and Pozuelo in Huelva, among other places.

Communities with stone-constructed dwellings appeared in the Bronze and Iron Ages and are widely attested in the region. The somewhat mythical and nebulous kingdom of Tartessos developed in the western region, that is, in the present-day provinces of Cádiz, Huelva and Sevilla, while the Iberians occupied the central and eastern areas.

Phoenician trading settlements were established along the southern coasts as early as the eighth century B.C., but their activities in this part of the Mediterranean were later supplanted by Punic interests.

Known to the Romans as Baetica and watered by the Baetis River, now the Quadalquivir, Andalucía was colonized and Romanized early compared to other regions of Spain, and it prospered in spite of barbaric tribes, first from Africa and then from Europe, who ranged the countryside and plundered the cities.

By the early eighth century A.D., the entire region was firmly under Arabic hegemony.

Andalucía is extremely rich in archaeological sites but poorly explored, documented, and maintained. A large number of sites, once excavated, have been left to the elements and the souvenir hunter. Wanton destruction of sites by bulldozing developers making way for apartment blocks, roads and holiday chalets in this fast-expanding tourist area make the Vandals, who pillaged the region in the fifth century, look relatively benign.

ALMERIA

In the south-east of the peninsula, a region of dry hills and sometime rivers, criss-crossed by mountain ranges and bordering the Mediterranean, Almería was occupied by Neolithic and Bronze Age cultures. According to some scholars, they emanated from the Eastern Mediterranean, the latter in search of metal deposits once abundant in the area. Cave sites, some with paintings (such as those at Ambrosio and Los Letreros) attest to these early inhabitants.

Of considerable importance in this connection is the third-millennium site of Los Millares (see under Gádor), with interesting remains, and the later Argar culture which acquired great significance throughout the southeast of the peninsula in the second millennium B.C. The latter was a semi-urban society with an economy based upon agriculture and mining which, for the past decade, has been the subject of intense study, especially with regard to its various offshoots or settlements, of which twenty-two are known in the region of Jumilla alone, with many more around Lorca and Cartagena in neighboring Murcia. There is, however, generally little or nothing left to see at these sites. Later, Phoenicians, Carthaginians, Romans and Arabs left their imprint in the area.

Albolodúy

Late Bronze Age site, Peñon de la Reina, situated on a high rocky hill across the Nacimiento river opposite town. Sometimes steep climb to site which takes about thirty-five minutes at moderate pace and is best approached up the left side of the hill.

Sights:
Foundational remains of Bronze Age oval houses and cisterns.

Location:
NW of Almería. Leave car at km 9 on the AL 451, just outside of town.

Almería

Called by the Arabs Al-Mariya, or "mirror of the sea," it supplanted the Moorish town of Bayyana as the major commercial city of the region (see under Pechina). It fell into Christian hands in 1488.

The Arabic fortress, begun by the Caliph of Córdoba, Abd-al-Rahman III, was enlarged by al-Mansur and completed by Hairan, the Taifa king of Almería, in the eleventh century. The site covers an area of 35,325 m². The church of Santiago El Viejo, of small proportions, was constructed in 1553 but contains a notable slim Roman tower 55 m high.

Sights:
Alcazaba, Roman tower.

Location:
In the city of Almería.

Antas
Ruins of the Bronze Age site of El Argar located opposite the town of Antas across the river of the same name. While of great historical significance, there is actually very little to see at the site, which covered a small plateau above the river. The ancient settlement dates back to about 1700 B.C. and was defended by stout walls on the sides where the river bank afforded no protection. About nine hundred fifty graves were discovered here. Human remains were interred in cist graves or in earthenware jars, generally individually, and with the deceased's jewellery or arms. The population had access to tin and made bronze tools and weapons. As in the case of Los Millares (see under Gádor), the extent of Eastern Mediterranean influences which may have shaped El Argar culture is controversial.

Sights:
Scant remains of rectangular stone houses, walls and necropolis.

Location:
NE of Almería. To reach Antas take N 340 S of Puerta Lumbreras. Just before Vera go S on AL 821. Site is situated on hill to left immediately before crossing bridge over river Antas into town.

Four kilometres from Antas at Lugarico Viejo is situated a five-thousand-year-old, little-excavated settlement with very slight outlines of walls and gravesites, located on a hill above Jauro. Not a lot is known about this pre-Argar site. Ask in village for exact location.

Barranquete, El
Neglected and overgrown Chalcolithic site on the edge of a ravine, badly eroded and little left to see.

Sights:
Copper Age settlement. Rock-cut cisterns for rainwater, tomb of megalithic type with roof fallen in, and stone foundational remains of both rectangular and round houses.

Location:
23 km E of Almería. Follow the AL 100 for ca. 21 km, then turn S on road to El Barranquete for 5 km. Site is situated on edge of the Rambla de Artal about 300 m beyond farmhouse on left. Farm has two large stones as gate. Walk to edge of Rambla about 200 m from road.

Cuevas de Almanzora

A number of Bronze Age sites lie in the vicinity but all are difficult to find and contain only scant remains. Nearby at Campos, virtually a one-farmhouse hamlet not on maps, is an ancient offshoot site of the El Argar culture. Fuente Alamo is a Bronze Age hilltop site situated 4 km NE of town in a maze of dry river beds. Excavations were carried out in 1977 and 1979 revealing remains of round and rectangular dwellings and graves dating back to about 2000 B.C.

Sights:

Bronze Age sites with remains of round and rectangular houses, cisterns and necropoli.

Location:

NE of Almería near Antas. For Campos, turn immediately left on gravel road upon leaving town toward Las Herrerías and after crossing bridge. Site located beside cortijo on right side of road to Campos. Fuente Alamo, not to be confused with town of same name in Murcia, is situated 4 km NE of the Cuevas de Almanzora between this town and Campos. In both cases one should inquire at the Ayuntamiento for a guide. Other Bronze Age sites in the area, such as Cabezo del Oficio and Tres Cabezos, could also be considered for a visit.

Dalias

Almeria: Dalias. Arab Baths

Moslem baths, Baños de la Reina, once somewhat restored but again derelict, are situated above the town on the banks of a stream. It is only a short walk to the site, which can be seen from the road at the top of the town. Nearby, at the end of the road, is the Nacimiento, a system of Moslem water channels derived from natural springs. Also seen here are the remains of a Moorish castle and the Ermita de los Dolores, built on the site of a Mezquita.

On a nearby hill W of town are some remnants of the Roman city of Murgis but of difficult access. (No road.) Inquire at Ayuntamiento.

Sights:

Remains of Moorish baths, water systems, and Alcázar.

Location:

W of Almería 34 km on the N 340, then 8 km N on the AL 400.

Gádor

Site of an important southern Iberian inscription, the Gádor Lead Tablet, discovered in a mine at Barranco del Rey. There is an Alcázar known as El Castillejo, constructed in the ninth and tenth centuries, and on the opposite side of the river is an Arabic tower.

Nearby are the ancient remains of the Early Bronze Age settlement of Los Millares, located on a triangular meseta above the river Andarax and which dates back to about 2300–1600 B.C. The settlement shows remains of fortifications, and a necropolis, and was located in one of the richest mining centres of the country. The dome-shaped chamber tombs and the metallurgical practices of the ancient population, characteristic of eastern Mediterranean peoples, have suggested to some experts an influx of settlers from the east. But both copper and stone tools have been found, implying to others an in situ development of a Chalcolithic culture, that is, transitional between the Neolithic and Bronze Ages. It is thought that about two thousand inhabitants occupied the site. The area is now fenced off and one is obliged to ask for the keys in Gádor. Try the Ayuntamiento first.

Sights:

Remains of circular houses, canals and defences, the latter consisting of a wall, a moat and remains of towers. The necropolis, situated outside the wall, contains circular, vaulted megalithic graves (tholoi or beehive-like tombs) covered with a false cupola, as well as interments in artificial caves.

Location:

N of Almería, the site is reached by taking the N 340 to Benahadux, then the N 324 W (left) 4 km to Gádor. Los Millares is 3 km NW of Gádor.

Herrerías, Las

Chalcolithic to Bronze Age site of Almizaraque, situated on a slight knoll among heavy thickets of growth and nearly fruitless to try to find without a guide although it is only about 200 m in front of the old, abandoned house of the archaeologist Luis Seret, who excavated the area. There are some remains of round houses but the site is heavily eroded, overgrown and has been neglected for decades. Not much left to see. A little to the north, on a larger hill, are some remains of cupola style graves of the same period.

Sights:

Scant remains of Copper Age site.

Location:

NE of Almería on N340 to Vera, then follow the N 332/AL160 to Las Herrerías. Just before entering town, follow signs to the campground of Las Rozas. Inquire here for location of site a short walk away.

Mojácar

Bronze Age site of Loma de Belmonte in the vicinity of Mojácar, discovered in the past decade and perhaps an offshoot settlement of Los Millares culture. It is located just outside of town near the Era del Lugar. There is, however, very little to see except a large caved-in and overgrown grave site. Many of the artifacts, such as stone axes, arrow heads and pottery, were surface finds and have been long since removed to museums.

Sights:
Slight remains of Early Bronze Age settlement.

Location:
NE of Almería. Take road from Mojácar toward Turre. Site is nearly on edge of town at 0.4 km after football stadium on left of road.

Pechina
In the vicinity of Pechina was the Iberian and Roman town of Urci, whose site remains undiscovered. Of interest, nevertheless, is the excavated Arabic town of Bayyana dating back to the ninth century. This was the old port of Almería before the town was relocated.

Sights:
Remains of Arabic town with streets, houses and walls. Site is enclosed by a fence but the key may be obtained at the Consejería de Cultura.

Location:
12 km N of Almería on the N 340.

Tabernas
An old Roman and later Moslem town with a ruined Alcazaba, the most important in the province after that of Almería. Just south of the town are the few remains of a Chalcolithic site on the spur of a hill, consisting of the ruins of round stone houses.

Sights:
Copper Age site and Alcazaba.

Location:
NE of Almería, 31 km on the N 340.

Vélez Blanco
The region contains many caves or rock shelters with prehistoric paintings such as Lavaderos de Tello, Estrecho de Santonge and Cortijo de los Treinta, but for the most part the pictures have all but disappeared.

La Cueva del Gabar, actually an abrigo, contains the best rock paintings of the region. It has two levels: in the lower, the pictures have all been destroyed by the smoke of shepherds' fires, while the upper part retains paintings in good condition. The site is unmarked at present and requires a guide and a ladder to reach the second level up a sheer rock face. Inquire at Ayuntamiento.

The Cueva de los Letreros is signposted on the highway from Vélez Rubio just before entering Vélez Blanco, where a dirt track in poor condition is followed for about 2 km. Also an abrigo, the site is fenced off and the paintings of human figures and animals and some astronomical signs, in poor condition, are extremly difficult to make out.

From a later period the town preserves many Arabic characteristics in the old section—the Morería. Repopulated by Christians in the sixteenth century, the Alcazaba was destroyed to build the castle.

Sights:
Rupestrian paintings.
Location:
N of Almería and W of Puerto Lumbreras on C 321/342 to Vélez Rubio, then N 5 km to Vélez Blanco.

Villaricos
On the north bank of the mouth of the river Almanzora there was once a Punic settlement, but there is little left to see as the site has been over-whelmed by a modern urbanization of holiday villas. Nearby, however, are some Punic graves built into a hillside. In spite of bars across the entrances to the rock-cut graves, the interiors of five of them are clearly visible, including niches for urns. Several of the larger ones have collapsed inward. There are also some slight excavations on nearby hilltop to the right.

Almeria: Villaricos. Punic Necropolis

Sight:
Punic necropolis.
Location:
Villaricos is situated ca. 100 km NE of Almería on the coast. Upon entering the town from the west (Cuevas de Almanzora), the site lies just before the urbanization, on left of road where the sign indicates the name of the town. Walk about 150 m across the field to the first knoll.

Other sites in the Province of Almería include **Adra**, W of Almería 53 km on the N 340. Once the Phoenician settlement of Abdera, it later became a Roman port and finally an Arabic town. Ruins of Alcázar, walls and towers. **Berja**, about 13 km NE of Adra, displays the ruins of a citadel and remains of Arabic cisterns. **Sorbas**, NE of Almería on N 340 about 66 km, has remains of an Alcázar.

CADIZ
This is the most southerly of the Spanish provinces. Of outstanding interest are the Roman ruins of the cities of Carteia and Baelo (Bolonia), and the new archaelogical park of Castillo de Doña Blanca incorporating excavations from prehistory down to Phoenician times. The province is liberally sprinkled with

traces of the past—for example, in the mountainous region around the town of Ubrique within a 50 km radius there are about one hundred ten ancient historic sites, most of which are, unfortunately, still unexcavated.

One elusive site, a reputedly Phoenician temple at Sancti Petri on the coast to the west of Chiclana de la Frontera, is said to be seen only at low tide.

Alcalá de los Gazules

Small town which retains much of its original Arabic character including the ruined Alcázar. Nearby is a cave site, Laja de los Hierros, containing prehistoric cave paintings. There are also other cave sites in the vicinity with rupestrian paintings but not all are open to the public at the present time.

Sights:
Alcázar and nearby rupestrian paintings.

Location:
E of Cádiz and NW of Algeciras 55 km on the C 440. For the availability of cave sites inquire at the Ayuntamiento.

Benalup de Sidonia

Nearby rock shelters, Cuevas del Tajo de las Figuras, with a variety of rock paintings, one of difficult access by rope. Both contain paintings of animals near the entrances. They will be signposted on the highway when excavations are finished but a healthy up-hill walk of about twenty minutes is required to reach the spot. Also in the vicinity, 8 km E of Casas Viejas, are more shelters with paintings, but many are in poor condition.

Sights:
Rupestrian paintings.

Location:
E of Cádiz, take the C 440 NW of Algeciras for 25.5 km, then the CA 212 to between km 18 and 19. The abrigos or rock shelters will be on the right, and can be seen from the road.

Bolonia

A Roman city was discovered here in 1920, and excavations have been going on with some interruptions since. The city, Baelo Claudia, dates back to the first century A.D. and appears to have been a thriving community dependent for part of its commercial life on the sea. The necropolis contained over a thousand graves, mostly of incineration, and marked by small stone monuments. By the fourth century, decay had set in as evidenced by the construction of small, shoddy stone buildings, and the abandonment of the theatre which was used as a rubbish dump and then a cemetery.

Sights:
Roman forum, houses, baths, walls, roads, gate, fish-salting vats, bridge, temples, basilica, theatre, and necropolis.

Location:
Take the N 340 Cádiz-Málaga. The site is signposted on the right of the highway about 16 km before Tarifa.

Bornos
Nearby Roman site of Carissa Aurelia, dating back to the first century B.C. Some of the area along the ridge has been excavated but not the Roman fort on top of the hill. The site is most interesting for its rock-cut graves, some in the shape of an "N" that contained three people. The necropolis also contains a stout wall through the centre, which suggests the poor were interred on one side and the wealthy on the other. One grave is in the form of a cross. The area is fenced and a guard/guide is on duty during normal hours.

In town are the ruins of an Alcázar and encircling fortified wall.

Sights:
Roman necropolis, remains of walls, well, Alcázar.

Location:
NE of Cádiz and of Arcos de la Frontera on N 342, 12 km. Take left turn after town opposite petrol station on right. Just before km 6, turn left at sign for Carisa. Excavation is on ridge 1 km at end of dirt road and about a 100 m walk uphill through a field.

Cádiz
First a Phoenician coastal town called Gadir, the city dates back to about the ninth century B.C. By the fifth century B.C. it was under the domination of the Carthaginians and the sometime headquarters of Hamilcar Barca, Hasdrubal and Hannibal. The city fell into the hands of the Romans in 206 B.C during the Second Punic War and was called Julia Augusta Gaditana or Gades. In the sixth century it suffered extensive damage and decline from the Visigoths who, as non-seafaring people, had little use for it. Arabs occupied the town in the eighth century, but it suffered further atrocities and abandonment in the wake of the Normans in the ninth century. In the thirteenth century, during the reign of Alfonso X, it was repopulated. The Roman theatre and Phoenician-Roman tombs, currently under excavation, will be restored and opened to the public at some future time. Of more immediate interest are the four Phoenician tombs and remains of a covered Roman aqueduct of the first century B.C., constructed by Balbo the Younger to bring water to the city.

Sights:
Phoenician tombs and Roman aqueduct.

Location:
Plaza de Hasdrubal. For other sites inquire at the Delegación Provincial de Cultura, Plaza de España 19.

Carteia
Roman colony founded, according to Livy, in 171 B.C. for the sons of Roman soldiers and Spanish women. The most important Roman towns were the *coloniae* or formal settlements for Roman citizens with individual plots of

land. Carteia seems to have been a major exporter of amphorae for the purpose of conveying the fish sauce, garum. It is situated over a large area and the visitor is required to spend some time walking in order to take in the scattered excavations. The area is fenced but the guard/guide is generally available with the keys at his house near the entrance. Some of the sights may be somewhat overgrown. Many of the stones from the ancient site ended up in the houses and other buildings of nearby San Roque and Algeciras.

Sights:

Roman theatre, forum, baths, walls and steps, garum factory, a Paleo-Christian basilica and Paleo-Christian grave site.

Location:

From the coastal N 340 Cádiz-Málaga, take the road toward La Linea and Gibraltar, turn right at sign for Puente Mayorga and go through town, cross bridge, and continue through industrial refining area for 2.8 km.

Medina Sidonia

The town appears to have been founded by Phoenicians with the name of Assido, and it was subsequently occupied by Romans, Byzantines and Visigoths. The addition of Medina, "city," was made by the Arabs who controlled the town until its capture by the Christians in 1264. There are a number of Moslem structures in evidence here, including the old walls of the town currently under reconstruction.

Sights:

Arco de la Pastora, a horseshoe arch and old Arabic gateway into the city; Arco de Belem, restored; Ermita de los Santos reputed to have tower of Visigothic origin located just outside and below town; Roman inscription in wall across the plaza from the Ayuntamiento; and columns of the temple of Hercules. A Roman statue is found on the ground floor of the Ayuntamiento.

Location:

E of Cádiz 21 km on the C 346.

Puerto de Santa María

In the town is the castle of San Marcos, constructed under the auspices of Alfonso X in the thirteenth century on the spot of the earlier mosque. Nearby are the sites of El Aculadero, which has yielded artifacts from the Paleolithic era, and Las Arenas, from which have come finds from Mesolithic times. There is little or nothing to see now, however, all objects having been removed.

A site of special interest is the archaeological park outside the city at Castillo de Doña Blanca, currently under excavations begun in 1979. Here, on a slight elevation by what was once a natural harbour, have been found structures, tools and ceramics of Phoenician and Punic vintage, dating from the eighth to the third centuries B.C., and various artifacts that suggest strong contacts with the ancient Greeks. Still to be excavated is an adjacent Chalcolithic or Copper Age site of the third millenium B.C.

Sights:

Phoenician and Carthaginian walls, remains of houses and two necropoli (*hypogeum* and *tumulu*). Museum in situ.

Location:
N of Cádiz ca. 20 km, then from town take the N IV N toward Jerez and turn off on road to El Portal. After 3 km turn right up unpaved road 100 m to site.

*Cadiz: Ubrique.
Roman Columbarium*

Tarifa
The most southern city of Spain and one of the first founded by the invading Arabs, Tarifa lies only about 14 km from the African coast. It always had special significance for the Arabs, some of whose monuments remain, such as the city wall and the castle of Guzmán el Bueno of the tenth century.

Sights:
Alcázar; Arabic wall; Torre de Guzmán; San Mateo, built on the site of the mosque, contains a Visigothic tablet, dated 674, which was found nearby.

Location:
SE of Cádiz and SW of Algeciras 21 km on N 340.

Ubrique
Small mountain town W of Ronda not far from the Acropolis of Ocurris on the hill referred to as El Salto de la Mora. The Roman name Ocurris seems to be derived from *hoc* and *curris*, or "this road." The site may have been, in part, a toll station for the nearby Roman road. The most interesting monument is the columbarium which, while in a fairly good state of preservation, has unfortunately been used over the years as a stable. The second floor is missing and the unkempt stones are somewhat overgrown.

In town is a ruined Almohade castle, and along the forested trail to the nearby Embalse de los Hurones stand the ruins of the Arabic castle of Fatima.

Sights:
Columbarium, remains of a small ornamental fountain, rock-cut steps, cistern (3 m deep), some remains of termas or baths, water conduits, slight remains of living quarters with various rooms.

Location:
E of Cádiz, leave Ubrique on the C 3331; exactly 1 km from petrol station where road is joined is a farm house on the right. Here, ask permission (always given) to climb Salto de la Mora. Follow path uphill on zigzag course but keeping power line pylons in view as they lead to the site. The first sight is the columbarium near the last pylon. About a fifteen-minute walk.

In the immediate area are remains of a Roman aqueduct; the Calzada de Ventamartín; the ancient fortress of the Venta del Pájaro; prehistoric ruins of Salto del Pollo, among about twenty other sites, all unexcavated at the present time. Guide recommended.

The traveller interested in Moslem sites may wish to note that numerous fortifications from this period exist in the province, such as those of **Algeciras**, opposite Gibraltar on the coastal road N 340, remains of an Arabic aqueduct, a little inland beside the railway. **Arcos de la Frontera**, NE of Cádiz on the N 342, a hillside town of pre-Roman vintage known to the Romans as Arcóbriga and to the Arabs as Medina Arkosh. The Alcázar, originally a Taifa fortress, was converted to a Christian castle by the counts of Arcos. Some of the Arabic walls and towers are still preserved. **Castellar de la Frontera**, Alcázar, E of Cádiz and N of Algeciras on N 340/C 3331, 20 km, then 7 km on secondary road to left. **Conil de la Frontera**, Torre de Guzmán, once part of the Arabic castle and raised on Roman foundations, about 33 km S of Cádiz on N 340. **Jimena de la Frontera**, Alcázar and underground granary, mostly from the eleventh century, and Arabic baths and octagonal tower from the twelfth century, E of Cádiz and N of Algeciras about 42 km on N 340/C 3331. **San Fernando**, 17 km S of Cádiz on the N IV, rebuilt Roman bridge, Puente Suazo, over the Caño de la Carraca. **Torre de Melgarejo**, reconstructed in the fourteenth century, ca. 20 km N of Cádiz, about 8 km E of Jerez. **Vejer de la Frontera**, S of Cádiz on N 340, 46 km at the mouth of the river Barbate, ruins of Alcázar dominating Cape Trafalgar. The local church is built over the old mosque.

CORDOBA

Situated in north-central Andalucía, the province is watered by the Guadalquivir river running from east to west and by many tributaries from the shielding pine-covered granite mountains of the Sierra Morena to the north of the river. To the south of the Gualdalquivir extend the undulating plains of the Campiña. This fertile area has always attracted settlers. Artifacts from the Paleolithic era, along with those of subsequent epochs, have been found on the banks of the river. Roman remains are well in evidence in several places, but the most outstanding extant sights in the province are from Moslem times, and include Medina de Azahara (the Arabic royal city) and the Great Mosque of Córdoba.

Alcaracejos

Remains of a Late Roman cemetery and the ruins of a Visigothic basilica (of A.D. 615, according to inscriptional material), situated outside of town on the Cerro del Germo over a very bad road. An eighth-century coin from the site suggests that the church functioned up to and perhaps into the Moslem period. About 100 m west of the church are the slight remains of an apparently Visigothic compound, with some small structures grouped around a central courtyard.

Sights:
Slight remains of Roman cemetery and Visigothic basilica.

Location:
Follow the N 432 N out of Córdoba for 51 km, then branch off to the right on the C 411 for 27 km. Inquire at the Ayuntamiento of Alcaracejos for local directions.

Baena

A ruined Arabic castle, of which the upper part (known as the Almedina) is nearly surrounded by Arabic walls with fifty-nine towers, dominates the town. It fell to the Christians in 1240. The town goes back to pre-Roman times when, according to Pliny, it may have had the name Iponuba and belonged to the Turdulos. About 2.5 km from town were the ruins of the old city, destroyed in the first century, B.C. and last excavated in 1923, whence came the Lion of Baena, now in the Archaeological Museum in Madrid.

Sights:

Arabic walls and ruined Alcázar.

Location:

61 km SE of Córdoba on the N 432 .

Bujalance

Originally a Roman site, this small town preserves little of its origins. There are a few stones of the Roman road, but nearly everything else has been removed. Of interest, however, are the remains of an Arabic fortress endowed with seven towers and constructed for Abd-al-Rahman in 935.

Sights:

Slight Roman remains and Alcazaba.

Location:

About 45 km E of Córdoba on the N 324.

Cabra

The church of San Juan Bautista, known locally as San Juan de Cerro, is reputedly one of the oldest churches in Andalucía, dating back originally to perhaps the seventh century. Located in the Plaza de Santa María la Mayor; the key may be obtained at the house to the right of the main portal.

Sight:

Early Medieval church.

Location:

SE of Córdoba. Once in Cabra, take the road marked for Llanos de San Juan and take first right turn to where road narrows. Church is on the right.

Castro del Río

Small town on the river Guadajoz which preserves the ruins of an Arabic castle, reputedly constructed on the foundations of a Roman fortress, and the remains of Roman walls.

Sights:

Alcázar and ruins of Roman walls.

Location:

Approximately 42 km SE of Córdoba on the N 432.

Córdoba

This bustling capital city was once an Iberian settlement which now lies in the area of today's cemetery of Nuestra Señora de la Salud and the municipal park of Cruz-Conde. It was on high level ground on the bank of the Guadalquivir river, SE of the present old city. Eleven strata were in evidence, beginning in the Late Bronze Age down to the most recent, of the third century B.C. An Iberian phase is clear from the rich number of artifacts and graffiti in the Southern Iberian script. Having passed to Carthaginian control, the town then fell to the Romans and became the capital of Hispania Ulterior.

For a time Córdoba was in the hands of the Byzantines, but was conquered by the Visigoths in 572. In the eighth century it was destined to become the capital of Moslem Spain and court of the caliphs in the west, and from this period survives the magnificent Great Mosque. In the tenth century the city reached its golden age of prosperity and culture. It was reconquered by Christian forces in 1236. While there are some Roman structures remaining in the city, most of the sites and sights relate to the Arabic epoch. Here, too, in the Jewish quarter are preserved some of the few remaining Sephardic buildings in the country.

Córdoba: An entrance to the Great Mosque

Sights:

Opposite the Mosque over the river Guadalquivir stands a 238 m-long bridge spanning sixteen arches of Roman origin, but rebuilt by Moslems and Christians. The city also preserves some sections of the Roman wall. Near the Ayuntamiento is a restored Roman temple. The Puerta de Sevilla in Córdoba is of Visigothic origin.

The Mezquita or mosque, partially converted to a Roman Catholic church, stands as one of the greatest symbols of Moslem times in Spain. On the river are the remains of Arabic mills and a noria or water wheel can be seen beside the river near the Mezquita.

The Alcázar de los Reyes Cristianos, situated by the Campo de los Mártires (where there were Arab baths) was constructed by command of Alfonso XI on the site of an Arabic castle. Now it contains a museum with Roman mosaics and a large Roman sarcophagus of the third century with decoration in relief.

In the calle de Maimonides, in the Jewish quarter, an ancient barrio dating back to the Moslem period—entered through the old Puerta de Almodóvar—are the remains of a synagogue.

Location:

These various sights and others are shown on local tourist maps of the city.

Medina de Azahara

This was the royal city occupied by the Ommiad Calif Abd-al-Rahman III. The site (Madinat al-Zahra) measures 1500 m by 750 m and was distributed over three terraces on the slopes of the Sierra Morena. It was surrounded by double bulwarks with towers. The construction of this lavish seat of royal indulgence was begun in 936 with about ten thousand labourers, and concluded in 960 when the Arabic court and administrative personnel moved in. A 16 km aqueduct supplied the water. The palatial city was besieged and destroyed by invading Almoravides from Morocco whose austere Moslem religious beliefs disdained luxuries and sumptuous living. Later, the site was used as a stone quarry for new edifices in Sevilla and Córdoba. Much restoration work is currently in progress.

Sights:

Mosques, administrative buildings, gardens, stables and troops' quarters, palaces, gates in the form of horseshoe arches, walls, fountains, walkways and water conduits, all in various states of preservation. Small museum in situ.

Location:

W of Córdoba on N 432 about 30 km, then N 17.5 km on secondary road. Signposted.

Córdoba: Medina de Azahara

Santa Cruz

Extensive and important hilltop site of Teba la Vieja, with stratigraphy showing habitation from the Copper Age, Iberian and Roman times down to the Moslem period. The area has been partially excavated. The site, neglected and abandoned, affords unhindered entrance.

Sights:

Remains of defensive walls, dwellings, cisterns, baths, streets.

Location:

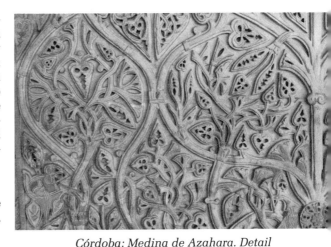

Córdoba: Medina de Azahara. Detail

SE of Córdoba about 24 km. From Santa Cruz take CO 271, a gravel road signposted for Teba. Pass km 5, and take next left fork marked for Casalillas and proceed several hundred metres to Huerta de Tebas on left. On right side of road is a gate marked Fuente de Ategua. Go through gate to end of path and climb hill. About 200 m to site. Alternatively, a dirt road on right, immediately after taking the left fork, leads to site around back of hill, but the road is impassable for ordinary vehicles.

Villa del Río

Alongside the highway in town stands an Alcázar which has been converted into a church, and 2 km E of town beside the modern bridge over the Arroyo del Salado is situated a small but charming five-spanned Roman bridge in a good state of preservation.

Sights:
Roman bridge and converted Alcázar.

Location:
E of Córdoba 55 km on the N IV.

Zuheros

Cave known as Cueva de Murciélagos (should not be confused with grotto of same name in the province of Granada), contains cave paintings. They are in poor condition and difficult to locate.

Sight:
Rupestrian paintings.

Location:
SE of Córdoba about 69 km on N 432; after Baena follow secondary road in direction of Luque and Zuheros. Inquire in Zuheros for guide.

Remains of Arabic strongholds in the province and other sites can also be found at **Aguilar de la Frontera**, Alcázar ruins, on N 331 S of Córdoba 72 km. **Almodóvar del Río**, 24 km SW of Cordoba on C431, impressive restored Alcázar on hill west of town, with powerful defensive battlements, walls and tower. The fortress appears to date back originally to the eighth century and was an important bulwark fortified by Abd-al-Rahman II. It fell to the Christian king, Fernando III, in 1240. **Belmez**, NW of Córdoba, 73 km on the N 432, Alcázar. **Carpio**, a large, square Moslem tower easily seen from the highway, situated E of Córdoba 33 km on the N IV. **Espejo**, 45 km SE of Córdoba, Roman bridge on the N side of town and adjacent, but now built-over Roman amphitheatre. **Fuenteobejuna** at La Loba, Roman silver mines, 93 km NW of Córdoba on N 432. **Iznájar**, Alcázar, SE of Córdoba on the C 334 on the E side of the Embalse of the same name. **Obejo**, N of Córdoba on N 432 about 30 km, then N for 17.5 km on secondary road. Alcázar. **Pedroche**, Roman bridge, 96 km N of Córdoba and 9 km NE of Pozoblanco. **Rute**; nearby, slight remains of Visigothic town on shores of the Embalse de Iznajal, but difficult to locate without guide; SE of Córdoba. Take the CO 210 off the N 331 S of Lucena to Rute and inquire at the Ayuntamiento. **Santa María de Trassierra**, a little NW of Córdoba on secondary road; Alcázar and ruins of an ancient mosque.

GRANADA

The last stronghold of the Arabs in Spain, the city of Granada fell to the Christian forces under Isabel la Católica in1492. It is also in the province of Granada, near Orce, that the oldest encampment in Europe has been found and it is here that one of the most remarkable discoveries concerning Neolithic times was made, near Albuñol in the Cueva de Murciélagos.

Although this cave site is one of the most famous in the country, there is now nothing to see except the cave itself. The name derives from the large number of bats that inhabit it. A dozen decorated Neolithic cadavers were found here, laid out in a semi-circle around a central figure of a woman also richly adorned with rings and necklaces. The bodies were accompanied by clay pottery, stone implements, esparto baskets and sandals, head gear and tunics of esparto grass, along with stone and bone knives, axes and arrow heads. Fifty cadavers were also found in another part of the cave with stone and bone armaments, and a few others were discovered in other areas. Near the entrance were three bodies, one of which wore a gold diadem. Everything was shattered and trampled to pieces, and in some cases thrown from the cave down the precipice by the first discoverers, a group of nineteenth-century miners seeking metal ore but finding instead what appeared to them to be the possibility of untold riches. Tucked away in the maze of arroyos, hills and thick growth, the cave is nearly impossible to find without a guide.

From Granada, also, comes the famous Dama de Baza of Iberian vintage, a superb sculpture of pre-Roman times; of course, from the more recent past, few structures can surpass the Alhambra in simple beauty.

Alhama de Granada

Near the town are thermal springs enjoyed by the Romans and later by the Arabs. A hotel was built over the site and the springs are still in use today. Some of the early hot water conduits are still in place outside the building, but there is now little to see of the ancient baths. More interesting perhaps is the archaic bridge across the river between the thermal baths and the highway.

Sights:
Slight remains of ancient thermal baths and bridge.

Location:
SW of Granada 53 km on the C 340. Baños de Alhama signposted from town of Alhama de Granada.

Almuñécar

Developing coastal resort town founded by the Phoenicians with the name of Sexi. In and around the town are several interesting historical sites all within easy reach.

Phoenician necropolis of Puente de Noy, excavated and visible behind a fence and under a tarpaulin cover, but all objects have been removed and only holes in the ground remain.

Cueva de los Siete Palacios, chambered rooms hollowed out of the rock and containing Phoenician and Roman remains. Museum in situ.

A two-level Roman aqueduct about 1 km north from town up the Rio Seco; another smaller Roman aqueduct about 4 km north in the village of Torrecuevas and used to bring water from the Sierra Nevada, two parts are visible. Roman columbarium (signposted as Columbario Romano) or funerary tower in fairly good state of preservation with twenty-six niches for urns, situated on road to Torrecuevas about 3 km from Almuñecar. Well-preserved Roman fish-curing compound or Factoría de Salazones, with numerous tanks in centre of town. Castillo de San Miguel, a ruined Alcázar, situated on the hill above the town.

Granada: Almuñecar. Roman Salting Industry

Sights:
Phoenician necropolis, rock-cut chambers, Roman aqueducts, columbarium, Roman fish-salting compound, Alcázar.

Location:
On the coastal road N 340 south of Granada.

Granada: Almuñecar. Roman Columbarium

Atarfe
Nearby ruins of Elvira, perhaps ancient Iberian Illiberis, with subterranean aqueduct and reputed traces of acropolis. Reported in some travel books, but guide required to find the unmarked site. The descent to the underground aqueduct is said to require a rope nearly 100 m long.

Sights:
Reputed Ibero-Roman remains of town.

Location:
NW of Granada ca. 12 km on N 432.

Baza

Originally Iberian Basti, the town was conquered by the Romans and again by the Arabs. It fell to the Christians in 1489. From the Iberian epoch comes the famous Dama de Baza, a fourth-century B.C. Iberian statue now in the Museum of Archaeology in Madrid.

Easily reached, 3 km E of town on left of highway N 342 toward Cúllar is the Iberian-Roman necropolis on the first knoll, in otherwise flat land, about 200 m from the road. Excavated but now somewhat eroded and overgrown.

Only a few pieces of wall remain from the Alcazaba in town, but the so-called Baños Arabes in the judería or Jewish quarter, signposted in the Plaza de Santiago, and currently under restoration, may be visited.

Sights:
Ibero-Roman necropolis and Medieval baths. Remains of Alcazaba.

Location:
On the N 342 NE of Granada.

Gabia la Grande

Ancient tomb in a field on the edge of town. The crypt is locked but keys may be obtained from the Ayuntamiento.

Sight:
Paleo-Christian crypt (hypogeum) of ca. third century.

Location:
Approx. 10 km SW of Granada on the C 340. Signposted.

Galera

The excavated cemetery or Necrópolis de Tútugi, consisting of scattered grave sites, is situated on the Cerro del Real next to the town, above the local cave houses and the river Orce, and dates back to the third to fifth centuries B.C. Open access but one must climb the hill, about a fifteen-minute walk. The tombs have been much despoiled, and in fact little remains of great interest. Another, older, pre-Roman necropolis is nearby, enclosed and undergoing excavation. Keys may be obtained from the Ayuntamiento.

Sights:
Pre-Roman necropoli.

Location:
NE of Granada, 127 km on the N 342, then 20.5 km on C 3329.

Gor

The town is the nearest point of reference, while the site is some distance away with no need to enter Gor itself. Closed to the public, the megalithic site can only be viewed from the outside.

Sight:
Megalithic domed grave site.

Location:

Follow the N 342 E from Granada past Guadix to the turn-off to Gor at 17 km. Continue on N 342 a little beyond turn-off, cross bridge over river Gor and take the first immediate right turn onto dirt road. This track ends after about 200 m and it is necessary to walk approx. 1500 m over very rough ground to site.

Granada

The world-famous and enchanting Arabic palaces and gardens of the Alhambra and Generalife in Granada, which include about forty-four splendid sights including walls, gates, towers, gardens, baths, fountains and exquisite architectural decoration, are beyond the scope of this guide book. They form the subject matter of countless other books and travel pamphlets. However, next to the Alhambra on the Albaicín (one of the hills of the city) are some excavations of walls revealing stratigraphy from the Late Bronze Age down to Arabic times. The gate to the Albaicín, Puerta de las Pesas, is from the eleventh century.

Iznalloz

Small town with several sites in the vicinity.

Sights:

Roman bridge and Alcázar on Tajo de la Hoz. Nearby also is the Cueva del Agua, a prehistoric site reached by an extremely bad road. Permission from the Ayuntamiento is required to enter.

Location:

N of Granada 31 km off the N 323 on the C 336. Inquire at Ayuntamiento.

Monachil

Excavated ancient settlement, Cerro de la Encina, is situated not far from the city of Granada, but it is now abandoned and somewhat overgrown.

Sight:

Neolithic and Bronze Age fortress and settlement.

Location:

Follow the GR 410 SE out of Granada in the direction of Huétor Vega for 7 km. Just before entering town, a modern cemetery is on the right and the hill or Cerro de la Encina on the left across the valley behind a derelict farmhouse. The site can be seen from the road and requires approximately a 600 m walk, some of it over rough ground.

Montefrío

The town has an Alcázar, but the most interesting site is prehistoric and outside of town some distance at Peña de los Gitanos. There is a dirt road up to the site, which lies partially among spaced-out trees and in an open field. Here are remains of dwellings (now just piles of stone), extensive dolmens (some well preserved), and other types of later Iberian stone graves. Some Roman remains have been reported in the same area.

Sights:
Alcázar. Neolithic to Copper Age settlement and necropoli.

Location:
Montefrío is NW of Granada on N 432, then W 11 km to Illora and N 18 km on secondary roads. Approx. 5 km out of town. on the GR 222 E toward Illora, site is signposted on left. Follow dirt track up hill through the cantera or stone quarry to end of road.

Orce
Hominid camp re-mains (El hombre de Orce) reported to be the oldest in Europe have been discov-ered on a cortijo in the vi-cinity of Venta de Micena near Orce, according to the director of the Paleological Institute of Sabadell, José Gibert. Fossilized remains of an elephant, rhinoceros and hyenas, among other animals, have also been un-covered at the site. More palpable, however, as far as something to see, are the Copper Age remains of round houses above the river Galera.

Granada: Montefrío. Dolmen, Peña de los Gitanos

Sights:
Paleolithic excavation and Copper Age settlement with remains of houses.

Location:
Orce is NE of Granada on the N 342 to Cúllar Baza, then N on C 3329 to Galera. Turn E toward Orce 5.3 km. On right is an arch inscribed El Marchal. About 100 m before this arch, turn right up rough dirt track and continue for 1 km to hermitage (which can be seen from the main road) beside which are the excavations. For Cerro de la Virgen, site of the hominid camp, go east from Orce and a little out of town, turn left at sign for Venta de Micena. Follow gravel road to church and turn left and left again at crossroads to the cortijo. Owner, from whom permission is needed to see the site, lives in Orce (inquire at the Ayuntamiento), but there is virtually nothing to see except some diggings.

Pinos Puente
The Bronze Age Ibero-Roman site, Cerro de los Infantes, is situated on a hill outside of town, while the ninth-century Arabic bridge, Puente Califal, is on the southern fringe of the town over the river Cubillas. Some guide books list the bridge as Visigothic and some as Roman. Travellers are warned by the local police not to leave their cars to view the bridge, which has a main horseshoe arch and two small side arches. This is a very dangerous section of the little city—the Barrio Gitano—where robberies are frequent.

Sights:
Ibero-Roman necropolis neglected and overgrown, Arabic bridge.
Location:
NW of Granada 17 km on N 432. To reach the necropolis travel 2 km NW of Pinos Puente on same road; site is signposted on right. Requires a short climb to hilltop through brush.

Purullena
Village consists of numerous troglodyte houses. Nearby are two historical sites, Cuesta de Negro and Balneario de Graena, with neglected and eroded Bronze Age remains of stone houses at the former and remains of rebuilt Arabic baths at the latter.
Sights:
Bronze Age settlement and Arabic baths.
Location:
Purullena is situated E of Granada and 6 km W of Guadix on the N 324. The baths, 2 km from town, are signposted in town on highway, while the pre-Roman remains are located 5 km NW of town. Travelling in direction of Granada, turn right on dirt road just past last ceramic shop on left. Go to cortijo and walk to top of hill. Steep climb in parts over rough ground.

Like other Andalucian provinces, Granada has its share of Arabic castles. Others not mentioned above can be found at **Castell de Ferro**, S of Granada and approx. 22 km from Motril E on the 340, ruins of Alcázar. **Guadix**, Iberian Acci and Arabic Wuad-Aix had originally a ninth-century Alcazaba and walls but the fortress has been rebuilt, E of Granada 58 km on N 342. **Huéscar**, remains of Alcazaba with little to see but the wall held up by supports. Perhaps of interest are the inscribed Roman stones incorporated into the wall with the inscriptions upside down, situated in the NE section of the province near the Murcian border, N of Baza 50 km on C 3329. **Illora**, remains of Alcázar on rock in centre of town which is NW of Granada 23 km on N 432, then W (left) 11 km on secondary road. **Laborcillas**, N of Granada 31 km on the 323, then E 20 km on the C 336. Reputed megalithic construction. **Lanchar**, castle of San Pedro, ruined Alcázar, 30 km W of Granada on N 342 just beyond airport. **Lanjarón**, Alcázar, S of Granada 40 km on N 323. **Loja**, Alcázar whose construction began in 895, once the stronghold dominating the valley and the access to Granada, located W of the capital 53 km on the N 342. **Moclín**, well-preserved Moslem remains, Alcázar and walls fortified by cylindrical towers, NW of Granada 31 km on N432 then E 4.5 km on secondary road. **Piñar**, 45 km N of Granada off the N 323 E (right) on the C 336, Alcázar. **Salobreña**, restored Alcázar and defensive walls, S of Granada on N 323 71 km and 15 km W of Almuñécar. **Vélez de Benaudalla**, S of Granada on the N 323 ca. 55 km near the coast, ruins of Alcázar.

HUELVA

The most westerly of the Andalucian provinces borders Portugal and is famous for its ancient mines, some of which are still worked today in large-scale operations such as the Río Tinto and Tharsis mines. The Río Tinto itself still runs reddish-brown with copper ore as it did in antiquity. Mining operations appear to have begun as early as the final phases of the Bronze Age and were continued by the Tartessians, whose legendary kingdom may have been centred in the province around the sixth century B.C. according to diverse artifacts found around the city of Huelva. Phoenicians coveted the mineral wealth of the region; they carried on extensive trade with the Tartessians and were, perhaps, responsible for the disappearance of this mysterious civilization.

From the much earlier Paleolithic period come a number of flaked stone tools for cutting and scraping, mostly from surface finds around the area. Polished stone tools from the Neolithic are also well documented from open-air sites and caves. Shown on some maps is the Cueva de la Mora north of Huelva in the jurisdiction (comarca) of Jabugo, where Paleolithic and Neolithic artifacts were discovered. First "excavated" in 1906, explosives were used to loosen up the encrusted accumulations of stalagmites.

Regarding the Bronze Age or Late Neolithic times, there are dozens of dolmens in the province, but some are only piles of rubble and others are unmarked, locked away in dense underbrush and forests and very difficult to locate even with a map. The largest concentration of these megalithic graves is found in the vicinity of El Pozuelo.

The capital city, Huelva, of Tartessian and Phoenician origin, was called Onuba. Another important town in antiquity, Ilipula (today Niebla)—known by classical geographers as Baeturia—was inhabited by the little-known Celtici. The area fell into the hands of the Romans in 194 B.C. and the mines, worked by thousands of slaves, became even more profitable especially as the Romans constructed a network of roads, most of which today are not easy to find, throughout the region.

Huelva became a major Roman port for the shipment of ore, and much later became one of the Arabic Taifas with the name of Guelbah, before succumbing to the Christian forces under Alfonso X in 1257.

Just 12 km from Huelva is the modest fifteenth-century Franciscan monastery of La Rábida, built on the foundations of an Almohade building, where Columbus was given shelter during his quest for money and ships

Cueva del Zancarrón de Soto

The site is not a cave as the name suggests, but a dolmen dating back roughly to about 2000 B.C. Discovered in 1923, it is covered by an artificial tumulus. The headstone is estimated to weigh about 21 tonnes and to have been brought from 32 km away. It has a 20 m-long corridor which leads to the rectangular burial chamber containing schematic stone engravings.

Sight:
Dolmen.

Location:
NW of Huelva, just off the N 431 between Niebla and San Juan del Puerto at km 619; signposted. The dirt road leading up to the site fords a stream which, after heavy rain, makes the passage hazardous.

Minas de Río Tinto

The open-pit mines of copper and iron ore are still in operation and to visit the ancient shafts and galleries worked in Roman times and before, permission is needed from the directer of the Río Tinto Mining Company by correspondence or in person.

Of interest to mining historians would be the new museum at the company offices (in process of implementation) with ancient mining artifacts, Roman statuary from the shafts, pottery, hammers, scrapers, chisels, etc. Mining paraphernalia from the entire province are being collected here. The museum contains photos of Roman shafts and stratigraphical layers dating back to the Bronze Age.

The mines of Río Tinto were scattered over a large area of about 85 km by 35 km in Roman times, with one of the major settlements at Corta del Lago, the Río Tinto of today, which is estimated to have produced two million tonnes of silver ore in antiquity. Scheduled for excavation, this Roman town is soon to disappear before the advancing mining operations.

Sights:
Ancient mines.

Location:
Take the N 435 N from Huelva and turn right on the C 421 approx. 8 km.

Niebla

This ancient town, Ilipula of the Celtici and Romans, situated beside the Río Tinto, became an episcopal seat under the Visigoths and later an independent Arabic kingdom. The stout walls resisted the advancing Christians under Alfonso X for over six months in the year 1262. The church of Santa María de la Granada, in which Christians (Mozarabes) worshipped even during Arabic times, is a restored edifice but with porticos containing Mozarabic details dating back to the tenth century. It was converted into a mosque during the reign of the Almohades and was redone in Gothic style in the fifteenth century. The

ruins of the church of San Martín are also reputed to be from the Moslem period.

About 3 km from Niebla on the 20 m-high hill called El Palmarón, was a Punic sepulchre, dynamited and looted in 1934. The well-cut stones are still there.

Sights:
Impressive Arabic walls, resting on Roman foundations, with forty-six towers and four gates or puertas (excavations at the

Huelva: Niebla. Roman Bridge over Río Tinto

Puerta de Sevilla) with horseshoe arches. Well-preserved Roman bridge over the Río Tinto. El D'esembarcadero, remains of some docks in the eastern part of the town on the banks of the river. Santa María de la Granada, Mozarabe church but with later (Gothic) additions.

Location:
NE of Huelva on the N 431.

Huelva: Niebla. Arabic Walls

Pozuelo

Near this small village, over a rough dirt road, stand three complexes of dolmens each on top of its separate hill. The first one encountered has three burial chambers but only one entrance passage, and is in a good state of preservaton. Two of the chambers have capstones in place. The second has seemingly four burial chambers, several passageways, one capstone in place and is in fair condition. The last is in poor condition with stones askew.

Sights:
Dolmens

Location:
Follow the N 435 N from Huelva, between Valverde and Zalamea turn off to right to Pozuelo. Just before entering village (before cemetery) take the dirt track to the right marked "dolmens." Go 2.2 km from sign and road splits with gate on left. Path on right through trees leads up hill about 100 m to first dolmen. From here the other two can be seen on their respective hills nearby.

Huelva: Pozuelo. Dolmen

San Bartolomé de la Torre

Situated on a hill by itself just outside of the town is a ruined, partially restored (fifty per cent) Punic tower. On the main street through town is a large millstone, possibly from Roman times.

Sight:
Punic tower.

Location:
Turn off the N 431 just W of Gibraleón N of Huelva and proceed on the C 443 14 km to the town.

Tharsis
Old copper mines dating back to Roman times, recently discovered, contain some ancient bits of walls. Mines are an ongoing operation and sightseers are not encouraged. If someone is particularly interested in mining history he or she may gain access to Phoenician and Roman sites by inquiring of the Tharsis mining company in writing.

Sights:
Ancient mines.

Location:
Turn off N 431 by Gibraleón N of Huelva and follow the C 443 for 32 km.

Other places of historical interest in the province are: **Almonaster la Real**, N of Huelva on N 435 approx. 90 km, then W on H 521 7 km. The church Ermita del Castillo was thought to have been constructed in the early tenth century as a mosque but converted to a church after the reconquest. **Aracena**, ruins of an Almohade castle, N of Huelva ca. 98 km on N 435, then E (right) on N 433 for 18 km. **Aroche**, ruins of Almoravide wall, castle and ramparts, N of Huelva on N 435 to junction with N 433, about 98 km, then W on N 433 approx. 24 km. **Ayamonte**, Alcázar, W. of Huelva on the Portuguese border. **Cortegana**, Alcázar, N of Huelva to N 433, 28 km due W of Aracena. **Dehesa, La**, N of Huelva on N 435 to Zalamea la Real, then E (right) to a few kilomentres N of Río Tinto on the H 501; remains of Roman necropolis. **Encinasola**, Alcázar, N of Huelva on N 435 to the junction with the secondary road H 211, left 23 km. **Gibraleón**, remains of Moslem fortress and walls, W of Huelva 16 km on N 431. **Sotiel Coronada**, NE of Huelva on N 435 then branch off to left on H 141 NW to town; some remains of Roman and pre-Roman mines. Ask for directions at Ayuntamiento. **Villalba del Alcor**, church of San Bartolomé, Almohade chapel, E of Huelva 35 km on N 431. **Zalamea la Real**, N of Huelva ca. 60 km on the N 435, in the hills to the SE lies an excavation of the hilltop Bronze Age settlement of Chinflón, however, there is little to see in situ.

JAEN

Always an important gateway on the north-south route of early peoples, the province of Jaén was inhabited by all the major historical cultures of the peninsula and contains about six hundred fifty known archaeological sites. The fertile area in the triangle east of the confluence of the Quadalquivir and Quadalimar rivers, which merge a little south of Bailén, has long been a desirable area. Well represented in the region are Bronze Age settlements of great antiquity. Here the Oretanos, an Iberian clan, cultivated the region, and the towns of Canena, Ibros and Rus were Iberian settlements. Here also ancient Cástulo was located and the battlegrounds where Carthaginians fought Romans for dominance of Baetica, causing a depopulation of Iberian tribes in the process. In the fifth century A.D. the area was again in violent turmoil as Germanic invaders passed through toward the south. Archaeologists have barely scratched the surface of this area, not to mention the many other known sites in the province.

The Cazorla mountains in Jaén are the source of the Guadalquivir river and many early settlements were spawned in its valley. Mining in the mountains and agriculture along the river and open hilly country were the major economic pursuits of the early communities.

Mining communities were also established in the Sierra Morena in the northern sector of the province, and in the south the Sierra Mágina offered caves and rock shelters to some of the earliest people, and impregnable mountain spurs for Iberian settlements.

Not unlike other Spanish provinces Jaén harbours numerous unexcavated sites that are potentially of great importance in the historical record. For example, surface finds south of Vilches on the spur of a meseta, at Santagón near the artificial lake of Guadalén, suggest an agricultural settlement here from perhaps as far back as 2000 B.C., near which the Romans established a camp or town, also unexcavated. In the vicinity of Giribaile, E of Linares, there are many signs of continuous habitation from the Bronze Age to the Arabs, but the area is little explored archaeologically.

Alcalá la Real

The vicinity is prolific in unexcavated Roman sites. At least three villas are known in the area but so far there is little to see. The mausoleum is in the NE sector of town near the water deposit of San Marcos and is of Roman appearance but of disputed date; it could be much later. In the same sector is a Roman bridge and remains of a Roman road reached by a rough dirt track. The Arabic castle, Fortaleza de la Mota, is from the fourteenth century.

Sights:
Mausoleum, Roman road and bridge.

Location:
Alcalá la Real is 75 km S of Jaén on the N 432.

Aldeaquemada

There are two caves—Peñón de la Tabla de Pochico and Prado de Azoque—with rupestrian paintings near here, but they are extremely difficult to find without a guide and have nearly faded out of existence. One contains repainted deer with antlers changed to horns. Inquire for directions at the Ayuntamiento.

Sights:
Cave sites with paintings.

Location:
N of Jaén and E of Despeñaperros on J 611, approx. 25 km.

Baeza

Excavations in progress of a Bronze Age site are located on the Paseo de las Murallas in the SW part of the town (Barrio Alcázar) beside the radio tower. The site has so far revealed several levels of habitation. The Fountain of the Lions in town is an Ibero-Roman monument from Cástulo. Remains of a mosque have been discovered in the cloister of the cathedral.

Sights:

Bronze Age settlement with remains of walls and cisterns, Ibero-Roman fountain, remnants of mosque.

Location:

NE of Jaén 48 km on the N 321.

Baños de la Encina

The town lies on a gentle hill in the Sierra Morena. There are rupestrian paintings in the natural refuge of Canforos de Peñarrubia belonging to the Bronze Age showing figures of deer and animal-taming scenes. But it is about a one-hour trek through a tangle of hilly country to the site. The Ayuntamiento will provide a guide.

A guide is also needed for Peñalosa, a Bronze Age site of about 1500 B.C. in the Sierra Morena, which requires about a fifteen-minute walk over about 1.5 km after leaving vehicle. Here may be seen remains of houses, walls, streets, forges, terraces (five excavated at time of writing) and connecting ramps and stairs. This was essentially a mining centre and there appear to be remains of buildings for processing minerals which were traded for agricultural products from neighbouring settlements. Access to the site is under improvement. Of interest in the same area is the hill of Navalmorquín with a walled mine from the Phoenician era. This can be reached at present with an all-terrain vehicle over a very poor road.

Artifacts from the area also indicate a Roman presence connected with the work of mining, but no specific Roman sites have been excavated.

Jaén: Baños de la Encina. Alcázar

The Arabic stronghold in the town was ordered constructed by Al-Hakam II and was completed in 968 according to the founding inscription at the gate (where the date recorded is the 357 Ramadan of the Hegira). The Alcázar is oval in shape with square towers and a double horseshoe gateway. The key may be obtained at the Ayuntamiento.

Sights:

Rupestrian paintings, Bronze Age site, Phoenician mine, Alcázar.

Location:

N of Jaén and N of Bailen 11 km on the N IV, then W on the J 504 for 6 km.

Castellar de Santisteban

The nearby site, Cuevas de Biche, was an Iberian sanctuary where votive figurines have been found along with earlier Copper and Bronze Age artifacts and later Roman fragments of columns and tombs. This rock sanctuary lies SE of Despeñaperros; it had five grottos ranged at the foot of a cliff. It is situated in an area of bronze production that probably began around the end of the sixth century B.C. The remains of dwellings are associated with the third century B.C. This centre and that of Despeñaperros seem to have produced most of the Iberian bronze work. Copper mines are located in the region along with lead mines, but the tin had to be transported from afar. There is now almost nothing left to see.

Sight:
Iberian sanctuary.

Location:
NE of Jaén on N 321/2 approx. 98 km to Villanueva del Arzobispo, then NW on J 622 20 km.

Ceal

Iberian necropolis (chamber tomb) covered over at present, but excavations expected to continue at some future date. Inquire at Escuela-Taller Arqueológico in Ubeda. The existence of Celtic graves in a lower level helped date the foundation of the settlement to the sixth century B.C.

Sight:
Iberian necropolis.

Location:
NE of Jaén, go E of Ubeda on N 322 for 10 km, then SE on J 314/C 323 to Quesada, beyond which take road W beyond Hinojares.

Despeñaperros

Famous cave, Cueva de las Muñecas, in and around which thousands of Iberian votive figurines were found, hence the name of the site (Cave of the Dolls). From the end of the sixth century B.C. there developed a school of bronze metallurgy which was to endure until the fourth century A.D., when the triumph of Christianity brought about the closing of pagan sanctuaries. During the course of these centuries pilgrims deposited a vast number of votive offerings (small bronze figurines) at this site. Nearby was once an Iberian settlement destroyed by the Romans. The sparse remains reveal a large inhabited area of rectangular houses with stone foundations and slate roofs. It was enclosed by a wall and two towers which flanked the gateway. There are some scant remains of gravesites. A fragment of the cyclopean wall is still visible. There is very little to see, however, except the grotto itself, which has a rock painted deer so faint a guide is required to point it out. In the nearby Cueva de los Organos there are rock paintings but a guide is needed to find them. Inquire at the Ayuntamiento of nearby Santa Elena, where there is also a rather uninteresting excavation of an Iberian settlement (Collada de los Jardines), done at the beginning of the century and since neglected.

Sights:
Iberian sanctuary, remnant of wall, rupestrian paintings.
Location:
N of Jaén. Take mountain road E toward Aldeaquemada off the N IV just N of Santa Elena. After km 5 marked beside road is a large curve from which one can see the cave and excavations on the left about 200 m away.

Giribaile
Its name derived from Gil Baile, a personal name, here are the so-called Cuevas de Espelunca where Roman, Visigothic and Arabic remains have been found. The site served as a defensive position guarding the Roman roads that crossed nearby, namely the Via Herculeum from Rome to Cádiz and the Camino Real from Toledo to Almería via Ubeda and Granada. There is little to see but the remains of the Arabic castle and stretch of ancient wall.

Sights:
Alcázar and earlier wall.
Location:
NE of Jaén and NE of Linares and a little S of Vilches on poor road.

Guardia de Jaén
Monte Salido is a small hill about 100 m S of the entry to the town, found by passing through an olive grove. On the hill are rock-hewn Visigothic graves whose contents have been removed to the museum in Jaén. The town also has the impressive remains of an eighth-century castle.

Sights:
Visigothic necropolis and Alcázar.
Location:
About 15 km SE of Jaén on the N 323.

Ibros
Once an Iberian fortress, the short but impressive remains of the cyclopean wall are still to be seen in the town.

Sight:
Cyclopean wall.
Location:
Approx. 4.5 km off the N 322 NW of Ubeda. The wall is signposted in the village.

Jaén
Iberian and Roman Auringis (the latter worked the local silver mines) but Jayyan, or "Route of the Caravans," to the Arabs, was no doubt due to its important geographical location. To be seen in the city are eleventh-century restored Arabic baths beneath the palace of Villardompardo, whose very size make them the most important in the country, with hot, temperate and cold

water pools. The Convento de Santo Domingo, once a Moslem palace, is now a school, and the Castillo de Santa Catalina on Monte Bernisa above the city, once a Roman fort and an Arabic castle, was restored by Fernando III, who conquered the city in 1246. It is now a parador.

Sights:
Arabic remains, baths and Alcázar.

Location:
In town.

Jimena
Nearby is located the Cueva de Graja, with rock paintings from the Chalcolithic period in fair-to-poor condition but easily seen.

In the recently discovered Cueva de Morrón are some rock paintings reputedly from Paleolithic times, and on the Cerro de Alcalá are the scant remains of an Iberian settlement.

The town has an Alcázar and the parochial church was built over the Arabic Mezquita.

Sights:
Rupestrian paintings, Iberian site, Alcázar.

Location:
The town is E of Jaén about 36 km on N 321/324/328. To see the Cueva de Graja, obtain key from the Ayuntamiento, go W out of town past petrol station and take right fork of road. Then right again immediately. One can drive as far as the football field and the cave is visible above it in the hillside. A rather steep 300 m climb. For other sites obtain permission and directions from the Ayuntamiento.

Linares
Near Linares, Cástulo (the ancient name known from Latin authors and coin inscriptions) is an extensive site of great potential but has been only partially excavated, and then not for many years. It was the birthplace of Imilca, wife of Hannibal, and occupied at one time or another by Iberians, Carthaginians (sites at present re-covered), Romans (villa complex approx. thirty per cent excavated), Visigoths (necropolis near cortijo), and Arabs (walls and tower standing). Here the Roman Scipio Africanus defeated the Carthaginians in 208 B.C. in the campaign to deny Hannibal, fighting in Italy, reinforcements from Spain.

Sights:
Roman villa with remains of houses and caldarium, road, Visigothic necropolis, Arabic walls and tower.

Location:
NE of Jaén and E of Bailén 17 km on N 322. Do not enter Linares, but follow road S to Torreblascopedro. After 2.5 km, Cástulo is signposted left. Proceed another 2.5 km then right 500 m to site and house for guard/guide.

Martos

From the Roman colony of Augusta Gemella (once Tucci of Iberian origin) there remain some Latin inscriptions on the rock above the town. Here are also some ruins of the Arabic fortress La Peña.

Sights:
Roman inscriptions, Alcázar.

Location:
SW of Jaén 24 km on N 321. Ask for directions in the Ayuntamiento.

Menjíbar

Ancient pre-Roman and Roman town at nearby Cerro de Maquiz. Roman remains consist of a tomb (hypogeum) or cistern (?) with two levels and remnants of Roman temple. Under the second level of the possible hypogeum are the remains of an Iberian settlement. The sites are neglected, unmarked and difficult to find in the middle of an extensive olive grove. There is virtually nothing to see of the Iberian town.

Sights:
Remains of Roman hypogeum (or cistern) and temple.

Location:
Mengíbar is N of Jaén 23.5 km on N 323. Take road E off highway opposite main entrance to town, pass railway tracks and cross over river, then take second unpaved road on right to just below hermitage. Walk up hill into olive groves; patience is required here.

Miraelrío

Some preliminary and urgent excavations at Cerro Del Salto have revealed slight remains of a fortified, agricultural Bronze Age site situated on a small meseta, but they are threatened by the waters of a projected dam nearby.

Sight:
Bronze Age site.

Location:
NE of Jaén, a little E of Linares, on the right bank of the river Guadalimar very near its intersection with the river Guadalén, and over rough dirt road. Best to check with the Escuela-Taller Arqeológico in the Ayuntamiento of Ubeda for map and permission to visit.

Peal de Becerro

In 1909, a large rectangular underground stone tomb was discovered by a farmer ploughing his field near Toya (ancient Tugia) on a hillock called Cerro de la Horca. The family wasted little time in cleaning out the sepulchre and selling the artifacts (ceramics, coins, jewellery, arms, etc.) in the neighbouring towns. Some have been recovered for the National Archaelogical Museum in Madrid.

The necropolis is nearly square and measures 5 m on each side and is divided into a central and four lateral chambers with niches for relics. Stone benches and tables supported the urns filled with the ashes of the deceased.

The architectural style of the tomb and the recovered artifacts—such as a Greek vase imported from Southern Italy with red figures on a black background and representing the god Bacchus attended by two winged spirits— suggest a good deal of influence from the eastern Mediterrean. The tomb appears to have been constructed and used from the fifth to second centuries B.C. by a southern Iberian tribe who were at that time under the economic domination of the Carthaginians.

The descent into the tomb is via a curved ramp of recent construction. The large stones of the site, quarried nearby behind the Cerro de Castillo de Toya, are well preserved, but a few have been replaced by new ones.

From the nearby village of Toya an Alcázar can be seen, built on the site of an Iberian (and later Roman) settlement belonging to the people who constructed the mausoleum. By the fountain in town are the remains of another settlement, older still but unexcavated.

Near the road between Ubeda and Peal de Becerro, just before crossing the bridge over the Guadalquivir, on the hill on the right hand side, is the Cerro del Gato where there are the scant remains of a flan-shaped Iberian fortress of the fourth century B.C. It seems to have marked the limits of the territory of the Toya people.

Sights:
Iberian hypogeum (largest of its type), Alcázar, slight remains of an Iberian fortress.

Location:
E of Jaén. Take secondary road toward Toya out of Peal de Becerro, where keys for the sepulchre may be obtained from the Ayuntamiento. Continue for 5 km to sign on right "Camara Sepulcral." Follow farm road 900 m to site.

Porcuna
Here, the Roman city of Obulco, situated on the southern edge of town, is under on-going excavations. The site is fenced and hidden by a row of garages and one should go to the Ayuntamiento for keys and information about local guides if desired. Only a small section of Obulco has been excavated.

On the neighbouring hill and easily seen from Obulco are the ruins of an older pre-Roman agricultural settlement.

Sights:
Roman town revealing remains of grain silos, pillars, streets, steps, dwellings, walls and baths. Nearby pre-Roman town, not currently under excavation, contains the remains of houses, walls and grain silos.

Location:
Porcuna is W of Jaén on N 324 about 42 km.

Quesada
Excellent remains of Roman villa, Pago de Bruñel Bajo, largely excavated with beautiful mosaics in rather good condition. Easy access by automobile right to the hilltop site.

Also near Quesada is the Cueva de la Encajera with rupestrian paintings in fair condition.

Sights:
Roman villa with mosaics, remains of columns, streets, baths, and dwellings. Nearby, rupestrian paintings.
Location:
E of Jaén and S of Peal de Becerro on the C 323 toward Quesada. At about 7 km is a sign, left, "Ruinas de Bruñel," go 4 km (toward Cazorla) to Bruñel. Sign on left reports that the keys (*llaves*) to the villa can be obtained at the Cortijo de José Zamora. Take first turning left and the farmhouse is the first on the left. Villa is less than 1 km further along same road and site can be seen from the cortijo.

Jaén: Quesada. Roman Villa Mosaic

The grottos containing the rupestrian paintings are located to the right of the road between Quesada and Pozo Alcón travelling south. They can be seen from the road.

Sabiote
On the edge of town is an Arabic castle converted to a palace. Beside the entrance to the palace is an excavated Bronze Age site, now abandoned, in poor condition and somewhat overgrown. Recent laying of underground cable to illuminate the palace was done through the excavations with little sensitivity to the relics of the past.

Sights:
Bronze Age site with remains of cisterns, walls and houses. Alcázar.
Location:
Sabiote lies NE of Jaén and 9 km NE of Ubeda on J 604.

Ubeda
At the time of writing, excavations were planned for a Bronze Age site in the Alcázar district of the city with a proposed completion date of 1992. Check with the Escuela-Taller Arqueológico in the Ayuntamiento.

Sights:
The city contains some Moslem and Mudéjar remains, such as the thirteenth-century Torre del Reloj (once part of the walls) and the Puerta de Losal.
Location:
Ubeda lies on the N 321 NE of Jaén ca. 60 km.

Ubeda la Vieja

This is not a town, but a hill on which some test shafts have been sunk. Situated in plain view of the road are the remains of a great wall about 40 m long and 10 m high which once enclosed the site. The various strata of the wall indicate Bronze Age, Iberian and Roman occupation of the area. Nearby and visible from here is a bridge over the Quadalquivir river built on Roman foundations but successively reconstructed by Visigoths, Arabs and Renaissance builders.

Sights:

Ancient wall, Roman foundations of bridge.

Location:

E of Jaén. Take the C 325 S from Ubeda to Donadio and just after crossing the Guadalquivir river turn E. Where road forks, go left and cross river again on Roman bridge. Immediately after bridge turn right and travel about 0.5 km and stop between first and second overhead electric power lines. Site is on hill at left. Climb up approx. 100 m to wall.

Valdecanales, Casa de

A rock sanctuary, Cerro de la Alcobilla, from Visigothic times, is the only one preserved in the south of Spain from that period. It contains a chapel of three naves cut out of the living rock with a *bóveda de cañón* (barrel vault) on square pilastres, with spaces for graves and incineration urns. There is some evidence that the site was also used by the Moslems.

Jaén: Ubeda la Vieja. Ibero-Roman Wall

Sight:

Visigothic rock-cut sanctuary.

Location:

At Canena, NE of Jaén and W of Ubeda on the N 322 (where there is an Arabic castle converted to a palace in the sixteenth century) ask for the *carril* (farm road) to Escuderos. At first cortijo (Varcuende) ask for road to Casa Abajo. From here walk across river bed in front of house; road leads to site about 100 m away. Unfortunately, it is very easy to get lost in the maze of farm roads en route and best to solicit a guide. Expert help can be found at Francis Electric and TV shop in Rus, the next little town.

Vilches

Archaeological finds on the hill of the castle, Cerro del Castillo, in Vilches indicate that the site dates back to Neolithic and Bronze Age times and was active during the Roman period. Some of the walls preserved in the ruins of the Arabic castle are of Iberian origin. These are about all there is to see from the remote past.

Sights:
Iberian walls, Alcázar.

Location:
N of Jaén. 14 km E of La Carolina on C 3217.

Further sights in the province include: **Alcaudete**, 48 km SW of Jaén on the N 321, ruins of an Alcázar. **Andújar**, on the N IV W of Bailen 27 km, the ancient bridge over the Quadalquivir river, near the modern one, contains fifteen original Roman spans. Here also may be seen an Alcázar rebuilt after the reconquest, and some remains of Arabic walls. **Bedmar**, E of Jaén just beyond Jimena on C 328, remains of ninth-century Alcázar. **Cambil**, 33 km SE of Jaén on the N 323/324, scant remains (foundations of walls) of tenth-century Alcázar. **Campillo de Arenas**, ca. 40 km SE of Jaén on N 323, slight Roman remains on the cortijos (farms) of Casablanca and Cañada de las Viñas as well as around the parochial church. **Cazorla**, E of Jaén and SE of Ubeda on C 322/ J 314 to the C 328, Alcázar, and beyond which at Puente de las Herrerías there is a reputedly Roman bridge. **Jodar**, 57 km E of Jaén on the N 321/325, Cerro de San Cristóbal, slight Ibero-Roman remains and two towers, one Arabic, one Christian. **Noalejo**, SE of Jaén on the N 323 on the Granada border, rupestrian paintings of Navalcán situated a few kilometres from the village. The paintings from the Neolithic period seem to involve a dance scene. **Segura de la Sierra**, in the Segura mountains well NE of Jaén, Alcázar.

There are many fortresses partially preserved in the province, a reminder that this was a highly disputed area during the Christian reconquest. In fact, nearly every town has some remnant of Moslem times it can call its own; a few others are Jabalquinto, Lupión, Cabra del Santo Cristo, Torreperogil, Iznatoraf, and Belmez de la Moraleda.

MALAGA

This is the smallest of the Andalucian provinces. Its Mediterranean coast line and parallel mountain ranges harbour Phoenician, Cathaginian and Roman remains, and in the fertile Antequera depression beyond the hills from the capital city of the same name are the great dolmens of Antequera, some of the most important prehistorical remains on the peninsula. To the east, in the Serranía de Ronda, a labyrinth of mountain formations around the small plateau on which rests the city of Ronda, are many relics of Roman and Arabic times.

There is potentially a great deal here to appreciate for its historical value; for example, the province contains nearly two hundred known Roman villas, most unexcavated, and about thirty dolmen remains—yet there is much that is sadly neglected, plundered, swallowed up in the urban sprawl, left unmarked, or that has simply vanished under some apartment complex or other. This process of destruction continues.

Of the millions of visitors to the Costa del Sol each year, few are likely to see or even hear of an ancient site apart from perhaps the highly profiled Alcazaba in Málaga—yet they are there if one knows where to look.

Alamos, los

Possible Roman villa currently being excavated. The actual villa associated with the vats and graves has so far not been found. Area will be covered over again in order to build modern houses.

Also near Torremolinos at Playamar are Roman baths, also slated to be covered over for modern construction. Roman ovens for the production of amphora are located in nearby La Carihuela, but their continued existence is somewhat more than precarious. Inquire at Ayuntamiento of Torremolinos or the Department of Archaeology at the University of Málaga for more information.

Sights:

Baths, necropolis, garum vats, ovens.

Location:

W of Málaga and a little E of Torremolinos, a few hundred metres from Los Alamos train station. Turn right off highway just W of km 229 and go under railway bridge, then first left and follow unpaved road ca. 300 m to site.

Antequera

Dating back to Roman times and before, the city has three magnificent, well-preserved dolmens nearby which themselves date back to the third millenium B.C. The first two are situated on a slight rise about 1 km from Antequera on the left of the Granada road. The third, Romeral, is about 4 km from town in the same direction but near the junction with the Lucena-Málaga highway.

The Cueva de Menga is the simplest of the tombs — consisting of only a covered gallery—and appears to be the oldest, dating back to about 2500 B.C. It measures 25 m in length, 6.5 m in width and nearly 3 m high from the present floor to the ceiling. On the last stone slab of the left wall are some engraved symbolic forms. The star engraved below is from a more recent period.

Fifty metres from Menga, Viera was discovered in1905 by the brothers Viera. It is constructed with smaller but better-cut

Málaga: Antequera. Cueva de Menga

stones. The grave has a 19 m-long corridor leading to the burial vault, with an average width of just over 1 m and a height of almost 2 m; it is still partly covered with earth. The chamber is a 1.8 m across and 2 m high.

Discovered about the same time as Viera, Romeral is different from the other two dolmens. The walls are made of small stones and mud bricks plus lime, while the ceiling consists of the usual megalithic flagstones. Also unusual is the rounded vault, reminiscent of the *tholos* in Crete. The entrance passage is 20.5 m long, 1.6 m wide on average and 1.4 m high. The vault has a diameter of 5.2 m and is 3.9 m high. This first vault has a smaller, second vault attached to it by a short corridor. The tomb, more complex than the others and the most recent dating back to about 1800 B.C., was restored in part after 1940 from its then-lamentable state. There are plans to establish an archaeological park on the site of the dolmens.

On the hill above the city of Antequera near the Alcazaba (of which only the Torre de Homenaje or castle keep and some walls remain) and beside the church of Santa María, are the remains of Roman baths, recently discovered under a parking lot and now under excavation begun in 1988. The site seems to substantiate the existence of the Roman city of Anticuaria, previously only alluded to in ancient literature.

"Carnicería de los Moros" refers to a Roman site on the right of the Granada road, just past the Cueva de Menga and beside the Instituto de Bachillerato. There are remains of a reservoir and arches which suggest part of a Roman temple.

Other Roman sites in the area include Prensa de Aceite, at Gallumber, W of the city, a settlement of the first century A.D.—2 km up a difficult forestry road and on currently private property—and Ciudad Romana, 6 km on the road to Bobadilla W of Antequera at Cortijo del Castillón, also on private property. In both cases inquire at the Escuela-Taller Arqueológico for permission to visit sites.

Sights:
Dolmens, Roman remains including baths, houses, walls, arches, cisterns and temples in various locations in and outside of town, remains of Alcazaba and Arabic walls.

Location:
Antequera lies 57 km due N of Málaga.

Ardales
About 5 km from the town is the cave of Doña Trinidad with Paleolithic paintings, but inquire at Ayuntamiento for permission to visit and to obtain guide. Here also are slight vestiges of the Iberian settlement of Turóbriga and of a Roman fortress, as well as ruins of the Alcázar with traces of walls and cisterns. Nearby are the ruins of Bobastro (see next entry)

Sights:
Rupestrian paintings, scant traces of Iberian and Roman settlements and remains of Alcázar.

Location:
NW of Málaga on the MA 441/442 and 25 km NW of Alora over poor roads.

Benaoján

Approx. 6 km beyond the town is the prehistoric cave of La Pileta, with red and black rupestrian paintings of fish, goats and bison among others. The cave is 1500 m long and the paintings are well back. Guide available at entrance during normal hours. Be prepared to spend some time here.

Sights:
Rupestrian paintings.

Location:
Go N of Ronda on road to Algodonales, C 339, and turn off left on the MA 549 toward Benaoján on a rather poor road. Cave 13 km from turning.

Bobastro, Ruinas de

En route to this site is the Mozarabe necropolis of Nuestra Señora de Villaverde de Ardales, a small cemetery of about a half dozen graves, fenced but visible, dating back to Moslem times. Signposted on right of road. Further along the same road are the remains of a Mozarabe church of about 898, partly cut from the rock, but now in near total ruin and only a pile of stones. General outlines of the church are still visible. Signposted on left of road, walk up rock-cut steps and follow path for about 150 m. At the end of the road, approx. 1 km beyond the reservoir, on top of hill on right, about 60 m, are the ruins of Bobastro, a fortress founded in 884 by Omar Ibn Hafsun supposedly as a rival to the Emirate of Córdoba; now there are only scant remains of the Arabic fortress, neglected and thickly overgrown.

Sights:
Mozarabe necropolis, rock-cut Mozarabe church and remnants of an Alcázar.

Location:
From the western suburbs of Málaga take road to Alora, and from there follow signs for Ruinas de Bobastro.

Estepona

Seaside tourist town called by the Arabs Estebuna and site of earlier Roman town. A little W of the city on the N 340 and on S side of road behind the urbanization Arroyo Vaquero are about half a dozen single and two double Roman graves. Neglected and overgrown site is about 50 m off road and scattered with rubbish.

There are the remains of an Arabic fortress in town, and ruins of the Aqueduct of Salduba, about one thousand years old, seen from the highway on right travelling E, on private property just out of town.

Sights:
Roman necropolis, Medieval aqueduct, Alcázar.

Location:
W of Málaga on the N 340.

Fuengirola

Originally named Suel, this popular seaside resort is overlooked by a castle on the hill W of the city. Its origins are controversial but it seems to have been a Punic or Roman site, rebuilt in the tenth century under the Caliph Abd-al Rahman III as a coastal stronghold against pirates. It was rebuilt again in 1730 and is currently under reconstruction.

To the E of the city in the village of Carvajal are the remains of the Roman site of Torreblanca del Sol. This appears to have once been a sumptuous villa dating back to the first century A.D. of which only the bath area (*termas*) has been excavated. In the fourth century the baths were converted into fish-salting tanks but the villa was abandoned in the fifth or sixth century. Part of the site was later used as a Visigothic burial ground and thirty-two tombs were discovered, all sacked and destroyed sometime in the past. Several are still visible. The villa is badly overgrown and for years neglected. It can be approached from the highway through a hole in the dilapidated fence after climbing a steep 3 m-high bank.

On the Paseo Marítimo in Los Boliches, just W of Fuengirola, stands a recently built "Roman Temple" where no temple existed. The stones for its modern construction, however, were found nearby and seem to have come from the Roman quarry at Mijas in the hills behind Fuengirola. It seems they were cut and transported to the coast, but no ship ever arrived to pick them up.

A stretch of the Calzada Romana that ran along the coast is, according to archaeological reports and tourist brochures, supposed to be on the hill opposite the castle, but it has never been excavated and there is nothing to see.

The Vikings conquered the town in 858 but left no trace of their passing. Fuengirola was "liberated" in 1485 by the Catholic monarchs.

Sights:
Roman baths, Visigothic graves and Alcázar.

Location:
Fuengirola is 30 km W of Málaga on the N 340.

Málaga

The first to arrive from abroad along the sunny shores of Málaga appear to have been the Phoenicians, who established trading centres and fish-curing industries and called the locality Malaka. Greeks came to trade also and, of course, the Carthaginians and Romans came to conquer. Byzantines occupied the area in the sixth century after the demise of the Roman Empire, but only for a short period. They were routed by the Visigoth Leovigildo in 570 when he captured the city. Less than a century and a half later it fell to the Arabs, who relinquished it to the Christians only in 1487.

At present, the second century Roman theatre in Málaga, the castle of Gibralfaro and the Alcazaba are undergoing restoration. The last is one of those magnificent fortresses from Arabic times whose walls dominate the city from the east and whose cool, sumptuous interior affords great pleasure to the traveller. It was constructed in the ninth century over the ruins of a Roman fortress and was completed in 1063. Stones from the Roman ruins including the theatre were used in its erection.

The fortress of Gibralfaro was first built by Abd-al-Rahman III on the hill where prehistoric remains have been found. The name derives from Jabal-Faruk, "lighthouse hill." There appears to have been a lighthouse earlier, perhaps Phoenician. The fortress was enlarged in the fourteenth century and was once connected to the Alcazaba. It may be again when restoration is completed.

Sights:
Roman theatre, Alcazaba and Gibralfaro. Museum in situ.

Location:
In the eastern section of the city.

Málaga: Alcazaba

Manilva
The Roman baths of Hedionda are situated in the valley below the hill town of Manilva. The high sulphur content baths can still be used but are now under an offensive concrete shell. Some small adjacent excavations of water channels are nearby. The site is a disappointment due to the artless attempt to preserve and improve it.

Nearby in the valley between the baths and the coastal highway is a one hundred-or-so metre stretch of aqueduct reputed to be of Roman origin.

Beyond Manilva in the hills are the partially excavated, heavily overgrown remains of a Roman villa complex sometimes referred to locally as Torrejón, once involved in the production of olive oil. The hilltop site, ca. 100 m wide and 300 m long, is difficult to find.

Sights:
Roman baths, aqueduct, Roman villa with remains of dwellings, walls (one stretch of cyclopean wall), cisterns, water conduits and pools (perhaps for oil).

Locations:
Manilva is W of Málaga. For the Roman baths signposted on the N 340 11 km SW of Estepona go N out of Manilva following signs for Roman Oasis Restaurant approx. 2 km. Turn right and follow poor dirt road past quarry down to river and where road splits (right to restaurant) go left about 1,500 m to baths. For the aqueduct, take steep, unpaved road down to river from village; site is on the left. For the Roman villa it is advisable to seek a guide in the town, but if one wishes to chance it take the MA 529 north of Manilva (same as for the Roman baths) toward Gaucín. Travel 9.3 km from edge of town, turn left up gravel road, drive to end of road where there is a farmhouse and walk about 1 km through fields straight ahead and then climb through fence and up the steep hill through the underbrush. On top of the hill is the site.

Marbella

Just W of the town on the grounds of the Hotel Puente Romano is a small Roman bridge over a stream and tucked away between the buildings. It is signposted on the main highway from Marbella to San Pedro de Alcántara.

The old city of Marbella preserves parts of the Arabic and Roman wall and two towers of the tenth century near the parochial church. The Alcazaba, on the site of an older Roman structure, has been partially restored and retains its walls, keep and patio.

Sights:
Roman bridge, and Arabic remains in town.

Location:
W of Málaga on the N 340.

Nerja

A little outside of town is the Cueva de Nerja, a large cave with high ceiling, and some faint, reputedly Paleolithic, cave paintings in the deep interior. The cave is well lighted and open during normal hours.

Sights:
Rupestrian paintings.

Location
E. of Málaga 53 km on N 340.

Puerta Duquesa

An urbanization with adjacent Roman cemetery, on W side, of about ten scattered graves in poor condition, some no more than a pile of stones, and nearby remains of a late Roman villa complex next to the eighteenth-century coastal fortress to the W of the urbanization. Excavated but neglected sites.

Sights:
Roman necropolis and villa with remnants of walls, foundations of dwellings, water conduits, well, baths, stone mill for grinding wheat.

Location:
W of Málaga and about 12 km SW of Estepona on the N 340.

Rincón de la Victoria

The large cave here, Cueva del Tesoro, with reputed Neolithic rock drawings, also served as a refuge for both Christians and Moslems at various times. At time of writing cave was closed to the public.

Sights:
Rupestrian paintings.

Location
7 km E of Málaga on N 340 in a park above the village.

Ronda

Roman Arunda, the town is known primarily for its Arabic remains. It became the capital of an Arabic emirate and remained independent until its capture by the Catholic monarchs in 1485. The Alcazaba was blown up by French troops during the Napoleonic wars. The town preserves many fine relics of its Moslem past including the walls and gateway, Puerta de Almocávar, with horseshoe arches, the principle entrance to the town in Arabic times; the Arco de Cristo, another entrance; and the Arabic baths (under restoration). These sights are from the thirteenth century and most others are of the fourteenth century or later.

Only a short distance from Ronda stands the remains of a Roman aqueduct and, further removed at **Ronda la Vieja**, is the large site of the Roman city of Acinipio founded on the ruins of a Phoenician town. Here partial excavations have revealed a number of interesting sights.

Sights:

Roman city of Acinipio, remains of theatre including the *fons scenae* (stage backdrop) and seats, a bit of the aqueduct, slight remains of dwellings and other structures below the theatre including relics of a Phoenician wall and foundations of a group of round stone houses. Sights in Ronda include Moslem walls, gates and baths.

Location:

W of Málaga, the Roman aqueduct is 1.7 km E of Ronda on the C 344 where it crosses the highway. The Roman city lies about 21 km from Ronda off the C 339 on MA 449. Signposted.

San Pedro de Alcántara

There is a Roman villa with mosaic floors in the vicinity near the mouth of the Río Verde, although the fenced site is uncared for and somewhat overgrown. The villa was reputedly destroyed in an earthquake of 365.

To the west of the villa, on the other side of the river, is Las Bóvedas, an eight-sided structure of which the nucleus is still preserved, as are part of the rooms that surround it. The building seems to belong to the third century A.D. Situated in the middle of the complex is a pool or cistern also consisting of eight sides. This central area has four accesses and four apses that may have served as places for decorative statues. The rooms around the core were also octagonal in shape. Ceilings were formed with vaulted domes.

The structure had an upper part consisting of an interior gallery that served as access to cubicles whose purpose is unknown. In this upper part was a cupola with a skylight that gave light to the centre of the building. On top of the upper floor was a flat terrace. Construction material was lime and sand mixed with pebbles from the beach to which it is adjacent. This combination in contact with air forms a very durable material. Las Bóvedas appears to have performed one of two purposes: a public bath, or a deposit of water at the end of a no-longer-existent aqueduct. The site may have been part of a Roman port.

There are some patchwork excavations around the structure revealing foundations of other buildings but the entire complex, so potentially interesting, is neglected, heavily overgrown and behind a stout fence, although the key may be obtained from the Ayuntamiento in Marbella.

Also in close proximity to the sites mentioned above (600 m from Las Bóvedas) is the Visigothic basilica of La Vega del Mar. Here, fenced off but clearly visible from all sides, are the foundation remains of an Early Christian church, the first recorded in Spain with a double apse. The church was rectangular in plan with three naves, a sacristy and baptistry. The baptismal font, fairly well preserved, is of large dimensions, since in those days the rite was performed by immersion. Within and around the basilica is the necropolis with about two hundred tombs of various types. The most common were constructed with brick. Many skeletons and accompanying personal objects, such as brooches, rings, coins, and clay receptacles, were removed from the graves to the National Museum of Archaeology in Madrid. Some artifacts are also in the Provincial Museum of Málaga and a very few are in the Archaeological Museum in Marbella. The most recent studies place the basilica in the sixth century.

Sights:

Roman villa with mosaics, Las Bóvedas of undetermined function, and Visigothic basilica with necropolis.

Location:

San Pedro de Alcántara is W of Málaga and 10 km W of Marbella on the N 340. For the villa, take road into Río Verde Villa urbanization to beach. Villa is on the right just before beach restaurant but hidden between modern houses. The basilica is situated in and obscured by a eucalyptus grove within the Linda Vista Playa urbanization. Las Bóvedas is nearby in Guadalmina Baja opposite restaurant Parque del Sol and large apartment block. All these sites are very near the beach and close to one another.

Torre del Mar

In the vicinity of the town are two Phoenician sites: a necropolis and a fish-curing industry, near to each other and easily accessible. The former consists of a small covered site with a half dozen excavated graves also known as the Phoenician tombs of Almayate and dating back to the sixth to fifth centuries

Málaga: Torre del Mar. Phoenician Tomb

B.C. The latter preserves a large wall and remains of other structures and dates from the eight to sixth centuries B.C. Both are fenced off but clearly visible.

Sights:

Phoenician necropolis and fish-curing factory.

Location:

Travelling W of town toward Málaga turn north (right) just after crossing bridge over the Río Vélez at km 269. About 0.5 km up dirt road on left is a fenced area with fruit trees. Enter gates and continue to farm. On right, on side of small hill is a covered hut with stone steps leading up to it and fenced in front. Inside are the tombs. The factoría is reached by veering right immediately after turn-off at km 269 along dirt track for 200 m. Signposted. The site is next to the Cortijo Toscano, identifiable by large palm tree in garden. Torre del Mar is E of Málaga on the N 340.

Torrox, Costa

Interesting complex of Roman sights all situated near the lighthouse and well signposted. They include the remains of a villa of the third century with walls and cisterns (the mosaics have disappeared); kilns and part of the heating system where containers for salted fish and garum were made; baths, first to second centuries, partially reconstructed showing individual rooms for hot, warm and cold baths, and a necropolis over the remains of a garum industry, of first to fourth centuries, whose containers were used as burial urns.

Sights:

Roman villa, ovens, baths, necropolis.

Location:

On the beach E of Málaga on the N 340, but not to be confused with Torrox in the hills north of highway.

Trayamar

Discovered in 1967, the Phoenician tomb here was once part of an extensive cemetery. In its original form it was constructed of stone blocks and had a wood and mud roof with a descending ramp. It is now enclosed in a locked brick building. The site pertains to the seventh century B.C. and sits on a small promontory around which is thought to have existed a Phoenician town. Excavations are in progress and have revealed rich finds which are now in the Archaeological Museum of Málaga.

Sight:

Phoenician tomb.

Location:

At Mezquitilla, E of Málaga on the N 340, take the MA 103 N toward Algarrobo 0.7 km to Residencia Trayamar on the right. Pass through gate and follow track to farmhouse at end. Here key to tomb can be obtained.

Villanueva de Algaidas

The grave site in the hills near the town dates back to the Chalcolithic period and was first excavated in 1976. It consists of seven neglected stone tombs in which excavations are scheduled to continue in the future. The chambers are elliptical in plan; the principal one is entered through a passage-way and a step down through a retangular stone-framed doorway. The second chamber leads off the first near the back.

Near the edge of town on the left bank of the Arroyo de Burriana in the face of the cliff is situated a rock-hewn church of two parts, the larger of which is the single nave church, the other a dwelling or vestry. This Medieval site, whose exact age is unknown, is adjacent to a ruined convent through which one must pass to reach it. The cave-like rooms of the church have been used as goat pens and are littered with debris. The anticipation and excitement upon entering this simple holy place is quickly tempered by the foul odour and layers of garbage.

Málaga: Villanueva de Algaidas. Rupestrian Church

Sights:
Copper Age necropolis, rock-hewn church.

Location:
N of Málaga and travelling N of Antequera on the N 331 turn E (right) on the MA 221 for 11 km to the town. Approx. 3 km before town turn N (left) by large Cortijo and follow dirt farm road. After fording a shallow stream, go halfway up hill, turn right, follow winding track 2 km and just before abandoned farmhouse take left fork in road for about 100 m through almond trees. Copper Age necropolis on top of hill. The rock-hewn church is situated 1 km from town on the right of the local road MA 203.

Other sites in the province of Málaga are numerous. The more accessible ones can be found at **Alora**, Alcázar, now site of local cemetery. NW of Málaga ca. 38 km off the MA 402, turn N (right) on to the C 337. **Archidona**, N of Málaga 57 km to Antequera and E (right) on N 342 14 km, Punic-Arabic castle converted into sanctuary of the Santísima Virgen de Gracia. **Benadalid**, SW of Ronda ca. 25 km on the C 341, remains of Alcázar, now a cemetery. **Cártama**, Alcázar and the sixteenth-century hermitage of Los Remedios built on site of former mosque, W of Málaga on the M 422. **Casarabonela**, in the mountains W of Málaga and E of Ronda on MA 402/403/404, traces of two Roman roads that once linked the two towns. **Casares**, ruins of hilltop Alcázar, NW of Estepona, the town dates back to Ibero-Phoenician beginnings and was called Lacipo. It takes its current name from Julius Caesar, who (the story goes) used the Baños of Hedionda in 61 B.C (see Manilva) to cure infectious hepatitis. Soon after, the baths became famous in Rome. **Coin**, founded by the Arabs in 929 on the remains of the Roman town of Lacibis, ruins of Alcázar, W of Málaga 36 km on C 344. **Comares**, Arabic reservoir, NE of Málaga and N of Rincón de la Victoria. **Cortes de la Frontera**, W of Málaga and SW of Ronda on MA 549 above the río Guadiaro, go 2 km N to Cortes del Viejo. Here are remains of Roman construction in the ruined walls and towers. **Gaucín**, W of Málaga and SW of Ronda 37 km on the C 341, Alcázar remains of El Aguila. **Mijas**, On the hill behind Fuengirola, W of Málaga on N 340 29 km then N (right) 8 km, Arabic walls. **Vélez-Málaga**, E of Málaga 32 km on the N 340, then N (left) 4 km on C 335, remains of Alcázar. **Zahara de la Sierra**, 34 km NW of Ronda just off the C 339, remains of Alcázar and bridge.

SEVILLA

This is the largest of the Andalucian provinces, with well-defined geographical features. The Sierra Morena mountains dominate the north while the depression of the Guadalquivir river valley occupies the centre and the Cordillera Subbética is situated in the south. The river called the Baetis by the Romans and the Wadi-el-Kebir by the Arabs is the vital artery of the province.

There are remains of prehistoric settlements throughout the province, ranging from cave sites to megalithic constructions. The great treasure of Carambolo, discovered on a small hill near the capital, Sevilla, in 1958 and comprising small gold chests, bracelets, brooches and a chain of exceptional beauty, appears to have been from the Tartessian period of about the sixth century B.C.

The most obvious reminders of past civilizations are the Roman remains and their presence, even today, seems to overwhelm the visitor at such places as Itálica and Carmona. Romanization of the region began with the defeat of the Carthaginians at Alcalá del Río (Ilipa) in 206 B.C. Prior to that time the area seems to have been under the sway of the mysterious Tartessians, who lost control of it to the Phoenicians and subsequent Carthaginians. With the defeat of the latter, the practical Roman Senate founded Itálica in 205 B.C. for its tired veterans.

The austere Germanic tribes who swept through the Guadalquivir valley, including the more permanent Visigoths, left little of substance and much wreckage behind. Not until the arrival of the autocratic and hedonistic Arab did the area again prosper, but with an entirely new style of architecture. Along with the Roman monuments, but in obvious contrast, are the ubiquitous Moslem signs of a different age.

Alcalá de Guadaira

The town site on the river of the same name was once a Chalcolithic settlement and later a Moslem stronghold called Al-kalat-Wad-Aira, which has changed little since the reconquest of the town in 1246. It has a large Almohade castle with eleven towers and subterranean corn magazines, cisterns and dungeon. On the river below are Roman and Arabic mills, and the bridge over the Guadaira river was rebuilt on Roman foundations.

Sights:
Rebult Roman mills and bridge, Alcazaba.

Location:
Approx. 20 km SE of Sevilla on N 334.

Sevilla: Alcalá de Guadaira. Alcazaba

Alcoleo del Río

Situated on Peña de la Sal, a hill adjacent to the highway to the E of town, the site, Arva, is known for its large quantities of amphorae. It is currently closed to the public.

Sights:
Roman ruins of Arva, arch, baths, necropolis.

Location:
NE of Sevilla on the C 431.

Carmona

Roman Carmo, lies in a strategic position on a hill above the fertile Guadalquivir depression, which has been occupied continuously since the Chalcolithic period. During the Roman epoch, the settlement reached its greatest splendour. The necropolis centres on the time from the end of the Republican period into the first century A.D., the dominant funeral rite being that of cremation. Situated in the west section of the city, the site, with about one thousand tombs (and, in the richer, stuc-coed chambers, fragments of paintings of flora and fauna), is one of the most important in the country. The Tumba del Elefante (for the representative stone elephant found here) allows a certain perspective on the funeral ceremonies of the times, with its burial chamber, bath, pantry, kitchen with chimney, and dining facilities for funeral feasts in three banquet rooms. The Tumba de Servilia has separate columbaria for the servants of the deceased. The richer graves contained a glass urn enclosed in a lead box within a stone container set in an underground chamber.

Sevilla: Carmona.
Tumba del Elefante
(courtesy of Bryan Pryce)

The most general type of tomb here is a quadrangular chamber hollowed out of the rock and entered by descending rock-cut steps. The chamber contains benches and niches for the funeral urns. This type of grave is well diffused throughout the Mediterranean, and those of Carmona appear to have their antecedents in the Punic cultural substratum of Spain.

More or less systematic excavations of the necropolis began in 1881, but the graves have often been plundered throughout their history. Pre-Roman sepulchres have also been discovered on the site. Across the road from the necropolis are the remains of the Roman amphitheatre.

In town is the Puerta de Sevilla, a double Roman entrance way forming part of the Alcázar de Abajo which was rebuilt during the Arabic domination. The horseshoe arches and the cistern were constructed in the ninth century. The site reputedly goes back to Tartessian times of the eighth century B.C. and was occupied and modified by the Carthaginians in the third century. The Puerta de Córdoba, flanked by two powerful but restored octagonal towers, contains elements of the Roman period. Through these gates ran the Roman road from Córdoba to Sevilla. The Alcázar de Arriba on top of the hill (now mostly ruins) is from Moslem times. It was converted by Pedro I into a palace after the reconquest of the town by Fernando III in 1247, but was abandoned after the earthquake of 1504. Part of it is now a national parador.

About 5 km from the city in the valley below is a ruined Roman bridge of five arches.

Sevilla: Carmona. Roman Urn Necropolis (courtesy of Bryan Pryce)

Sights:
Two circular mausolea, Tumba del Elefante, Tumba de los Cuatro Departamentos, Tumba de las Guirnaldas, Tumba de Servilia, Mausoleo Cuadrangular, Tumba de las Cuatro Columnas, and Tumba de Postumio. Museum in situ. These are only the most spectacular sights; there are many more.

Besides the necropolis, there are the Roman fortress of la Puerta de Sevilla, La Puerta de Córdoba, the amphitheatre, Alcázar.

Location:
Carmona lies 33 km E of Sevilla on the N IV.

Ecija
Ecija, on the left bank of the river Genil, is the site of Roman Astigi. A Roman amphitheatre is covered by the bull ring and there is a reputedly Roman necropolis nearby. The town was the seat of a Visigothic bishop, but its walls were built by the Arabs. It was conquered by Christian forces in 1263. Some remains of an Arabic wall are still in place and in the eighteenth-century church of Santa Cruz, built on the site of an earlier Visigothic cathedral and later mosque, is a Visigothic sarcophagus and Arabic inscriptions recording the establishment of public fountains in 929 and 977, the latter a gift from the Basque Princess Subh, mother of Hisham II. In the Ayuntamiento is a beautiful second-century Roman mosaic.

Sights:
A few, scant Roman, Visigothic and Arabic remains.

Location:
E of Sevilla on the N IV 92 km.

Gandul

The town has some Arabic walls and towers of the twelfth century. Nearby is a megalithic tomb of los Alcores in fair condition (others reputed to be in the area).

Sights:

Dolmen, some Arabic remains.

Location:

SE of Sevilla on N 334 approx. 20 km, signposted on left. Go up rough unpaved road to fork and then right for about 2 km.

Herrera

Roman villa with excellent mosaics; one of them—of two boxers and referee, nearly intact with vivid colours—was only recently discovered during the construction of an irrigation canal near the town. The villa dates back to the second century as indicated by coins found at the site, and seems to be part of a much larger complex still to be excavated. Its name is unknown, but it was clearly the home of a wealthy Roman. Excavations were begun in January of 1990 under the auspices of the University of Sevilla.

Sights:

Roman villa with baths, patios, rooms, caldarium and mosaics.

Location:

E of Sevilla on N 334 116 km to Estepa. Site is N just outside Herrera on the W side of the road C 338 from Estepa.

Itálica

Founded by Scipio Africanus in 205 B.C. for veterans of the Second Punic War, Itálica was the first Roman *colonia* in Spain and the birthplace of the emperors Trajan and Hadrian. From the remains it seems to have been prosperous, the inhabitants well off. The area most visible is the luxurious urban development of the northern quarter, with paved streets and porticos and the amphitheatre, the fourth largest in the Roman Empire, with seating for thirty thousand spectators.

The old city, the *vetus urbs,* remained intact while, in the second century, a new town, *nova urbs,* was added, seemingly under the auspices of the Emperor Hadrian.

The city declined in the fifth century and fell into ruins during the Arabic epoch, seemingly due in part to the change in course of the river Guadalquivir which deprived this city of its port and shifted the commercial activity to Sevilla. Much of the site was used as a quarry for construction both locally and in Sevilla.

The population of this apparently wealthy city was about ten thousand. The site is rather extensive and is partially covered by the modern town of Santiponce, in which stands the Roman theatre a few minutes away from the main excavated area. The reconstruction of the theatre (with modern steps and brick columns) is distinctly out of character.

Sights:

Remains of Roman houses, streets, patios, mosaics, statues and fountains, walls, gate to the city, sewer systems, water deposit, baths, forum, large amphitheatre, theatre, Paleo-Christian necropolis and a small museum in situ.

Location:

At Santiponce 9 km N of Sevilla on N 630.

Osuna

Ibero-Roman Urso, was the centre of Pompeian resistance to Julius Caesar in the civil war which ended in 45 B.C. The Roman remains are situated on the hill above the present town near the old sixteenth-century university, with its blue and white tiled towers. Along the Camino de las Cuevas, a Roman funerary avenue at the top of the hill, are fantastic sandstone configurations in the form of artificial caves and grottos quarried since Roman times or earlier. Today many of these are used to store sunflower seeds from the local farms, or as houses. On the hill, but along a very poor unpaved road, are some slight traces of a Roman fortress, and in a field nearby are the remnants of a theatre. Little of it remains above ground. After the Arabic domination of the city, it was reconquered by Fernando III in 1239. Pre-Roman, Roman, Visigothic and Arabic artifacts are housed in the Torre del Aqua, a defensive bastion of the old Medieval wall, today the museum.

Sights:

Caves excavated from the rock, Roman necropolis, remains of a Roman theatre.

Location:

SE of Sevilla on the N 334.

Setefilla

Behind the Ermita de Nuestra Señora de Setefilla (a place of pilgrimage where the Virgin was allegedly seen) are the ruins of an Alcázar. The hilltop castle and hermitage can be seen from the town down on the plain. Reported in some guides are Bronze Age and Tartesssian tumuli at the foot of Mesa de Setefilla (between town and castle). The site, however, has been covered over (*tapada*) and there is nothing to see but a wheat field.

Sights:

Ruins of Alcázar, cisterns, walls and tower.

Location:

NE of Sevilla 50 km on C 341 to Lora del Río. Just E of town turn off to left (north) on small paved road to Setefilla. Bypass village and continue to hermitage and castle.

Sevilla

Remains of Campaniforme pottery probably originating in or near Carmona have been found in Sevilla, indicating Neolithic settlements in the area. Similarly, discoveries of what appear to have been Tartessian gold jewellery in El Carambolo, a suburb of the city, suggest that these little-known people occupied the ancient site of Sevilla. As early as the fifth century B.C. or a little before, Phoenicians took control of the region, followed by their kinsmen the Carthaginians—they both maintained active trade with southern Spain. Following the Carthaginian defeat at the hands of the Romans in 206 B.C. at Alcalá del Río, the province of Baetica began the period of Romanization. Julius Caesar founded a colony at Sevilla (or Hispalis, as it was called in 45 B.C.) and it was given the name Colonia Julia Romula. Surrounding walls were then built by the Romans, but only a few bits are visible today. Most of the ancient ruins lie under the modern city. The city fell to the Vandals in 411, but soon after the Visigoths gained authority and Sevilla became a focal point of culture under the sainted archbishops Leander and Isidore. With the Arabic conquest in 712 the city was given the name Ibila, the forerunner of its modern name. The Berber dynasty of the Almohades controlled the city in the twelfth century, and it is to this time that most of the preserved Moslem remains relate. Fernando III reconquered the city in 1248.

Sights:

The Barrio Santa Cruz, located behind the Alcázar, is the old Jewish quarter. It contains dwellings and Christian churches converted from synagogues.

There are some Roman columns and an aqueduct in the Calle Luis Montoto but most of the sights are from Moslem times, such as the Giralda, the Torre de Oro, the Mudéjar style Alcázar, and the Puerta de Macarena and walls.

Lying close about Sevilla are several sites of interest, all of which can be easily visited from the city. **Alcalá del Río**,14 km N on the C 431, remains of a Roman colony: thermal baths and necropolis, but currently covered over. Some remains of Roman and Arabic walls. **Aznalcázar**, SW 21 km on SE 620/621, Roman bridge over the river Guadimar. **Bollullos de la Mitación**,14 km W, the hermitage Cuatrovita, once an Almohade mosque, preserves the notable restored minaret of the twelfth century. **Coria del Río**,15 km S, with reputedly Phoenician remains. **Guillena**, 24 km N, reputed dolmens in the area, the best known being Las Canteras with corridor and circular burial chamber. Difficult to find. Inquire at Ayuntamiento. The bridge over the Bureba is said to rest on Roman foundations. **Valencia de la Concepción**, about 7 km W on the SE 510, a Chalcolithic and Bronze Age settlement NE of the town; some excavations but not a lot to see. SE of Valencina on the road to Castilleja de la Cuesta is the large chambered Copper Age tomb (dolmen) of the so-called Cueva de Matarrudilla.

Villanueva del Río y Minas

Beyond the town, about 9 km N into the hills on a poor, unpaved road, is Castillo de Mulva, the remains of the Roman mining town of Munigua. It is situated on the top of a hill on an older pre-Roman town. On the highest part of the town stand remains of a Roman religious sanctuary.

Sights:

Remains of houses, sanctuary, mausoleum, forum, late Roman walls.

Location:

NE of Sevilla on C 431 to Villanueva del Río y Minas, then N on dirt track 9 km from town. Site is signposted on the other side of the bridge over the river.

Other sites in the province include: **Constantina**, Arabic quarter, NE of Sevilla on C 431 to Lora del Río ca. 70 km, then N (left) on the C 432. **Estepa**, E of Osuna (and E of Sevilla) on the N 334, once a Neolithic and later Roman settlement of Ostippo, keep of the Alcázar. **Las Navas de la Concepción**, NE of Sevilla follow route to Constantina, then go E on the secondary SE 141, ruins of Alcázar, Castillo de la Armada. **Lora del Río**, NE of Sevilla go ca. 70 km on the C 431. Preserves some stretches of Arabic wall and an Alcázar. **Marchena**, ca. 59 km SE of Seville on N 334, are remains of Arabic walls. **Morón de la Frontera**, Alcázar, 67 km SE of Sevilla on the C 342 and 47 km from Alcalá de Guadaira. The fortress and walls originated with the Phoenicians and were reinforced by the Romans and Arabs. They were blown up by the French in 1812. The keep and some towers are all that remain. **Sanlúcar la Mayor**, Arabic Alcázar and walls, W of Sevilla

Sevilla: Villanueva del Río y Minas. Mulva

approx. 12 km on N 431. **Santa Olalla del Cala**, N of Sevilla ca. 80 km on N 630, the road between Sevilla and Mérida, ruined Alcázar. **Utrera**, Roman Utricula, SE of Sevilla on the C 432 about 35 km, remains of Alcázar and Roman bridge.

GIBRALTAR

Recent excavations at Gibraltar have revealed large numbers of very early and well-made flint tools, evidence of camp-fires and cooked meals, and the bones of animals which appear to have contributed to Neanderthal man's diet. The material has been unearthed inside a cave on the southeast tip of the Rock immediately adjacent to the sea. The site is regarded by many as one of the most important prehistoric caves in the world, whose contents, when fully analysed, may add considerably to our knowledge of Neanderthal social and economic life. The cave seems to have been occupied intermittently for over one hundred thousand years, first by Neanderthals and later by Homo sapiens, modern man. The cave may contain some vital clues as to the extinction or amalgamation of the earlier race.

Paleolithic human remains from Forbes Quarry at Gibraltar, on the northern slope of the Rock, but with no record of stratigraphic position or associated fossils, represent the most complete so far found on the peninsula. They are the remains of a woman's skull discovered in 1848. The cranium was assigned to the Neanderthal grouping.

Another discovery in 1919, at a site opposite Devil Tower, contained Pleistocene artifacts and animal remains.

In Europe modern humans replaced Neanderthal types about forty thousand years ago. Some scholars suspect that Neanderthals may have persisted in southern Spain a little longer than elsewhere, perhaps driven to this once-remote part of Europe by Homo sapiens. Archaeologists working at the Gibraltar site, the first excavation of this kind in about forty years of a Neanderthal in situ settlement in southern Europe, hope to learn more about their daily life and correlate climatic changes and their effect on human behaviour over a period of about one thousand centuries.

ARAGON

The region of Aragón originally was a small territory around Jaca at the foot of the Pyrenean mountains. It now consists of three provinces: Huesca, the most northern (Alto Aragón), Teruel, the most southern, and Zaragoza between them. Except for the fertile areas of the northern mountains and the river valleys, the land is generally harsh and dry. Many small and poor villages dot the landscape. Zaragoza, the largest of the Aragonese cities, is situated on the Ebro River and has always served as a crossroads between north-south and east-west. The 910 km-long Ebro River has played a major role in the settlement patterns of the region.

In the Pyrenean foothills and mountains of the north various dolmens have withstood the passing millennia, and in the southern hills of Teruel abundant Levantine cave paintings attest to man's presence from even earlier periods of time. Neolithic, Bronze and Iron Age settlements have been uncovered throughout the Ebro depression. About the eighth century B.C., the use of iron was

introduced into Aragón by central European Celts moving southward across the Pyrenees.

The region was, for all practical purposes, Romanized by the time of the foundation of Caesaraugusta (today Zaragoza) in 24 B.C. Often, as happened elsewhere, existing Celtic settlements were occupied by the Romans and became Roman towns, such as Zaragoza, Bilbilis near Calatayud, Osca (today Huesca) and Turiaso (present-day Tarazona).

Arabic influence in Aragón, strongest in the south, diminishes toward the north and the mountains, both in numbers of Moslems once living in the area and in the length of time they remained in the region. Some of the best Moslem traditions in Mudéjar art are preserved in the provinces of Zaragoza and Teruel.

HUESCA

This province of Alto Aragón contains two major cities, Huesca, the capital and Jaca, near the French frontier, the old capital of the province. The only site so far discovered representative of Paleolithic art is the Cueva de la Fuente del Trucho. Of Neolithic times not a great deal is known except that the period appears to have persisted longer here (down to about 2500 B.C.) than in many other regions of the peninsula which were more acccessible to outside influences. Only one site has been studied in detail, the Cueva de Chaves, where a body was found folded into a circular but small hole (*fossa*) in the floor.

Rupestrian Levantine art from the Neolithic period is generally dated between 7000 and 4500 B.C. It is primarily found in the gorges that constitute the upper valley of the river Vero. Mostly deer were painted, but there are also some goats, occasionally other animals and a few isolated human figures. The colours were generally reddish brown, with black being rare.

The distribution of megalithic monuments in Huesca shows two main groups, both in the north: one is in the foothills of the Pyrenees while the other, the more numerous, is in the mountains proper. They are all simple in design with few variations: a single chamber, more or less square, with vertical or upright stones covered over by a horizontal stone slab. These dolmen builders of the Alto Aragón were no doubt pastoral people, of little wealth, living in small communities. The majority of the megaliths are unmarked, off the roads in wild terrain, difficult to find without local guides and often badly eroded and collapsed.

Bronze and Iron Age sites are found mostly in Lower Huesca on the plains, on top of knolls or hills for defensive reasons. The two main pre-Roman Celtic clans in the area were the Iacetani around Jaca, who appear to have arrived in Spain through the Pyrenees, and the Ilergetes, who occupied the flat lands in the vicinity of Huesca and who seem to have arrived there from the Mediterrean coastal belt, displaced, perhaps, by the Iberians.

The Romans have left traces throughout the region, mostly in and around the capital, but almost nothing in the Pyrenees, whose high peaks and deep, often snow-laden valleys they seem to have avoided. Similarly, the Arabs preferred the warmer, open lands to the south, leaving the high country to the independent, untamable mountain people.

Because of the lack of Moslemization in Huesca, Christian monasteries and churches flourished and were some of the first whose architectural attributes were heavily influenced by the Romanesque styles from across the Pyrenees.

Colungo

The shallow Cueva de la Fuente del Trucho near the town is the only cave in the province with paleolithic paintings. They consist of various heads of horses, representations of hands in negative and a few other signs.

Sights:
Rupestrian paintings.

Location:
E of Huesca on the N 240, then N on HU 340 to Colungo. Inquire at Ayuntamiento for permission to view the site.

Fraga

Near the town on the banks of the river Cinca is situated the Roman settlement Villa Fortunati of the second to fourth centuries. The site also continued to function after this period, however. At the villa were found the ruins of an early Christian convent of about the year 600 and a small Visigothic basilica of the same period. Here also are interesting mosaics, some covered by a shed and others protected under a layer of sand. Inquire at the farmhouse adjacent to the villa and just a few metres off the road for permission to enter.

A few kilowmetres away is a hilltop Iberian town of about 500 B.C. The Iberian necropolis lies on the side of the hill facing the river, but there is little to see except a few small, unadorned tombstones lying chaotically here and there, and a few overgrown burial cavities in the ground.

Sights:
Remains of Roman villa with walls, temple, altar, atrium, fish-pond, well, living room overlooking river, and heating system, waiting room, mosaics, cisterns mostly covered over by Visigothic basilica, and necropolis of Visi-gothic period.

The nearby Iberian settlement displays stone walls, remains of houses, necropolis and large cistern.

Huesca: Fraga. Villa Fortunati

Location:
Fraga is SE of Huesca and SW of Lérida on the N 11 about 27 km. From Fraga take road HU 872 NW out of town along left bank of river Cinca toward Zaidín. The Iberian site is approx. 3.5 km from town and the Roman villa 1 km further on. Both sites are signposted on left of road. For the Iberian settlement, park by sign and climb steep hill opposite to the top.

Huesca

Once a Celtic settlement in Roman times, the town rose to some prominence as Urbis Victrix Osca. It was a battleground between Sertorius and Sulla.
Sertorius founded a school here designed to educate the sons of native chiefs.
(The location of the school corresponds to the present site of the Archaeological
Museum on the hill above town). Later, Huesca became an important Arabic
fortified town. It was retaken by Pedro I of Aragón in 1096. There are a number
of small archaeological diggings around the city, ranging from an Iron Age
necropolis of 800 to 500 B.C., to Roman structures. The excavations are often
covered over after they have been plotted and artifacts removed. Inquire at
Archaeological Museum or the Tourist Office for open sites.

Sights:

Stretches of Roman wall and various small excavations scattered throughout the city.

Location:

In the city of Huesca.

Loarre

Protected by a thick wall with cylindrical towers, the castle was constructed in the eleventh century by Sancho Ramírez I of Aragón on the
foundations of the Roman fortress of Calagurris Fibularia. Later it was to
become an Augustinian monastery. It has been somewhat restored with keep,
towers and walls. Its purpose was to contain the Moslem threat from the south.

Sight:

Castillo de Loarre.

Location:

NW of Huesca on N 240, then N at Esqedas on HU 312 or continue via
Ayerbe to site.

San Juan de la Peña

Benedictine monastery inserted under the overhanging cliff and documented in the tenth century. Impressive location. The cloister is covered by the
natural vaulting of the rock cliff. The interior consists of one nave and three
apses, the latter carved from the rock. Some twenty-seven sarcophagi of the
early kings of Aragón are found here dating back to the eleventh century,
including those of Ramiro I, Sancho Ramírez and, it is thought, that of Doña
Jimena, wife of the Cid. Mozarabic features include horseshoe arches.

Sight:

Monasterio de San Juan de la Peña.

Location:

Follow the N 330 W from Jaca 11 km, then S, signposted on highway.

Santa Cruz de la Serós

Romanesque church with a tall square tower of ca.1095 remaining from the
monastery founded here in 992, but its little neighbour, San Caprasio, is dated
848.

Sights:
Ninth-century church of San Caprasio and eleventh-century Santa Cruz.

Location:
W of Jaca 11 km then S (left) 4 km, signposted for San Juan de la Peña.

Siresa

The site denoted as Siresa pertains to the mountain village of Hecho and is noted for the monastery of San Pedro founded in 833. Only the church constructed in 1082 during the reign of Sancho Ramírez is preserved. It consists of a single nave and apse.

Sight:
Monasterio de San Pedro.

Location:
NW from Huesca on the N 240 to Puente la Reina de Jaca, then N on the HU 210 to Hecho. Site is just beyond.

Arabic forces in Huesca were never very strong and their stay relatively short. They did, nevertheless, leave some monuments behind, such as the Alcázar at **Alquézar** E of Huesca on the N 240 ca. 30 km, then N (left) on HU 340 11 km. **Jaca**, N of Huesca on the N 330 approx. 72 km. The site was occupied by the Romans in 194 B.C. and surrounded by a wall, some remains of which may still be seen. Overrun by the Moslems in 716, the town was retaken in 810. **Obarra**, NE of Huesca and ca. 15 km NE of Calvera, reached via the HU 940, tenth century monastery of Santa María de Obarra with an eleventh century Catalán-Lombardic-style church. **Ruesta**, NW of Huesca near Leyre but on the south side of the Embalse de Yesa, Arabic fortress abandoned in the tenth century. Rebuilt ca. 1017 by the Navarrese. The entire town of Ruesta was abandoned in 1959. **Sallent de Gallego**, take the N 330 N of Huesca to Sabiñánigo, then go N on the C 136 to town, Roman bridge.

TERUEL

The province is situated in the extreme south of the Aragón region. In the centre and south of the province are located Las Serranías Ibéricas (the Iberian Mountains), a tangled mass of often-wooded hills and peaks interlaced with deep rocky gorges, while in the north is a more barren area of depressions, sandstone mesetas and isolated hills formed by the meanderings of the ancient Ebro river.

Apart from some apparent quartzite hand axes and scrapers from the period, there is so far little cultural evidence of the passage of Paleolithic man through the region. The only habitation find to date assuring that Paleolithic man was present is the grotto of Eudovigas near Alacón, excavated in 1970.

The Mesolithic period is somewhat better represented, and new cultural elements corresponding to the Neolithic appear in the province, with some evidence of pottery usage such as was found at La Botiquería dels Moros.

One of the cultural manifestations of the Mesolithic and Neolithic phases in the Iberian mountains is that of the Arte Rupestre Levantino or Levantine Rock Art which appears to have been practised well into the Bronze Age. This cultural phase in Teruel, and indeed in all of Aragón, is little known generally through lack of systematic excavations and, of course, as everywhere, due to the non-durable nature of building material employed in the agricultural and pastoral villages of the times. At present few Bronze Age fortifications are known in the province. At Alto Batán an artificial moat and a pile of stones are preserved that could have constituted a wall at the most easily accessible part of the settlement, and at El Cabezo del Cuervo near Alcañiz there appears to be the remains of a wall surrounding the small hilltop site.

With the coming of the Celtic peoples from central Europe and the initiation of the Iron Age, the cultural climate of the region changed considerably; for example, from burial in tumuli to incineration and burial in urns. In the valley of the Ebro the local Iberians, Europeanized, lived in communities called Celtiberian by the Romans.

The presence of Rome in the province is not well documented, and the absence of Roman excavations further impedes any substantive knowlege of their activities in the region. In the year 472 Visigothic troops occupied the Ebro Valley (with resistance from the Hispano-Romans) but their presence left hardly any material trace, with the exception of a few artifacts.

Of the approximately seven hundred archaeological sites known in the province—most unexcavated—only a few of the more interesting and accessible ones are given here. The majority of those mentioned in the following pages pertain to prehistoric rupestrian paintings and Iberian settlements.

Albarracín

The oldest section of the walls and fortifications of this small Medieval mountain town, stretching from the cathedral of Santa María and the Alcázar to the city hall, date back before the year 1000. Other sections are from the eleventh century.

About 5 km from town is a cluster of grottos in a setting of pines and large red boulders, in which can be seen prehistoric paintings of the Levantine style. Of the three easily accessible sites, Cueva del Navazo, Cueva de Callejón de Plau and Cueva de La Losilla, the first is the best. All are abrigos or grottos with entrances fenced off to the public, but with reasonably distinguishable pictures a few metres beyond the grills.

Teruel: Albarracín. Rupestrian Painting

There are numerous other such sites in the Serranía de Albarracín depicting animals and hunters but most are unmarked and difficult to find without a guide.

Sights:

Ancient walls, Alcázar, three easily accessible abrigos with rupestrian paintings.

Location:

Approx. 37 km W of Teruel on the TE 901. The rock paintings are S of town on road to Bezas and signposted.

Teruel: Albarracín. Rupestrian Painting

Alcañiz

Rock paintings are found at the grotto of Val de Charco del Agua Amarga some distance from town near the village of Valdeagorfa.

Alcañiz el Viejo, an Ibero-Roman hilltop site of El Palau, lies about 3 km outside of town. The settlement and rock-cut necropolis, partially excavated in 1928, appears to have survived in various phases from about the fourth century B.C. to about the fifth century A.D. The actual state of the excavation is very poor, having been many times worked over by treasure seekers.

Next to the twelfth-century castle in town are some excavations of the previous castle or fortification which, it is said, dates back to the eighth or ninth century.

For the rupestrian paintings it is advisable to seek the guide in Valdeagorfa. He is more than willing to go and will, upon his own insistance, spray water through the protective iron grill to enhance the colours of the very faded paintings of people and animals nearly indistinguishable from the rock without it. This is, of course, against all the rules as it only causes the paintings to deteriorate further.

The guide will explain that several patches of bare rock among the figures are there because a hunter, some years ago, stopped by and blasted some of the figures of animals with his shotgun. In other cases souvenir hunters have chiselled figures out of the rock, and even the grill work has not deterred some of these modern barbarians who use car jacks to pry the bars apart. These prehistoric paintings, discovered about seventy-five years ago, are some of the most famous in the country, but they have lost nearly all their brightness.

In the vicinity of Alcañiz there are numerous other sites but many are not easy to find, let alone visit. The intrepid may wish to note the following, however: **Cabezo del Moro**, Ibero-Roman town of about the fourth century B.C. to the first century A.D., excavated in 1927, remains of walls and houses. **Cabezo Rojo**, Iberian settlement destroyed in the first century B.C. at a time coinciding with the Sertorian wars. **Cascarujo, El**, an ancient (Iron Age) settlement on the banks of the river Guadalope, excavated in 1931, with remnants of walls, several streets and foundations of houses and a necropolis. **Taratrato, El**, Iberian settlement, probably abandoned by the third century B.C., excavated in the 1920s but very little to see except the remnants of walls and houses. There are still other sites tucked away in the hills but most with only a few stones and bits of ceramic material remaining.

Sights:
Rupestrian paintings, Iberian and Roman necropolis.

Location:
To see the rock paintings take the N 420 SE of Alcañiz and turn of on TE 711, to Valdeagorfa 15 km . From here the directions are complicated over a 10 km maze of farm tracks for about one half hour—inquire in the village for the guide.

Alloza
The Iberian settlement of El Castelillo, discovered and excavated in the 1950s and more systematically in the 1960s, appears to have begun its existence in the sixth century B.C. and ended in the first half of the second century B.C. It seems to have reached its highest cultural point in the third century. The site has yielded many finds of high quality painted ceramics. The dwellings were generally rectangular and distributed around the sides of the hill, sometimes set into hewn-out rock. Erosion on the steep sides of the hill has contributed to the despoilment of the site.

Sights:
Iberian settlement, remains of dwellings.

Location:
NE of Teruel, Alloza lies 16 km E of Oliete on the TE 133 and W of Alcañiz on the TE 131. The site is 3 km W of town on a 676 m-high ridge above the river Escuriza. Poor roads; inquire at Ayuntamiento for quide.

Azaila
One km beyond the village at Cabezo de Alcalá stand the remains of a heavily restored hilltop Ibero-Roman town of the first century B.C. built on the site of an earlier village. Excavation here began near the end of the nineteenth century and continued sporadically into the 1960s. The site was first occupied, probably in the seventh century B.C., by people of the Hallstatt culture (Celts) whose cemetery is found at the base of the hill. Having been successively built over, little is known of the early settlement. It appears to have been destroyed around 218 B.C. during the Second Punic War. A second city was built, which corresponds to Iberianization and Romanization of the site almost simultaneously, at least from our perspective. It was again destroyed about 76 to 72 B.C. during the Sertorian civil wars.

A third city was raised on the ashes of the previous one and fortifications were improved, including a moat and drawbridge and a double ring of walls. That it was firmly of the Roman cultural persuasion is amply clear from the temple, the baths and type of houses and ceramic material of the period. The town was again destroyed in the year 49 after the battle of Ilerda, and its population removed.

Sights:
Remains of Roman temple, baths (almost nothing to see), defensive moat, water conduits, foundations of dwellings, steps and streets. Iberian burial chambers constructed with stones and nearby Celtic necropolis, of mixed-type graves, which is sliced through by a road. A few of the graves have been reconstructed.

Teruel: Azaila. Iberian Burial Chamber

Location:
Azaila lies NE of Teruel and SE of Zaragoza on the N 232 ca. 57 km.

Bezas
Just before this village on the road from Albarracín are three grottos, with prehistoric paintings which require a little effort to find. Each has only several figures but two sites are reasonably clear, while in the third the paintings have nearly disappeared.

Sights:
Rupestrian paintings.

Location:
W of Teruel and about 2 km before entering Bezas on the TE 900 from Albarracín is a sign for *pinturas rupestres* on north (left) side of road. Opposite is a car park. This is the only sign, which soon leaves the visitor a choice of several possible trails, and often the frustrated seeker returns to the car unfulfilled. But walk down rough path in front of sign to creek bed. Follow stream left about 50 m and cross over to go up valley directly opposite. Continue up narrow path between the rock cliffs on either side for about 200 m (ca. 600–700 m from road). First abrigo on left slightly above, enclosed by iron grill. Facing it, there are two more in side of cliff on right but not visible behind brush until reached. All three are on the left side of the gorge going up.

Calaceite
The excavated Iberian village of San Antonio, signposted in town as Poblado Ibérico, lies about 1 km south up a dirt road on top of a nearby hill on which is also located the Hermitage of San Antonio. The excavations took place between 1902 and 1919, exposing the city plan and fortifications and rich finds of Iberian, Greek and Campanian ceramics from the fifth to second centuries B.C. The town

was destroyed and abandoned sometime a little before 200 B.C. It is one of the most important Iberian sites in Aragón, and well preserved.

Also south of Calaceite, on a small hill of easy access called Les Umbries, are the remains of an Iberian settlement dating to sixth and fifth centuries B.C.

Sights:

Iberian settlement with remains of dwellings, defensive walls, moat, and streets. At Les Umbries are remnants of square houses.

Teruel: Calaceite. Iberian Settlement

Location:

Calaceite is situated NE of Teruel on the N 420, about 37 km out of Alcañiz toward Tarragona. As is often the case, the sign for the site in town points the visitor initially in the general direction, after which no more information is forthcoming. Take first slip road (dirt but at present under repair) off to right and travel to top of hill where road forks, left to Iberian site, right to Hermitage.

Calomarde

The village church situated on main road has Roman stones embedded in the walls, one of which has a Latin inscription. Others have decorative, (possibly Visigothic) designs.

Sights:

Roman inscribed stone and other ancient motifs in wall of church.

Location:

Site on TE 903 SW of Albarracín on route to Frías de Albarracín.

Cretas

NW of the town on a low hill lie the remains of an Iberian settlement contemporary with that of the Iberian site of Calaceite and called Els Castellans. Judging from the pottery at the site it appears to have functioned between the sixth and second centuries B.C. The town layout consisted of a central street with houses on both sides and access by stone-hewn steps.

Sights:

Iberian settlement with remains of street, houses, and defensive walls.

Location:

NE of Teruel and E of Alcañiz 37 km on N 420, then S on TE 301 for 12 km.

Frías de Albarracín

Some on-going summer excavations of Bronze Age site on hilltop in town. Brief two-minute walk to top of hill. Not much to see, apart from the view, except some evidence of ancient camp fires and numerous shards.

Sight:
Bronze Age settlement.

Location:
On the TE 903 W of Teruel ca. 60 km.

Hinojosa de Jarque

A few remains of an Ibero-Roman town, name unknown, lying on a small hill, La Muela, on the right bank of the river Aliaga. Much of the site has been ruined by ploughing, but some walls and dwellings remain. The town persisted to the second or third centuries A.D.

Just before this town is another site called Cuevas de Almudén, where there was an Iberian settlement. Some clandestine diggings have occurred here but most finds have been on the surface, and there is at present precious little to see except for some ashes, a bit of wall and many scattered pieces of adobe. The site is on the hill near the cemetery.

Sights:
Ibero-Roman town, slight remains of walls and floors.

Location:
N of Teruel on the N 420, then E on TE 820. Inquire at Ayuntamiento.

Mazaleón

There are several grottos with prehistoric paintings far back in the mountains around the town, but a guide is recommended to find them. Another beside the road N of town about 2 km and mentioned in some tourist brochures has been completely destroyed by treasure seekers. There is virtually nothing to see.

Across the river from the town on the hill, behind and around the Hermitage, are the remains of an Iberian settlement with some slight remnants of dwellings and tombs. Not a great deal to see apart from the usual splendid views from Iberian hilltop sites.

Sights:
Scant remains of an Iberian settlement.

Location:
NE of Teruel ca. 7 km N off the N 420 on the TE 720 E of Alcañiz and 119 km W of Tarragona. The rutted dirt track to the hilltop site is difficult for a vehicle but a non-demanding 500 m walk.

Oliete

The Iberian site of El Palomar lies 1 km away from the town and 60 m above the opposite (left) bank of the Río Martín. Some of the remains of the settlement have been eaten away by a gravel quarry. Excavations were begun in the 1940s but more systematic diggings began only in 1977. So far, four well-paved streets and about thirty dwellings have been uncovered—some with second floors, judging from the remains of stairs. Under some of the houses graves of children and animals have been found . The site yielded rich finds of Iberian and Campanian pottery and continued in existence until the first century B.C., after which it appears to have been abandoned.

Sights:
Iberian settlement with remains of houses and streets.

Location:
The town is situated NE of Teruel and W of Alcañiz on the TE 133 ca. 17 km W of Alloza.

Teruel
Iberian town of Turba, destroyed by the Romans in 218 B.C. in response to the destruction of Sagunto by Hannibal. Little from ancient history remains except for a bit of Roman aqueduct between Teruel and Albarracín, near Cella.

Ibero-Roman settlement of Alto Chacón, with a roughly paved central street with houses on both sides. In the southern section part of the wall is preserved. The site was excavated between 1969 and 1976, yielding a great deal of pottery, both local and imported, weapons, jewellery and sixteen coins. The settlement seems to have flourished from the fifth century B.C. to the first century A.D.

Sights:
Iberian settlement, remains of dwellings, streets and wall.

Location:
4 km W of the city, on the extreme western part of the Muela de Teruel above the right bank of the river Guadalaviar.

Tormón
Grotto, Barranco de las Olivanas, discovered in 1926 with thirty-three human and animal figures painted in reds and blacks. Some deer have been repainted as cattle reflecting, perhaps, a change in cult.

Sights:
Rupestrian paintings.

Location:
SW of Teruel and due S of Bezas from which Tormón is approached. Ask for directions in the Ayuntamiento.

Villastar
On a large rock face, Peñalba de Villastar, a group of inscriptions chiselled into the stone in the Celtiberian language, but employing Iberian letters, are preserved. Other inscriptions are in Latin.

Sight:
Celtiberian and Latin inscriptions in the living rock.
Location:
SW of Teruel about 10 km on the N 420 near Villastar.

Further Iberian sites and several dozen once-inhabited prehistoric caves and grottos, of which many have remains of rupestrian artwork, are to be found in the vicinity of **Alacón**, NE of Teruel on the secondary road TE 110 out of Muniesa. **Alcaine**, situated NE of Teruel and W of Alcañiz, rupestrian art at Cañada de Marco on the right bank of the Río Martín, 1.5 km from town. Among the paintings is a figure of a man surrounded by a herd of goats. Also at Cabezo de la Ermita are the poor remains of an Iberian settlement with a few remnants of walls. **Almohaja**, NW of Teruel W off the N 234 , nearby at Peña de la Albarda and some 100 m away at the Abrigo de los Tioticos are rupestrian paintings. **Andorra**, hilltop Iberian settlement at El Castillo de la Cerrada on the right bank of the river Regallo NE of Teruel on the TE 130 near Alloza, remains of buildings and stone walls, fifth to second centuries B.C. **Arcos de las Salinas**, S of Teruel by the Valencian border on the TE 600, at Cabezo de las Herrerías on the right bank of the river Arcos and on a large rocky spur, are the remains of an Iberian settlement with remnants of an iron smelter and walls. The town seems to have been abandoned in the third century B.C. There is another Iberian site nearby at Cabecico Royo, but with practically nothing to see. **Caminreal**, NW of Teruel ca. 63 km on the N 234 and 2 km from the centre of town. Celtiberian ruins of La Caridad on a slight elevation above the río Jiloca. Discovered in 1977 and first excavated in 1984–86, walls and foundations of buildings and roadways remain. The most important building so far discovered is the so-called Casa Likinete, which might have borne the name of the owner, as found on an inscription. It is an 850 m^2 house with a 15.5 m by 15 m atrium and sixteen rooms around it. Some had mosaics. **Hijar**, NE of Teruel on the N 232, 13 km S of Azaila, Iberian settlement El Castillejo de la Romana of the third to first century B.C. on an isolated hill in the vicinity of the town, with a central street and remains of dwellings distributed on both sides. Under one of the dwellings the graves of four children were found. There are two small but beautiful Roman bridges, one at **Luco de Jiloca** N of Teruel on the N 234 and a little S of Daroca, and the other at nearby **Calamocha** ca. 25 km S. The former has a central arch and smaller lateral arches, while the latter consists of one arch and is partly in ruins. **Los Olmos**, NE of Teruel and W of Alcañiz on the N 420, small early Iron Age site of about the sixth century B.C. situated on the river Alchoza, where slight remains of dwellings can be observed. **Puertomingalvo**, hilltop Iberian settlement with remains of dwellings, defensive walls and three circular towers, E of Teruel off the C 232 and TE 811.

ZARAGOZA

The province is somewhat triangular in shape, with the apex touching the Pyrenees between Huesca and Navarra in the north, the base resting on Teruel in the south. It is watered by the Ebro river flowing from the NW to the SE. The Iberian mountains lie in the western section of the province, and the Catalán Cordillera in the east.

There are many vestiges of Neolithic, Bronze and Iron Age cultures in the province and some slight Iberian remains, but the most visible monuments in situ attest to the vigorous industry of Romans and Arabs.

Botorrita

Remains of Celtibero-Roman Contrebia Belaisca on the hill known as Cabezo de las Minas. The Celtic settlement was conquered by the Romans during the Celtiberian wars with Rome in 143 B.C. Most of the inhabitants fled to Termes (modern Tiermes) and Numantia, towns which later also fell to the Romans. The site is small and occupies a knoll near Botorrita, but is well known for the discovery of an inscription written in the Hispano-Celtic language using Iberian orthographic signs.

Sights:

Large mud brick buildings of unknown function, a collapsed colonnade presumably of Roman inspiration, remnants of dwellings, steps and walls.

Location:

Approx. 21 km S of Zaragoza on the N 330 turn left onto the Z 100 for Botorrita. At top of hill instead of going right into town, take sharp left and follow gravel road about 1 km to site which can be viewed through fence. To enter obtain keys from Mayor (Alcalde) in town.

Calatayud

The second largest city in the province, once the capital, takes its name from the eighth-century Arabic castle, Qalat-Ayud or Castle of Ayud. The fortified complex is much deteriorated but still impressive, with extensive walls that link up other strongholds on the neighbouring hills. The river valley below was cultivated by the Arabs, who left a complete system of irrigation. The town returned to Christian hands in 1120 when it was conquered by Alfonso I of Aragón, and the defeated Moslem population took up residence in the Barrio de la Morería, a labrynth of streets and alleyways below the castle.

Near the town are the Celtibero-Roman ruins of Bilbilis on the hill known as Cerro de Bámbola. The ancient town and religious centre was the birthplace of the Latin poet Martial and the scene of a victory by Metellus Pius over Quintus Sertorius in 73 B.C. The site is somewhat spoiled by over-zealous reconstruction.

Sights:

Remains of Celtibero-Roman town with forum, temples, remnants of theatre, baths, streets, dwellings and porticos.

Alcazaba with remains of keep, walls, towers, and various strongholds. Some reconstruction.

Location:

Calatayud lies on the N 11 SW of Zaragoza. For Bibilis take the N 234 out of town, direction Soria, and take right fork just outside town signposted Embid de la Ribera. Go 1.5 km along this gravel road to sign on left for Bilbilis. Take left, go up steep hill and follow road for 1.4 km to gate. From here walk to site about 200 m away.

Caspe

Remains of Roman mausoleum at top of hill beside church of Santa María la Mayor. What is left of the structure (cut stone wall) is well preserved.

Sight:
Roman mausoleum

Location:
SE of Zaragoza on the N 11, then take the C 230 from Bujaraloz 33 km S to Caspe.

Chiprana

Remains of Roman mausoleum, tomb of Fabia Severa, in the wall of the hermitage known as Ermita de la Consolación.

Sight:
Roman mausoleum.

Location
Follow the C 221 W of Caspe or E of Azaila to Chiprana. Site lies close by the Ayuntamiento on opposite side of street.

Fabara

Roman mausoleum of L. Aemilius Lupus, completely intact and said to be the best in Spain. Fenced but in full view in a field with several stone coffins outside.

Nearby at El Roquizal del Rullo are the remains of a Celtic settlement with remnants of fourteen stone houses, wall and streets. Inquire at Ayuntamiento for directions.

Zaragoza: Fabara. Roman Mausoleum

Sights:
Roman mausoleum and Celtic village.

Location:
Roman site signposted from Fabara, which lies off the C 221 on the Z 720 ca. 21 km SE of Caspe.

Layana

Near the town are the hilltop Roman remains of Los Bañales (Roman name unknown). The most spectacular sight is the baths situated just over the tip of the hill in front of the abandoned church. The site appears to have been an agricultural town of some wealth, judging from the remains.

Zaragoza: Layana. Los Bañales

Sights:

Remains of Roman town with well-preserved and partially restored indoor and outdoor baths, water conduits, temple (two pillars standing), dwellings, steps, remnants of aqueduct.

Location:

Approx.1.5 km out of Layana on farm road travelling E. The town lies NW of Zaragoza and NE of Sádaba a few kilometres on the Z 552.

Monreal de Ariza

On Cerro Vila outside of town are the remains of the Roman town of Arcóbriga, constructed on an earlier Celtiberian settlement. Here is a large excavation running along a ridge above the valley floor, with the ruins of a basilica measuring 31 m by 7.6 m and a single line of columns down the centre. A small room 5.33 m by 4.4 m opened off the rear wall. This is an interesting and extensive (400–500 m from end to end) site, but at present neglected and somewhat overgrown.

Sights:

Walls, cisterns, foundations of houses, basilica, graves and fairly well-preserved baths.

Location:

Turn off the N 11 from Zaragoza beyond Calatayud about 50 km left (S) on road to Monreal de Ariza, go 2.2 km and take rough dirt farm track to right up the hill. Continue to crossroad at 1.6 km and across valley, past shepherds' hut on left and up ridge (switchback) for ca. 585 m. At top on the right is parking. Walk along ridge about 50 m straight ahead into site which gets more interesting further along.

Sádaba

Remains of second century mausoleum of the Atilii family, referred to locally as Altar de los Moros, approached by dirt road and surrounded by heavy chain link fence, making photos difficult. Only the façade is still standing.

Nearby are the remains of a fourth-century Late Roman monument, perhaps a columbarium, called the Synagoga (Synagogue) for which purpose it may have been used for a time. The structure, in shambles, roofless and with broken walls, has two interior and two exterior apses. The site is fenced only on three sides. Walk around to the back.

The castle in town with a well-preserved exterior is from the thirteenth century.

Sights:
Roman mausoleum and synagogue (?).

Location:
The mausoleum lies ca. 3 km NE of the town toward Layana and is do، a farm track to the left. For the other site take the same road and turn right immediately before the canal. Follow the roadway along the canal for 1.5 km and turn right into field. Building is 100 m away.

Sofuentes
Roman tombstones of the Atilii family encorporated into an eleventh- or twelfth-century tower (according to the lady who lives in it) on the edge of town. Some of the stones have bas-relief heads and geometric designs, and one at the back of the building has the name of the Atilii family engraved on it. A head was chiselled off one stone by present owners, as it was in the way of the gate for the chicken coop which is also in the tower.

Sights:
Engraved stones of a Roman mausoleum.

Location:
NW of Zaragoza, follow the C 127 from Sádaba toward Sos del Rey Católico and turn off left at signpost for Sofuentes.

Velilla de Ebro
Extensive remains of Roman veterans' colony of Celsa on hill overlooking fertile valley of the Ebro and abandoned in 58 A.D. Partially excavated; in situ museum planned. Many of the stones of the ancient town were redeployed in building the nearby church and the farm houses which are on the site.

Sights:
Remains of wide paved streets, large living quarters and shops.

Location:
Approx. 50 km SE of Zaragoza on the N 232, then branch off left, then left again to Gelsa on the Z 700. Just beyond, sign points right to Vella de Ebro. Pass this turn and take first right (about 10 m and signposted "Excavaciones") on gravel road. Continue for ca. 400 m to site.

Zaragoza
The town was once a Celtiberian settlement of the Sedetani known as Salduie (the name appears on ancient coins) and as Salduba by the Romans, who made it into a colony for the veterans of the latest Cantabrian wars sometime around 19 to 15 B.C., and referred to it as Caesaraugusta—hence the current name. Some sections of the Roman defensive wall and towers, once 3 km in length, constructed in the last quarter of the first century B.C., remnants of the theatre located between the streets of Verónica and Pedro Joaquín Soler and some slight remains of Roman baths in the calle San Juan, as well as the forum in the Plaza de la Seo, are still visible. The Paleo-Christian crypt in the

cathedral, with scenes from the New Testament, indicates the presence of Christian communities in the city before the fourth century. From 472 to 714 the town was under the jurisdiction of the Visigoths.

The name was later corrupted by the Arabs to Sarakusta when they conquered the city in 714. There are sparse remains of an Arabic palace of 918, La Zuda, in the Plaza de César Augusto, residence of the Moslem governors of the region. La Palacio de la Aljafería on the Avenida de Madrid is one of the most important architectural monuments of the Hispano-Moslem period, with construction begun about 864 but successively reformed. Remains of Jewish baths of ca. 1250 are in the calle Coso.

The city fell back into Christian hands when Alfonso I of Aragón reconquered it in 1118. New archaeological finds are constantly being discovered under the surface of the modern city when new construction takes place.

Sights:
Roman, Paleo-Christian, Arabic and Jewish remains.

Location:
In town.

Other sites of interest in the province are located at **Alfajarín**, ruins of Arabic castle in southern outskirts of Zaragoza. **Fuendetodos**, very slight remains (pile of stones) of an Arabic castle and walls (most of the stones were used in local building), S of Zaragoza on the C 221. **Juslibol**, across river from Zaragoza with nearby Iberian settlement 2–3 km beyond town, some excavations behind castle on hill above Ebro river. Difficult to find; inquire at Ayuntamiento. **Lécera**, pre-Roman settlement of which only traces still exist on a hill 200 m E of town, S of Zaragoza ca. 50 km on the C 222. **Mequinenza**, small town on the N bank of Ebro river with Iberian graves in the vicinity E of Zaragoza on the C 231 in the extreme eastern section of the province. Inquire at Ayuntamiento for directions. **Muel**, Roman fountains, now site of attractive park and waterfall, and the Hermitage of Nuestra Señora de la Fuente, built on site SW of Zaragoza on N 330 ca. 28 km. **Rueda de Jalón**, Arabic castle of Rota on the C 302 N of La Almunia de Doña Gadina and W of Zaragoza situated on a high rock cliff above village.

Throughout the Jalón valley at such places as **Alhama de Aragón, Ateca, La Almunia de Doña Godina, Calatayud, Calatorao,** and **Terrer** are many Mudéjar structures, mostly towers of charm and beauty, some leaning at seemingly precarious angles.

ASTURIAS

The region of Asturias is geographically conterminous with the province of Oviedo.

OVIEDO

The province sits on a vast rugged mass of limestone mountains, the Cantabrians, and is particularly prodigious in prehistoric material and evidence of the cultural evolution of its inhabitants. Paleolithic art, with its world of symbols and representations of animals engraved or painted on the walls of caves and rock shelters, reflects the obscure rituals celebrated by these early hunting-collecting societies as an expression of their unknown mythology.

Near the end of the Paleolithic period and primarily during the Magdalenian phase, some fifteen thousand years ago, cave art reached its highest degree of quality. In the final phase, the Azilien, it seems to have degenerated in quantity and quality, and the economy switched somewhat to the collection of mollusks, whose remains have been found in impressive depths in some habitation sites. During this period, objects were fashioned in stone and bone and, no doubt, in more perishable materials such as wood and hides. Only much later, during the Neolithic period, was durable baked clay employed in the making of pottery.

Perhaps as early as the fourth millenium B.C. a great permutation occurred in the northern cultures with the building of the monolithic structures in the form of dolmens and tumuli, a custom which appears to have spread from

Portugal and Galicia into Asturias. In the second millenium B.C. the first use of metal as a prime material for the fabrication of jewellery and weapons began, although stone working was not abandoned.

For those interested in the prehistory of northern Spain, a good place to begin is at the cave of Tito Bustillo, on the outskirts of Ribadesella, with its well-preserved cave paintings and in situ museum depicting the physical and cultural phases of man and the distribution of prehistoric sites in the province at given points in time. There were many caves utilized by Paleolithic man but there is now little to see except the caves themselves, as all artifacts have been removed. Some other outstanding caves with rupestrian paintings are Candamo, El Pindal and El Buxu.

The Celtic tribes that later occupied Asturias around 500 B.C. remained relatively isolated from the events and peoples that influenced the southern part of the peninsula (e.g., Greeks, Phoenicians, Carthaginians), and were only brought under control of the Roman legions about two centuries after the south had been Romanized.

It was to Asturias, the land of the Asturs, that the Visigoths fled after their defeat by the Arabs in 711, and from Asturias that the reconquest began with the alleged battle of Covadonga in 722. Here, too, the Asturian society gave rise to new styles in architecture which had no precedents in Europe. Some of the original buildings are still preserved in and near Oviedo, at Las Regueras, at Lena, Valdediós and Villaviciosa.

Cangas de Onis

This small town, nestled in picturesque mountain scenery, has the reputation of being the starting point of the reconquest of Spain from Moslem rule. There is a charming Medieval bridge on Roman foundations over the river Stella, seen at the entrance to the town from the north, and within the town is the Hermitage of Santa Cruz, constructed in 775 by Fávila, son of Pelayo. It was rebuilt in the seventeenth century. Under the building and visible through a large hole in the floor is a Bronze Age dolmen with prehistoric engravings.

Nearby is the Cave of Buxu, with engravings and paintings dating back around fifteen thousand years. It contains tectiforms and naturalistic drawings of stags, horses, an ibex, and a bison over a metre in length and outlined in black.

Further along is the holy cave of Covadonga (Cuevahonda) where, in about 722 (dates are controversial), the Moslems suffered their first defeat at the hands of Pelayo (d. 737), whose sarcophagus lies in a recess of the cave. His wife, Gaudiosa, is also reputed to be buried here. Their daughter, Ermesinda, along with her husband Alfonso I (d. 757), are supposed to be buried in the rebuilt chapel.

Sights:

Nearby Paleolithic Cave of Buxu with rupestrian paintings; Medieval bridge on Roman foundations; Early Christian Hermitage of Santa Cruz over a dolmen, and Cave of Covadonga with sarcophagus of Pelayo.

Location:

Cangas de Onis is located E of Oviedo on N 634, 56 km to Arriondas then S on C 637 approx. 7 km (signposted). Hermitage and dolmen are in town and key can be obtained from Ayuntamiento on main street. Bridge also in town.

Cave of Buxu is 2.5 km off the C 6312, signposted. It requires a fifteen-minute walk up a mountain path, with steps up to the cave at the end. Guide and key are obtained in the village below, also signposted. Covadonga is reached by following the C 6312 branching off S after 4 km on the O 220 for 7 km.

Coaña

One of the most important and well-preserved Celtic sites in Spain with remains of round stone houses and other artifacts. Like other castros, it was apparently Romanized (Roman coins were found on the site), but is considered a typical Celtic village. Materials recovered were from the first to third centuries.

Asturias: Castro de Coaña (courtesy of Bryan Pryce)

Sights:

Celtic castro with remains of houses, grinding stones and funeral urns; remnants of a road, cistern and cattle enclosure.

Location:

W of Oviedo. Take the N 634 from Ribadeo E to El Espin. Just before the river Navia, go S on C 644 for 5 km. Signposted.

Gijón

Once a Roman town, Gijón was the residence of Asturian kings in the eighth century but was largely destroyed by fire in the fourteenth century and again during the civil war. Some Roman remains have been found here, and there are some on-going excavations.

Sights:

Sections of Roman wall and thermal baths.

Location:

Gijón is NE of Oviedo. The baths are entered with a guide from the Jovellana Museum which is just around the corner from them. No charge. The wall and excavations are adjacent to the baths.

Gobiendes

The church of Santiago de Gobiendes was constructed in the ninth century during the reign of Alfonso II.

Sight:

Early Christian church.

Location:

NE of Oviedo and approx. 18 km W of Ribadesella on N 632, turn right (S) at km 23 for 3.8 km. Signposted.

Lago

Nearby, the Cueva de Juan Rata on the Río del Oro is an important example of a Roman mining camp and hard-rock mine. Several kilometres away are the remains of a Roman aqueduct and water storage tanks. Another Roman gold mine is found at Alto Aristebano near Naraval, NE of Lago.

Sights:

Roman gold mines and remains of aqueduct.

Location:

Lago lies SW of Oviedo on the C 630. The mine at Puerto de Palo is located about 5 km away to the NE. Naraval lies W of Oviedo, due south of Luarca on the O 751.

Lena

The ninth-century church of Santa Cristina de Lena is attributed to the same architect of Ramiro I who worked on Santa María de Naranco and San Miguel de Lillo (see Oviedo). It is richly decorated with Visigothic motifs and with an exceptional iconostasis. Each of the four sides of the rectangular nave have external projecting structures.

Sight:

Ninth-century Asturian church.

Location:

Approx. 40 km S of Oviedo on the N 630. Turn off at Pola de Lena, where church is well signposted. Obtain keys at house at bottom of hill where path up to the church begins.

Asturias: Llanes. Peña Tu

Llanes

Large, natural stone column of Peña-Tu on top of hill with Bronze Age symbols dating back to the middle of the second millenium B.C. Enclosed by sturdy fence but easily visible.

Also on the coastal road near Llanes, between Posedo and Celorio, are two caves: the first, a rock shelter about 1 km N of the town, contains prehistoric occupation deposits; 200 m beyond is a decorated cave of two galleries with engravings drawn with fingers in the clay walls of the left one. The only discernible engraving is the outline of the head and back of a boar, about 35 cm in length. Also near the town is the single-room cave of San Antonio, in which a horse is drawn in black outline, about 37 cm in length, on the back wall.

Sights:
Peña-Tu, Bronze Age reliefs and rupestrian paintings.

Location:
Llanes is E of Oviedo, just beyond km 295 on the N 634 from Llanes toward Santander, turn S (right) for Peña-Tu. Signposted. Navigable track for 0.5 km, then follow pathway another 0.5 km uphill to site.

Mohias
Small, Celtic site situated on a knoll, partially excavated but now neglected, eroded and overgrown with remains of a dozen square and round houses and some badly deteriorating walls.

Sights:
Celtic castro, remnants of walls and houses.

Location:
W of Oviedo take the N 634 W from Navia toward Ribadeo. Cross the river Navia, turn right on road signposted for Ortiguera. Go 0.5 km past hospital then left down unpaved road to lumber mill. Walk 200 m further on.

Asturias: Oviedo.
Santa María de Naranco

Oviedo
In the year 761 the Benedictines founded a monastery on the site of the present city and Fruila I, the fourth king of Asturias, built a palace and church beside it. When Alfonso II came to the throne in 791, he established the royal court at Oviedo where it remained until the tenth century, at which time it was transferred to León. The city was the centre of the Christian-Moslem conflict between 810 and 924.

The city has several Asturian pre-Romanesque buildings corresponding to the periods of the most important of the early monarchs: Alfonso II, 791–842; Ramiro I, 842–850; and Alfonso III, 866–911.

Segments of the town walls, constructed under Alfonso II in the eighth century, are still visible. On the edge of the city and within 100 m of each other are two early Christian buildings of Asturian pre-Romanesque style which date back to the ninth century: Santa María de Naranco was originally the palace of King Ramiro I, but was amplified and converted into a church in the thirteenth century. It underwent some restoration in the present century. San Miguel de Lillo, a cruciform basilica with unusual windows, has also undergone some reconstruction but preserves much of its original structure.

The cathedral, begun in the fourteenth century on the site of an early church—founded about 781 and enlarged by Alfonso II in 802—preserves only the Cámara Santa of the earlier structures with historical relics, and that has been restored since it was dynamited in 1934 during the miners' uprising.

Asturias: Santa María de Naranco (courtesy of Bryan Pryce)

There are several other noteworthy churches of the ninth century in and near Oviedo, such as La Foncalada, constructed during the reign of Alfonso III, Santa María de Bendones, ninth-century church a little south of the city, San Tirso in the Calle Santa Ana, originally built by Alfonso II but rebuilt. Just E of the city is a Roman bridge over the river Nora and another just S at Olloniego, once over the river Nalón but now over dry land due to a change in the course of the river.

Asturias: Oviedo. San Miguel de Lillo

Sights:

Roman bridges near the city; ninth-century palace of Santa María de Naranco with rooms and baths on the main floor and a great hall on the upper floor; ninth-century church of San Miguel de Lillo with interesting decoration; ninth-century San Julián de los Prados, constructed during the time of Alfonso II, 30 m by 25 m (largest pre-Romanesque church in Spain); San Pedro de Nora, ninth-century church partly restored, and several others restored or rebuilt; Cámara Santa in the Cathedral.

Location:

Roman bridges at Colloto on the N 634 a few kilometres E of the city and at Olloniego a few kilometres S. Santa María de Naranco and San Miguel de Lillo are ca. 3 km N of town on Monte Naranco, but well signposted. San Julián de los Prados is NE of the city in Santullano, a suburb of Oviedo. San Pedro de Nora is situated 12.5 km W of Oviedo on N 634, 2 km after turning N (right) toward San Pedro. The Cathedral is situated in the Plaza de Alfonso II in the centre of town.

Panes

Near the town is a Mozarabe chapel of about the year 1000 but in ruins, roof caved in and heavily overgrown. Also nearby is the cave of La Loja, a single gallery about 90 m long containing naturalistic engravings, mostly of cows. They are on the right wall, some distance into the cave and about 5 m above the present floor level. Another cave nearby, Llonin, with paintings and drawings, is currently closed to the public.

Sights:

Remains of Mozarabe church, rupestrian paintings.

Location:

E of Oviedo on the N 634 to Unguera, then S on the N 621. Just beyond town on the right in a field stands the remains of the church. After passing through town, and below the hamlet of Del Marzo on the N side of the road at the entrance to a rock defile, is the cave of La Loja.

Pimiango

Nearby Cueva del Pindal in the cliffs with a wide gallery 360 m long. Paleolithic figures of twenty-eight animals and a series of horizontal red signs are found in a round chamber some 18 m from the entrance. Drawings in poor condition. Site is supposed to be open all year round.

Sights:

Rupestrian paintings.

Location:

E from Oviedo on N 634 turn N (left) at 4 km W of Unquera to Pimiango. Here, cave is well signposted, including where to obtain key.

Pola de Allande

Hilltop Celtic site, Castro de San Chuis, with excavated remains of generally round stone houses, and Santa María de Célon, a pre-Romanesque ninth-century church with fourteenth-century murals.

Sights:

Celtic castro and ninth-century Asturian church.

Location:

From Oviedo take the N 634 W ca. 58 km to La Espina. Then follow the C 630 S via Tineo to Pola de Allande.

Pravia

At Santianes de Pravia, 3 km from the town, there was once the residence of the kings of Asturias in the eighth century (774–783). Here is situated the oldest church in the province, with three naves and a wooden roof currently under restoration. To the right of the entrance is an enormous baptismal font that also dates back to pre-Romanesque times.

Sight:
Eighth-century Asturian church.

Location:
W of Oviedo on N 634 to Grado, then N on C 632 to Pravia. Take by-road N toward Muros and then right fork to Santianes de Pravia.

Priesca

Tenth-century church of San Salvador, founded in 921, situated in village on top of hill. The church was burned down and restored. Little remains of the original, but some Mozarabe and Asturian features are still present.

Sight:
Rebuilt tenth-century Asturian church.

Location:
NE of Oviedo. Follow route to Valdediós and continue on the C 638 to Villaviciosa. Here, pick up the N 632 E to the turn-off to Priesca, a short distance off highway on an unpaved, farm road.

Ribadesella

Discovered only in 1968, the original entrance to the cave of Tito Bustillo was reopened in 1969 (after a landslide that had occurred thousands of years ago), and a year later, another artificial entrance was created by drilling a 165 m-long tunnel which shortened the 3 km distance from town, some of which had to be done on foot. The new tunnel is now the entrance for visitors. A 540 m walk through the main gallery of the cave culminates in a chamber at the junction of three passageways, one to the original entrance. Here were the general living quarters of prehistoric man, according to the artifacts found in the area, and here also is the painting of a large horse, now rather obscured due to past flood waters that sometimes covered it. To the left, a gallery leads to a large chamber of painted animals, some of which are over 2 m long and date back to between twelve and twenty thousand years ago (dates differ). Animals portrayed are horses and deer, including reindeer, in red, black and violet, the latter from a natural mineral in the cave. There are also paintings and engravings along the route to the above-mentioned chamber. This is one of the few caves in the north with prehistoric drawings that the visitor can count on being open to the public. There is a museum in situ.

The Cueva de les Pedroses, a little NW of Ribadesella outside the village of El Carmen, contains drawn representations of deer and bulls.

Sights:
Rupestrian paintings.

Location:
Ribadesella is on the coast NE of Oviedo ca. 80 km on the N 634, and the cave entrance is on the edge of town on the W bank of the river Sella.

San Roman
The Cueva de Candamo contains several chambers leading to a large hall with some sixty Paleolithic engraved and painted figures of horses, bulls, stags, oxen, bison and ibex. The best is a shaded engraving, over a metre in length, of a stag with spears in its flank. There are also two human figures, one engraved, the other a drawn ithyphallic figure in heavy black outline. At time of writing, the cave was closed to the public.

Sights:
Rupestrian paintings.

Location:
Follow the N 634 W of Oviedo 26 km to Grado, then turn N (right) on C 632 to San Roman.

Tuñón
Simple abbey church of San Adriano de Tuñón, built in 891 during the reign of Alfonso III and restored in 1106. It consists of three naves and contains remnants of murals dating back to its origins.

Sight:
Ninth-century Asturian church.

Location:
Take the N 634 W of Oviedo ca. 12 km, then go S on O 424 ca. 8 km to Tuñón.

Valdediós
Located here is the ninth-century church of San Salvador de Valdediós, consecrated in 893 and showing traces of its original frescos. The design of the horseshoe arch and other Visigothic features are thought to have been brought by Mozarabe refugees from the south. The church stands adjacent to the ruins of the thirteenth-century Cistercian monastery of Santa María.

Asturias: Valdediós. San Salvador

Sight:

Ninth-century Asturian church.

Location:

Follow the N 534 E from Oviedo and branch left at La Secada on C 638 and continue to Valdediós ca. 15 km.

Besides those already mentioned, there are other Roman bridges and early churches in the province. For example, **El Haya**, remains of Roman bridge over the Desfiladero del Cares on the Ruta de los Picos de Europe. E of Oviedo, take N 634 to Unquera, go S to Panes on N 621 then W on C 6312. There is a rebuilt Roman bridge at **Peñaflor**, W of Oviedo on the N 634 over the river Nalón some 6 km before Grado. The Puente del Romanón spans the river Nora at **Pola de Siero** on the N 634 a little E of Oviedo, and is located beside the railway between the hectometres 182 and 183. It has the characteristics of a Roman bridge. Near **Trubia** are the remains of the Roman Puente de Udrión over the Nalón. Note also that a little S of Trubia is the pre-Romanesque church of Miguel de Bárzana. Beside the village of **Villanueva de Santo Adriano**, S of Trubia on the O 430, is situated a single-arch bridge, which appears to be of Roman origin, over the river Trubia. At **Viñon** is the tenth-century church of San Julián. Take N 634 E from Oviedo to La Secada, then left on C 638 to Amandi and follow the O 121 to Viñon.

The Roman bridge at **Infiesto**, listed in some guide books, is now non-existent, having been blown up in the civil war of 1936.

CANTABRIA

As the name of the region implies, it is mostly occupied by the Cantabrian mountains, with their great limestone peaks, sheer stone walls and deeply scored valleys, whose northern boundaries fall away into the sea. The mountain range of which Cantabria is part extends roughly 480 km along the Bay of Biscay from the Pyrenees to Cape Finisterre. The mountains are rich in minerals, especially coal and iron; the Ebro river arises on the southeastern slopes.

The area was home to European tribes during the last great ice age of the Quaternary period and their remains abound in the many caves in the region, from that of Altamira near Santillana del Mar—once called the Sistine Chapel of Quaternary art for its magnificent cave paintings—to many lesser-known sites such as Puente Viesgo, Ramales, Novales and Valles.

Later events that had a profound impact elsewhere on the peninsula scarcely influenced this rugged and nearly inaccessible region that forms a stone wall cutting off the Castilian meseta from the sea. There are as yet no known pre-Roman remains of ancient towns, necropoli or structures of importance in the mountainous area.

The major thrust of Roman conquest began in earnest in 26–25 B.C. Augustus sent a fleet to conquer the Cantabrians in coordination with attacks from the south, and centred his military base at present-day Santander. In the

mountains behind the base the Romans found rich iron ore deposits, but in general the area was given much less importance than the Roman settlements on the other side of the mountains, such as at Castro Urdiales (Roman Flavióbriga) and Retortillo, near Reinosa, called Julióbriga.

Cantabrian tribes were apparently not enamoured with Roman ways and fighting erupted on numerous occasions. The last serious resistance was a major rebellion in 19 B.C. The final drama after two hundred years of nearly continuous warfare was played out in these mountains of the north.

The Cantabrians accepted the new Christian faith slowly, but in time monasteries were founded in remote places and during the period of Moslem conquests, as Christian immigration into the area increased, cave sites were hollowed out to serve as sanctuaries. Arab forces never seemed to have ventured into the lofty Cantabrian uplands.

This is the region par excellence of Paleolithic cave remains, especially those with rock paintings. While mostly of animals hunted at the time, many cave paintings show various (no doubt ritual) designs and in some are the impressions of human hands (in negative) in which the hand was placed on the wall of the cave and paint applied around it, leaving the print clear and unmistakable. Presumably this representation signified human power over that of the animals.

The Cantabrian Cordillera served not only Paleolithic societies with their caves and shelters, but later peoples also found refuge in the dense mountains. The Romans came, too—not for the same reasons, but to complete their conquest of the peninsula. Many Christians, fleeing from the Moslem onslaught as it flowed northward, found solace in the bosom of the protective peaks.

SANTANDER

The province of Santander is geographically conterminous with the region.

Arce

The cave of Santián on the road between Santander and Torrelavega, about 5 km from the sea, is a narrow cleft between two rocks, with a winding gallery some 200 m long, about 2 m wide, and 3 m high throughout much of its length. The paintings are grouped into two panels about 130 m from the entrance, and are unusual in that they consist of symbols representing hands or feet on the end of long stick-like limbs with variations of clubs and tridents. There are about fifteen painted in red, about 30 cm in length, as well as other symbols in the cave.

Sights:
Rupestrian paintings.

Location:
SW of Santander on N 611. Ask for key at local bar upon entering town.

Arredondo

Church of San Juan de Socueva, situated on the side of a steep mountain, has a single, rectangular nave and horseshoe arches. In front of the entrance is a modern church.

Sight:
Visigothic rupestrian church.

Location:
27 km SE of Santander on the S 531.

Arroyuelos

Small village with an-
cient Visigothic church of
two storeys, carved out of
the rock cliff at end of town
(where road ends and be-
comes a farm track). On the
side of the church are half
a dozen graves chiselled
from the rock.

Sights:
Visigothic rupestrian
church and necropolis.

Location:
S of Santander on N
623 ca. 92 km, then W on

Cantabria. Arroyuelos. Rupestrian Church

BU 631 to San Martín de Eline, 10 km. Arroyuelos is signposted from there. Ask
for key at first house on left upon entering village.

Barros

At the small church hermitage of the Virgen de la Rueda a large stone
circular disc (*rueda*) was found. It now resides in a barred enclosure next to the
church. The designs on the stone clearly indicate some aspect of sun worship,
but opinions differ as to its Roman or Celtic origin.

Sight:
Large ancient stele.

Location:
Turn off the N 611 S of Santander at km 174 by petrol station and go back
over old highway (N) into town. The church and disc are on right of road into
town.

Busta, La

Next to the village is the Cueva de las Aguas, a small, unattended and
unpretentious opening at ground level in the face of a cliff. It is said in the
village that the cave has no known termination. The faded prehistoric paintings
in the recesses of the unlit cavern are difficult to find, as is a guide.

Sights:
Rupestrian paintings.

Location:

SW of Santander, take the N 634 W from Torrelavega and turn right just beyond Barcenaciones to La Busta. Cave in cliff across field at end of village.

Cantabria: Cadalso. Rupestrian Church

Cadalso

Very small, early Christian church excavated out of the rock on side of road, somewhat restored in 1923. Alongside are several graves cut from the solid rock.

Sights:

Rupestrian church and rock-hewn graves.

Location:

South of Santander on N 623 , then W on S 612. Church is between San Martín de Eline and Polientes. Signposted.

Gayangos

At Peña de los Moros, near the village, are several dozen rock-cut graves on top of a rather precipitous outcropping which requires a vertical climb of about 5 m, using hand and foot holds. The site is heavily overgrown.

Sight:

Early Christian graves.

Location:

S of Santander, beyond Ramales on the C 629. Difficult to find. Ask in town for guide or at km 83 follow indistinct path on W side of road (left going N) for about 2 km in a SW direction to watering trough. Proceed another 50 m or 60 m to prominent outcropping on right and look for hand holds on face of rock.

Lebeña

The church of Santa María de Lebeña dates back to the ninth or early tenth century (one account gives the date as 925). The overall plan is in the shape of a Greek cross, and the interior arches are in Mozarabe style. The capitals are Visigothic, showing the leaves of the acanthus palm tree. Of particular interest is the vertical stone in front of the altar piece which, only a few years ago, was employed as a step up to the altar. When it was lifted and turned over, the circular stele was found on the underside. The stone appears to represent a form of sun worship, to be about two thousand years old and of Celtic origin. In the lower left hand corner is a small stick-like figure of a human painted on with a mixture of blood and ash.

Sights:
Early Christian-Mozarabe church and Celtic engraved sun stone.

Location:
SW of Santander and nearly due South of Unquera, best approached by the N 621 from Unquera, 32 km, to Lebeña. Church signposted in town.

Cantabria. Santa María de Lebeña

Novales
The cave called Las Aguas lies in the valley below Novales a little less than 1 km SW of the town. It consists of a single gallery ca. 100 m long, and contains one panel of engravings and red signs on the left wall, a few metres from the end. The principal figure is an engraving of a bison's head.

Sights:
Rupestrian paintings.

Location:
Approx. 35 km SW of Santander near Santillana del Mar on the S 482.

Puente Viesgo
Situated on a hill behind the town, the Cueva del Castillo is the only one of four caves in the area currently open to the public. It consists of several galleries with a total length of about 300 m. There are forty-four fairly clear hand stencils (hands in negative), some well-preserved tectiform signs, and a number of animal paintings and engravings. The latter are generally small and indistinct (cows, horses, bison, deer, an ibex and a chamois). The most famous of the paintings is the red outline of an elephant or mammoth in the depth of the cave, about 30 m beyond the last chamber. (At time of writing, this section was closed to public.) The cave was inhabited from the Lower Paleolithic to the Bronze Age (Neanderthal to Cro-Magnon) as attested by the successive layers of habitation excavated on the cave floor. The earliest drawings are reputed to go back twenty-five thousand years, the more recent a mere fifteen thousand years. Guide at site.

The other caves in the immediate vicinity with rupestrian paintings are Las Chimeneas, so called for its vertical descents into the hillside; Las Monedas, the name derived from a hoard of fifteenth-century coins found inside; and Pasiega, 2 km from Puente Viesgo on the steep face of the hill, which also contains the cave of Castillo. It has two entrances which provide separate visits to different parts of the cave when open. Here, among well-preserved animal paintings, is a small, conventionalized human figure, rather rare in the northern caves.

Sights:

Rupestrian paintings.

Location:

SE of Santander on the N 623. Caves are signposted in town.

Ramales de la Victoria

A few km S of the village are a series of caves, one of which, Cueva de Covalanas near the top of the hill, contains two long galleries and preserves fairly good Paleolithic paintings of hinds, a horse, an ox, a bull and some of the symbols of the usual type. A herd of deer, the principal painting of the cave, is depicted in graceful movement of artistic interest for the time.

Also, among the caves of this vicinity, is La Haza consisting of a small, round room with paintings of somewhat faded horses in blotted red line, high on the wall.

Sights:

Rupestrian paintings.

Location:

36 km SE of Santander on C 629 S of Ramales. Signposted beside road. Ask for guide at Ayuntamiento.

Retortillo

Roman town of Julióbriga currently under excavation, and excavated Roman villa on left of road just before entering town. Alongside the ancient townsite, and adjacent to the twelfth-century church, there are also some Early Christian tombs.

Sights:

Ruins of Roman city with remains of houses. Nearby Roman villa and Early Christian graves.

Location:

SE of Santander, take the N 611 75 km to Reinosa, then SE to Retortillo. Signposted.

Santillana del Mar

For many years this town has played host to visitors from all over the world who have come to the Cueva de Altamira, the most famous cave in the country, for prehistoric paintings. (There is a facsimile at the National Archaeological Museum in Madrid.) Now, due to deterioration of the paintings, it can only be visited by small groups of no more than eight and only after permission is requested at least six months in advance. Even then permission may be denied. Requests may be sent to Centro de Investigación y Museo de Altamira, 39330 Santillana del Mar, Cantabria, España.

One of the first caves to be discovered, in the year 1879, it also contains the finest cave art in the form of about twenty painted representatives of bison, horses, bulls and boars. Most of the paintings are grouped in one room of the cave about 30 m from the entrance. They are said to date back about thirteen thousand years or a little more. Museum in situ.

Sights:
Rupestrian paintings.

Location:
35 km W of Santander on the N 611, then right on the C 316 about 9.5 km (but signposted from Santander).

Suano
Under the village church Early Christian graves were discovered and may be seen from inside the building which is open to the public for Sunday Mass. Otherwise, the key must be obtained from the Carmelite convent in Reinosa. Also near the village is an Early Christian cave church about half an hour's walk into the hills. For guide, go to Ayuntamiento.

Sights:
Rupestrian church and Early Christian graves.

Location:
Going S from Santander on N 611, take turn-off W just S of Reinosa for Suano. Signposted.

Tarriba
Near this town is situated the cave of Horno de la Peña, with Paleolithic paintings. The cave also contains a number of engravings, many of which were lightly traced in the clay of the wall by a finger but damaged after discovery. They seem to be predominantly horses, but of various styles and periods.

Sights:
Rupestrian paintings and engravings.

Location:
SW of Santander on N 611 approx. 10 km. S of Torrelavega; take S 602 E (left) from Samahoz toward Puente Viesgo. Ask at Ayuntamiento for key to cave.

Valles
Near the village is the Cueva de la Clotilde, in the area of many other caves, which contains several fairly clear schematic animal finger drawings of bulls with square, vertically striped bodies, twisted horns and pointed feet. The cave has been recently closed to the public.

Sights:
Rupestrian paintings.

Location:
SW of Santander at Torrelavega take the N 634 to Valles and obtain key to cave (if open) at the Ayuntamiento.

Other cave sites in the province of Santander with Paleolithic paintings (but which may be closed to the public—one can inquire) are: **Cueva de El Pendo**, take the N 611 out of Santander and turn off left at Arce to Escobedo, about 3 km. Go through town and take right turn up hill to Barrio La Fuente (1 km). The cave contains a single panel of engravings, of which the only decipherable one is that of two birds with their backs superimposed. The best were removed to the Archaeological Museum in Santander. Ask for key and directions in village. **Cueva de Pozalagua**, E of Santander and E of Ramales on the C 6210, go to the signposted border of Santander and Viscaya and ask for key at houses on right. Cave is across the road and up the hill. Near Miera is the **Cueva de Salitré**, one of two adjoining caves which consists of a single corridor about 160 m long with a few poorly-preserved paintings. S of Santander on the S 554, then right on secondary road to Miera.

There are other caves in the province containing paintings besides those mentioned above, but most are difficult of access and often contain barely-discernible representations of animals or uninterpretable signs.

At the entrance to **La Calera**, a village of three or four farm houses SE of Santander, stands a little Roman bridge of one span and 11 m long, still used for local traffic. To find it, take the C 629 S of Ramales and turn E (left) to La Calera at bottom of long hill.

Santa María del Hito, archaeological excavation of Medieval cemetery by left side of road which cuts through it. The church to which it belongs is across roadway. A little further along at **Las Presillas de Bricia** are the remains of an early Christian rock-hewn church, some distance to the left of the road. Follow directions for Arroyuelos. Both sites are just beyond on the same road. Ask in village for church.

CASTILLA - LA MANCHA

A broad expanse of territory in the centre of the peninsula, the region is made up of the five provinces of Albacete, Ciudad Real, Cuenca, Guadalajara, and Toledo. Apart from the city of Toledo, much of this area remains relatively unruffled by tourists. It might be thought that the high, flat, arid plains and extremes of climate of La Mancha (the largest uniform natural region of the country, of which Ciudad Real is the centre) would also have tended to discourage ancient settlers, yet there are a number of exceptionally interesting sites in the area. Places of interest in the region include three major Roman cities near Cañaveruelas, Saelices and Valeria (all in the province of Cuenca), the Roman complex at Carranque in the province of Toledo (a recent and most important discovery), a large Iberian site near Hellín in Albacete, the grotto with excellent rock paintings near Fuencaliente in Ciudad Real and a cave near Riba de Saelices in Guadalajara with unique Paleolithic drawings. Nor is the region

without the ubiquitous dolmens—sites that are often associated with areas closer to the coasts.

All phases of Spanish history, from Paleolithic times to the Arab kingdoms of the Middle Ages, are represented in Castilla - La Mancha, yet it is an area that travellers tend to hurry through on the way to somewhere else. Perhaps the distant horizon of the dry, endless plain of La Mancha that never seems to come much closer has something to do with it. But off the beaten track from Madrid to Málaga, the region is also well-endowed with forested mountains and cool river valleys.

ALBACETE

Except for the Sierra de Alcaraz in the southwest and some hilly country in the south and southeast, the province is generally rather flat. Infrequent rainfall leaves a desiccated landscape devoid of forests. The most populous city is Albacete (derived from Arabic Al Basite, "plains"), the capital, with about two hundred thousand inhabitants.

There is ample evidence that early man, from Paleolithic times (when the climate must have been wetter) onward, moved through the area establishing camps here and there, especially along the ancient water courses. Rupestrian paintings clearly attest to Neolithic or Bronze Age cultures in the province, and the Iberians established some of their most inland settlements here.

The Romans found the area suitable for wheat-growing and other agricultural pursuits, as did the Arabs around whose strongholds small farming communities developed.

Alpera

On the hill near the town is situated the Cueva de la Vieja with prehistoric paintings, the oldest dating back about ten thousand years and others much younger. Paintings in this rock shelter or grotto must be viewed through a protective iron grill, but faded animal forms and human figures can be distinguished. One frieze depicts a man in a feathered head-dress and bulls with added antlers. In the vicinity of Alpera are other grottos with rock paintings, such as the Cueva del Queso, Fuente de la Arena, Cueva negra de Meca and Cueva del Rey Moro, but they are not easy to find. Inquire at Ayuntamiento.

Sights:
Rupestrian paintings in the Levantine style.

Location:
Turn off the N 430 Albacete to Almansa road just before km 576 onto AB 860 to Alpera. Obtain key to grotto in town at no. 1, calle de Seda (off Plaza de la Iglesia). Route to Cueva de la Vieja is signposted from town.

Bonete

At El Amarejo, are the remains of an excavated Iberian hillside terraced village with foundations of some dwellings visible. All artifacts have been removed. Site is easily accessible, but there is not a great deal to see.

Sight:
Iberian settlement.

Location:
E of Albacete just off the N 430. Take road out of town toward Montealegre del Castillo and just before km 6, signposted, turn south (right) on unpaved road. Site on conical flat-topped hill ca. 1 km from turnoff. Hill can be seen from the main highway N 430 on right just before turnoff to Bonete.

Hellín

There is a Roman villa here, discovered in 1925. Mosaics from the site are in the local museum. The remains of the villa are north of the central core of the town on one of the hills of the city. It has been built over with modern houses, factories and roads. There is little left.

South of the town is the Cueva de Minateda, actually a grotto or abrigo with faint cave paintings difficult to distinguish. The

Albacete: Hellín. Tolmo de Minateda

abrigo, just below the summit of a hill, requires a strenuous climb and is fenced off.

Also south of the town is a large Iberian site, Tolmo de Minateda, of more than passing interest. Situated on top of a large triangular rock above vertical cliffs, the site was occupied for about fifteen hundred years, beginning in the fifth century B.C. when Iberians settled there, down to Arabic occupation

which ended in the eleventh century. Well chosen for its strategic position, the settlements here dominated the route from Alcalá de Henares (Roman Complutum) in the province of Madrid to Cartagena (Roman Cartago Nova) on the Mediterranean. The modern highway follows the same course past the site. Excavations were first carried out in 1946. It is expected that eventually the area will be laid out with pathways and indicators, but at present nothing is marked or signposted and the remains are heavily overgrown.

Little is known about the settlement between the second and fourth centuries A.D. but at the end of the fourth or beginning of the fifth century, the approach to the hill was fortified—no doubt owing to the instability of the times—using stones, blocks, capitals and other sundry materials taken generally from houses, perhaps already in ruins or demolished for the purpose.

Sights:

Rupestrian paintings in poor condition. Iberian-Roman-Arabic settlement. From Iberian times, rock-cut steps, stone ramp with wheel ruts, rock-hewn chair (probably observation point), cisterns, Ibero-Roman necropoli of incineration, stone inscriptions, remains of dwellings and walls, rock-cut wine or oil presses and silos. Early Christian graves. Arabic remains are fewer, but include dwellings and a portal to the town. Shards from all epochs are in great abundance.

In the city of Hellín itself are the remains of an Alcázar.

Location:

Hellín is S of Albacete on the N 301. The Cueva de Minateda is signposted on the N 301 ca. 9.5 km S of Hellín on the right (going S) just before dry river bed and bridge. Follow secondary road 1.5 km and cave can be seen on right high on a hill.

For Tolmo de Minateda see above, but cross over dry river bed. Site is on hill on right of N 301 immediately after bridge. Walk around to right of hill for access.

Inquiries can be made at the Taller Arqueológico in Hellín as well as for El Tesorico, an Iberian necropolis in the vicinity and a recent excavation of a Bronze Age and later Iberian site, with remains of a cyclopean wall and monumental entrance-way between Hellín and Albatana to the NE off the C 3212.

Hoya-Gonzalo

Nearby at El Camino de la Cruz is an Iberian necropolis of the fifth century B.C. where thirty-three rock-hewn tombs have been excavated. Also in the vicinity is Los Villares, another Iberian necropolis of the fifth to fourth centuries B.C.

Sights:

Iberian necropoli.

Location:

E of Albacete on the N 430 ca. 20 km, then N (left) on the AB 883 ca. 4 km.

Isso

Near the town of Isso are three bridges in various states of preservation, assumed to be Roman. One of the bridges over the river Mundo is situated just outside Isso, a little up-river from the old mill of Falcón, and may have served to connect the plains around the town with the Camino Real (thought to have passed through Isso from Hellín) toward Elche de la Sierra, W of the town, and ultimately to Andalucía. (Some fragments of a Roman road have been uncovered in the town.) The well-preserved bridge is 35 m long and 4 m wide with three arches. At the S end of the bridge are remains (paving stones) of the Roman road. A second bridge, also over the Mundo and near Falcón, is several hundred metres down river from the first and appears to be older than the other. Only one of its original two or three arches remains. A third bridge with one arch, near the exit from town, is situated over a stream by the remains of the Alcázar and the church of Santiago, and may have been built for local commercial purposes.

Sights:
Remains of Roman bridges.

Location:
Take the C 3212 S of Albacete and SW of Hellín 3.5 km. Go through town, continue and cross river Mundo. Immediately after bridge, turn left on unpaved road to end. The other bridges are at El Falcón where there are also remains of an aqueduct.

Munera
Remains of a Bronze Age settlement, Torre del Quintanar, on a cliff dominating the valley of the river Quintanar. In the highest part is a double enclosure of stone. Outside this fortified zone are remains of dwellings. Radiocarbon dating places the settlement about 1700 B.C.

Sights:
Bronze Age settlement, walls and dwellings, possible necropolis.

Location:
W of Albacete on the N 430. For directions, inquire at Ayuntamiento. There are slight remains of several other Bronze Age sites in the area.

Nerpio
Nearby rock shelters with Levantine style prehistoric paintings such as Abrigo de la Fuente del Sapo, Castillo de Taibona with animal figures and vegetable motifs, Torcal de las Bojadillas, a group of six rock shelters with paintings of animal and human figures and Solana de las Covachas, a group of ten abrigos, some containing paintings of animals and human figures. All date back to Neolithic times.

Sights:
Rupestrian paintings.

Location:
S of Albacete and SW of Hellín on C 3212 to Elche de la Sierra, then C 3211 SE to Las Murtas. Next take C 415 S to Moratalla and pick up the 703 W to Nerpio. Leaving Nerpio by the road W to Pedanía de Pedro Andrés 8 km (which is at the end of the road), continue on a private road to Noguera ca. 2 km. From here take the path toward the SE following the creek bed toward the hill beyond. Not a difficult walk. Above the right bank of the creek are the grottos of Solana de las Covachas. For information on other local grottos with paintings, inquire at the Ayuntamiento.

Ossa de Montiel

Rock shelter, La Tinaja, on whose walls are some schematic engravings possibly related to nearby megalithic remains.

Sights:

Megalithic site and grotto engravings.

Location:

W of Albacete on the N 430. Inquire for directions at Ayuntamiento.

Near the city of **Albacete** there have been various finds dating back to the Bronze Age such as El Acequión, a settlement with double walls and a central habitation zone. Here also was an Iberian settlement dating back to the fourth to third centuries B.C., with remains of stone houses. This site and others nearby such as Las Peñuelas at **Pozo Cañada**, a little south of the city on the N 301, with remains of tower and dwellings, are best visited by obtaining permission, directions and information about state of preservation from the Archaeological Museum in Albacete.

Other sites in the province of Albacete include those at **Alcaraz**, ruins of an Alcázar on the N 322 SW of Albacete 79 km. Rupestrian paintings can be found near **Almansa**, 72 km E of Albacete on the N 430. Inquire at Ayuntamiento for El Abrigo de Ladera del Monte Murgrón. There is also a spectacular Alcázar on the hill dominating the town and easily seen from the highway. Near **Ayna**, SW of Albacete on C 3211 ca. 60 km, are Levantine rock paintings in the Cueva del Niño dating back to Late Neolithic or Early Bronze Age times. Excavations show evidence of Paleolithic inhabitants. **Chinchilla de Monte Aragón**, once an Ibero-Roman and later Arabic settlement, is 14 km E of Albacete on the N 430. The Iberian necropolis of Pozo Moro is now covered over, but around the town are numerous dwellings carved out of the tufa. Most are now abandoned and fast disappearing due to quarrying. The fifteenth-century castle on hill above town was constructed on the site of a Roman fort. **Santuario de Belén**, Arabic irrigation canals (*acequias arabes*) run alongside the sanctuary. Most of the stone channel is still in place, bringing water down from a natural spring. Take N 430 from Albacete E toward Almansa to km 578, sanctuary signposted on right. Follow poor, dirt road, across railway tracks and continue short distance to site.

CIUDAD REAL

The area is generally flat, high and dry, but with mountainous areas of the Sierra Morena in the south and southwest. The major river, the Guadiana, flows from east to west.

The province contains Paleolithic and a very few Neolithic open-air sites, but without durable structures; consequently there is, for the most part, nothing left to see for the general traveller with the exception of the fine cave paintings near Fuencaliente.

Later Bronze and Iron Age settlements offer more concrete remains but they are not always easy to find without a guide. Visible in situ Roman remains in the province are few, most sites are from Medieval times.

Albaladejo

At Puente de la Olmilla is a Roman villa, dated to the fourth century A.D., with various structures and hallways paved with mosaics around an interior patio. There are also other rooms with mosaics and some slight remains of walls painted with murals. The bridge of Carromolón, reputed to be Roman, may be Medieval.

Sights:
Roman villa and bridge.

Location:
SE of Ciudad Real, take the C 415 E from Valdepeñas to Villanueva and turn S (right) 14 km on secondary road.

Alcázar de San Juan

Excavations at Motilla de los Romeros revealed remains of a large tower rebuilt several times, and evidence of walls from the Middle Bronze period (1650 to 1340 B.C.). From the final phase of the Bronze Age is the necropolis of La Vega on the right bank of the river Cigüela, where ceramic urns were deposited in small fossae. Little remains to see, however.

At Casa de las Motillas de Pedro Alonso a central structure or tower has also been uncovered around which were other smaller structures whose material seems to date back to the Middle Bronze Age, but again there is little left to see.

In town are the remains of a Roman villa with walls, hypocaustum and mosaics with geometric patterns.

Sights:
Bronze Age settlement, necropolis and Roman villa.

Location:
Follow the N 420 NE of Ciudad Real, cross the N IV, continue 21 km.

Alhambra

On the hillside below the town and alongside the highway, a reputedly Roman necropolis was discovered in 1989, and excavations are on-going. Site is unmarked but easy to find, and consists of a number of graves stretching 100 m or more along the base of the hill. A granite sarcophagus was also found. On the hilltop in full view and near a Roman crossroads is an Alcázar.

Sights:
Late Roman or Early Christian rock-hewn necropolis. Alcázar.

Location:
E of Ciudad Real and the N IV on the N 430. Necropolis on left of highway about 100 m beyond petrol station. Easy access.

Almodóvar del Campo

La Bienvenida was a Roman city identified with ancient Sisapo which pertains to several phases, Imperial and Late Roman. Excavations have revealed, among other things, the outbuildings of a grand, Roman house with porticos. An older, Iberian level, dating back to the fourth century B.C., has also been uncovered.

Sights:
Remains of Ibero-Roman town.
Location:
SSE of Ciudad Real on N 420 to Puertollano, then W on the C 424 ca. 7 km.

Ciudad Real

The city was founded by Alfonso X in 1252 but little remains of the old walls and one hundred twenty towers except the Puerta de Toledo, a Mudéjar gate. In the vicinity of the city are several Paleolithic and Bronze Age sites pertaining to surface finds, but with virtually nothing to see. A large Iberian fortress, Oppidum de Alarcos, has undergone some excavations revealing walls, street, entrance way and urn-incineration tombs. At Alarcos, a few km SW of city beside the river Guadiana, the remains of a rectangular Alcazaba with towers, dwellings and streets have been excavated.

Sights:
Iberian fortress and Arabic Alcazaba.
Location:
For permission and directions to visit sites, inquire at the Diputación Provincial in the city.

Ciudad Real: Puerta de Toledo

Damiel

Motilla de Azuer, Bronze Age settlement and fortress with remains of large central tower surrounded by two lines of concentric walls and dwellings. Inside the walls are fifteen inhumation tombs. The site is dated between 1750 and 1300 B.C. Also, at Motilla de las Cañas is another Bronze Age site similar to that of Motilla de Azuer with a central tower, several times destroyed by fire and dating to 1600–1400 B.C. Here, as well, is a circular fortified Iberian settlement, excavated and dating back to the fourth century B.C., on top of which were constructed several Medieval buildings.

Sights:
Bronze Age and Iberian settlements.
Location:
NE of Ciudad Real on the N 420/430 to Damiel. Bronze Age site 9 km E of Damiel on the banks of the river Azuer. Sites unmarked and difficult to find. Inquire at Ayuntamiento for guide.

Fuencaliente

The grotto named Peña Escrita contains excellent, unspoiled clear paintings easily seen through the iron grill. The schematic representations, mostly in red, of flora, fauna, solar symbols, tectiforms, and human forms have been tentatively dated to Neolithic or Early Bronze Age, but could be much younger. They appear almost as picture writing, precursors of orthographic systems.

Sights:
Rupestrian paintings.

Location:

S of Ciudad Real on N 420 to Puertollano. Continue on the N 420 ca. 60 km to Fuencaliente. Site is N of town 1.5 km signposted on E (left) side of highway. Go to top of hill and turn right and follow paved road to end, ca. 4 km. Walk past chain barrier and take trail immediately to left up mountain, about 250 m. Site can be seen from road.

Ciudad Real: Fuencaliente. Peña Escrita

Other grottos in the area are La Batanera, more difficult to find, and with fair paintings, reached by continuing straight ahead at top of hill for ca. 2.3 km over poor, unpaved road and then walking. It is situated beside a waterfall known as Chorrera de los Batanes and cannot be seen from road. For Cueva de la Sierpe and its rupestrian paintings, it is best to inquire at the Ayuntamiento.

Granátula de Calatrava

Ceramic material from the Bronze Age has been found at Cerro Domínguez, an ancient hilltop village near the river Jabalón, along with evidence of an Iron Age settlement. Roman and Medieval finds confirm a long period of occupation of the hill down to the twelfth century A.D. Excavations have uncovered some remnants of walls and dwellings but there is little to see here. The bridge over the Jabalón river toward Calzada de Calatrava is reputed to be originally Roman.

Sights:
Roman and earlier settlements.

Location:
SE of Ciudad Real to Almagro on the C 415, then S on the C 417.

Other ancient sites of interest in the province are at **Almadén**, SW of Ciudad Real on the C 424 with various rock shelters in the vicinity containing prehistoric paintings, such as Cueva de la Solana del Puerto de las Viñas, Puerto Palacios and Reboco del Chorrillo. Here also are the ruins of an Alcázar. **Almagro**, 26 km SE of Ciudad Real on the C 415, Motilla de los Palacios, Middle Bronze Age site with a small central enclosure, dwellings and a large fossa from which many human bones were extracted, now little to see. **Argamasilla de Alba**, E of Ciudad Real and about 30 km NE of Manzanares on the CR 132, Alcázar, Castillo de Peñarroya. **Carrión de la Calatrava** or Calatrava la Vieja, ca. 1 km N of Ciudad Real on the N 401, turn off NE (right) for ca. 3 km. Arabic ruins with excavated Alcázar from the ninth and tenth centuries. **Chillón**, Alcázar, SW of Ciudad Real and 4 km NW of Almadén. **Malagón**, Alcázar N of Ciudad Real on N 401, ca. 24 km. **Membrilla**, E of Ciudad Real and a little SE of Manzanares on the N 430, Motilla de la Virgen del Espino, near the Azuer river W of town, Bronze Age site dated by carbon-14 to about 1470 B.C., but nearly completely destroyed. **Motilla de Santa María del Retamar**, SW of Ciudad Real, 48 km on the N 420, Bronze Age site with remnants of walls and dwellings.

CUENCA

Situated nearly in the centre of the peninsula, the province presents three distinct geographical zones: La Serranía, a mountainous region of clear water and rocky defiles, the origins of the Tajo and Júcar rivers, and where a number of Bronze and Iron Age sites have been found, especially cemeteries (but nothing now remains of them); La Alcarría, area of gentle hills and valleys more suitable to the Romans; and La Mancha in the south, an extensive dry, flat plain.

Three major Roman cities are found within a short distance of each other in the province of Cuenca: Ercávica, Segóbriga and Valera. All preserve important ruins and have been at least partially excavated.

Albalete de las Noguera

At Fuente de los Baños is a necropolis of the third to fifth centuries, consisting of rock-cut graves and others constructed with stone slabs. There were twenty-two graves of the two types but there is now little to see as the site has been, and is still being, destroyed by an encroaching gravel quarry. Parts of only four tombs remain at present.

Sight:
Paleo-Christian necropolis.

Location:
N of Cuenca ca. 45 km on N 320, branch right on CU 904. Turn right just before bridge into town onto dirt farm road, go left where farm road forks. Site on slight elevation on right ca. 2 km out of town.

Alconchal de la Estrella

Cerro de la Virgen de la Cuesta, Late Bronze Age settlement with remains of wells and silos and the ruins of an Iberian village occupied from the fourth century B.C. to the first century A.D. Later Roman town with remnants of walls of dwellings about 80 cm thick. The site appears rich in potential and some of the configuration of the settlement can be seen from the lay of the land, but so far there are only small excavation areas and not a great deal to see. Area littered with shards.

Sights:
Bronze Age, and Ibero-Roman remains of settlements.

Location:

SW of Cuenca, take the N 420 to Villalgordo del Marquesado, turn W (right) on secondary CU 330 to village with Medieval castle on height. Continue through village ca. 2 km to site at hermitage on a hill which can be seen from the village.

Cañaveruelas

Near the village are the remnants of a hilltop Celtiberian village, Ercávica, at Castro de Santaver, and the extensive remains of a Roman city from Republican times. The Roman forum was built over the earlier Celtic village. In the so-called Casa del Médico or Surgeon's House were discovered surgical instruments; also found and removed were Celtic and Roman ceramics, objects of ivory and bone, swords, coins and inscriptions. The town was, no doubt, the centre of local agricultural activity.

Sights:

Celtibero-Roman town, with remains of houses, cisterns, unexcavated theatre, forum with slight remains of Paleo-Christian basilica, temple, baths, bodega (or wine cave), wash-board of natural rock, Casa del Médico with wells (11 m and 13.5 m deep), streets, etc. Pre-Roman rock-cut tombs on hillside just to right of gate into city. Off to the right, ca. 500 m before reaching gate is a Medieval necropolis.

Location:

NW of Cuenca on the N 320 branching off W (left) on the CU 214 which follows the shoreline of the Embalse de Buendía. Ercávica lies 4 km W of town over unpaved farm roads. Site fenced off. Seek guard/guide and key in

Cuenca: Cañaveruelas. Ercávica. Roman Forum

village at cafe-bar, or his house behind bar. There are other remains of Celtic castros on the neighbouring hills which require strenuous walks and preferably a guide.

Cañete

Pajaroncillo, settlement dating back to the first Iron Age, judging from hand-made painted pottery of the Hallstatt type. Urn necropolis and Iberian village with remains of stone and adobe construction.

Sight:

Iron Age settlement.

Location:
E of Cuenca on the N 420 ca. 71 km. Inquire at Ayuntamiento for location and permission to visit.

Castellar, El
A very picturesque humpback Roman bridge over the river Júcar (seen from the old highway above it) has one major span, one minor span, and is still usable on foot.

Cuenca: Castellar. Roman Bridge

Sight:
Roman bridge.

Location:
Take the N 430 SW of Cuenca ca. 30 km to where highway crosses river. Bridge is 100 m down stretch of old road running S alongside the river and the power station.

Huete
Some Paleolithic finds were made at Terrazas de los Ríos Mayor y Cuevas (nothing to see), and at Cerro Alvar Fáñez was a Roman settlement dating back to the first century B.C. and continuing until the third century A.D. Roman mining construction was discovered at Minas de Lapis Especularis.

Sights:
Roman settlement. At El Castillo are further excavations showing various levels of habitation, and the remains of a caliphal tower.

Location:
W of Cuenca on the N 400 ca. 57 km, turn N (right) on the C 202 to Huete. Opposite town, entering from the south, turn E (right) on Camino Valparaiso and go 1 km (crossing railway). Roman excavations on hill on left. Walk up.

Saelices
Cabeza del Griego, Roman agricultural town of Segóbriga, from Republican and Imperial times situated on a hill once containing about one thousand houses and six thousand inhabitants. The Roman city was built over an earlier Celtiberian town of which nothing but some wall and remnants of a portal remain. The name of the town derives from Celtic *seg-*, "victory," and *-briga*, "town" or "fort." Much of the area has been excavated but there is still a great deal to be done. The town was on a major Roman road from Alcalá de Henares (ancient Complutum), in the province of Madrid to Cartagena in Murcia.

Sights:

Roman necropolis of first century, theatre and amphitheatre, remains of baths, water conduits and wall niches, ruins of large Roman tomb, walls, streets, foundations of dwellings, aqueduct, temple to Diana, restored Hispano-Visigothic basilica. Small museum in situ behind which is a Hispano-Visigothic necropolis.

Location:

SW of Cuenca on the N 111 at km 103, just E of Saelices, turn off onto CU 304 for 4 km. Signposted.

Cuenca: Saelices. Segóbriga. Roman Baths

Valeria

Roman town of Valeria on hill beside village and below castle ruins currently under excavation. A modern graveyard occupies the centre of the site.

Sights:

Remains of Roman houses, walls, cisterns, aqueduct, forum platforms, basilica and nymphaeum.

Cuenca: Saelices. Segóbriga. Roman Theatre

Location:

Follow the N 320 S from Cuenca ca. 32 km and take secondary road W ca. 14 km to Valeria.

Villar del Humo

In the vicinity of the town a dozen groups of rock paintings have been discovered with figures of humans, some with bows, and animals, totalling over one hundred seventy. In the grotto Peña del Escrito is a well-preserved naturalistic bull and lassoed horse, among other figures.

Sights:

Rupestrian paintings.

Location:

SE of Cuenca on the N 420, turn S (right) onto the CU 501 branching off N (left) at Cardenete for 17 km. Inquire at Ayuntamiento for permission and directions to visit sites.

Villas Viejas

Fosos de Bayona, Iberian settlement of the fourth to first centuries B.C. with three defensive walls and various towers, subterranean galleries and wells, and two streets parallel to the walls. Inside the fortified zone a cache of arms and coins was discovered, as well as a necropolis which has disappeared under a ploughed field. The site is partially excavated but much of it covered over again. Now little to see but general outlines of the ancient site and some underground galleries and stretches of wall.

Sight:

Iberian settlement.

Location:

SW of Cuenca on N 111 a little E of Saelices, turn S (right) at km 111, go through farm and walk up small hill on left.

There are several other sites of ancient historical interest in the province; one, Fuente de la Mota is located near **Barchín del Hoya**. Iberian settlement dated between the fourth and second centuries B.C., excavated and part of the wall is visible. S of Cuenca off the N 111. Take the CU 714 just W of Motilla to Omedilla de Alarcón (where there is no longer an ancient necropolis reported in some tourist guides), and turn N (right) just beyond town to Barchín del Hoyo. El Colmenar near **Landete**, is a hilltop settlement of the Middle Bronze period dated by carbon-14 to about 1600 B.C. Some slight remains of defensive works including two towers and three terraces supported by rubble-work walls may be seen. E of Cuenca 87 km on the N 420 to Salvacañete, then SE on CU 500 for 33 km. Inquire at Ayuntamiento.

GUADALAJARA

Watered by the rivers Henares and Tajo, the province is generally hilly. Ancient sites from Paleolithic times onward including dolmens and menhirs have been discovered, but many of the remains have been either re-covered, not excavated, or have simply disappeared.

Celtic peoples inhabited the area, and among their remains is the Luzaga Bronze, an important written inscription recording the Hispano-Celtic language. There were also scores of Roman remains, especially villas or farmsteads which capitalized on the agricultural potential of the area, but little is left. The best sights are perhaps those of Cueva de los Casares, with its singular cave paintings and the Visigothic Recopolis near Zorita de los Canes.

Aguilar de Anguita

Near the town stands the remains of another of the ubiquitous peninsular dolmens. The passageway and the polygonal tombstones are mostly upright, but the capstone is missing. Thirty-five interments were found within this grave reputedly dating back to ca. 3000 B.C. The site is fenced off, neglected and overgrown. A few hundred metres away is an uprooted menhir, banished from a farmer's field, and lying beside the road. On top of the hill, across the highway from the town, are some slight remains (bits of walls and towers) of a probable Roman camp, but it is up a difficult farm road and not easy to find.

In the vicinity are also a number of Iron Age sites both settlements and cemeteries, but they have either been covered over or obliterated by treasure-seekers.

Sights:

Dolmen in rather poor condition, uprooted menhir and slight Roman remains.

Location:

Take the N 11 NE from Guadalajara then branch E (right) on the N 211 a few km to the town. Continue through town and take the first unpaved road to left where, after ca. 2 km, a hermitage is seen on left. Just before the hermitage stands the dolmen on the right, in the middle of a field. The menhir is lying on the right of the road before reaching the dolmen. For Roman remains, inquire in town as a guide is recommended.

Bochones

El Tesoro, excavated Roman villa of Late Imperial times.

Sights:

Roman villa with small pool, hypocaustum, water channels, walls.

Location:

N of Guadalajara and a little N of Atienza on the GU 15, ca. 7 km.

Espinosa de Henares

Medieval town lying at the confluence of the Henares and Allendre rivers. Along the valley of the Henares passed the ancient Roman road connecting Mérida and Zaragoza. Espinosa corresponded to the way station (*mansion*) of Caesada. The remains of the small urban Roman complex and the earlier Celtic settlement that was here have been identified from surface finds or excavated and covered over. Still to be seen in the vicinity are Roman bridges, one over a stream beside the Caserio de Tejer (on private property), another, much restored, crosses the river Henares, and a third is over the river Sorbe. These bridges served the road between Guadalajara (Arriaca), Espinosa (Caesada) and Sigüenza (Segontia).

At Pico Buitre a Bronze Age site was discovered along the river Henares, dated by carbon-14 to between 1040 and 950 B.C., with remains of walls and dwellings, but the site has been re-covered.

Sights:
Roman bridges.

Location:
Take the N 11 NE from Guadalajara to Torija, then W on the GU 190, 9 km to Torre del Burgo, 4.5 km N to Hita, then W on GU 144 for 13 km to Espinosa. Inquire at Ayuntamiento for directions to bridges.

Guadalajara
Ancient Arriaca, the city was founded in pre-Roman times. From this and the Roman period little remains to be seen. It was subjugated by the Arabs and called Uad-al-Hayar or "river of stones" (hence the name), and retaken by Christian forces in 1085. The old Mezquita was converted to the Church of Santa María de la Fuente in Mudéjar style and is one of the best examples of this kind of architecture in the country, with horseshoe portals, columns and a tower that was once the minaret. The powerfully constructed Arabic bridge from the tenth century was built on Roman foundations and can best be appreciated from the Parque del Río adjacent to the bridge, on the downstream side.

Sights:
Mudéjar church and Arabic bridge.

Location:
In town.

Luzaga
Some slight and now neglected excavations of the pre-Roman Celtic town may be seen at the end of the town square behind a small tower, and by the cemetery. A Celtic necropolis of some eighteen hundred or more urn interments and dating back to the fourth through second centuries B.C. was excavated here, but there is little left, as the unprotected sites were picked clean. The ancient settlement is the origin of an important bronze tablet written in the first century B.C. in the Hispano-Celtic language and Iberian script.

Sight:
Celtic settlement.

Location:
Follow the N 11 NE of Guadalajara 78 km. Turn S (right) at Alcolea del Pinar onto GU 950, 7.5 km to town.

Mazarete
Nearby in the pine forest is a menhir called El Huso, "the Spindle," but it is difficult to find over 2.5 km of poor forestry roads. Inquire at Ayuntamiento in village or at Blanca de Solonillos in forest, nearer the site.

Sight:
Menhir.

Location:
Take the N 11 from Guadalajara NE and the N 211 to Mazarete, then follow GU 944 to Blanca de Solonillos.

Muriel
Rock shelter with Bronze Age paintings of human figures and geometric designs.

Sights:
Rupestrian paintings.

Location:
N of Guadalajara on the secondary GU 143 at the N end of the Embalse de Beleña.

Riba de Saelices
Seen in the distance from the hill in the village, the Cueva de los Casares, on the right bank of the river Salado, contains 168 engravings dating back to about eighteen thousand years ago. Along with the representations of flora and fauna (many fish as well as rabbits and birds), the cave is unique in the world for its anthropomorphic presentation of a copulation scene under the watchful eye of a witch with the mask of a mammoth. This and other scenes, for instance that of a pregnant woman, show a certain preoccupation with fertility and have led to a better understanding of human concerns in such remote times. The cave has been known for over two centuries, but only protected recently. Many of the engravings consequently have been defaced.

To visit the cave, make an appointment with the guide Emilio Morena (Tel 39 17 09). The rock engravings are situated about 200 m inside the cave, which maintains a temperature of fifteen degrees. The visit lasts three hours and warm, old clothes are recommended. A maximum of six people are admitted at any one time.

At Santa María del Espino, a village just N of Riba de Saelices, is the Cueva de la Hoz, beside the river Salado with Paleolithic cave paintings of horses and (in another gallery) engravings of four deer.

Sights:
Prehistoric rupestrian engravings and paintings.

Location:
Follow the N 11 NW from Guadalajara and turn SW (right) on the CU 950 beyond Luzaga ca. 16 km. For Cueva de la Hoz, inquire about permission to visit at the Ayuntamiento.

Villacadima
El Portalón is a grotto half-way up the hillside containing some Neolithic paintings, in reddish colour, of human beings and a quadruped. On the hillside opposite are a few small rock shelters with some indistinct paintings.

Sights:
Rupestrian paintings.

Location:
Well N of Guadalajara and just off the C 114 near the provincial boundary with Soria.

Zorita de los Canes

Above the village stands an oblong Alcázar begun in the ninth century. It has tenth-century walls, but towers and ramparts are from various epochs. On the opposite hill of Cerro de la Oliva are the ruins of the Visigothic Recopolis where excavations were begun in 1944, partially uncovering an important city founded by King Leovigildo in 578 in honour of his son Reccarede (hence the name Recopolis). The site is unusual for a Visigothic city in that it had no Roman antecedents. On the ruins a twelfth-century Romanesque chapel was constructed, itself now in ruins.

Sights:
Remains of Visigothic town (Recopolis) including walls, basilica and royal palace, small dwellings and storage silos. Arabic walls and Alcázar in town.

Location:
From Guadalajara travel SW on N 320, then on C 200 to Zorita de los Canes ca. 51 km. For Recopolis, turn left immediately upon entry to village through archway and follow steadily deteriorating road around town to Cerro de la Oliva. A ruined chapel at the site can be seen on the hill from the distance.

The province of Guadalajara is actually fairly rich in ancient sites; for example, within a 30 km or so radius of Alcolea del Pinar on the N 11 NW of Guadalajara are several dozen sites, but most, especially Bronze and Iron Age necropoli and settle-

Guadalajara: Zorita de los Canes. Alcázar

ments, have been covered over or destroyed by careless excavations and souvenir hunters. Many settlements are known from surface finds, and still others from caves and rock shelters and the pottery associated with them. Some of the more important sites, or what is left of them (and that may, in some cases, be nothing), are located at or near the following: **Alcolea de las Peñas**, N of Guadalajara and N of Atienza on C 101, Celtic settlement and necropolis. **Alcuneza**, NE of Guadalajara on C 204, urn necropolis of the seventh to fourth centuries B.C. **Atienza**, Altillo de Cerropozo, third century B.C. Celtic urn necropolis, ca. 84 km N of Guadalajara off the C 114. **Clares**, NE of Guadalajara on the N 211 a little N of Mazarete, urn necropolis of the fifth to fourth centuries B.C. **Cogolludo**,

N of Guadalajara, turn off the C 101 N (left) on GU 144 to Espinosa de Henares and follow the GU 150, site referred to as La Loma del Lomo, remains of Bronze Age site consisting mainly of holes excavated in the rock and used as dwellings, silos and graves. **Embid**, NE of Guadalajara on C 211, go N off the N 211 at Molina de Aragón ca. 26 km, Bronze Age settlement of Fuente Estaca dated by carbon-14 back to about 800 B.C., slight remains of dwellings. **Fuensaviñán**, NE of Guadalajara just off the N 11 S (right) a short distance after Algora, Roman necropolis. **Guijosa**, NE of Guadalajara and NE of Sigüenza on secondary road, fortified Celtic hilltop village, remains of walls and an Arabic settlement of Los Castillos, with dwellings hewn from the sandstone, stairs and cisterns, along with La Cerradilla, Moslem necropolis. **Humanes**, settlement and necropolis of Valmatón of the fourth to third centuries B.C. with natural and artificial defenses, a little N of Guadalajara on the secondary GU 132. **Palazuelos**, El Altillo de la Horca, seventh-century Visigothic necropolis, NE of Guadalajara on C 114 NW of Sigüenza and nearby (ca. 1 km) **Carabias**, urn necropolis of El Tesoro of the seventh to third centuries B.C. **Pelegrina**, Los Castillejos, Iron Age village with two lines of walls, the inside with attached dwellings, the outer composed of large cut stones set without mortar, ca. 64 km NE of Guadalajara on N 11, then N (left) on road to Sigüenza. **Prados Redondos**, E of Guadalajara off the N 211, turn S (right) just after Molina de Aragón on secondary road; Ibero-Roman settlement, La Coronilla, showing excavated walls and rectangular dwellings, storage silos and infantile interments. **Sigüenza**, 74 km NE of Guadalajara, judería just below the entrance to castle (now a parador). **Torresaviñán**, NE of Guadalajara ca. 64 km on N 11 near Fuensaviñán, La Cabezada, fourth- to third-century B.C. urn necropolis. **Trillos**, E of Guadalajara on GU 990 on river Tajo, Ermita de San Martín,

Guadalajara: Zorita de los Canes. Recopolis

Visigothic necropolis. **Yunta, El**, E of Guadalajara and S of Embid off the N 211 turn NE (left) at Molina de Aragón ca. 21 km, pre-Roman necropolis of about one hundred tombs of various types.

TOLEDO

The province of Toledo, one of the most centrally situated in the peninsula, contains few Paleolithic, Neolithic and Chalcolithic sites. The oldest vestiges of man are located at Mocejón, on a hill near the river Tajo where Musterian materials have been found, and at Pinedo, where the terraced site on the right bank of the same river has revealed tools and animal bones dated to the

Achelense epoch. In the province of Toledo, approaching from the south, one begins to enter the territory of the Verracos' culture, of which there are a few remnants. The majority of archaeological remains in the province date back to Roman and Medieval times.

Azután

Large double-ringed Dolmen de Azután (although the dolmen is closer to the town of Puente del Arzobispo) dating back to the Bronze Age, excavated, huge chamber and entrance-way with most stones upright but cap stone missing.

Sight:
Dolmen.

Location:
S of Talavera de la Reina on the N V to Oropesa, continue S (left) on the TO 701; on W side of road (right) at km 49 stands the dolmen.

Carranque

On-going excavations of eighteen-room Roman villa, Santa María de Abajo, many with mosaics of geometrical designs and hunting scenes, heating system and adjacent remains of dwellings and possible mills. Area of the mosaics is fenced off but in full view. Across the generally fordable (by foot) river Guadarrama on the Carranque side stands a Roman windmill—a rather rare specimen—once used to grind wheat. Upon entering the area, the first sight is the remains of the Early Christian basilica on the left, near the river. The Roman villa is 1 km beyond along the same road which forks twice, stay to the left. The area is strewn with shards from centuries of habitation.

One of the most important in the province, the site is eventually to be opened to the public as an archaeological park.

Near Carranque, at Casarrubios del Monte, a short stretch of Roman road has been recently excavated.

Toledo: Carranque. Early Christian Basilica

Sights:
Roman villa, windmill, Early Christian basilica, Roman road.

Location:
About 30 km S of Madrid on the N 401, go W (right) at Torrejón de la Calzada onto C 404. Continue 12 km to town and turn left on dirt road ca. 350 m after petrol station (after crossing the river Guadarrama). Follow dirt track 3.3 km to site. From Toledo, travel N (direction

Madrid) on the N 401 to Torrejón de la Calzada. The road to Carranque is 20 km from Yuncos W (left) off the N 401, Toledo to Madrid.

Casalgordo

Remains of Visigothic church, San Pedro de la Mata, of ca. 675, with horseshoe arch entranceway. Constructed during the reign of Wamba, it belongs to a similar series of churches built in the latter part of the seventh century, such as Santa Comba de Bande and San Pedro de la Nave. Of this one, in ruins, there are only some arches and walls standing.

Sight:
Visigothic church.

Location:
Take the N 401 S of Toledo 21.5 km; site is ca. 4 km SW of town over heavily rutted farm track. Keep to right when track forks. Unmarked.

Consuegra

Remains of long, Roman dam, broken at one end where stream passes through. Interesting but neglected site. Farm buildings erected against dam structure.

Sight:
Roman dam.

Location:
From Toledo go SE on C 400, ca. 63 km to Consuegra. Then TO 233 7 km SW toward Urda. Signposted 5 km from Urda. Turn off road onto farm track ca. 300 m; dam is on left.

Herencias, Las

Arroyo Manzanas, excavated Final Bronze Age to Roman period site on hill above the river Tajo near town, with some remains of dwellings and walls. Found here was a granite stele with engravings of human figures wearing helmets and carrying lances and shields, along with a horse-drawn chariot. It is datable to ca. 700 B.C. Site may be covered over. Other neglected and overgrown excavations (tombs) in town by river. Inquire at Ayuntamiento.

Sight:
Bronze Age to Roman settlement.

Location:
S of Talavera de la Reina on C 503. Excavation on E (left) side of road on hill between km 126 and 127. Requires strenuous walk uphill.

Illescas

Iron Age (Celtic) site of El Cerrón dating back to the fourth to second centuries B.C., where the remains of a series of dwellings on rectangular foundations with stone socles and adobe walls painted red have been excavated. Discovered here was a relief with representations of two carts pulled by horses, guided by coachmen and followed by a griffin.

Sights:
Iron Age settlement and sanctuary.

Location:
Illescas is about half way on the N 401 Toledo to Madrid road. The site lies ca. 1.5 km away along farm track. Leave town from S going parallel with highway but past and behind warehouses on W (right) side.

Malpica del Tajo
Roman villa, Las Tamujas, various rooms pertaining to the bath complex excavated. The mosaics have disappeared. Little to see although there are also slight remains of a fourth-century Paleo-Christian basilica.

Sights:
Roman villa, remnants of basilica.

Location:
W of Toledo and E of Talavera de la Reina on N V 29 km, then SE on the C 502 then S (right) on the CO 762 ca. 2 km.

Melque
Pre-Roman settlement originally, but there is little left. There appear to be remains of a Roman villa complex, a small dam and collapsed bridge, and remnants of houses and walls. Pottery finds in excavations under the church indicate Roman presence at the site but the structures could be later.

The Mozarabe church, Santa María de Melque of around the ninth century, with horseshoe arches and somewhat restored, seems to have been inhabited during Visigothic times, judging from the marble objects found inside. It was later used as a fortress for a time during the Moslem epoch.

Toledo: Santa María de Melque

Sights:
Roman or Late Roman/ Visigothic remains and Mozarabe church.

Location:
SE of Toledo on the C 401, then N (right) at cross-roads with the C 403 past San Martín de Montalbán ca. 4 km (km stone 31/32) to farm road on right; signposted Santa María de Melque, 3.2 km. Farmhouse on site.

Navalmoralejo
Los Vascos, a Moslem city of the ninth to twelfth centuries, situated on a hill and walled with towers. Outside the walls are the baths and necropolis, the

graves marked with stone pillars. Inside are streets, drains and remnants of houses. The site is fairly extensive and very interesting in that it contrasts sharply with the splendour of Moslem Spain seen elsewhere, such as at Córdoba and Granada. Los Vascos is considered to have had a rather poor standard of living. Under the Arabic town were found remains of an older Roman settlement.

Toledo: Navalmoralejo. Los Vascos. Arab Tombs

Sights:

Remains of a walled Arabic city with external baths and necropolis.

Location:

W of Toledo and S of Oropesa on the TO 70, follow highway to crossroads W to Navalmoralejo, but take farm road E (left) to ruins. Proceed 5 km on farm track, turn right by first farm and again right by second farm, then immediately left to top of hill and take left fork. Marvellous site, diabolical road.

Talavera de la Reina

Ancient Talabriga, Roman, slight Visigothic remnants of construction material scattered about and Arabic remains attest to the long-standing importance of the city. In the arcaded Plaza Mayor stands the Arco de San Pedro, once a Roman gateway and among the houses of the city rise the Torres Albarranas, relics of the tenth-century Arabic wall.

Sights:

Roman gate and relics of Arabic wall.

Location:

W of Toledo on the N V from Madrid.

Toledo

One time capital of the Carpetani, the town, Toletum, was subdued by the Romans in 192 B.C. By the middle of the sixth century, it became the capital of the Visigothic kingdom and a castle was built on the site of the present-day Alcázar. Captured by the Arabs in 712, the city became a centre of trade, attracting Mozarabe Christians and Jews. It was retaken by Christian forces under Alfonso VI in 1085. The city is replete with history and in situ sights going back to Roman times. The walls of the city show the influences of Roman, Visigothic and Arabic periods.

Sights:

Remains of the Roman circus with a capacity for twenty thousand persons; amphitheatre in the suburb of Las Covachuelas and remnants of aqueduct upstream from the Puente de Alcántara; second-century necropolis at Vega Baja and perhaps later Moslem tombs; Santa Eulalia, Mozarabe church but founded in 589, contains Visigothic column and horseshoe arches; Puente de Alcántara, (*kantara* "bridge"), rebuilt by the Arabs in 866 with recently discovered Visigothic and Arab pilastres (but present structure dates mostly from the thirteenth and fourteenth centuries); the Puerta Bisagra, the only gate remaining of the Arabic wall constructed in ninth century (*bab* "gate" and *sahra* "wasteland"); Iglesia del Santo Cristo de la Luz, the ancient mosque of Bab-el-Mardoun with Visigothic capitals probably from an early building, constructed in 999, and numerous other later edifices.

Two Jewish synagogues, remains of the old judería, also are in the city: the older is Santa María la Blanca with horseshoe arches and Mudéjar decoration; the second is a fourteenth-century synagogue of El Tránsito, begun on orders by Samuel Levi, treasurer of Pedro I of Castilla.

Location:

In the city.

Vegas de San Antonio, Las

Large fourth-century Roman mausoleum with two outside octagonal walls and a half pyramid-shaped centre below ground. The site is totally unkempt, full of debris and garbage and hardly recognizable as an interesting and beautiful Roman tomb.

Sight:

Octagonal Roman mausoleum.

Location:

W of Toledo and a little E of Talavera de la Reina, from which one may take the TO 742 S and proceed E (left) on secondary road past La Puebla Nueva to Las Vegas. Site is situated 1.3 km out of town from Ayuntamiento to left of unpaved road in orchard.

Other sites in the province, some of which are still in the prospective stage and which may contain in situ remains are located at **Alcaudete de la Jara**, Late Roman villa and mosaics with geometrical designs and tombs, currently covered over. NW of Toledo on N 403 to N V then W to Talavera de la Reina and turn S (left) to Alcaudete on the C 503 ca. 20 km. **Arisgotas**, Los Hitos, excavated Visigothic basilica of the eighth century, S of Toledo on the N 401 to Orgaz, then 6 km W on secondary road. **Belvis de la Jara**, El Carpio, Bronze Age necropolis, W of Toledo to Talavera then S 18 km on the C 503. **Castillo de Bayuela**, Cerro del Obispo, Bronze Age necropolis, NW of Toledo on the N 403 40 km, then W 23 km on the N V to Los Nogales. From here go N (right) 11 km on the TO 924. **Coral de Amaguer**, Cerro del Castillo-Gollino, Iron Age settlement, excavated street, dwellings and the perimeter of the wall, E of Toledo ca. 50 km on N 400, then go SE to Ocaña and pick up the N 301 38 km to Coral. **Erustes**, Paleo-Christian sarcophagus of the fourth century, NW of Toledo 40 km on N 403,

W on N V ca. 14 km and turn S (left) on TO 763. **La Estrella**, La Aldehuela, Bronze Age necropolis with corridor and chamber, W of Toledo near border with Cáceres on TO 702. **Layos**, Paleo-Christian sarcophagi of the fourth century, 9 km S of Toledo on the TO 781. **Orgaz**, Roman bridge, 34 km S of Toledo on N 401. **San Martín de Pusa**, Valle del Arcipreste, a Bronze Age inhumation tomb, W of Toledo on C 401 to Los Navalmorales (ca. 70 km) then N (right) on TO 742 9 km. **Santa Cruz de la Zarza**, Las Esperillas, Iron Age necropolis with rock-cut tombs, E of Toledo on the N 400 ca. 120 km. **Yeles**, Iron Age urn necropolis, NE of Toledo on the N 401 to Illescas, then E (right) on the TO 424. **Yuncos**, Bronze Age necropolis, N of Toledo ca. 28 km on the N 401.

CASTILLA Y LEON

This large area, now encompassing the previous historical regions of Castilla la Vieja (minus Santander) and León into one administrative unit, consists of the nine provinces of Avila, Burgos, León, Palencia, Salamanca, Segovia, Soria, Valladolid and Zamora. The topography is varied between mountains and high plains and, like Castilla - La Mancha, it only lacks a sea coast. Cutting the region in nearly two equal halves is the river Duero, flowing from east to west on its way to the Atlantic.

Paleolithic, Neolithic and Bronze Age in situ remains in this section of the country are less in evidence than in the coastal regions of the peninsula, but the region does display sites from these periods, such as the dolmens of Salamanca.

Predominant, however, were Iron Age Celtic settlements, which eventually succumbed to the Roman legions, beginning a new era in the life of the northern meseta. Perhaps the most outstanding remains from this period are the Celto-Roman cities of Numancia and Tiermes in Soria, the Roman city of Clunia

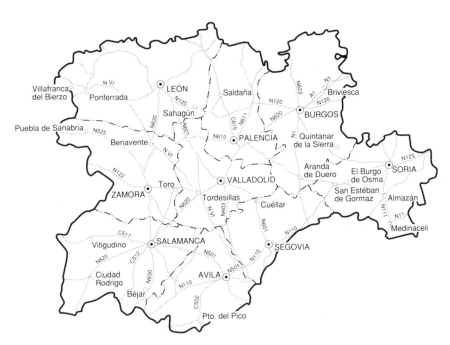

in Burgos, the aqueduct in Segovia (an engineering marvel), the Roman road in Avila, and the villas in Palencia, with their memorable mosaics.

Visigoths occupied the region but their numbers were relatively small and their impact on the culture of the area correspondingly so. The area has several Visigothic churches—for example, one at Campillo in Zamora, another at Baños de Cerrato in Palencia.

Arabs and their Berber allies left no great legacy behind during their short sojourn in the area, as they were soon obliged to pull back beyond the Duero river toward the south, but their later influence is readily seen in such places as the Mozarabe churches, many in the province of León, and in the Mudéjar decoration of the monastery of Las Huelgas in Burgos and the convent of Santa Clara at Tordesillas in Valladolid.

In the ninth century the Kingdom of León, propelled forward by Christian advances, reached to the Duero. In the same century, Burgos was repopulated with Christian settlers as the inexorable process of southward expansion continued, resulting in the reconquest of the north and eventually the entire country.

AVILA

Situated in the SW of the region, the northern section consists of a plain which climbs up to a series of mountain ranges culminating in the Sierra de Gredos in the extreme south, before dropping off abruptly to the valley of the Tiétar. The high and often heavily glaciated land did not attract Paleolithic man in any numbers. From the lower Paleolithic, only one site is known, situated on a terrace of the river Trabancos near Narros del Castillo in the W of the province, where primitive stone tools were discovered in 1974. Such tools have been found in a few other places in the province but sites have not been defined.

The lack of man-made material and sites during the Middle and Upper Paleolithic have led some archaeologists to believe that the region was depopulated between 120,000 and 10,000 B.C. Neolithic sites, also rare, are seemingly the result of migrations from the S of the peninsula into an unpopulated area. One of the few sites is La Peña del Bardal at Diego Alvaro, excavated in the 1920s, revealing artifacts associated with the period, and the base of a round stone hut.

With the advent of the Chalcolithic era, ancient monuments become more numerous as seen, for example, by the dolmen at Bernúy Salinero near the city of Avila which belongs to this period, along with the large aligned stones on the farm of San Simones at Muñogalindo, a little SE of Avila. Settlements are found at Peña el Aguila near Muñogalindo, excavated in 1973, Cerro Herbero y Sonsoles near Avila, el Alto del Quemado in Narrillos del Alamo, and la Cueva del Gato near Muñopepe, as attested by ceramics and other artifacts from the time.

In the province of Avila the Bronze Age is represented primarily by the sites at Sanchorreja, a little W of the capital, Berrueco in the SW and Cardeñosa just N of Avila where the hill, El Cerro de las Cogotas gave its name to the earliest settlement, Cogotas I. Here, Bronze Age artifacts were discovered along with a decorated pottery whose type and technique of production appears to have spread throughout the peninsula. The second phase of settlement, Cogotas II, or Cultura de los Castros, pertained to the Iron Age. During this period the province was occupied by the Vettones, a Celtic people who tended toward peaceful relations with Rome. Some of their settlements may be seen near Cardeñosa, Candeleda, Charmartín de la Sierra, Sanchorreja, Medinilla and Solosancho.

There are about thirty-five known Roman sites in the province, but most have left only vestiges of their former existence. They consist of villas, roads, bridges, sanctuaries and necropoli.

Widely scattered traces of Visigothic necropoli and other objects confirm their presence in Avila, but the remains are few; the most important is the necropolis of El Tiemblo.

Avila

Once a Celtic settlement and later a Roman camp, little remains of the early period. The great Medieval wall, with its eighty-eight towers, dating back to the eleventh century, seems to reflect the contours of the Roman camp and to contain some stones of Roman origin from other sites. At the entrance to the town, on the Salamanca highway, is a Roman bridge over the river Adaja, alongside the modern one.

Several verracos can be seen in the city and standing outside the walls. All are not indigenous to the site, however, some having been transported there from the Celtic Iron Age settlement near Cardeñosa.

Sights:
Celtic zoomorphic sculptures and Roman bridge.

Location:
In and on the edge of town.

Bernúy-Salinero

Only recently discovered and excavated in March of 1990, the small dolmen near the village is a fairly good specimen, with all stones standing in upright position. Cap stone is missing.

Sight:
Dolmen.

Location:
Upon leaving Avila on the N 110, pass under the railway bridge and take first right turn which leads to Bernúy along road divergent but nearly parallel with the N 110. Travel for 7 km and with village in view, turn left on gravel road before entering. Proceed around back of farm, passing through gate with cattle grid, and continue ca. 500 m. The dolmen stands in the middle of an open field.

Candeleda

The hillside Iron Age village of El Raso, covering some twenty hectares, contains extensive remains of quadrangular and round houses and some remnants of walls and defensive trench. There is also a partially excavated urn-burial necropolis which encompasses the fourth to third centuries B.C. A large area of the castro has been excavated, first in the 1950s, and work is still in progress. There are two sites on left of road and another on the right and up the hill. The villages seems to have housed about three thousand people. It is thought to have been abandoned in the second half of the first century B.C. when the region was pacified by Caesar. The area commands impressive views of the Sierra de Gredos in the river valley below. The sites are fenced off but are in full view from all sides.

There are some reputed Iron Age rock paintings in the area.

Sights:
Celtic Iron Age village with numerous remains of structures and necropolis.

Location:
On C 501 SW of Avila and N of Oropesa 30 km. Take the C 501 W of town ca. 5 km, then N on road to El Raso, signposted Castro de El Raso. Take gravel road on right upon entry to El Raso and proceed three bumpy kilometres on the forestry road up mountain.

Cardeñosa
Nearby is a fortified Iron Age village, Las Cogotas, dating from approx. 700 to 220 B.C. The castro is situated on a hilltop with panoramic views and was surrounded by a double belt of walls, much of which is still intact. Several entrances to the village are in evidence. About 100 m away is the necropolis with 1,456 graves which were excavated, after a fashion, in 1930. The unadorned, rough stones, marking the shallow burial holes, each once containing an urn with the ashes of the dead, have been left thrown about on the ground with no attempt to give the site a semblance of the way it was. The surface of the ground is littered with shards, but the three verracos found here were removed to Avila. The guard/guide is informative and, if not at the site, can be reached in town.

Sights:
Bronze and Iron Age remains of walls and dwellings. Iron Age necropolis.

Location:
From Avila, take the Salamanca highway a little out of town and turn right on small road marked for Cardeñosa. Just before km 5, turn right onto unpaved road marked by sign for Castro Las Cogotas. Continue on road to end, 4 km.

Chamartín de la Sierra
Nearby is situated the Castro de la Mesa de Miranda, an Iron Age settlement, and La Osera, the necropolis. The sites were discovered in 1930 and excavated in 1932 and 1945. The castro preserves some of the three walled enclosures, the upper one for the confinement of cattle, with remains of towers and portals. From here comes the verraco that is now in the village of Chamartín, while two others remain at the site. The necropolis, one of the most important for the period in the region, yielded 2,230 incineration graves with the accompanying artifacts. In some of the tombs the urns were deposited in a chamber and covered over with a mound of stones.

Sights:
Iron Age settlement and necropolis.
Location:
Approx. 30 km W of Avila on the AV 110, site is located 2.5 km N of town. It is of moderately difficult access over rough and hilly ground. Inquire at Ayuntamiento for best route.

Medinilla
Situated in the foothills of the Sierra de Gredos in the vicinity of the town was a Neolithic, and later Celtic settlement, Cerro de Berrueco, but nothing is to be seen of the former and very little of the latter.
Sight:
Celtic castro.
Location:
SW of Avila 81 km on the N 110 to El Barco de Avila, then take the C 500 N ca. 13 km to Becedas. From here follow secondary road N to Medinilla.

Ojos Albos
Found here at Peña Mingubela is one of the few examples of schematic rock art in the province, located in a natural abrigo at an elevation of 1,300 m. The small human figures in the paintings, with lances and swords, are depicted in war scenes, but many other symbols are no longer intelligible and of controversial interpretation. In many cases, the red dye has faded considerably and the paintings are very faint.
Sights:
Rupestrian paintings.
Location:
NE of Avila ca. 14 km on N 110, fork E 2 km to village. Inquire in village for guide.

Puerto del Pico
Long stretches of Roman road, the finest in the country, some parts restored, ascend to the Puerto del Pico 1,352 m high, sometimes in a series of switchbacks. Most of it is

Avila: Puerto del Pico. Roman Road

on the S side of the mountains and can be clearly seen on a good day from the summit of the pass. The road is ca. 6 m wide and well built. It runs parallel in many places to the modern highway.
Sight:
Roman road.

Location:
SW of Avila on C 502 between Mombeltrán and the Puerto (pass).

Solosancho

Iron Age hilltop castro of Ulaca, known since 1896 but not systematically excavated until the 1970s. It preserves the remains of a wall with towers around the site, enclosing nearly sixty hectares. In some parts near the entrances, the stones reach cyclopean dimensions. Inside are two areas excavated from the rock: the so-called Altar de Sacrificios, and the Fragua (forge). The latter seems to have been a large oven, while the former seems to have been a place for cult activities. Disseminated over the top of the hill are parts of walls and foundations of stone houses, some with several rooms. An isolated tomb was uncovered in 1950 but the necropolis of the castro has not been found. There is a verraco in the Solosancho town square from the site.

Close by are the remnants of a Paleo-Christian and Visigothic community near Villaviciosa at Cabeza de Navasangil, excavated in 1977 and 1979. Of the ancient wall and primitive dwellings composed of rubble-work, almost nothing remains, making the site difficult to find. Inquire for guide in village.

Sights:
Iron Age castro, walls and dwellings, verraco in town.

Location:
On the C 502 SW of Avila 22 km. At Solosancho go 2.3 km S (left) to the hamlet of Villaviciosa, but just before entering, turn left on dirt road which passes behind houses, and right at first crossing. Go left again at second crossing and proceed ca. 250 m further to open area on farm road. From here climb mountain on right. Thirty-five- to forty-minute walk. Site is behind mountain.

Tiemblo, El

Of the few Visigothic necropoli in the province, the one near El Tiemblo at Llano de las Palomas is the best known. Excavated in 1960, it had long before been despoiled by treasure seekers. The twenty coffins are composed of granite stone slabs covered with flagstones. The head of the deceased was oriented west. There is now little to see of this seventh-century site, abandoned after the Moslem invasion, except some holes. It is difficult to find among the trees and bushes. Inquire at the Archaeological Museum in Avila.

Sight:
Visigothic necropolis.

Location:
S of Avila on the N 403 ca. 40 km.

Toros de Guisando

The Toros are four very large verracos standing in a row at the site of a ruined fifteenth-century inn near the Avila-Madrid provincial boundary. One of them has been broken and repaired, but the others are in excellent condition, just as they were made by the Iron Age Celtic people. This is the most important verraco "herd" in the country.

Sights:
Four verracos.

Location:
Follow the N 403 SE from Avila for San Martín de Valdeiglesias (province of Madrid). Site is signposted.

Other sites in the province, but sometimes with very little to see, are found at or near **Arévalo**, the nearby thirteenth-century church of Lugareja is in Mudéjar style, as are the bridges over the rivers Arevalillo and Adaja. **Burgohonda**, S of Avila 36 km on the AV 900, tenth- and eleventh-century tombs. **Diego Alvaro**, W of Avila 56 km on N 501, then S 33 km on C 610, a Visigothic site excavated in 1956 where small nuclei of the remains of dwellings

Avila: Toros de Guisando

date back to the sixth and seventh centuries (at El Castrillo, los Caralillos, Cerro de Espino, Los Molinos, Campo de los Moros, La Casa, etc.). At **Niharra**, SW of Avila ca. 12 km on C 502, are the slight remains of a Roman villa. There were a number of Roman villas in the province, but most have been covered over or all the contents removed. **Sanchorreja**, nearby Celtic settlement of Los Castillejos on hill, but little left to see. W of Avila on AV 110, just before Chamartín, turn S on secondary road to village. **San Juan de la Nava**, Early Christian necropolis around the church of El Murueco, ca. 21 km S of Avila on the N 403.

BURGOS
Crossed by the Upper Ebro river in the north and the Duero in the south, the province spans the intermediate zone linking the northern meseta with the Cantabrian mountains. The inland province records some of the earliest remains of man on the peninsula and some Upper Paleolithic cave paintings. The Romans found the area of interest for agricultural settlements, and the province contains plentiful remains of Roman bridges, vestiges of roads, Roman camps and towns.

The area appears to have had a large Visigothic population after the end of the fifth century, and some Visigothic buildings are still in evidence, such as Santa María de las Viñas.

The capital city, Burgos, was supposed to have been founded by one Diego Porcelos who, in the ninth century, built a castle on the banks of the Arlanzón during the reign of of Alfonso III as a check to the Moslem advance.

The splendid monastery of Silos is a fitting tribute to the Middle Ages.

Burgos holds the essence of Medieval Spain during the long period of the reconquest in the larger-than-life personalities of Count Fernán González, founder of the county of Burgos in the tenth century, and the Cid, acclaimed as the nation's greatest warrior.

During this period also the province and the city of Burgos played host to the many thousands of European pilgrims on their way to the shrine at Santiago de Compostela, bringing with them them the ideas that would herald the new styles in Romanesque and Gothic architecture of later centuries.

Atapuerca

Cave site with paleontological excavations where human remains have been found dating back two hundred fifty thousand years. Guide recommended.

Sight:
Cave with Paleolithic excavations.

Location:
E of Burgos between the N 120 and N 1 take secondary road between Zalduendo and Quintanapalla.

Baños de Valdearados

Excavated Roman villa on edge of town, open entry across field, neglected and somewhat overgrown, mosaics removed and under cover in village awaiting restoration. For access to mosaics, see the mayor for key.

Sights:
Roman villa, graves, remnants of dwellings, baths and mosaics.

Location:
S of Burgos and a little NE of Aranda de Duero on the BU 910. Unmarked site on W edge of town in field.

Castrojeriz

This was the location of one of Caesar's camps, which was excavated and covered over. Now a wheat field. The general configuration of the camp may be seen, however, along with bits of wall here and there.

Sights:
Roman camp, some remnants of walls.

Location:
Approx. 26 km SW of Burgos on N 620, then turn NW (right) on BU 401 for 15.5 km. Site across road from Colegiata on edge of town.

Clunia

The remains of Roman Clunia cover the entire top of a plateau. The city had about thirty thousand inhabitants and only a small portion has so far been uncovered. The theatre, carved out of the hillside at the entrance to town, held around nine thousand spectators. The stage is in ruins, but the seating arrangement is largely intact. Just past the theatre, on the right of the road, are the largely reconstructed public baths. The city had two forums (one excavated), and was built over subterranean water deposits. There is a Romanesque church on the site, adjacent to the excavated forum. A Roman bridge is located nearby at Coruña del Conde.

Sights:
Remains of Roman theatre, public baths, palatial villa and mosaics, forum, dwellings, private baths (hot, tepid and cold), cisterns, Roman basilica, Roman bridge.

Location:
S of Burgos and 19.5 km E of Aranda de Duero to Peñarando de Duero, then N on C 111 12 km. Just beyond town turn left, signposted. The bridge is N of Peñarando de Duero on the C 111, E of Aranda de Duero.

Covarrubias
Old Tower of Doña Urraca (d. 1126), daughter of Alfonso VI (d. 1109) and wife of Alfonso el Batallador, the Battler. Currently privately owned (inherited), with cafe in lower part. Seek owner's permission if visit to upper levels is desired.

Sight:
Tower of Doña Urraca.

Location:
From N 234 Burgos to Soria, turn S (right) at Horigüela ca. 13 km on C 110.

Faido
Tiny restored village with several interesting artificial caves in the vicinity. For the church of Virgen de la Peña, built into the rock, acquire key in village and walk up path ca. 200 m. On left, before reaching church, is a cave with tombs. Directly across the valley in plain view are several more artificial caves hewn from the rock.

Sights:
Early Christian artificial caves.

Location:
E of Burgos take the L 122 S of Vitoria 17.5 km, then follow signs for Bernedo. After passing Argote, there is a crossroad signposted for Faido, 3.7 km, and Cuevas Artificiales.

Frías
Dominated by church and castle, the town has two Roman bridges nearby. The first of nine spans, some of which have been rebuilt, is found by taking the castle road and following the river Ebro. A defensive tower was added to the middle of the bridge. The other is encountered before entering the town from Oña, standing opposite a shrine with two Roman columns in front and a privately owned Romanesque church by the side of the road on the hill. The bridge has a single span and is much deteriorated.

Sights:
Roman bridges.

Location:
NE of Burgos, follow the N 1 to Briviesca and take the BU 510 to Oña. From here take road toward Barcina de los Montes to turn-off for Frías ca. 9 km. Signposted.

Laño
Just before town, at entrance to valley, there are artificial caves on both sides. On the right, Las Gobas, and on the left, Santorkaria. See the mayor for keys. Man-made caves excavated from the rock served various functions. They were used as dwellings or burial sites, and sometimes as sanctuaries or places of worship.

Burgos: Laño. Artificial Caves

Sights:
Artificial caves.

Location:
SE of Burgos and S of Vitoria. Take L 122 to Bernedo and a few km after Argote, pass above Albaina to a crossroad. Turn right to Laño 1.6 km. Close to Faido.

Lara de los Infantes
On a high, flat hill and visible from the town are the remains of a Celtic settlement, Castro de Peña Lara. Part of the climb can be made by an all-terrain vehicle, otherwise it is a long, steep hike of about two hours, with only some remnants of walls and dwellings at the end of it. Also from the town, but on a closer and less formidable hill, are the ruins of the tenth-century castle of Fernán González, founder of Castilla la Vieja, or Old Castille, but only one wall remains standing. Nearby is Quintanilla de las Viñas (see entry below).

Sights:
Iron Age castro and tenth-century castle.

Location:
Take the N 234 E from Burgos to Mambrillas de Lara, and turn N (left) through Campolara to Lara de los Infantes.

Lences
Attractive but deteriorating Roman bridge over the river Homino with one span, beside church and road at entrance to village.

Sight:
Roman bridge.

Location:

E of Burgos to Briviesca and take BU 510 to Cornudilla. Go left on BU 502 to Pozo de la Sal, then S 1.5 km and take right hand road to Lences. Not signposted.

Penches

Near the town is a cave with small, sealed entrance on left of the road to Frías, which can easily be missed among the trees and brush. Inside are paintings of animals. A light is required, as are the keys to the site which at the present time are with the Ayuntamiento of Oña.

Sights:

Rupestrian paintings.

Location:

NE of Burgos and N of Briviesca to Oña. Take road to Penches (road toward Frías), and 1.5 km after the town, on left above road—not signposted—is the cave.

Puentelarrá

Large, hillside rock-cut cemetery and sanctuary hewn out of the stone above the Ebro river. Site contains over one hundred closely packed graves of all dimensions, and is surrounded by a dilapidated fence with large holes in it. Graves have been excavated and everything removed, but still impressive site in peaceful setting.

Sights:

Anthropomorphic rock-cut tombs and sanctuary.

Location:

NE of Burgos on the A 1 to exit 5 ca. 86 km, then C 122 to the town, ca. 13 km. Go S out of town, cross Ebro river and take turn to right up farm road to Finca Tejuela. Follow road in a few metres; then, when it splits, take left fork (right goes to farm), and continue 600 m and take first right. 1.4 km further on is the necropolis on the right.

Quintanar de la Sierra

About 126 graves clustered together and hewn from the solid rock in this area of pine trees and tranquility present an impressive sight. The graves are sometimes in groups of three or four (perhaps a

Burgos: Quintaner de la Sierra. Rock-cut Tombs

family), others are alone, and range in size from infants to adults. Compared to those at Puentelarrá, they are somewhat shallow, averaging perhaps about 20 cm. Many are cut to the configuration of the body, with space for the head.

Sights:
Anthropomorphic rock-cut tombs.

Location:
Travel SE of Burgos on the N 234 and at Salas de los Infantes, take road E to Quintanar 25 km to Hermitage (Ermita de Revenga). Take left turn into church park and continue 400 m down gravel road from gate to second outcropping of rock on left. Tombs are here; site not marked.

Quintanilla de las Viñas

Small, seventh-century Visigothic hermitage of Santa María de Lara. The church, built on the site of a Roman villa and necropolis, was once shaped in

the form of a cross, but was partially destroyed. There are some Roman columns in the church. On the outside wall is a three-band stone relief. To enter the church, find guide for key in village. House signposted. (See also Lara de los Infantes.)

Sight:
Visigothic church.

Location:
3.5 km N (left) off the N 234 Burgos to Soria.

Burgos: Quintanilla de la Viñas.
Santa María de Lara. Visigothic Relief

San Pedro de Arlanza

The monastery was begun in 912 and finished in the twelfth century. It was the original resting place of Fernán González (d. 970), whose castle is not far away (see Lara de los Infantes). The older structures are built over with Romanesque and Gothic designs. The monastery is at present in a general state of ruin, but is under restoration. Visigothic stone work and early graves are in evidence.

The building is situated on the banks of the river in the beautiful Arlanza valley, and a stream, from which the monks caught their fish for dinner, runs through the kitchen.

On the hill above stands an older, ruined hermitage under which Roman and Visigothic remains have been found.

Sights:
Tenth-century monastery and nearby older hermitage.

Location:
From the N 234 Burgos to Soria highway, turn S at Hortigüela on the C 110. Approx. 5 km.

Santibáñez del Val
Tenth-century Hermitage of Santa Cecilia on hill above river outside of town. Well signposted. Roman bridge, in poor condition and very dilapidated, across the Mataviejas river.

Sights:
Roman bridge and tenth-century hermitage.

Location:
Take the N 234 Burgos to Soria road and go west on BU 903 past Santo Domingo de Silos and toward Covarrubias. 7 km W of Santo Domingo is Santibáñez del Val.

Santo Domingo de Silos
Monastery supposedly founded by Visigothic king Reccared in 593. There is a Visigothic portal to left of door to cloister. The *Glosas Silensis*, tenth-century Latin documents glossed in Spanish representing some of the earliest forms of the written vernacular, are from here, but are now in the British Museum.

Sight:
Pre-tenth-century monastery.

Location:
Take the N 234 Burgos to Soria road and turn W south of Salas de Infantes at Hacinas onto the BU 903 to Santo Domingo, 13.5 km.

Sasamón
Remains of crenellated Roman wall and square tower with ogival arches. Nearby Roman bridge (Puente San Miguel) with two spans over river Brullés and Roman bridge with four spans over the same river a short distance away.

Neither bridge is usable for transport but may be crossed on foot. At the larger bridge, 100 m or so of Roman road with paving stones may be seen before it disappears into the fields.

Sights:
Roman bridges, wall and road.

Location:
NW of Burgos on N 120 ca. 30 km to Olmillos de Sasamón, then BU 640 for 2 km. Town is signposted. The Puente San Miguel is ca. 2 km out of town on the BU 620, just beyond the three crosses and standing archway of Romanesque church. The other bridge is ca. 1.5 km from town on the road to Villasidro.

Tosantos

Virgen de la Peña. Church hewn from the rock on hill above village. The modern façade is visible from highway. Key in town, although at time of writing, no-one seemed to know exactly who had it. Inquire at the bar.

Sight:
Church in the rock.

Location:
E of Burgos on N 120 approx. 35 km, between km 71 and 72.

The capital city, **Burgos**, preserves some pure Mudéjar decoration in the so-called claustrillas and the chapel of Santiago de la Asunción in the Cistercian Monastery of Las Huelgas, founded in the twelfth century.

There is a Roman bridge at **Gumiel de Hizán** near Baños de Valdearados, 11 km N of Aranda de Duero on the N 1. Other sites in the province include **Oña** with nearby Roman bridge over the river Oca, which seems to have been completely destroyed except for one arch, and another Roman bridge built next to it. This also appears to have been partly destroyed and rebuilt in the Middle Ages. On entering the town through the Arco de la Estrella, the Calle Barruso is seen to the left. This was the principal street of the old Jewish quarter. The second house on the right of this street (off the Plaza Mayor) is thought to have been the synagogue. From Briviesca, take BU 510 approx. 22 km N to Oña.

About 60 km N of Burgos ca. 44 km on the N 623, after the village of Valdelateja, a rural road leads off to the abandoned hamlet of **Siero**. On top of an enormous rock that dominates the village is a tiny chapel dedicated to Santa Centona and Santa Helena, who were martyred during the time of Diocletian and worshipped throughout the Middle Ages. There is an inscription with the Germanic names of Fredenandus and Gutina, who seem to have been a Visigothic couple who apparently had the chapel built or restored. It appears to date back to the seventh century. At **Tordómar** stands a Roman bridge, S of Burgos on N 1 ca. 35 km almost to Lermar, then W on C110.

LEON

South of the capital the undulating plains stretch to the horizon, while to the north the land climbs rapidly into the foothills and mountains of the Cordillera Cantábrica. Various rivers from the mountains supply water to the province. The western and hilly section of the province, El Bierzo, is watered by the river Sil, famous for its gold-bearing sands. Ancient Asturians, tribes of uncertain affinities, once inhabited the highlands and have left some traces of their passing on the southern plains.

Pre-Roman remains are not in great abundance in this province, but there are some rock shelters with prehistoric paintings. The most visible remains, however, are of Roman vintage, consisting of towns, walls, villas, bridges and mines.

Neither Visigoths nor Arabs made much direct impact on the area. In fact, many Christians who fled the Moslem domination of the south came to León. During the reigns of Alfonso III and his successors García I and Ramiro II in the ninth and tenth centuries, there appeared in Leonese territory a series of Mozarabe churches, unique in their characteristics. Unfortunately, some have been disfigured by subsequent additions, and others remain in ruins.

Astorga

A Roman military base at the beginning of the Cantabrian Wars, Astorga grew into an administrative centre and a Roman town. Under the Emperor Augustus, Roman Asturica Augusta (Astorga) was linked to Mérida in the south by the famous Camino de la Plata. By the third century A.D there was a substantial Christian community in the city, and by the ninth century it was an important stopping point on the Camino de Santiago.

Sights:
Late Roman city walls with funerary stelae and cryptoporticus.

Location:
C 46 km W of León on the N 120.

León: Astorga. Roman Wall

Castrocalbón

On a hill overlooking the town are the ruins of a Roman fort, with a small portion of the walls standing along with remnants of the entrance portico.

Sights:
Remains of Roman fort.

Location:
SW of León and SW of La Bañeza ca. 15 km on the LE 110. Remains on hill above town.

Compludo

Situated on the site established by the earliest Bierzan Visigothic monks is an early forge (herrería de Compludo) which is still functional.

Sight:
Iron forge from the seventh century.

Location:
W of León. Take the LE 142 SE out of Ponferrada. At Acebo take right fork in road to Compludo.

León

Capital of the province, the city dates back to 68 A.D. when the Roman Emperor Galba established a camp here for the Seventh Roman Legion (hence the name León) to protect the local mines and to inhibit the Asturian tribes from moving southward. A wall, 6 m thick, was built around the town in 250, but little of it has survived. The town was destroyed by the Moslem al-Mansur in 988 and subsequently rebuilt.

The Roman villa on the edge of town dates back to the third to fourth centuries, enclosed in a building with mosaics and sculptures. The church (Iglesia del Salvador de Palaz del Rey) next to the Plaza de Conde, the oldest in the city, dates back to the tenth century. It was constructed in the reign of Ramiro II and preserves the remains of a Mozarabic chapel. Only the transept and four columns of arches are recognizable.

Sights:

Late Roman city walls, Roman villa of Navatejera with mosaics, and early church.

Location:

Sites in town except the villa of Navatejera. Take LE 311 N of town ca. 3 km to Navatejera. Villa is signposted just past village.

Médulas, Las

An impressive site some 25 km from Ponferrada near the village of Las Médulas where an entire mountain was washed away to extract its gold, leaving a panorama of gullies, caves, tunnels and perpendicular rock faces. The mining continued throughout the second to fourth centuries and was carried out by thousands of slaves. An estimated nine hundred tonnes of gold were extracted. Water, to sluice the gold, was brought to the site by a system of aqueducts, and the so-called *ruina montium* method was employed, which consisted of releasing great gushes of water through a series of constructed galleries inside the mountain, flushing out the rock, soil and minerals and collapsing the tunnels. The water carried the ore to panning lakes where it was separated. The gold was sent to Astorga and despatched southward over the Camino de la Plata to Mérida, then on to Sevilla and Cádiz for shipment to Rome. Below the mines lies the village of Carucedo and adjacent lake created by the Romans. There are also some Roman remains in town and remnants of aqueducts in the vicinity.

León: Las Médulas. Roman Mines

Sight:

Las Médulas: enormous Roman open pit gold mine.

Location:

W of León. After Ponferrada take the N 120 S to Caruedo. Site is signposted.

Mellanzos

Mozarabe church of San Miguel de la Escalada. The site was chosen by monks from Córdoba who arrived in León with their abbot during the Moslem hegemony in the south, seeking the protection of Alfonso III. They rebuilt the small, seventh-century Visigothic church, which was damaged in 988 when al-Mansur plundered the region. In 1886 it was restored. With its numerous exterior and interior horseshoe arches, the church is one of the most graceful of the Leonese pre-Romanesque Mozarabic buildings.

Sight:
Tenth-century Mozarabe church.

Location:
S of León c. 11 km on the N 601. Turn E (left) at Villarente on LE 213 to Mellanzos.

Peñalba
Santuario de Santiago de Peñalba, Mozarabe church constructed by Córdoban monks dates back to 931. Beautiful example of Leonese Mozarabic architecture, and considered the best in the province.

Sight:
Tenth-century Mozarabe church.

Location:
W of León take LE 161 S of Ponferrada ca. 7 km to San Esteban. Then take left fork to Peñalba ca. 14 km. The church is in the centre of town.

León: Ponferrada.
San Tomás de las Ollas

Pieros
Near the village is situated Castro de la Ventosa, a pre-Roman Asturian fortress, once called Bergidum (which gave rise to the name of the region: Bierzo). Some stretches of wall are preserved.

Sights:
Remnants of Asturian hilltop fortress.

Location:
West of León, Pieros is ca. 6 km E of Villafranca del Bierzo. Take dirt farm track on right directly after village and continue taking right hand roads until top of hill. Then a short but somewhat strenuous walk.

Ponferrada
Mozarabe church of San Tomás de los Ollas, built between 931 and 937, has nine Arabic-style horseshoe arches and Visigothic architectural elements, such as a single nave. More Arabic in style than that

of Escalada, and more simple than that of Peñalba, the church once belonged to the monastery of San Pedro de Montes.

Sight:
Tenth-century Mozarabic church.

Location:
W of León the church is signposted by the hospital near the first entrance into Ponferrada off the N VI. The key may be obtained from the house no. 6 next to the church.

Sésamo
Rock paintings near the village (that section of the village on the left of the highway) require about a forty-minute climb, past water deposit, up to the rock face at the top of the mountain.

Sight:
Rupestrian paintings.

Location:
W of León. Take the LE 711 N out of Ponferrada for ca. 25 km. Site unmarked. Strenuous climb up mountain to rock paintings. Approximate location of site can be seen from village if pointed out. Inquire of residents.

Villasabariego
Castro de Villasabariego, the ancient Asturian town site of Lancia. Excavated area is about 50 m by 100 m, all that is visible of a once large pre-Roman town. The site, fenced off but clearly visible from all sides, rests on a hilltop overlooking the river Porma and the N 501 highway, although it must be approached from behind. A few decades ago there were many more ruins on the hill around the excavated site, but treasure seekers have removed virtually everything.

Sights:
Small excavated area of Asturian city, walls, foundations of dwellings, water conduits.

Location:
Follow the N 601 S of León to just before Mansilla de las Mulas and before crossing river Esla. Follow secondary road and take left at Villafalé and left again to Villasabariego. Go through village and take dirt road to left and continue approx. 2 km. Site can also be reached by taking left off the N 501 S on dirt road ca. 1 km just beyond Puente Villarente.

Other interesting historical sites in the province are **Balouta**, N of Ponferrada on the 711/712, which is an area of Pallozas (Celtic straw-roofed houses). In the town of **Bembibre**, on the N VI León to Ponferrada, is the church of San Pedro, built on the site of a synagogue, but no trace of the former structure is readily visible. **Boñar**, N of León 25 km on N 630 then E on the C 626 30 km, San Adrian de Boñar, constructed in 920 by Count Guisvado and his wife Leuvina and dedicated to San Adrian and Santa Natalia. An inscription in the church dates back to 980, and is all that is left of the period. The present church is much later.

Campo de Villavidel, 25 km S of León. The town lies near the confluence of the rivers Esla and Bernesga. In the jurisdiction of the town is a Roman villa of the fourth to fifth centuries, discovered in 1981 and excavated in 1982. The site yielded mosaics of hunting and fishing motifs, among others.

La Iglesia Rupestre de Villamoros, 4 km from León in the locality of **Villamoros de las Regueras** and half way up the mountain at the so-called Cueva de San Martín, was noted in the tenth century. It is the only rock-cut church in the province. It has a rectangular nave, a semi-circular apse and a horseshoe arch. It is abandoned and difficult to reach.

PALENCIA

Watered by the Carrión and Pisuerga rivers, the province is high and somewhat arid, lying in the lee of the Cantabrian range to the north. The Tierra de Campos dominates the landscape to the southeast, a tableland which it shares with León and Valladolid. It is primarily an agricultural region of austere, sweeping plains and distant mountains, and did not attract numerous ancient peoples as did other more agreeable areas. The capital, ancient Pallantia, dating back to the Celtic Vacceos, later became a Roman city, only to be destroyed by invading Germanic tribes. It functioned as a Visigothic centre, but was not greatly rebuilt until 1035 by Sancho the Great of Navarra.

The two most interesting sites are located at Quintanilla de la Cueza and at Pedrosa de la Vega (see Saldaña).

Baños de Cerrato

The Visigothic church of San Juan Bautista (or San Juan de Baños de Cerrato), built by Recesvinth in 661, is still preserved although once nearly destroyed and now much altered. It was constructed from stone quarried from Roman sites.

Palencia: Baños de Cerrato. San Juan Bautista

Sight:
Seventh-century Visigothic basilica.

Location:
S of Palencia just off the N 620, the church is signposted in town.

Frómista

The eleventh-century Romanesque church of San Martín contains richly adorned capitals, which include Roman pagan themes that presumably came from an earlier building.

Sights:
Capitals with pagan themes.

Location:
Ca. 32 km N of Palencia on the N 511. Church is signposted.

Olleros de Pisuerga

Entirely hewn from the rock, the Medieval church has two naves. Adjacent are rock-cut graves. Roman artifacts have been found on the hill behind the church, but nothing remains of the Roman site except rock-cut steps.

Sights:
Rock-hewn church and graves.

Location:
N of Palencia on the N 611, turn off into village a few kilometres S of Aguilar de Campóo. Church is signposted.

Palencia

The fourteenth-century cathedral was constructed over the remains of a Visigothic church of the seventh century. It was restored in the eleventh century and serves as a crypt, which contains the tomb of Queen Doña Urraca. It is difficult to enter, however, being available to the public only a few days a year. Otherwise special permission is needed from church officials.

On the western edge of the city is a reputedly Roman bridge, still in use, over the river Carrión.

Sights:
Visigothic remains and rebuilt Roman bridge.

Location:
In town.

Quintanilla de la Cueza

Roman villa, not far from La Olmeda (see Saldaña), discovered in 1970, dates

back to the first century A.D. and was in operation until the fourth century. The site is under cover and viewed from catwalks, from which may be seen the many rooms with mosaic floors, the heating system (hypocaustum) of the villa (rooms were warmed with hot air under the floors, as is still done in some rural Spanish houses), and some remains of the interior walls.

Palencia: Quintanilla de la Cueza. La Olmeda. Roman Villa

Sights:
Roman villa, mosaics and hypocaustum.

Location:
From Carrión de los Condes, N of Palencia on the C 615, follow N 120 W 15 km to Cervatos de la Cueza. Continue N on same road to Quintanilla de la Cueza. Villa is signposted outside of town.

Saldaña
Near La Olmeda, at Pedrosa de la Vega, is a large, late Roman villa—the centre of an agricultural enterprise—discovered by the owner of the property in 1968. The rooms of the villa opened onto a central rectangular patio with four galleries of mosaics. Similarly, almost all the rooms contained mosaics of geometrical designs, plants, figures and hunting scenes. A central theme is the Unveiling of Achilles by Ulysses in the women's quarters of Licomedes on Skiros.

The mosaics found here are as good as any so far discovered in the Roman world, and certainly the best in Spain.

At each corner of the villa stood a tower, and between them, on the south side, was a portico with columns. Of this there is little to see, nor of the hot baths on the north side. Virtually nothing remains of the necropolis found near the building, whose objects are displayed in the museum in Saldaña, once a Roman town.

The villa, one of the finest and wealthiest of the Late Empire, appears to have flourished from the fourth to the sixth century, when it was ruined by a fire.

Sights:
Roman villa and superb mosaics.

Palencia: Saldaña. Pedroza de la Vega. Roman Villa

Location:
N of Palencia, take the C 615 from Carrión de los Condes N toward Saldaña. Villa is signposted 5 km before town.

Santa María de Valverde
Rock-hewn church with bell tower constructed on top of rock, and rock-cut graves around church, some tiny infant interments.

Sights:
Rupestrian church and necropolis.

Location:
N of Palencia and just a little N of Aguilar de Campóo, take road SE from Quintanilla de las Torres to Santa María de Valverde. Church is signposted.

Further sites of historical interest in the province are **Aguilar de Campóo**, N of Palencia on the N 611, Medieval town first mentioned with the founding of a Benedictine monastery, but Celtic and Roman finds indicate a much older village. On the Puerta de Reinosa is a Hebraic inscription from the fourteenth century. Signposted from town is the Cueva de las Francesas at Revilla de Pomar. Interesting cave of great beauty, but containing no paintings. **Arenillas de San Pelayo**, N of Palencia on N 611 75 km to Herrera de Pisuerga, then ca. 7 km W, the church of the old convent contains a Visigothic baptismal font with friezes. **Menhir de Sansón**, a lone menhir stands in a field below a church on a hill some 700 or 800 m behind it. The name derives from the legend that alludes to a strong man, Samson, who threw the stone in anger from the hill where the church is located—it landed in the field and remained upright. N of Palencia on the N 611 several hundred metres off the highway, a little beyond Aguilar de Campóo. Signposted, but misleading. The menhir lies to the right of the highway (going N) some 100 m or so before the sign for it.

Caution at **Venta de Baños**: a Roman villa with beautiful mosaics is sometimes mentioned in the travel guides. It is covered over and *hors de vue*.

Palencia: Menhir de Sansón

SALAMANCA

The province is dry and mostly arid, with rolling hills throughout the central and eastern sections. In the south lies the western portion of the Sierra de Gredos, and to the southwest rises the Sierra de la Peña de Francia. The major river, the Tormes, traverses the province to flow into the Duero, which forms part of the border with Portugal. Other important rivers, the Huebra, the Yeltes and the Agueda, are all tributaries of the Duero.

Lower Paleolithic quartzite tools have been found in the vicinity of the capital and cave paintings from the Neolithic period have been discovered in the southern and western parts of the province, but the most palpable manifestations of early cultures in the area are the numerous dolmens, Iron Age castros and their concomitant verracos, and the remains of Roman civilization.

Alba de Tormes

There are prehistoric terraces, La Maya, along the Tormes river near the road from Alba de Tormes en route to Fresno Alhandiga, on the right bank of the river by Galisancho. The site is located between Santa Teresa de Tormes and the river, but there is little to see. A dolmen is situated on the same road between Alba de Tormes and Fresno Alhandiga.

Parallel with the main highway 4 km NW of Alba de Tormes is ca. 200 m of Roman road (*calzada romana*) on left side heading SE, visible but unexcavated.

Sights:
Prehistoric terraces, dolmen, Roman road.

Location:
Alba de Tormes is 23 km SE from Salamanca on the C 510. From here take the SA 120 S toward Fresno Alhandiga. Inquire at Ayuntamiento of Galisancho for directions.

Alberca, La
Neolithic rock paintings of goats, fish, lines and dots are found in the Batuecas valley, a little south of this Medieval mountain village.

Sights:
Rupestrian paintings.

Location:
SW of Salamanca on the C 512, then on to the SA 210 at Vecinos to Tamames. Follow the SA 202 to La Alberca. From there, a very winding road leads down into the Valle de Batuecas. A guide is recommended for the four-hour walk to the cave site. Inquire at the Hotel Batuecas in La Alberca.

Béjar
Nearby Roman remains include bridge, long stretch of road and mile-stones, part of the Via de la Plata between Mérida and Astorga. In town are reputed Arabic walls, restored in the twelfth century, enclosing the southern end of Béjar.

Sights:
Roman road and bridge, Roman milestones, Arabic walls.

Location:
S of Salamanca on the N 630 ca. 73 km. For the Calzada de Béjar, take the C 515 out of Béjar 8.5 km. The Roman bridge is beside the road, as is the Roman road itself and a pillar. One pillar is inside an abandoned stable next to the bridge.

Ciudad Rodrigo
Town of Medieval appearance on the banks of the river Agueda and, according to artifacts found here (including a verraco), site of an Iron Age castro. In Roman times the village was called Augustóbriga. Remains of Roman columns are found at the entrance to the town and a restored Roman bridge spans the river Agueda; the latter is best appreciated from the old castle (now a Parador) situated on a hill in town above the river. The verraco stands at the entrance to the castle.

Sights:
Roman bridge, columnata and verraco.

Location:
Approx. 89 km SW of Salamanca on the N 620.

Fuenteguinaldo

Interesting Iron Age ruins of Urueña (or Irueña) in strategic position on hill above the river Agueda. The site appears to have been inhabited until late in the Middle Ages. It is situated on a private farm and could be dangerous due to numerous large and aggressive bulls freely roaming the area.

Sights:
Iron Age village, extensive defensive walls and remains of dwellings.

Location:
Take the C 526 S of Ciudad Rodrigo and branch right just after El Bodón to Fuenteguinaldo, pass through town and follow dirt track for 5.3 km of dust to private farm where site is located. Gate difficult to find in the trees and brush, and may be locked. Inquire in village at pharmacy for owner before going.

Ledesma

Situated on a hill above the river Tormes, the Medieval town may have begun life as a Celtic castro. It was occupied successively by the Romans and the Arabs who were there until 1085, when troops of Alfonso VI pushed them back beyond the river Tajo.

In the town beside the wall is a verraco, which seems to have been brought from somewhere else. Near the Tormes, east of the town, is a menhir removed from a site in a field, west of the town. Also reported on the left side of the road to Golpeja, just before km 1 in a rocky outcropping, are some signs of crosses, horseshoes and other symbols that may date back to prehistoric times.

The Romans seem to have left little here, but the walls are half Roman and half Medieval, and there is a milestone, almost illegible, at the north façade of the Church of Santa Elena. The bridge over the Tormes appears to have been originally Roman, but it was destroyed during the War of Independence and later rebuilt. At one end of it is an old hermitage. There are some remains of reputedly Roman baths near this bridge. There is another Roman bridge outside of the town, the Puente Mocha, somewhat restored, and beside it is part of the ancient road from Ledesma to Zamora.

Sights:
Celtic menhir and verraco, Roman bridge of Mocha, Roman road and remains of ancient baths and walls.

Location:
Approx. 35 km W of Salamanca on SA 300. Puente Mocha is 2 km out of town on the old road to Zamora SA 310, where it crosses the Ribera de Cañeda.

Lumbrales

Iron Age settlement, Las Merchanas, on right bank of river Camaces. Defensive wall, in some places 2 m high, is still preserved along with two portals.

Inside have been found Neolithic axes and millstones, tiles and coins from the Roman Imperial Age. In Lumbrales there are two verracos by the Via Publica.

Sights:
Iron Age settlement, walls and portals, verracos.

Location:
W of Salamanca ca. 70 km on C 517, the town is on the C 517 W of Vitigudino. The site is between Lumbrales and Cerralbo on right bank of river. It requires walking through heavily treed area and brush, and is difficult to find. Inquire in town at Ayuntamiento for a guide.

Salamanca
Once the site of a castro, the village on the river Tormes was occupied by Hannibal in the year 220 B.C. but soon fell into the hands of the Romans. The most obvious ancient sight in the city is the bridge spanning the river Tormes and still used for pedestrian traffic. The half of the bridge nearest the town is Roman, the other half was rebuilt in the seventeenth century after a ruinous flood in 1626. In the centre of the bridge stands a verraco.

There are also remains of the Roman defensive wall that once surrounded the town. The Visigoths left only slight traces of their sojourn in Salamanca in the form of a few artifacts. Conquered by the Arabs, the city was retaken by Christian forces in 1085.

Salamanca: Roman Bridge

Sights:
Roman bridge, walls and verraco.

Location:
In town.

Saldeana
Castillo de Saldeana, isolated and fortified hilltop Celtic castro protected on three sides by the river Yeltes and on the fourth by a wall. Site is nearly 1 km in length, but rather narrow. Inside are the remains of circular and rectangular houses and a large number of stones in disarray. The Romans conquered the town and referred to it as Saltus Dianae, or Sanctuary of Diana, but no temple has yet been definitely identified. Roman inscriptions and coins have been found at the site.

Sights:
Iron Age village, remains of walls and dwellings.

Location:
W of Salamanca on C 517, turn N (left) just beyond Cerralbo on secondary road ca. 8 km. Site is reached by a path 50 m beyond the town (first left), and

continuing on foot for about 2 km through fields and over fences and up the hill. Difficult access.

San Julián de Valmuza

Remains of a Roman villa or possibly a town, at present unexcavated. By scraping back the earth beside the overgrown Roman graves, a mosaic floor can be seen. Here, also, is the entrance to a long underground passage which (reputedly) leads to a neighbouring hill. The site is on a private farm, reached by turning off the main road near an ancient and ruined bridge which may have been Roman (ca. 200 m on left of highway) and which is no longer over a waterway.

Salamanca: San Julián de Valmuza.
Mosaic from Roman Villa (unexcavated)

Sights:

Unexcavated remains of Roman settlement with mosaics and graves. Nearby ancient bridge.

Location:

Take the C 620 from Salamanca toward Ciudad Rodrigo. After km 248, turn left (by ancient, ruined bridge). Follow unpaved road along to private farm 4 km, turning left and fording small stream into farmyard, just after "El Palacio."

Villaseco

Nearly intact dolmen on the ranch called Muelleres, all stones present but entry or passageway stones somewhat dislodged. Reputedly the finest example of a dolmen in the province.

Sight:

Dolmen.

Location:

Follow the C 517 W of Salamanca approx. 44 km. At 4 km W of the hamlet of Villaseco is a stone entrance gate to the ranch on right. Cross over cattle grid and proceed up to farmhouse for directions. One can drive or walk to site across fields from the house, ca. 2 km.

Yecla de Yeltes

Iron Age site, large, impressive hilltop fortified area of stone walls and remains of dwellings, but neglected and very overgrown. Known locally as Yecla la Vieja, the defensive wall in some places is preserved up to 2 m in height. On the Yecla river, the original settlement appears to date back to the Bronze Age. The fortress was conquered by the Romans. A hermitage, Virgen del Castillo, now stands in the middle of it.

Sights:
Iron Age fortified site with remains of walls, dwellings and streets.

Location:
W of Salamanca, take the SA 321 S of Vitigudino to Yelca de Yeltes, ca. 7 km. Site is 1 km beyond town toward Villavieja.

Other ancient sites of interest in the province include **Aldeavieja de Tormes**, dolmen, take the N 630 S from Salamanca and turn E just before Guijuela to Aldeavieja on the Embalse de Santa Teresa. Inquire in village for site. **Herguijuela**, W of Salamanca and S of Ciudad Rodrigo ca. 16 km, nearby walled Chalcolithic site, El Castillo, about a two-hour walk. Inquire in village for directions. **Juzbado**, verraco on private farm of Olmillos on SA 300, Salamanca to Ledesma, ca. 29 km. just after town. **Montemayor del Río**, S of Salamanca and S of Béjar off the N 630 W (right), Roman bridge. **La Peña**, Chalcolithic site with shelters at bottom of an enormous, curious rock outcropping that stands out on the landscape. Artifacts found here but nothing left to see of actual remains. Site located N of Vitigudino, just off the SA 314 ca. 21 km. **Pereña**, continue beyond La Peña approx. 8 km and pass through town and uphill to Nuestra Señora del Castillo, site of many cultures from Chalcolithic to Roman, in a very singular spot near the Arribes of the river Duero and overlooking Portugal. Virtually nothing left to see of the site, but spectacular scenery amidst huge boulders. **Villamayor**, on the C 517 Salamanca to Vitigudino just beyond town remains of dolmen on S (left) side of road between km stones 28 and 29. Poor condition, no stones left standing. **Vitigudino**, Humos de Masueco, reputed to have rupestrian paintings, but very complicated to find. Inquire in town at Ayuntamiento or in La Peña. **Zafrón**, dolmen situated behind church in a field with standing circular stones, but entrance way obliterated. Take C 517 from Salamanca toward Vitigudino.

SEGOVIA

The province is located in the SE part of the region and watered by the Eresma and Cega rivers. The northern area consists of extensive, often pine-covered plains, while the southern part rises to the wooded Sierra de Guadarrama. Although the province is replete with Medieval castles and other sights, there are no longer many ancient sites to be seen, most having been either destroyed or covered over. Cave paintings at Prádena attest to the presence of prehistoric troglodytes in the area but most in situ remains are from Roman times.

Aguilafuente

Excavated Roman villa with visible floor plan and some walls about 0.5 m high and once belonging to a presumably wealthy owner. The site has been neglected for years, and is now somewhat eroded and picked clean.

Sight:
Roman villa.

Location:
N of Segovia and NW of Tuérgano on the SG 222 ca. 12 km. Passing through

Sauguillos de Cabezas toward Aquilafuente site is just before km 10 on the right in a field about 200 m from the road.

Castilnovo
Privately owned castle, reputedly erected by Abd-al-Rahman I and enlarged in later centuries.

Sight:
Alcázar

Location:
NE of Segovia on the N 110 for 25 km and turning off on the SG 233 towards Sepúlveda, castle is E (right) of the crossroads with the C 112.

Duratón
Reputedly Visigothic necropolis across the road from the Romanesque church over the bridge on the edge of the village. There is little to see except some exposed stone coffins and a few tombstones incorporated into the wall behind the church. Capitals in church cloisters contain Visigothic style motifs.

Sights:
Visigothic stone coffins.

Location:
NE of Segovia and a little E of Sepúlveda.

Segovia: Roman Aqueduct

Prádena
Cueva de Prádena, containing cave paintings, is situated a little outside of town on a gentle rise of ground.

Sights:
Rupestrian paintings.

Location:
NE of Segovia on the N 110, signposted. Cave has been closed to the public for alterations. Inquire at the Ayuntamiento in town.

Segovia
Ancient Celtic centre of resistance against the Romans, the town was conquered in 80 B.C. and destroyed. Presumably due to its favourable position, it was rebuilt by the Romans and became an important town on the site of military crossroads. The aqueduct, one of the most outstanding extant monuments of the Roman period, was constructed with uncemented limestone blocks in the second half of the first century. It is about 728 m long, 29 m high and rests on 118 arches.

Under the Arabs, the town was a flourishing textile centre but was repeatedly conquered and reconquered until taken definitively by Alfonso VI in 1079.

Sight:
Roman aqueduct.

Location
In the city.

Of interest also in the province of Segovia is the town of **Coca** with a well-preserved fifteenth-century castle—a masterpiece of Mudéjar work—and the tower of San Nicolas; both constitute fine examples of the Arabic legacy. From Moslem times, the Arco de la Villa, the well-preserved entrance to the city, remains.

Similarly, at **Cuellar**, one of the important centres of Hispano-Arabic architecture, can be found several Mudéjar style churches dating back to the thirteenth century.

Reported in some tourist guides are the now non-existent Visigothic necropoli of **Madrona**—excavated

Segovia: Roman Aqueduct
(courtesy of Bryan Pryce)

in the 1920s—just a little SW of Segovia on N 110, that of **Ventosillo**, ca. 57 km NE of the capital off N 110, and the covered-over Roman villa of Tejeras near **Pedraza**, also NE of Segovia off N 110.

SORIA

High, pine-covered mountains, Picos de Urbión and the Sierra Cebolera, situated in the north of the province, are the source of many streams and rivers including the Duero. To the east looms the Sierra de Moncayo. An elevated plateau forms the centre and rolling hills make up the south. Some parts of the province are arid, others wooded. From Paleolithic times, with finds at Ambrona and Torralba, to the once-important Celto-Roman cities of Numancia and Tiermes, and down to the Arabic castle at Gormaz, the province has much to offer.

The area was home to the Arevacos, Celtic clans who gave so much trouble to the Roman legions by refusing to be submissive. They cost Rome huge expenditures in manpower and money, and caused more than a few Roman youths to dodge the draft for a war in which if the enemy did not kill you, the ice-bound winters or the sizzling hot summers might.

Agreda

Situated on a rocky crag with a ruined castle, the town shows ample signs of Roman and Arabic times. There was also an old Jewish quarter here along the banks of the river Queiles, opposite the Christian community, and on the side of the hill on which the castle stands was a Morería, or Arab quarter. Scene of many battles between Moslems and Christians, the town fell permanently into Christian hands through the efforts of Alfonso El Batallador.

Approx. 15 km to the SE at Muro de Agreda stands a short stretch of a large wall, all that is left of Roman Augustóbriga.

Sights:

Tenth-century Arabic walls and horseshoe arch entrances, Jewish and Arab quarters. Nearby stretch of Roman wall.

Location:

E of Soria 55 km on the N 122. Follow signs in town for Puente Califas. Muro de Agreda requires a turn to the S (right) off N 122 ca. 38 km just after Matalebreras on road to Olvedo. Go 4 km, then turn left. Signposted.

Ambrona y Torralba

Sporadic excavations of Paleolithic sites in the area of the Sierra Ministra east of Medinaceli have been continuing since the turn of the century. Primitive stone tools and animal bones of those killed for food suggest that man may have occupied the area as much as half a million years ago. While there is nothing much for the non-specialist to see at the actual excavations except shallow depressions where the soil has been scooped away in a search for ancient remains, there is a paleontological museum in situ outside Ambrona, displaying, among other things, three hundred thousand-year-old elephant bones and tusks. No human remains have been found, but there is evidence of human habitation at the site.

Sight:

Paleolithic campsite.

Location:

S of Soria off the N 111 and E of Medinaceli. Museum signposted on highway. Take the SO 133 off N 111 S of Medinaceli to Torralba, then N to Ambrona.

Berlanga de Duero

Nearby, in Casillas   de Berlanga, on a hill, stands the eleventh-century Mozarabe church of San Baudelio, which is one of the best of its kind. The strange and altogether surprising inside of the church resembles, on a small scale, the Great Mosque of Córdoba. The main chapel is situated in the apse, reached by five steps and through a horseshoe arch. There are also the faded remains of twelfth-century murals, with Romanesque, religious, Mozarabic and profane themes covering the walls, the traces of the originals which were sold and ended up in places like New York. Some were returned to the Prado Museum in Madrid in 1957. The well-preserved judería extends from the Mirador de las Monjas to the Calle de Jeraiz.

Sights:
Mozarabic hermitage and judería.

Location:
SW of Soria. Go 35 km on N 111 to Almazán, then 28 km W on C 116, then 4 km S on the SO 104 to Berlanga. Continue 8.5 km S of town on the SO 152. Church signposted on highway.

Soria: Berlanga de Duero. San Baudelio.

Burgo de Osma, El

Nearby ancient Uxama was an oppidum of the Arevacos (Celts), with an extensive necropolis of incineration. It participated in the wars of Sertorius and was taken over by the Romans, gaining great importance due to its location on the Via Asturica from Astorga to Zaragoza. Roman excavations are in evidence along the right bank of the River Ucero and on the Cerro Castro. It was the most important town after Clunia in the region. In the Middle Ages, the populace moved down off the hill to the river where the town of Osma was begun.

The city was taken by the Moslems and was repopulated in 912 by Gonzalo Tellez, becoming one of the defensive sites along the river Duero against Moslem attacks. It was finally incorporated into Christian hands in the eleventh century when the Caliphate of Córdoba disintegrated into Taifas. Excavations began in 1976 and have continued off and on until the present.

Sights:
Roman forum, baths, cisterns, water canals, houses, streets, luxury villas. Celtiberian necropolis. Tenth-century Alcázar.

Location:
SW of Soria 56 km on the N 122. Osma is the old part of the town. Just before entering it, between km 216 and 217, take dirt path on right to top of hill.

Cuevas de Soria

Discovered in the second decade of the twentieth century, in the fields near the village of Cuevas de Soria, were the remains of a sumptuous Roman villa. The site was first excavated in 1928–29. The outlines of the walls revealed a large, central patio surrounded by columns, a large living area and on the sides, smaller rooms and passageways. The floors were covered with rich mosaics (polychrome) of complicated and varied geometrical designs, never repeated. The total surface area was 1,400 m^2. Several mosaics were removed to the National Archaeological Museum in Madrid, but the remainder are in place. They have been covered over with sand, but the guard will sweep some away for the appreciative visitor.

The area is to be covered with protective roofings and the mosaics restored (currently bits are missing). Excavations since 1980 have exposed the baths and other structures. The villa appears to date back to the third to fourth centuries, and to have been abandoned in a controlled or non-violent manner. The villa seems to have been superimposed on an earlier structure, perhaps a villa of about 150 to 225 A.D.

The site is by the river, protected by hills which give it its micro-climate conducive to a good growing season. The surrounding area housed an abundant pre-Roman population as, for example, in the northern hills, where the Celtic castro of Izana, excavated decades ago, was located. To the south, much ancient pottery has been found.

Sights:
Mosaics, baths, evidence of walls, columns and central patio.

Location:
Take the SO 100 SW of Soria. Turn right (W) at Quintana Redonda and the villa is 5 km beyond. Signposted.

Gormaz
The castle of Gormaz is situated on a notable hill on the right bank of the Duero. The site has witnessed the passage of numerous cultures, having been first occupied by people near the end of the Bronze Age. According to artifacts from the location, the hill, over 100 m in length, seems to have contained two settlements, one at each end.

This period was followed by a Celtic Iron Age culture and once again it was located at both extremes of the hilltop. The necropolis of Quintanas and the abundance of Celtiberian pottery indicates fairly intensive settlement in this cultural phase. The site seems to have been in use up to the fourth century. The Romans did not occupy the site as far as is known.

In a fold of the hill, the Hermitage of San Miguel has been identified as originally Visigothic. Part of it, as well as the Roman villas that must have been in the area, have been reused in the construction of the Alcázar. The walls of the castle with twenty-one towers and twin keeps, seen from 50 km away, are very dominant on the landscape and make up an impressive advance of the Moslem culture toward the north. The castle was constructed in the tenth century, and its great south portal is an example of the grand architectural style of the Ommiads. Part of the structure is older, and appears to have had additions in

Soria: Gormaz. Caliphal Castle

the tenth century (altered in the thirteenth and fourteenth centuries). It was the largest castle in Western Europe. After 1059, the castle was occupied by Christians and was reputedly handed over to the Cid by Alfonso VI in 1087. Today, after having been used as a prison and later by soldiers in the Carlist Wars, it is an abandoned ruin.

Sights:
Caliphal castle, double horseshoe arch entrance, remains of walls and twenty-four towers, remains of keep, weaponry room, cistern, engraved stones —the centre one Celtiberian, the other two, Arabic

Location:
Take the N 122 SW of Soria 56 km to El Burgo de Osma. Then go S on SO 160 15 km to Gormaz.

Medinaceli
The town is situated on one of the higher hills of the area and the site, in the Ebro valley intersecting the Jalón valley, was strategically located on a natural trade route. It is thought that on a hill nearby was the Celtiberian city of Ocilis, cited by classical historians and conquered by the Romans in 152 B.C. In Roman times, Medinaceli became important as a point on the Via 25 of the itinerary of Antonio that united Mérida and Zaragoza. Traces of this road are said to still remain in the area.

The town was repopulated in 946 by the Arabs under the name of Madinat Salim (hence its modern name), and under Abd-al-Rahman III the walls were rebuilt and the Alcazaba constructed. Christian forces under Alfonso the Battler definitively retook the town in 1123.

Besides excavations in the Plaza Mayor, which reveal an original Bronze Age settlement, a Celtiberian castro, Roman, Arabic and finally a Medieval town,

Soria: Medinaceli. Roman Arch

Roman remains also include a well-preserved triumphal arch, the only one in Spain with three arches, the central one for carts, the two flanking ones for pedestrians.

Sights:
Roman arch, walls (Roman and Arabic), Alcazaba, Arabic gate (Puerta Arabe) and various levels of occupation in the on-going excavations.

Location:
On the N 111 S of Soria 74 km. Monumental part of the city on hill 2.5 km from centre of town.

Numancia

A Celtic city of the Arevacos, Numancia (Roman Numantia) is situated on a knoll above the river Duero (originally a prehistoric site). It resisted Roman domination for years, finally falling to Scipio Aemilianus after a long siege in 133 B.C. The Romans constructed a wall, towers and seven camps around the city and virtually starved it into submission.

Excavations were begun around the beginning of this century. Most of what is visible today belongs to the period of Roman occupation. Not all of the site has been excavated and some has been covered over to protect against deterioration. Nothing is left of the Roman wall of circumvallation, nor of the Roman camps, although they are identified by markers on the surrounding hills. Many of the stones were re-employed to build the nearby church of the Martyrs and other buildings. Similarly, little is left of the town's defensive wall except for some remnants near the entrance to the site.

There are some slight remains of a Roman tower (*atalaya*) ca. 6 km away.

Sights:

Remains of Roman baths, water conduits, dwellings (one with peristyle), streets, cisterns, silos, subterranean rooms, cellars, interior walls and some remains, especially near the entrance, of the exterior wall. Small museum in situ.

Location:

Follow the N 111 N from Soria 7 km to Garray. Site is signposted.

Pedro

Village in the Sierra de las Cabras with a modest stone chapel thought to date back to the seventh century. It is comprised of a single apse of ca. 6 m^2 and a nave of 17 m by a little over 7 m.

Sight:

Visigothic chapel.

Location:

Follow the N 122 W of Soria to San Esteban de Gormaz, then E 4 km. Just before reaching Montejo de Tiermes, take dirt road S (right) to Pedro.

Tiermes

Like Numancia, Termancia was another city of the Arevacos, and of great importance to the Celtic resistance to Roman domination. Excavations have been more or less continuous since 1975 and have turned up many Celtic, but mostly Roman, remains. The aqueduct and the so-called Casa del Acueducto were built in the first and second centuries. Some of the water was carried into the city via a subterranean gallery that contains four cylindrical air shafts to the upper surface. The Casa del Acuaducto consists of a peristyle "impluvium" or rain-water basin, surrounded by dwellings, some with wall murals.

Roman walls date back to the third century. A necropolis was found nearby, beside the river Manzanares. The site seems to have been occupied until the sixth century.

To the west of the city lies the Celtic section which was protected by steep cliffs and walls.

A ruined thirteenth-century Romanesque church is situated on the site.

Sights:

Celto-Roman city with remains of dwellings, walls, aqueduct and water conduits hewn from the rock, tunnel through cliff into the town, necropolis, and museum in situ. There are also caves nearby with traces of rupestrian paintings. Inquire at museum.

Location:

SW of Soria. Follow the N 122 from Soria and turn S (left) at San Esteban de Gormaz toward Montejo de Tiermes. Site well signposted.

Soria: Tiermes. Celto-Roman City

A few other sites of interest in the province are found at **Aldealpozo**, E of Soria ca. 20 km on the N 122, the church has an eleventh-century military tower. **Almarza**, ca. 20 km N of Soria on the N 111, nearby Castro de Zarranzano, small excavated Celtic village, stone base of a round house 6 m in diameter and part of defensive wall. **Caracena**, SW of Soria and ca. 24 km S of El Burgo de Osma, some slight remains of Los Tomos de Caracena, a Bronze Age pastoral settlement once of wood and grass huts and several graves. Little to see; guide recommended.

Fuensaúco ca. 13 km E of Soria and 0.3 km N of the N 122, Celtic village of El Castillejo on a small hill, 0.5 km SE of the town, first excavated in 1928 and in subsequent periods but not a good deal to see. Some remains of dwellings. **Langa de Duero**, Arabic tower above town on the N 122 ca. 86 km SW of Soria. **San Esteban de Gormaz**, site of numerous Christian and Moslem skirmishes, an imposing Alcázar overlooking the town and the church of San Miguel of 1081, one of the earliest known in the province. The town lies on the N 122 69 km SW of Soria.

Soria, Jewish tombstones and inscriptions from the thirteenth century in the monastery of San Juan de Duero on the edge of the city, whose church was constructed in 1134 and which has a unique cloister. **Ucero**, W of Soria and ca. 14 km N of El Burgo de Osma, necropolis of San Martín. Excavations began in 1980 showing burial sites of different phases from the Iron Age to Medieval times. Much was destroyed through ploughing of the land for agricultural purposes. There is little to see.

VALLADOLID

The high, rolling and arid landscape of the province appears not to have been conducive to the needs of prehistoric settlers in spite of the rivers Duero and Pisuerga that cross the land and amalgamate a little SW of Simancas. The region is conspicuous by the absence of Chalcolithic and Bronze Age sites, but with the arrival of the Celts, metal artifacts became much more plentiful.

The Celtic Vacceos were the dominant group in the area but did not long remain in any one settlement, judging from their habitation sites. Nomadic in temperament, two or three generations in any one place seemed to suffice, although in places such as Soto de Medinilla (see below), they constructed long, rectangular adobe houses, produced ceramics and metal objects such as axes, and engaged in agriculture.

According to a text by Diodorus Siculus (d. ca. 21 B.C.), the Celts in this area practised a kind of collective agriculture in which each year the fields were divided by lot between the various families and the common harvest was allotted to each family according to its needs.

Of the over 550 archaeological sites catalogued in the province from prehistorical finds to Medieval times, very few offer anything to see in situ.

Almenara de Adaja

Partially excavated, last time in 1969, neglected remains of a small Roman villa lie on the flat, open, dust-blown plain near the village. There is a large central atrium, rectangular in shape, and two large rooms plus the remains of the triclinium, but not a lot to see except the foundations of these areas. By brushing away the sand on the floor of the rooms, mosaics appear underneath. Some contain vegetable motifs, others swastikas. The sand, of course, should be replaced after viewing. The villa seems to have been abandoned at the beginning of the Germanic invasions.

Sights:
Roman villa and mosaics.

Location:
S of Valladolid off the N 403, 12 km S of Olmedo. Turn W (right) after km 138 ca. 1 km. Site in wheat field about 100 m off road to left coming from Almenara. Rusted-out sign in field locates the site.

Cabezón de Pisuerga

Roman villa of Santa Cruz, situated on the right bank of the river Pisuerga in the Granja (farm) Santa Cruz. The site is approachable over unpaved farm roads to within about 1 km, then on foot through the fields. It contains very little—a vaulted chamber, a bit of wall, and stones in disarray (mosaics and other objects having been removed)—and is heavily overgrown. Recommended only for those with a burning interest.

Sights:
Scant remains of Roman villa.

Location:
For Cabezón, take the signposted road off the Valladolid to Burgos highway. The site is 3 km S of the town. Ask at farmhouse for directions.

San Cebrián de Mazote
The church of San Cebrián de Mazote, ca. 915, is a large, three-nave restored Mozarabic structure with typical wooden roof and horseshoe arches. It has marble columns and most interesting capitals, some from unknown Roman constructions, others of Visigothic or Asturian tradition, not unlike those at Oviedo and Escalada. Still others are of Mozarabic tradition common to the Leonese Mozarabic churches.

Sight:
Mozarabic church.

Location:
W of Valladolid, take the C 611 N from Tordesillas to Torrelobotón, then NW 12.5 km to Mazote on secondary road (or, take the N VI NW from Tordesillas ca. 28.5 km and turn E ca. 5 km to town).

Wamba
The church of Santa María de Wamba is situated in the village and not far from Mazote. It was here that the Visigothic king Recesvinto, leaving his court in Toledo, came to die, and here also his successor, the nobleman Wamba, was elected. The present church was constructed in 928 using material from the earlier Visigothic church in which Recesvinto was buried. Later thirteenth-century restructurings have considerably altered the original. Currently the church is undergoing excavations and restoration and is closed to the public. The excavations in the courtyard and under the building have revealed human remains, possibly of the Visigothic period.

Sight:
Mozarabic church of the tenth century.

Location:
Follow the N 601 NW from Valladolid a short distance and turn W (left) on the VA 514 to Wamba about 18 km from the capital.

Valladolid: Wamba.
Santa María de Wamba. Tomb

Sites reported in some tourist books include **San Pedro de Latarce**, site of a Roman camp and bridge NW of Valladolid and ca. 40 km NW of Tordesillas off the N VI. The bridge has been demolished and replaced with a modern one, and outlines of the camp can only be seen with a good deal of imagination. Roman stones are incorporated in the wall of the castle there. **Soto de Medinilla**, outside of Valladolid, ca. 3 km on secondary road to Cabezón to the NE and on the bank of the river Pisuerga on a farm, is reputedly the most important Iron Age site in the province. It is, however, under 2 m of earth, having been excavated and re-covered. Owner will show some ceramics and Iron Age tools recovered there subsequently. Similarly, the Visigothic cemetery of **Boecillo**, a little S of Valladolid on the N 403, is now under a wheat field, and the Iron Age and Roman remains reported in the vicinity of **Simancas**, 11 km SW of Valladolid on the N 620, are no longer to be found. At **Tordesillas**, ca. 30 km SW of Valladolid on the N 620, is the one-time palace, now the convent of Santa Cruz, which preserves examples of pure Mudéjar style architecture.

ZAMORA

Watered by the river Duero flowing from east to west across the southern portion and the tributaries of the Esla and Tera from the north, the province, bordering Portugal on the west, exhibits a great contrast between the eastern plains and the western mountains. Occupied by Celtic peoples, the area formed part of the Cultura de los Verracos.

Of the various archaeologial sites in the province few offer much to see in situ. The Romans left a legacy of roads and bridges, the Visigoths a church, and although the river Duero formed for a time the boundary between Moslems and Christians, Arabic influence in the area was weak and short-lived.

Benavente

There are two Roman bridges near the town; one is on the right just before entering on the N VI coming from Madrid. It was once an impressive structure of five spans of which only three, in poor condition, remain. The west end of the bridge has been totally obliterated by modern highway construction. The heavily overgrown ruin is now located a little west of the river Esla over which it once stood.

Another small bridge of one arch is over the river Eria just off the C 620 beside the modern bridge. It is just below the National Parador, from which it may be seen.

Sights:
Roman bridges.

Location;
On the outskirts of Benavente.

Zamora: Benavente. Roman Bridge

Campillo

Visigothic church, San Pedro de la Nave, moved to present location in 1930–32 from nearby area flooded by waters of a dam. Built in the shape of a cross it is an exceptional seventh-century (somewhat restored) church containing noteworthy capitals inside. In the NW corner of the cross they depict Daniel in the lions' den, and in the SW corner they show the sacrifice of Isaac.

Sight:
Visigothic church.

Location:
Follow the C 620 from Zamora toward Orense. At ca. 12 km turn N (right) toward Campillo. Well signposted but rough road for 10 km. The key to the church can be obtained in the hamlet.

Puebla de Sanabria

Roman bridge alongside the modern one upon entering town, with five spans over the river Tera. It is still used for pedestrian traffic.

Sight:
Roman bridge.

Location:
NW of Zamora and W of Benavente off the N 525.

Toro

A verraco guards the entrance to the town from the E and stands as silent testimony to the ancient Celtic (Vacceo) town of Albocela, on a bluff over the river Duero. To the west of the Colegiata, begun in 1160, stood the old judería or Jewish quarter.

Sights:
Verraco, Jewish quarter.

Location:
E of Zamora ca. 33 km on the N 122.

Fermoselle, SW of Zamora on the C 527 ca. 61 km, may also be of interest with its Hermitage of Santo Cristo del Pino which preserves a small window with two arches from the Visigothic or Mozarabic epochs. The city of **Zamora** has a Jewish inscription in the wall near the Plaza de Santa Ana, N of the city centre. There are also several eleventh- and twelfth-century churches, some of which are rebuilt older temples, such as Santa María la Nueva and San Cipriano (built in 1025 but many times remodeled); Santa María la Nueva of the twelfth century appears to date back originally to the seventh century, but little is preserved from either period.

CATALUNA

The region comprises four provinces: Barcelona, Gerona, Lérida and Tarragona, stretching from the Pyrenees southward along the Mediterranean to Castellón de la Plana. The area is watered by numerous streams but the principal rivers are the Ebro, the Segre and the Cinca, all of which attracted early settlements. The name of the province seems to derive from the period of Visigothic influence when the area was called Gothalania.

Cataluña has always been one of the principal gateways into Spain from Europe and trade along its coasts has been active since Greek times. The area contains numerous archaeological sites from all epochs. There are, for example, about fifty-five known caves and grottos with rupestrian art in the region, with many of these in the area of Ulldecona and elsewhere in the province of Tarragona.

The presence of Neanderthal man has been found in Cataluña at Bañolas, and Upper Paleolithic remains of man are known from various cave sites such as those at Seriña in the province of Gerona. Cardial pottery and other artifacts found in caves on Montserrat show the presence of Neolithic cultures.

The northern coasts of the region embrace Greek settlements, extensions of those found in Southern France, the most important having been at Ampurias or Greek Emporión (Catalán Empúries).

Urnfields are found all through the area, consisting of cemeteries of a uniform nature in which the ashes of the dead were deposited in ceramic urns and sometimes protected with an overlay of stones (but not true monuments) and dating back to about the ninth century B.C., representing the first Indo-European penetrations into the peninsula.

Some of the best-preserved Iberian remains in the country are located at Ullastret in the the province of Gerona, but their ancient settlements are found throughout the region.

The Romans first arrived in Cataluña in 218 B.C. and left their presence in the form of villas and towns and necropli as they did elsewhere on the peninsula, with the most interesting remains at Emporión, at Tarragona, and Olérdola, the latter in the province of Barcelona.

Churches and other remains of Visigothic times may be seen in this Catalán region, and due to the lack of Moslem enthusiasm for the solitary and often snow-bound Pyrenean valleys and their relatively short-lived domination of Cataluña, Early Christian churches and monasteries flourished. Many of their ruins are still there to visit.

With the tenth and eleventh centuries a new style of architecture, the Romanesque, common to much of Europe, entered the region and made itself at home.

BARCELONA

The province consists of pine-covered hills, rugged coasts and some fertile plains. The mountain masses of Montseny north of the capital, and that of the formidable Montserrat to the northeast where there is evidence of Neolithic communities, provided defensible settlements for early inhabitants, as did the hills along the Mediterranean coast. The province was home to Iberian tribes such as the Layetani in the vicinity of the present-day capital and there is substantial evidence of many Iberian settlements in the hills around the Llobregat Delta. The landscape then was somewhat different from today's as, just south of the capital around Castelldefels, the sea reached almost to the hills where now there is a wide stretch of flat land.

After 218 B.C. numerous Roman villas were established which were not unlike the current Catalán *masias*—country houses where a family (with slaves in Roman times) lived, dedicated to agricultural endeavours. In the Baix Llobregat are relics of many such villas: one in Viladecans and another in Papiol produced amphorae for commerical purposes. There is little left to see of these enterprises, however.

For a long while during the Middle Ages, the Macizo de Garraf south of Barcelona was a no-man's land between the Franks and the Arabs.

Arenys del Mar

Nearby Iberian settlement, designated by the name Torre dels Encantats, has been known since 1881 but has not been systematically excavated. The site pertained to the Layetani and still visible are parts of a wall that enclosed the settlement and nearby towers, all of which are on private property. Arrangements for a visit can be made at the Ayuntamiento.

Sights:
Iberian wall and towers.

Location:
38 km NE of Barcelona on the coastal route N 11.

Badalona
Roman settlement of Baetula of second to fourth century B.C. The Iberian town of the Layetani that must have been in the area with the name Baitolo (according to Iberian coin legends) has not been found. On the Puntigal, a cliff W of town, is a carved inscription to Apollo.

Sights:
Roman baths, tabernae, rock-cut inscription.

Location:
NE of Barcelona on the N 11. Excavations on outskirts of town.

Barcelona
The city is situated on a plain between the Llobregat and Besós rivers and lies between the mountains and the sea. According to tradition it was founded by Carthaginians in the third century B.C. and supposedly derives its name from the founder, Hamilcar Barca. There was an earlier Iberian settlement at the site.

During the time of Augustus, the town became the Roman colony of Barcino, and four columns of a Corinthian temple dedicated to Augustus still remain inside the headquarters of the Centro Excursionista de Cataluña. Destroyed by the Franks in 263, the town was retaken by the Romans and defended by a 10 m-high wall with numerous towers. It appears to have been constructed in great haste using anything at hand including works of art, pieces of which have been found in excavations. By this time the town had mostly replaced Tarragona as the capital of Hispania Citerior. In 415 the Visigoths captured it and made it their headquarters for a time. Conquered by the Arabs in 713, it was retaken by troops of Charlemagne in 801. From 874, the Counts of Barcelona were independent rulers of the city.

Sights:
Columns of Roman temple, Late Roman walls, and behind the cathedral subterranean galleries with extensive remains of the Roman and Visigothic town. Excavations are on-going including a fourth-century Christian basilica. On the outskirts of the city are three churches of Visigothic style thought to have been constructed before the ninth century. Slight remains of judería in old centre of the city documented in ninth century, along with Hebrew inscription in the wall of the quarter.

Location:
In and around the city.

Other Iberian sites around the city with some excavations but not a lot to see include: **Sardanyola del Valles**, at Turo de Can Oliver, 12 km N of Barcelona and 5 km NW of Puig Castellar, excavations in the 1920s. **San Just Desvern**, Penya del Moro, 10 km NW of Barcelona and 2 km north of the town, excavations since 1972, thriving Iberian town of the Layetani; here, as at Ullastret, activity was begun in the sixth century and ended around the end of the third or beginning of the second century B.C. Greek imported ceramics were found in abundance. **Sant Vicenç de Horta**, 5 km W of the Penya de Moro and 12 km W of Barcelona, the Iberian settlement is found on the hill of Puig Castellar NW of the city near the bank of the river Llobregat and over the bridge of Molins de Rei. Some excavation in 1957 and 1962 uncovered rich pottery finds dating to a relatively short period (150–50 B.C.).

Cabrera de Mar

The Iberian site of Iluro (oppidum) lies on the S side of the mountain range at the foot of the village of Castillo de Burriac. It was an unusual, tiered town facing the sea some 4 km away and formed a large triangle, the tip of which clings to the crest of a hill, now occupied by a Medieval castle. The eastern wall still stands. After Ullastret this walled site was the most technically advanced, and was apparently influenced by the builders of Ullastret. The name of the town on Iberian coin legends was Ilturo. The inhabitants belonged to the Layetani tribe. Excavation began in 1885. According to ceramic material the site was occupied from the sixth century to the beginning of the first century B.C. Greek vases here date to the third century B.C.

Sights:

Remains of Iberian wall, dwellings and streets.

Location:

Approximately 25 km NW from Barcelona on coastal road N 11 and 3 km inland from Mataró.

Caldas de Montbuy (Montbui)

Roman town with large, well-preserved, impressive and partially reconstructed baths beside the spa.

Sights:

Roman baths.

Location

NW of Barcelona on the B 143, baths signposted.

Barcelona: Caldas de Montbuy. Roman baths

Castelldefels

The castle and the pre-Romanesque church on the hill above the once-incipient agricultural village of Castelldefels were constructed in the tenth century. Both have undergone restoration in 1990.

Sights:
Tenth-century church and castle.

Location:
Approximately 20 km SW of Barcelona on the C 246.

Garriga, La

Remains of small Roman villa adjacent to the highway on the farm of Can Terrés, neglected and overgrown. The villa is small, with a dozen or so rooms and remains of walls, large and small baths and stone steps leading down into them.

The twelfth-century Church of Santa María del Camí contains Visigothic motifs on the doorway.

In the area there is also a Roman mosaic in a field in Can Pericas on the road S of town, just past the Romanesque church of San Andrea de Sanalus. In the vicinity is the Early Christian Church of Sant Cristofol.

Sights:
Roman villa with remains of rooms, walls, baths, stone steps; mosaic; churches with Visigothic elements.

Location:
On N 152 N of Barcelona ca. 20 km. Once at La Garriga, go on road out of town toward Granollers and between km 34 and 35 on E side of road are remains of a Roman villa, part of private farm of Can Terrés.

On W side of road is the house, and the church of Santa María del Camí is adjacent. Ask permission to enter (owners are usually there on weekdays). Sant Cristofol is reached by taking the road of the Empresa SATI. Ask for the Camino de Sant Cristofol (this is a very bad road).

Manresa

Roman mausoleum, Torre del Breny, at San Vicenç de Castellet just S of Manresa in suburb beside railway track. Splendid structure, well-preserved, fenced but clearly visible. Part of roof missing. Two internal chambers.

Barcelona: Manresa. San Vicenç de Horta. Torre de Breny. Roman mausoleum

There are also many dolmens in this area but they are difficult to find. For more information inquire at Centre d'estudis del Bages, Museu Comarcal de Manresa.

Sight:
Roman mausoleum.

Location:
NW of Barcelona on C 1411, 10 km beyond Montserrat.

Martorell

Roman humpback bridge, Pont del Diable, over the river Llobregat, restored in 1768, blown up during the civil war, rebuilt and used today as a pedestrian crossing. Triumphal arch at end of bridge.

Sights:
Roman bridge and triumphal arch.

Location:
NW of Barcelona ca. 24 km on A 7 to exit 25, or follow the N 11. Bridge signposted.

Mataró

Impressive Roman remains enclosed in covered building, open in winter 11.00–14.00 h and in summer (June–Sept.) 17.00–20.00 h.

Sights:
Roman villa with mosaics, basilica and tower.

Location:
27 km NE of Barcelona on coastal N 11. Site is on left before entering town.

Olérdola

Large Ibero-Roman wall of the second century B.C. and Medieval walls of the ninth and tenth centuries, as well as a ninth-century Mozarabic chapel. Systematic excavations began in 1921. The hilltop site appears to go back to prehistoric times but its development as a town came with the Romans. It was abandoned also during Roman times (Pax Romana) when the inhabitants moved to the valleys. It was repopulated in the Middle Ages, but was destroyed during the Moslem invasions of the region in the early twelfth century. Much of the site has been restored since the 1920s.

Sights:
Remains of Roman towers, walls, large cistern, necropolis, ninth-century chapel. Small museum in situ.

Location:
Follow coastal road C 246 SW of Barcelona to Sitges 43 km, take B 211 ca. 11 km to Olérdola. Alternatively follow the A 7 (motorway) to Vilafranca del Pinedès and from there take B 211 ca. 10 km to site.

Roda de Ter

Iberian and Medieval settlements of L'Esquerda, where systematic excavations began in 1977. From hand-made and grooved ceramics the site has been dated back to the eighth to seventh centuries B.C. after which it was abandoned. In the fourth century B.C. the settlement was refortified with a 6 m-thick wall. At the end of the third century the site was again abandoned and the wall and dwellings were destroyed. During the second to first centuries B.C. it was repopulated and another wall built (the one seen today) and utilized by later Medieval inhabitants. Then it was once again abandoned. Not a good deal is known about this latter occupation of the site, since much of it was effaced through agricultural use. According to documents the remains of the settlement were employed again in the ninth century (826) when the Carolingian Franks fortified key areas of the river Ter against the advancing Arabs. Since wood was used for the fortifications, there is little archaeological evidence from this period. From the tenth century there are references to a church and a necropolis of anthropomorphic tombs hewn from the rock. These can be seen today. Much of the visible remains are from this period. The settlement was again abandoned in the thirteenth century when the inhabitants moved to the new, more convenient site of Roda de Ter.

Sights:
Some Iberian remnants, walls and dwellings, Medieval necropolis and remains of dwellings.

Location:
N of Barcelona ca. 87 km and NE of Vic on the C 153 ca. 9 km. Site is on the meander of the river Ter as it passes through Roda.

San Cugat del Valles

The town is on the site of Castrum Octavianum of the Roman epoch. The Benedictine Abbey of San Cugat is thought to be one of the oldest in the country and said to have been founded by Charlemagne or Louis le Débonair. Here also are the recently discovered remains of a small Visigothic basilica.

Sights:
Reputedly ninth-century Benedictine abbey (but much altered), and Visigothic remains of a church.

Location:
10 km N of Barcelona beyond Tibidabo.

Santa Coloma de Gramanet

An Iberian site lies on the left bank of the river Besos on the 300 m-high Puig Castellar, Ceramic finds indicate a thriving town in the third to second centuries B.C.

Sights:
Iberian settlement, remains of dwellings and walls.

Location:
9 km N of Barcelona and across motorway from Badalona, suburb of the city.

Terrassa (Tarrasa)

Ancient Egara, Early Christian Medieval church complex of Sant Pere (sixth to seventh century); church of Santa María has ninth-century apse and a tenth-century painted stone retablo, octagonal baptistry and floor mosaics. The church of San Miguel, originally built before the year 450, was reconstructed in the ninth century. The marble columns of the baptistry have some Roman capitals. The churches have been much altered in later years.

Roman bridge (rebuilt) leading over the gorge to the ecclesiastical complex.

Sights:

Pre-ninth century Visigothic-style churches. Roman bridge.

Location:

N of Barcelona ca. 22 km on N 150 (or on Motorway) Signposted in town as "Conjunt Medieval."

Vallgorguina

Small but well-preserved dolmen, seven standing stones and capstone in place, no gallery entrance.

Sight:

Dolmen.

Location:

Take exit 11 off motorway N of Barcelona toward Arenys de Mar. Just before km 13 is a sign for dolmen on right. Follow unpaved road 1.5 km, then walk to top of small hill on left.

Vich

The town rests on an Iberian settlement of the Ausetani, taken over first by the Romans and later by the Visigoths. The Arabs destroyed it and for about a century the town was abandoned. It was repopulated in 878. The restored Roman temple in town was built around the beginning of the second century, but for hundreds of years its existence was not known as it was surrounded by and formed part of the castle of Montcadas, constructed in the eleventh century. The walls of the temple made up the interior patio of the castle.

For anyone who desires an interesting walk, a special route has been mapped out from the Cathedral in Vich, past the Roman temple ending at the eleventh-century monastery of Sant Pere de Casserres some 18 km away. Besides an eleventh-century Romanesque church en route and very scenic countryside, the trail passes several archaeological sites. In front of the hermitage of Sant Jordi, 3.9 km from town stands the dolmen of Puigseslloses and further on at 10 km are remains of an Iberian settlement. Nearby is the hermitage of Sant Feliuet, with a tenth-century nave (reconstructed in the twelfth century). An itinerary can be obtained from the tourist office in the Plaza Mayor.

Sights:

Restored Roman temple and other sites (dolmen, Iberian settlement, churches) outside of town.

Location:

N of Barcelona 67 km on the N 152.

Other sites in the province include **Collbató**, NW of Barcelona off the N 11, ca. 13 km NW of Martorell near foot of Montserrat, Iberian settlement of Les Soleies. It is situated 3 km N of the town on the slope of the mountain. **Moià**, N of Barcelona ca. 40 km on the B 143 prehistoric habitation sites in the vicinity such as the Cova del Toll, Cova de les Teixoneres, Cova de Fontscalents and about thirty-five more which have been excavated and ceramics and artifacts removed. Little to see. In the area are also to be found various dolmens but most are in a poor state of preservaton, some completly destroyed. One of the better preserved dolmens is located at **Puig Rodó** N of the town.

Further sites in the vicinity include **L'Estany**, with megalithic tombs, N of Barcelona to Moià (see above), then 9 km N on secondary road. **Mura** N of Barcelona to Terrassa, then N on secondary road ca. 20 km. with a pre-Romanesque church of Marquet (Santa María de Matadars). **Pedret**, NW of Barcelona and 3 km NE of Berga off the C 1411, small Mozarabe church of the tenth century, once covered with murals. **Sallent**, N of Barcelona on C 1411 (ca. 13 km N of Manresa) with Iberian ruins. For details and locations inquire at the Museo Arqueológico y Paleontológico in Moià. **San Pere de Ribes**, 5 km N of Sitges on B 211, tenth century castle. **Tiana**, NE of Barcelona and NW of Badalona on secondary road, Roman villa some parts of which were occupied until the fifth century but now somewhat covered over by a Medieval farm-house; not much to see. **Vilanova de Sau**, N of Barcelona on N 152 and E of Vich on the N 141, Upper Paleolithic settlement, situated at foot of large cliff, ca. 11,500 years old, with on-going excavation. Currently closed to public. Inquire at Ayuntamiento. **Villanueva y Geltrú**, W of Barcelona on C 246 and 8 km W of Sitges on the coast has some excavations of the Greco-Roman site of Darró.

GERONA

The province lies among the foothills of the Pyrenees, bordering the Mediterranean and France. This fertile area of mountain streams, volcanic soil and defensible heights was coveted by ancient peoples. The discovery of an ancient human jaw bone (now in the Archaelogical Museum of Bañolas) in 1887 in the vicinity of Lake Bañolas indicates man's presence in the area around one hundred thousand years ago. The fossilized remains of elephants, hippopotami and long toothed tigers have also been unearthed in the area dating back to a little over one million years ago.

In the northwestern section of the province, specifically around Olot in the Garrotxa district, cylindrical cones of now extinct volcanic activity rise above the valley floors.

There are numerous dolmens in the area attesting to Neolithic and Bronze Age cultures, but most are difficult to find in the dense growth of the mountain sides.

On the coast at Emporión is the only example so far in Spain of a Greek urban settlement, although others are suspected from literary sources and may still be found. At Rosas, for example, there may be the remains of a Greek town or trading post under the Roman and later remains of the Ciudadela.

Gerona is also a land of Early Christian churches and monasteries built during the Moslem occupation of the south.

Bañolas

The town grew up around the monastery of Saint Esteve, founded in 815 by Benedictine monks who came across the mountains with Charlemagne's troops. In Porqueres (on W bank of lake), a suburb of Bañolas, are the remains of a ninth-century castle on private property opposite the twelfth-century Romanesque church of Santa María. It is mentioned in tourist literature but is, at least at the present time, not available for viewing. Church is well worth a visit.

At Pujarno, 5 km S of Porqueres, near the Roman villa of Vilauba, is a large dolmen but difficult to find without a guide. The modest peristyle villa of Vilauba, discovered in 1932, currently under excavation, alongside the road (fenced off), has remains of walls and dwellings, and pink concrete floors. The villa appears to have been in operation from the first to seventh centuries. In the area are also a few remains of an eighth-century convent on the hill above the lookout point (or "mirador") overlooking the lake.

Sights:
Remains of dolmen, Roman villa, eighth-century convent and ninth-century castle.

Location:
Bañolas lies on the C 150, 16 km NW of Gerona. For more information to sites inquire at the Archaeoogical Museum in town.

Besalú

Small Medieval town with fine Romanesque buildings, many from the twelfth century, and restored bridge, although the town dates back to Iberian times according to ceramic finds.

There was once a Hebrew community in the town whose presence can be noted in the Miqwah or Jewish baths of the eleventh century. Rectangular in plan, situated on the left bank of the river Fluviá, the structure is unique in Spain. It had running water from the river and a thermal spring which has long

since disappeared . Restoration began in 1964. It is known that Besalú also had a synagogue but its location has not been established.

Sights:
Jewish baths.

Location:
NW of Gerona ca. 30 km on the C 150.

Gerona: Besalú. Jewish baths

Caldas de Malavella

The spa town was known in Roman times by the name Aquis Vocontis. A water-bottling plant has utilized part of the Roman wall of the ancient baths for its own use, but site is undergoing some restoration. Subterranean vaults were recently closed to the public. Both the pool, measuring 4.75 m by 4.4 m, and its descending stone steps, are well preserved. Beside the sanctuary of San Mauricio there are some slight remains of a Roman fortress.

Sights:
Roman baths, pool, walls and subterranean chambers, remnants of fortress.

Location:
S of Gerona on the N 11 16 km, then E 3 km on GE 673 to town. Signposted.

Emporión

The monuments at this excellent site come from three different epochs: Iberian, Greek and Roman. Of the original Iberian settlement little is known, but Greeks and Romans left their indelible mark dating back to nearly 600 B.C., when the first Aegean traders arrived and developed a small commercial port. During the fifth century B.C., no doubt due to increased trade, the colony grew into a city. During the fourth century its prosperity and independence is evident in the fact that the city minted its own silver coins with the legend EM. In the conflict between Carthage and Rome the city of Emporión sided with the latter. It was here the Romans landed the legions in 218 B.C. to interdict Hannibal's supply lines, and here they consolidated their power until the rise of the new city of Tarraco (Tarragona) placed them in a more advanced position. Greek independence gave way to Romanization as settlers followed the soldiers to the new land.

During the latter part of the first century B.C. and the early part of the following century the city achieved its greatest splendour, which coincided

Gerona: Emporión. Roman mosaic

with agricultural expansion in the hinterland to which the Romans contributed through the establishment of rustic villas.

The city declined in the second century and was nearly abandoned by the end of the third. (According to Strabo the first nucleus of Greek population was on an island, the Paleapolis, just offshore from the present site, now a small rise in the land where San Martí d'Empúries, to give the Catalán name, now stands.)

Sights:

There are about thirty sights here. Some of them are: Greek gate, alley, tower, and guardhouse, (fourth century B.C.), remains of dwellings, forum, agora or public square, capitoline temple, port and south Roman gate, amphitheatre, palaestra or gymnasium, cyclopean wall, cisterns, Greek market with arcades (second century B.C.) and other walls, jetty, necropolis, mosaics, one with Greek inscription, precinct of temple of Zeus-Serapis (first century B.C.), commercial taverns, salting plant, cryptoporticus (second century), temples, roads, baths, Paleo-Christian church (fifth to seventh centuries), statues, and museum in situ.

Location:

N of Gerona on A 7/N 11 to exit 5; 16 km E to La Escala. Signposted.

Gerona

Roman Gerunda, the city appears to have been of Iberian origin as the town walls seem to be of part-Iberian as well as Roman construction. During the Moslem domination it was temporarily recaptured by Charlemagne in 785. Beside the high altar in the church of San Feliú, are Roman and Paleo-Christian sarcophagi and nearby are the so-called Arab baths (twelfth-century Mudéjar). Remains of the interesting judería are W and SW of the cathedral.

Sights:

Roman and perhaps Iberian town walls and Roman and Paleo-Christian sarcophagi. Judería.

Location:

In town.

Jonquera, La

Many dolmens are situated in the area, but many have also been destroyed while others are difficult to find (a few are marked by name and an arrow pointing in their direction). Most notable and easy to find are dolmens of E'an Boleta (group of three) and C'an Nadal. For more information on local dolmens and guide inquire at Bar Tomás in the main square of Cantallops.

Sights:

Dolmens.

Location:

N of Gerona on the A 7 or N 11. Go S of town on N 11 ca. 1 km, turn E (left) for Cantallops ca. 3.5 km and watch for sign (right) for dolmens.

Lloret de Mar

At Puig de Castellet is a small, third-century B.C. Iberian fortified hilltop town in the middle of an urban development, excavated but unattended. Gate ajar.

Sights:

Iberian fortified settlement, remains of dwellings, walls, stone-cut steps.

Location:
Coastal town S of Gerona on the GE 682. In town follow road up behind football stadium to Avenida Puig de Castellet and the urbanization of Roca Grossa. Take left fork and continue to top of hill, ca. 1 km. Signposted at site.

Pontós

Surface finds have suggested a large Iberian town and excavations are scheduled beginning in summer of 1990. The site is on a private farm but will eventually be opened to public. Meanwhile, owner is pleased to show visitors some of the artifacts from area stored on his estate. (Some excavation took place in 1974, exposing a little of the ancient wall, but site re-covered.) The ceramic finds here, as at Ullastret, place the town between the sixth and second centuries B.C. A quantity of Greek wares have been dated to the fourth century B.C. The site lies on an ancient road from France to Tarragona.

Sight:
Iberian settlement.

Location:
Take the N 11 N of Gerona ca. 23 km (12 km S of Figueras) and turn W (left) on secondary road marked for Pontós, ca 3 km. From town proceed 2.5 km to stone cross on left side of road and electrical hut on right. Take gravel road on right to farm.

Romanya de la Selva

Megalithic tomb of about 2000 B.C., Cova d'en Dayna on the slopes of the Sierra de les Cavarres. The dolmen stands within an outer ring of about 40 standing stones. Excellent specimen.

Sight:
Dolmen.

Location:
SE of Gerona on C 250 to just past Llagostera, then NE on secondary road to Romanya. Dolmen beside road and signposted.

Rosas

The city occupies the site of of the Greek colony of Rhodes. La Ciudadella, at the entrance to the town, once a fortified monastery constructed in 1022 and blown up by the French in 1814, preserves some ancient structures.

Sights:
Some Late Roman buildings.

Location:
NE of Gerona and E of Figueras on C 260 ca. 17 km.

Santa Pau

Attractive Medieval town and castle in midst of volcanic craters with nearby ninth-century Sanctuarios dels Arcs, a shabby, unkempt building with dingy bar, swimming pool and lodgings. Rather a disappointment. Near the monastery, 800 m E in a field, stands a menhir.

Sights:
Ninth-century monastery and ancient menhir.

Location:
NW of Gerona and W of Bañolas on GE 524 ca. 24 km. Just before entering town ca.1 km, menhir is on right and can be seen from road and monastery, signposted, is just beyond on left, down unpaved road.

Sant Juliá de Boada.
Small pre-Romanesque single-nave church, somewhat restored. Keys to church may be obtained from adjacent farmhouse.

Sight:
Visigothic style church.

Location:
E of Gerona and N of Palafrugell on the GE 651 go W on GE 650, 3 km to village. Signposted on road.

Gerona: Sant Juliá de Boada

Seriña (Serinya)
Near the village is an ongoing excavation of a Neolithic site and necropolis, Coves del Reclau. Enclosed behind fence and under roof, little can be seen from outside; key may be obtained in Bañolas but visits only for groups.

Sight:
Neolithic site.

Location:
NW of Gerona, and N of Bañolas 6 km on C 150, ca. 1 km before entering town Bar les Covas is on right, go ca. 200 m up dirt road by bar parallel with highway. Site on left hidden among the trees.

Tossa de Mar
Large Roman villa complex, Els Ametllers or Villa Vitalis, with mosaics and bath area visible, owned by Vitalis who had his name and portrait preserved on a mosaic at the entrance to the public rooms. The inscription reads "SALVO VITALE/ felix turissa." It is situated across the street from the Casa de la Cultura on the side of a hill. Unattended.

Sights:
Remains of Roman villa with mosaics, baths, dwellings.
Location:
SE of Gerona on C 250 to San Feliu, then S along coast 23 km.

Ullastret
Remains of Iberian town situated on the Puig de Sant Andreu. It is the best preserved in the region. Situated on a knoll above an ancient (now dry) lake, it lies in an area of rolling hills 10 km from the sea and 14 km from Emporión. Its cyclopean defensive walls and towers, rectangular foundations of houses, silos, cisterns bored out of bedrock, and its gate offer an absorbing impression of Iberian life. Activity in the town probably enjoyed its greatest splendour during the latter years of the fifth century B.C. but in the fourth century much of it was destroyed by fire. Decline set in during the third century B.C. and the town was abandoned soon after. Iberian inscriptions and Greek graffiti were found here datable from the fourth to third centuries B.C. Systematic excavation of the site was begun in 1947 and many of the important finds are located in a small museum in situ. The name of this city of the Indika tribe is unknown. The site has been sporadically occupied since Upper Paleolithic times.

Sights:
Remains of Iberian town, defensive walls, gate, dwellings, streets, cisterns, silos, small museum in situ.

Location:
E of Gerona on C 255 16 km, then GE 642 to Serra de Daró and the GE 644 to Ullastret. Signposted.

Some other sites in the province include: **Camprodón**, restored monastic church of San Pedro, tenth century, NE of Ripoll on the C 151. **Castellfollit de la Roca** on the C 150 NW of Gerona, scant remains of Roman bridge. **Oix**, take the C 150 NW of Gerona and turn N (right) 9 km just before entering Castellfollit de la Roca. Very winding and narrow road from highway to village. Upon entering Oix over stream, single span humpback bridge is on the right, neglected but charming, reputed to be from Roman epoch. **Palafrugell**, E of Gerona on C 255 37 km, remains of Arabic castle. **Palamós**, El Castell, Iberian village, unkempt, nearly totally destroyed with a few remnants of walls and floors of houses on cone-shaped hill adjacent to the sea. E of Gerona on coastal road and N of San Feliu 12 km. On the C 255 toward Palamós from Palafrugell, go E on small road, signposted for Playa Castell and Benelux camping (ca. 2 km from Palamós). At fork take right-hand road to beach. Site about 500 m N from parking area. **Ripoll**, NW of Gerona on the C 150 or N of Vich on the N 152. Benedictine monastery founded in 888, consecrated in 935 and rebuilt after fire in 1835. **San Feliu de Guixoles**, Benedictine monastery with some tenth-century towers and Porta Ferrada, built on site of fifth-century Christian edifice of which there are only remnants. SE of Gerona 36 km to coast on C 250.

Near **San Julia de Ramis**, a little NW of Gerona are supposed to be the remains of a Neolithic necropolis, La Cova de les Goges, and an Iberian settlement. **Sant Aniol**, NW of Gerona and Bañolas over poor road, reputedly ninth-century church. **Vilarblareix**, S of Gerona 8 km on autoroute, exit 7; Roman mausoleum in poor repair.

LÉRIDA (LLEIDA)

The province extends from the fertile plains of the southern portion northward deep into the most rustic and mountainous area of the Pyrenees to the French border. The principal rivers are the Segre, which flows through the capital, and the Cinca further west. They join SW of the city and flow into the great Ebro river.

Lérida is the ancient territory of the Iberian Ilergetes and their two leaders, Indibil and Mandonio, who rose in revolt against the Romans in 205 B.C. The legions put down the uprising and tightened their occupation of the southern and central areas of the province, but the Romans had little use for the mountainous north where their monuments are almost non-existent.

The area fell to the Arabs in A.D. 714 and became the petty Moslem kingdom of Lareda. Christian liberation arrived in 1149 in the form of Ramón Berengar IV of Barcelona. During the time of the Moslem occupation a number of Early Christian churches and monasteries were constructed in the high and remote Pyrenees valleys, snow-bound and isolated for many months of the year.

Cogul

About 0.5 km from the town on the banks of the little Set river is situated the so-called Cueva de los Moros, discovered in 1908. The unique paintings and seven engravings of this rock shelter or abrigo display forty-five black and red figures, both animal and human, including what appears to be a phallic dance in which ten female figures dance around a tumescent male. It is thought the shelter served as a sanctuary or a site for sacred rituals for many centuries, judging from the paintings of a later (Bronze age) epoch, beside the older ones and Iberian and first-century B.C. Roman inscriptions. There is now unfortunately little to see. The pigments of the paintings have faded considerably, mostly through abuse in the past few decades. In one case, an archaeologist hacked out niches in the rock wall of the shelter to support scaffolding to better view the paintings near the ceiling. The site is now behind a locked gate, and the visitor should inquire at the Ayuntamiento of Cogul for the guardian of the paintings in order to enter. A replica of the scenes has been produced on a stone face outside the cave.

Nearby are the Iberian rock-cut tombs of Saladar, consisting of rectangular and rounded graves. They are not easy to find and may require some searching around rocky crags.

Sights:

Rupestrian paintings, Iberian and Roman inscriptions and Iberian tombs.

Location:

21 km S of Lérida, follow the L 7020 from Lérida to Artesa de Lérida 10 km and continue on the LV 7021 11 km S to Cogul. Site 0.5 km from town, signposted. Iberian tombs 1.2 km further on same road among rocky hills on the left.

Lérida (Lleida)

Ancient Iltirda, the city was the major settlement of the Ilergetes, an Iberian tribe. The town was taken in 49 B.C. by Julius Caesar, who defeated Pompey's generals Afranius and Petreius there.

Sights:

Roman foundations of bridge over the river Segre and the castle of Zuda, an old fortress of Arabic origin with square towers.

Location:

In town.

Serós

The basilica of Bobalà and surrounding ecclesiastical complex was violently destroyed in the second half of the eighth century during Moslem civil wars against the authority of Córdoba, according to artifacts and charred remains found at the site. Utilizing much more wood in their construction than was the case in later times, the buildings were already some four hundred years old when the complex was destroyed. It seems to have been partially resettled for a short time after the fire and apparent sacking. Inside and around the church are numerous Paleo-Christian and Visigothic graves and sarcophagi. Almost nothing was found in the graves, since the practice at the time was to be buried in only a simple sheet with no adornments, in order to appear poor and humble before the Almighty.

The site was a military camp during the civil war of 1936-39 and was further ruined by trenches and shelling. Covered over by natural causes and completely forgotten until this century, it has great importance for the cultural history of the period in both the artifacts and the physical remains of buildings and tombs of a rural, pre-Visigothic village. Excavations were begun in 1943.

In the vicinity of Serós are reputedly two prehis-

Lérida: Serós. Bobalá. Paleo-Christian complex

toric necropoli, one excavated (Roques de Sant Formatge), the other not. There are also the remains of an Iberian tower called Torre dels Moros or d'Algorfa, built with cyclopean blocks of stone.

Also of interest is the convent of Avinganga founded by Saint Joan de Mata of the Order of the Holy Trinity for the purpose of redemption of Christians who were captive in Moslem territory. The church, situated 2 km from Serós on the banks of the river Segre, was constructed in 1202 and abandoned in 1835. It is in a poor state of repair.

Sights:

Remains of ecclesiastical complex including Paleo-Christian and Visigothic basilica, dwellings, walls and necropolis.

Location:

SW of Lérida 23 km and SE of Fraga, the town is situated on the C 242. Continue past town toward Maials. 2 km, cross bridge over the river Segre and turn immediately E (left) on unpaved road ca. 0.5 km. Site on left on the left bank of the river behind chain link fence.

Solsona

Near the town (Roman Setelix) was an Iberian mint whose coins carried the legend *iltir'kesken* ("of the Iberian tribe Ilergetes"). Directly S of the town is the high ground of Castellvell in the area of the farmstead Sotaterra, on which an Ibero-Roman settlement was excavated in 1923–24. Ceramic finds indicate an occupation date of the fourth to second centuries B.C. Iberian graffiti and Campanian ceramics were also discovered in the area.

Sights:

Iberian site, Roman baths, pool and sewer system.

Location:

NE of Lérida on the C 1313 to Basella 84 km, then E on L 301 25 km to Solsona. Inquire at Ayuntamiento for details and locations.

Soses

Iberian hilltop site known as Gegut, with some remains of dwellings and cisterns, but not a lot to see. Under excavation. Marked, but unexcavated Roman villa is located at the base of a neighbouring hill. There is a nearby Medieval site currently (1990) under excavation called locally La Farmacia dels Moros.

Sights:

Iberian settlement, unexcavated Roman villa and Medieval village.

Location:

SW of Lérida ca. 20 km between Soses and Serós on gravel road. S of town 3 km along the river Cinca. All sites are situated on cliff side of road, whose heights can be reached by dirt track through orchards. Ca. 400 m you will reach site of the Roman villa and 200 m further is the Iberian site on top of the next hill. Signposted.

Tournabous

Iberian town, Moli d'Espigol, site with on-going excavations. Ceramic finds around the area indicate settlements from the Late Bronze Age to Visigothic times. The site has been known for many decades and was for a time used as a quarry for construction in town. The Iberian settlement was only one in a long succession here. It thrived between the fourth and second centuries B.C. but many of the structures were ruined through ploughing.

Sights:
Iberian settlement, remains of dwellings, defensive walls, water conduits, streets and stone-cut steps.

Location:
E of Lérida 44 km on the N 11, then N 10 km on C 148. Site just outside of town ca. 0.6 km on unpaved road. Easily accessible, but fenced. Ask for keys at the Ayuntamiento in town.

Route of early churches, N of Lérida and SE of Vielha, on C 147: San Pére del Burgel, located at **Escaló**, cross bridge and proceed down road parallel with river, then follow pathway up hill taking left fork at split, remains of eleventh-century monastery with remnants of ninth-century church. Santa María d'Aneu, at **Unarr**e near Esterri d'Aneu, cross bridge and take right fork in road, then turn right again. Church on private land but

Lérida: Escaló. San Pére del Burgal

signposted. Parts of church reputedly of the ninth century, but structure primarily Romanesque. San Joan d'Isil, situated off C 147 on small road going N of **Sorpe**, original ninth-century church situated close to river.

Other sites in the province are located at **Ager**, take C 1313 28 km N of Lérida and go a further 35 km N of Balaguer on the L 904, remains of Roman wall. **Agramunt**, 15 km N of Tárrega which is 44 km NE of Lérida on N 11, Plaque with Jewish inscription on the Ateneo. **Albesa**, ca. 16 km N of Lérida on secondary road, Roman villa of Romeral. **Almenar**, 25 km N of Lérida on the N 230, Alcázar. **Balaguer**, Caliphal fortress of the ninth century, but used up to the fourteenth by the Counts of Urgell. Little remains of the ninth-century structure. Approx. 28 km NE of Lérida on the C 1313. From the hilltop site one can see the

Lérida: Sorpe. San Joan d'Isil

privately-owned castle of La Rápita, also once an Arabic stronghold. **Calaf**, E of Lérida on N 11 to Cerveral 56 km, then NE on N 141 26 km, ruins of Alcázar. **Coll de Nargo**, NW of Lérida on the C 1313 and 28 km from Seo de Urgell, pre-Romanesque church. **Isona**, NW of Lérida and E of Tremp 19 km, scant sections of a Roman wall. **Llanera**, NE of Lérida and S of Solsona, large megalithic tomb embedded in hill, cap stone in place and stones forming right side of passage way standing. **Margalef**, village on the S rim of the Pla d'Urgell SE of Lérida on the N 240 toward Tarragona, nearby Iberian settlement with foundations of dwellings and a street, ceramic fragments date the occupancy of the site from the fourth to second centuries B.C. **Os de Balaguer**, ca. 19 km N of Balaguer on the L 904, naturalistic and schematic rock art in poor condition. **Rubio**, vestiges of an Iberian settlement, NE of Lérida on the C 1313 ca. 129 km to Adrall, then W (left) on the C 146 ca. 30 km. **San Cerní**, N of Lérida on C 147 and a little SE of Tremp on secondary road, three dolmens in the vicinity but all in poor condition. **Sarroca**, S of Lérida on the C 242 ca.12 km remains of Alcázar. **Sidamón (Sidamunt)**, situated 18 km E of Lérida on the N 11, has nearby remains of Iberian settlement, excavated in 1915. Some architectural remains, but not much. Ceramic finds of imported pottery date back to the fourth to second centuries B.C. About 100 B.C. the settlement was abandoned. **Tremp**, N of Lérida on the C 147 approx. 86 km, ninth-century parish church. **Viella**, directly N of Lérida near the French border; the church of Gausach contains a Roman stele.

TARRAGONA

The most southerly area of Cataluña, the coastal flatlands are backed by ridges of mountains running more or less parallel the length of the province. The Ebro river flows through the mountain valleys to issue into the Mediterranean southeast of the capital, where it has formed through the millenia a large delta.

The province contains abundant rock shelters and caves in the mountainous areas with prehistoric paintings but many are difficult to find without guides and often entail a full-day excursion. Similarly, Iberian settlements are numerous here, but once again many are in difficult locations from the point of view of accessibilty. Generally, Roman remains are accessible, and the province has numerous sites, with most of the best situated in and around the capital.

Alcanar
Small hilltop Iberian settlement of the seventh to second centuries B.C. Arabic tower in town.

Sights:
Iberian settlement, remains of defensive walls and dwellings. Arabic tower.

Location:
SW of Tarrgaona on the coastal N 340 or the A 7 motorway. Take road from town 5 km NW toward Ulldecana and turn off to the right on gravel road marked for Ermita del Remedio 0.5 km. Follow path from hermitage leading to top of hill ca. 100 m. Iberian settlement marked at pathway.

Arco de Bará

Not a town but a site, the Arco de Bará is a second-century Roman triumphal arch 12.28 m in height with a span of 5 m and four fluted pilastres on either face. It was built during the reign of the Emperor Trajan, in the year 107, and was damaged during the civil war but later restored.

Sight:
Roman triumphal arch.

Location:
On right of the N 340 going from Vendrell (ca. 8 km) to Tarragona (ca. 20 km).

Constantí

Nearby is the so-called Mausoleo de Centcelles (restored), of great artistic interest, especially the mosaics in the vaulted ceilings with biblical scenes such as Daniel in the lions' den and Jonah and the whale.

Sights:
Remains of fourth- to fifth-century villa complex including mosaics and mausoleum.

Location:
5 km NW of Tarragona, well signposted.

Fontcaldes

Remains of a small Iberian kiln on the edge of the village. Site excavated and enclosed, must be viewed through small, barred window. It is on private property but owner amenable. Not much to see. Arches over furnaces have disappeared. The Iberian settlement that must have been in the vicinity has not been found.

Sight:
Iberian kiln.

Location:
N of Tarragona on the N 240 ca. 22 km.

Perelló

Nearby rock paintings from Neolithic times at Cabra Feixet. Paintings of goat, deer, detail of a deer's head, and a man are in fair to poor condition.

Sights:
Rupestrian paintings.

Location:
SW of Tarragona on the N 340 and NE of Tortosa ca. 18 km. From where C 235 joins the N 340. Site is signposted on road. Ca. 12 km to site but road deteriorates badly the last few kilometres.

Tarragona

Roman Tarraco (a name adopted from an earlier Iberian toponym), by the river Francoli, was occupied by the Romans and extends out from a 70 m-high hill where they established a base in the year 218 B.C. In 45 B.C. the city was elevated to the status of a colony by Julius Caesar. In the upper part of the city 1000 m of Roman wall are preserved, constructed on a base that may have been Iberian. On the archaeological walk around the old walled and fortified perimeter, the visitor can see much of the remains of the imperial city. In the lower part of town, in the Roman-Christian necropolis, discovered in 1923, is a fourth-century basilica with three naves, semi-circular apse, mosaic floors and over one thousand tombs.

Tarragona: Roman aqueduct

The Roman theatre lies below the hill near the beach, and the well - preserved aqueduct (Acueducto de les Ferreres, known locally as Puente del Diablo) 4 km away in the hinterland behind the town and thought to have been constructed during the time of Trajan, is a work of superb engineering. It is 217 m long.

The nearby Torre de los Escipiones, a mausoleum of the first or second century A.D. would appear to have little to do with Scipio. It is a square monument almost 9 m high with two badly damaged male figures in high relief and traces of an inscription.

Tarragona: Paleo-Christian necropolis

Christianity appears to have taken root rapidly in ancient Tarraco, and tradition maintains that Saint Paul preached in the city during a stay in Spain. The Paleo-Christian cemetery seems to support the contention of an early and strong base for the belief, and contains burials from luxurious sarcophagi to modest tombs made of tiles and amphorae in which children were buried.

Sights:
Cyclopean walls enclosing old city, remains of Roman forum mostly still buried under the town, theatre, amphitheatre, nearby aqueduct, vestiges of circus, Roman gateway and remains of Roman dwellings and streets, Paleo-Christian basilica, Roman-Christian cemetery of the third to seventh centuries, sculptured Paleo-Christian sarcophagus in the cathedral, Torre de los Escipiones (Roman mausoleum), Hebrew inscription near the Plaza de la Seu at No. 6, Escribanias (in the old judería).

Location:
Most sites in town. Torre de los Escipiones is situated 6 km NE of the city on the N 340. To reach the aqueduct, take the N 240 out of Tarragona and immediately after motorway crosses overhead, turn right on dirt track about 0.5 km to aqueduct. (It can be seen from the motorway.)

Tivissa
Iberian settlement of Castellet de Banyoles with spectacular views overlooking the river Ebro. The site is unattended and overgrown, and consists mostly of foundations of dwellings and the stone entrance gate.

There are also rock shelters or abrigos in the vicinity with prehistoric paintings at Barranco Font de la Vilella, but in poor condition. Guide is recommended.

Sights:
Iberian settlement, remains of walls and dwellings, rupestrian paintings.

Location:
Travel SW from Tarragona on the coastal N 340 to Miami Plaja, then W (right) 23 km on the T 304 to Tivissa, site ca. 4 km W of town down dirt track ca. 2 km, signposted. When road splits take right fork. For rupestrian paintings inquire at Ayuntamiento for guide.

Tortosa
Roman Julia Augusta Dertosa, was colonized on the site of an Iberian settlement. There are a few Roman columns on the grounds of the castle. The town remained in Arabic hands until 1148 when it was reconquered by Ramón Berengar IV. It was one of the early towns to be inhabited by Jewish families and a stone inscribed in Latin, Greek and Hebrew indicates their presence there in the eighth century. In the tenth century there were thirty families.

Sights
Some Roman columns, Arabic castle (now parador) and old Jewish quarter. Stone inscription is in the convent of the Dominicans.

Location:
In town.

Ulldecona
Prehistoric rock paintings in three rock shelters (Abrigo de la Esperanza) in the face of the cliff along a pathway requiring a walk of about 300 m and

climbing a ladder at each one. The abrigos are in a row; the first, with two ladders end-to-end, is the most precarious, and this one, along with the second, has very faded and difficult-to-distinguish paintings. The third shelter is the best, with clear paintings of men and animals.

Sights:
Rupestrian paintings.

Location:
SW of Tarragona and S of Tortosa follow the T 331 N from town and just before Les Ventalles take road W (left) leading to Ermità, M. D. de la Pietat. 2 km. Abrigos behind church approx 0.3 km in side of rock cliffs.

Other sites in the province include: **Altafulla**, on the coastal N 340 NE of Tarragona ca. 10 km, remains of a Roman house. **Arbolí**, Cova del Cingle, rock paintings of the Neolithic era, W of Tarragona and 16 km NW of Reus off the C 242. **Batea**, W of Tarragona off the N 420 on the the C 221 ca. 7 km beyond Gandesa, remains of Iberian settlement, Tossal de Moro and Arabic Alcázar. **Caseres**, W of Tarragona just off the N 420, Iberian settlement on hill above town, no road and little to see, i.e., remains of a few dwellings. **Felix**, Alcázar, W of Tarragona on the N 420 ca. 76 km, then N on the N 280. **Miravete**, Alcázar, on the N 420 W of Tarragona ca. 63 km. **El Molar**, near the town are the slight ruins of a Celtic settlement nearly totally destroyed, with only impressions in the ground and a few stones. Evidence of much clandestine digging. W of Tarragona on N 420 to Mora la Nova, then N 5 km to García and take the T 731 to El Molar. **Morera de Montsant**, W of Tarragona in the Serra de Montsant, off the C 242 onto secondary road, remains of Arabic tower. **Pinell de Brai**, El, SW of Tarragona off the N 230 after Tortosa and just before Gandesa onto the secondary T 324, Iberian settlement by the Ermita de Santa Magdalena and Arabic tower. **Rojals**, N of Tarragona on the N 420 and a little S of L'Espluga de Francolí, rupestrian paintings of the Neolithic period. **Sant Jaume dels Domenys**, NE of Tarragona and N of Vendrell on the secondary T 212, slight remains of Roman aqueduct. **Torre de L'Espanyol, La**, W of Tarragona off the T 303 on secondary road E at Vinebre. Roman fountain. **Vandellos**, Neolithic rock paintings, take the T 304 off motorway at Miami Plaje 23 km S of Tarragona, sites can be reached by automobile over mountain roads, but guide recommended. **Vilarrodona**, N of Tarragona off the A2 at exit 11, Roman mausoleum. **Vinebre**, SW of Tarragona and N of Mora la Nova on the N 230. Go S on road toward Mora 1.5 km to sign for Ermità de San Miguel on left. Follow road to church a few metres beyond which is the site, Iberian settlement, slight remains of dwellings and walls.

EXTREMADURA

In the southwestern region of the country bordering Portugal, Extremadura consists of two provinces; Badajoz and Cáceres. From the northern slopes of the Sierra de Gredos to the southern mountains of the Sierra Morena much of the area consists of arid plains or rolling hills. Extensive cultivation has only come with modern irrigation projects. Badajoz is watered by the Guadiana river and Cáceres by the river Tajo.

The presence of ancient cultures in the region is seen in the remains of dolmens and other finds, and the beginnings of metallurgy are associated with pastoral people or herd-tending societies, rather than agricultural or crop-raising communities.

Much of the area was later occupied by the so-called Lusitanians, whose territory appears to have extended from the Atlantic coasts of central Portugal

well into present-day Spanish Extremadura. (In general terms the area of northern Portugal belonged to the Galaicos and the south to the Tartessians and later Celticos, the latter a people of basically Celtic origin.)

Roman interest in the region centred around agricultural activities, mostly the cultivation of cereals, and administrative control of Lusitania from Augusta Emerita, today, Mérida. (In 27 B.C. Rome partitioned Ulterior Spain into two provinces, Lusitania and Baetica).

Moslems and Jews have left their mark on the quiet towns of the country with the various Alcázars and the towns such as Hervás where the Jewish quarter is still much as it was before the fifteenth century.

BADAJOZ

On the border with Portugal and watered by the Guadiana river, the province is mostly a land of dry rolling hills except where modern irrigation projects are in effect. Among many other sites, the province preserves the ancient Roman city of Augusta Emerita (Mérida), once the capital of Lusitania and now one of the most important and impressive of peninsular Roman towns. Wheat was the most valuable commodity from the area for Rome, and most of the ancient sights date back to Roman Imperial times, but earlier traces of man are present, for example, in the form of prehistoric artifacts and remains of dolmens.

Alange

Modern spa town with an imposing Alcázar captured from the Moslems by the Knights Templars. Below, in the lower part of the town, are well- preserved Roman baths with three circular rooms, each with a cupola, pool and marble steps and still in use today.

Sights:

Roman baths and Alcázar.

Location:

After crossing Roman bridge out of Mérida turn left and follow signs for San Antonio Alange about 18 km to the SE.

Badajoz

Situated on the river Guadiana 6 km E of the Portuguese border and capital of the province, the site dates back to Celtic times, but the in situ remains of the city are predominately of Arabic origin, although prehistoric and Roman artifacts are found in the vicinity.

The Alcazaba and walls were partially reconstructed after the reconquest in 1229; the eight-sided Atalaya (or Torre de Apéndiz) built by the Almohades is known locally as the Espantaperros. La Galera, an old mosque now the Archaeological Museum, contains some Roman columns and Visigothic capitals.

Sights:

Alcazaba and other Moslem remains.

Location:
In town.

Burguillos de Cerro
A small, modest rectangular church was discovered here in in 1897. In the nave, measuring ca. 11 m by 8.5 m, were found a baptismal bath, flagsones and a small votive Visigothic bronze cross with an inscription relating to an offering to the church. It is assumed that the church functioned in Visigothic times.

Sight:
Early Christian church.

Location:
SW of Badajoz on the C 4311, between Zafra and Jerez de los Caballeros.

Casas de Reina
1.5 km E of town stands a Roman theatre in a field, seats and part of stage area excavated and partially but thoughtlessly restored, with modern-looking steps in seating area. Small excavations behind the theatre have revealed foundations of dwellings. Remnants of stone columns are lying about. The site, known locally as Los Paredones, was used as a stone quarry, leading to the destruction of the wall of the *fons scenae*. Very little is known about the ancient population of the area, although Ptolemy mentioned the town as being in the territory of the Turdetani.

A plausible view maintains that the pre-Roman inhabitants occupied the hill (where the Alcázar now stands), then moved down into the new Roman town, only to revert to the heights later when troubled times began. Evidence for this stems from the remains of a Visigothic basilica, some of whose decorative elements are preserved in the later-built Alcázar.

The construction of the Roman town appears linked to the Roman road

Badajoz: Casas de Reina. Roman theatre

from ancient Mérida through Ecija (Astigi) to Sevilla (Hispalis). The town was situated at the bifurcation of the road (seen from aerial photographs), one in the direction of Ecija the other toward Azuaga, where the Roman town of Regina existed and where a Roman sewer and bit of road have been excavated.

The theatre was situated in the NW section of town and built into the side of a gently sloping hill. It seems to have fallen into disuse in the fourth century. Excavations began in 1978, although a little work was done previously.

On the hill overlooking the Roman site is the ruined Alcázar, with a poor dirt roadway leading up to it. At nearby Llerena are Arabic walls currently under restoration.

Sights:

Roman theatre and ruined Alcázar, Arabic walls.

Location:

SE of Badajoz, continue on the N 432 SE of Zafra, 35 km to Llerena, take the C 432 ca. 6 km SW to town. Continue past town 1.7 km and take dirt road on left toward railroad station (Estación f.c.) 1 km from where monument can be seen. Site is signposted in town.

Jerez de los Caballeros

About 5 km NW of the town is the Dolmen de Toniñuelo, engraved with solar symbols.

Sights:

Dolmen.

Location

S of Badajoz near the junction of the N 435 and the C 4311.

Medellín

Roman Metellinum was named after the Roman consul Metellus Pius in 80 B.C. The town was recaptured from the Arabs by the Knights of the Order of Santiago in 1229. The castle on the hill was constructed after the reconquest. The Roman site is covered by part of the town and castle, showing only a few sections of Roman wall and the incomplete theatre on the W slope below the fortress. The stones of the theatre, which once had the seating capacity for about three thousand, were used in the construction of the castle and the Medieval church of Santiago built over the back of the stage.

Sights:

Remnants of Roman theatre and walls.

Location:

Travelling E from Mérida ca. 50 km on the N V turn S (right) on the C 520 at Santa Amalia and follow signs for Medellín.

Mérida

One of the best-preserved Roman towns in Spain, and once the capital of ancient Lusitania, the city was founded by Publius Carisius in 25 B.C. for Roman veterans of the Hispanic wars. Its size was increased in 69 A.D. with an influx of settlers from Rome. A remarkable feature is the survival of its extensive stone-constructed drainage system under the modern town, which was laid out in the typical Roman grid-iron plan, divided into regular blocks (*insulae*). The populace enjoyed a large circus, amphitheatre and theatre, still well-preserved. Of great interest also is the temple in the middle of town, dedicated to the worship of the emperor.

Situated on the river Guadiana, the Roman bridge into Mérida is still used today. During the Visigothic period the town continued to flourish, but fell to the Moslems in 713. In 1220 it came back into Christian hands, reconquered by Alfonso IX of León.

Nearby are further Roman remains at Lago Proserpina, a Roman dam with possible remains of seats along bulkheads, for spectators of water sports.

Sights:

Roman: theatre, amphitheatre, villas, columbarium, house of Mithradates, Trajan's arch, circus, bridge over Guadiana river (792 m, some arches rebuilt in 686), bridge over river Albarregas

Badajoz: Mérida. Roman theatre

with Roman foundations (125 m), temple dedicated to emperor (mistakenly to Diana) and a temple to Serepis (remains only), aqueduct "los milagros," aqueduct "San Lazaro," dam at Lago Proserpina, wall along river at Alcazaba.

Paleo- and Early Christian: church of Santa Eulalia (Visigothic capitals in nave, Roman material in porch, rebuilt in thirteenth century), remains of basilica and graves, Visigothic columns and relics in national parador, Visigothic cistern in the Alcazaba.

Arabic: Alcazaba (from Roman to Visigothic to Arabic), new aqueduct dates from Arabic times.

Location:

Mérida is E of Badajoz on the N V/E 4 62 km. All sights are in or around the city and signposted. Lago Proserpina is 10 km NW of the town (signposted). Pantano Cornalvo, 10 km NE of Mérida on the river Albarregas is also reputedly of Roman origin. Signposted.

Badajoz: Mérida.
Detail of Roman theatre

Santos de Maimona, Los

Roman Segeda Angurina, a hilltop Roman fort dating from the time of Trajan.

Sights:
Roman fort with remains of walls and cisterns.

Location:
S of Mérida on E (left) side of road where the N 630 and the N 435 intersect. Can be seen from highway. No path up recently reforested hillside.

Badajoz: Zalamea de la Serena

Zalamea de la Serena

Roman tomb situated under two exceedingly high columns which dominate the town. The tallest one is made even taller by a stork's nest. It is located in the Plaza Mayor. There are also some Roman pilastres and columns incorporated into the tower of the parochial church which appear to have come from a previous Roman temple.

Sights:
Roman mausoleum and other architectural remains.

Location
Take the N V E from Mérida 33 km to Santa Amalia, then S on C 520 15 km to Don Benito. Continue ca. 32.5 km on BA 624 to Quintana de la Serena and then follow BA 632 to Zalamea de la Serena.

Other historical sites in the province include: **Albuquerque**, N of Badajoz on C 530 ca. 46 km, 2 km W of which are rupestrian paintings at Risco de San Blas. **Fuente de Cantos**, take the N 432 from Badajoz to 7 km beyond Zafra, follow the N 630 S for 18.5 km, a Roman hilltop site containing remains of houses but difficult to find and easy to get lost among maze of often deeply rutted farm roads, about a 0.5 km walk to top of hill. Inquire at Ayuntamiento. **Medina de los Torres**, take the N 342 SE from Badajoz to Zafra and go S on secondary road, 10 km, Alcázar. **Montemolín**, follow the N 432 SE from Badajoz to 7 km past Zafra then go 18.5 km S on the N 630 to Fuente de Cantos, then SE on secondary road 14 km, Alcázar. **San Pedro de Mérida**, village 15 km E of Mérida on the N V, remains of modest church built ca. A.D. 600. **Zafra**, 79 km SE of Badajoz on N 432, Alcázar, disfigured by later construction, now a parador.

CACERES

The verdant Sierra de Gredos mountains lie to the NE, and to the N are the Sierra de Gata. The central and southern parts of the province are generally arid, except along the water courses and where modern irrigation projects have been established. Traces of prehistoric man are found in the area (such as the rock paintings of La Cueva de Maltravieso), as are remains of later Celtic peoples and the ubiquitous Romans.

Alcántara

Roman Norba Caesares, (Arabic Al-Kantara) has nearby one of the most spectacular examples of Roman bridges preserved throughout the Empire. Constructed entirely of granite blocks without the use of mortar, it spans the Tajo river and is 194 m long, 8 m wide and with six arches (these measurements differ with every account). It stands ca. 60 m above the river and is still used for traffic. The bridge, partially rebuilt, was constructed in A.D. 105 by the architect Caius Iulius. In the centre is a triumphal arch to Trajan, and a small temple dedicated to the emperor stands at the end of the bridge.

Sights:
Roman bridge, triumphal arch and temple.

Location:
Site about 50 km NW of Cáceres. Take the N 521 W of Cáceres ca. 12 km and turn off N (right) on the C 523 to Alcántara.

Cáceres: Alcántara. Roman bridge

Alconétar

Impressive ruined second-century Roman bridge, once 290 m long, less than half of which is still standing.

Sight:
Roman bridge.

Location:
N of Cáceres 40 km on the N 630, signposted on road at site.

Aldeanueva del Camino

Steeply arched Roman bridge in the middle of the village, a few metres from the main square. The town was originally situated on the Camino de la Plata.

Sight:
Small Roman bridge.

Location:
N of Cáceres on the N 630 from Plasencia to Béjar. Turn off at km 438.

Baños de Montemayor

Just a little N of town, beside the highway, on the right hand side going N are the remains of a Roman road. Paving stones are clearly visible and there is a commemorative plaque.

Sight:
Stretch of Roman road.

Location:
N of Plasencia on the N 630 between km 425 and 426 and just before the Salamanca provincial boundary.

Cáceres el Viejo

Site of Roman camp built during the Sertorian Wars in A.D. 79 by Q. Cecilius Metellus and often mentioned in guide books. The configuration of the camp shows up well in aerial photographs but the visitor on the ground finds precious little to see: a small water reservoir and a few stones. The site, on private property, was excavated and covered over.

Sights:
Scarcely discernible outlines of a Roman encampment.

Location:
Approx 3.5 km N of city of Cáceres on road to Torrejón el Rubio on left of road. Farmhouse on site.

Cáceres

Originally a Celtic settlement occupied by the Romans in 54 B.C. under the name of Colonia Norbensis Caesarina, but with the Moslem occupation in the ninth century it became Al-Cazires. Disputed by various factions, the defenses of the city were in a constant state of renovation. The monumental or old section of the town preserves walls whose fundamental structures are of Roman origin, but which were largely reconstructed by the Almohades. In 1170 the city was retaken and later incorporated into the Christian kingdom of León.

The old and once-important judería has disapppeared, but was located between El Arco de Cristo and La Casa de las Veletas. The hermitage of San Antonio was constructed on the site of the synagogue.

Sights:
Roman and Moslem walls, Roman statue of the goddess Ceres in the Torre del Bujaco (or Reloj), Torre del Postigo and Torre Redonda of Almohade construction on Celto-Roman base, Arco de Cristo, a Roman portal and Casa de Veletas, former Moslem Alcázar, now Archaeological Museum.

Location:
In the old section of the city, i.e. Recinto Antiguo.

Cáparra

Ruins of the Roman city of Capera on the Camino de la Plata with four-sided arch (double arch) with inscription, one of two in existence (the other one in North Africa). Near the arch, which stands at the entrance to the unexcavated town, are some slight remains of the defensive wall and the Roman road.

Adjacent to the site is the *finca* (farm) Casablanca, a private ranch. One corner of the farmhouse is supported by a Roman pillar and other relics of Roman times are inside, such as a statue, milliarium and inscriptions (one in honour of Nero) and a Roman block for chopping off heads. Inquire of owner. Nearby is the small, unobtrusive Roman bridge over the river Amboz.

Sights:

Four-sided arch Roman arch and various Roman artifacts at farmhouse, Roman bridge.

Location:

From the N 630 N from Cáceres turn W (left) 18 km beyond Plasencia and continue 4 km, site marked.

Cáceres: Cáparra. Roman arch

Coria

The ancient Celtic settlement of Caura, Roman Caurium, has a well-preserved Roman wall of granite blocks, 8 m thick and 480 m long, and four gates, flanked by towers, leading into the old part of city. For a while the town was a centre of resistance against Rome under Viriathus and his Lusitanian followers. It prospered under the Visigoths, and during Moslem domination in the ninth century it became the capital of an independent kingdom. During the reign of Alfonso VIII it fell back into Christian hands. Below town is an old bridge on Roman foundations. The castle was constructed in the twelfth century.

Sights:

Roman wall (one of the best preserved in the country), portals and bridge.

Location:

68 km N of Cáceres, turn N (left) of the N 630 at Alconétar onto the C 526 for Coria.

Hervás

Situated in the NW section of town is the picturesque, well-preserved Jewish quarter, with typical narrow streets, hanging flower pots and plaque in Hebrew. At the bottom of the main street stands a Roman bridge, of one arch, which is still used.

Sights:
Jewish quarter and Roman bridge.

Location:
3 km off the N 630 E (right) N of Cáceres and N of Plasencia, signposted on highway.

Cáceres: Hervás. Jewish quarter

Segura de Toro

In the centre of the village is a Celtic verraco and a Roman capital, and just before entering the village down a dirt road off to the right 1.3 km is a small Roman bridge over the river Eljas along with remains of the ancient road.

Sights:
Verraco, Roman capital, Roman bridge and stretch of road.

Location:
Off the N 630 N of Cáceres turn E (right) at km 438 after Aldeanueva, 4.5 km along road to village.

Trujillo

The Roman and Arabic town reverted to Christian rule in the thirteenth century. The eleventh-century castle, constructed on the site of a Roman fortress, retains rectangular Arabic towers, and W of it is a restored Arabic cistern. Behind the pharmacy at no. 14 Calle Tiendas stood the old Synagogue, part of the entrance to which may be seen on request. Behind the Puerta de San Andrés is a public bath from the time of Augustus.

Sights:
Roman public bath, Arabic and Jewish remains.

Location:
E of Cáceres 49 km on the N 521.

Valencia de Alcántara

Situated on the Portuguese border with thirteenth-century Alcázar. There are reputedly some remains of the Roman city Julia Contrasta in the vicinity. Over the Peje stream stands the remains of a Roman aqueduct.

Sights:

Roman aqueduct and Alcázar.

Location:

Follow the C 521 W and then the C 523 NW of Cáceres, approx. 100 km.

Other sites in the province include: **Bohonal de Ibor**, nearby six Corinthian columns of a portico on the banks of the Embalse de Valdecañas, removed from the submerged ruins of Roman Talavera la Vieja when site was flooded by a dam. E of Cáceres take the CC 713 S (right) off the N V 3.5 km beyond Navalmoral. **Cañaveral** on the N 630 ca. 45 km N of Cáceres, Moslem tower. **Galisteo**, turn W 8 km S of Plasencia off the N 630, Arabic walls and castle. **Ibahernando**, SE of Cáceres and S of Trujillo, ca. 16 km on secondary road off the N V, nearby ruins of Visigothic basilica and necropolis recently discovered, inquire in town.

Note that the mountainous region just south of Béjar (Salamanca) en route to Plasencia (Cáceres) and traversed by a Roman road was once well endowed with Roman towns and spas, and many of the ancient bridges still stand. The town of Plasencia, site of Roman Dulcis Placida, is shown on some maps as having a Roman aqueduct. The town was completely destroyed by the Arabs and resettled in the twelfth century and fortified. Some of these fortifications are still standing. There is also an aqueduct, but it is from the Medieval period.

GALICIA

The NW corner of Spain is made up of four provinces: La Coruña, Lugo, Orense and Pontevedra. In spite of periods of glaciation, northwestern Spain appears to have enjoyed an oceanic climate, permitting a stable population throughout the quaternary. Paleolithic artifacts have been found in abundance along the river Miño, from Tuy to its mouth at La Guarda, as well as in other localities. Neolithic and Chalcolithic artifacts are more common, many from burial sites such as megalithic tombs. The Neolithic period lasted longer in Galicia than in many other parts of the country, and in some respects was continued by the Celts up to the time of the Roman conquest. Celtic villages often became Roman towns and continued their existence into modern times as reflected by onomastics with castro in the name. Metal working was not

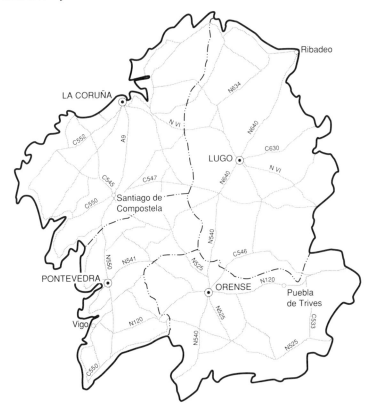

unknown, however, and copper artifacts are known from the Chalcolithic period, along with gold and bronze jewellery from the beginning of the Metal Ages.

The root form of the name of Galicia (Gal-) is related to Celtic names elsewhere such as Gales (Wales) and Gaulia (Gaul), carried to remote places by a people with a common Indo-European language.

The first Roman expedition of conquest in the northwest was that of Decimus Junius Brutus in 138–136 B.C. when, after a military action in Lusitania defeating the rebellious tribes of the Serra da Estrela, he crossed the Limia and Miño rivers and turned inland, ravaging the countryside. Resistance to Roman occupation nevertheless continued until 26 B.C.

The Romans were not slow in developing a system of communications to facilitate their access into the mineral-rich region. One road to Lugo entered the area through Cabreiro from Astorga (which was later much used by the pilgrims to Santiago), a second followed the course of the gold-bearing valley of the river Sil (said to have been the Klondike of the Roman Empire), and a third opened a route along the lower Miño river and followed the contour of the rías through Pontevedra. Important bridges along the routes are in some cases still intact, such as El Puente Pedriña, much of the foundations of the Puente de Bibey, and the large bridge at Orense. Nor were the Romans slack in exploiting the mineral waters of settlements such as Lugo, Burgos de Orense and Caldas de Cuntis. They walled their important towns (as seen at Lugo,) established sanctuaries or temples such as at Santa Eulalia de Bóveda, and built the great lighthouse at La Coruña for their maritime commerce. They left behind cemeteries like the one recently discovered at Orense, and many coins and inscriptions throughout the region.

The rejection of the Celtic and Roman gods and the introduction of the new religion spread rapidly throughout the northwest. Oftentimes churches were built on the site of a castro, which demonstrated the triumph of Christianity over the pagan cults. Widely accepted also was the doctrine of Priscillian, a Galician Bishop of Avila. Priscillianism endured from the fourth to the sixth centuries before the heretical doctrine was extirpated. The period coincided with the presence of the the Swabians, the Germanic tribe who ruled the region for 176 years from 409 until they were defeated in battle by the Visigoths in 585.

The Moslem invasion of the country spent itself before reaching Galicia, but the area was under constant threat from Arabs and the seafaring Normans who attacked and sacked the coasts in 967. In 997 the great Moslem general al-Mansur, using the Roman roads along the Rías Bajas, attacked and burned Santiago de Compostela before retiring. The town had for two hundred years before been the sanctuary of Santiago (Saint James), whose bones were allegedly discovered here. His appearance, at least in spirit, and his nickname Matamoros, "Moor Killer," were a great unifying force for the poor and hard-pressed Christian communities in northern Spain, and brought much-needed capital from beyond the Pyrenees by an endless procession of pilgrims.

CORUNA, LA

The capital of the province, La Coruña, is the largest town in Galicia, but perhaps the best known is Santiago de Compostela because of its long-standing association with Saint James and the end of the journey to his shrine for millions of pilgrims over the centuries. It was also the site of a pre-Roman Celtic castro, later a Roman camp and finally a Swabian settlement, and many of the remains attesting to these earlier stages have been found under the cathedral. With the alleged discovery of the bones of the Saint early in the ninth century the backwater town rose to special prominence—special enough at any rate for the Arab, al-Mansur, to boldly sack it.

Prehistoric artifacts and megalithic constructions, mostly in the form of dolmens, clearly indicate the existence of cultures dating back to the Neolithic or Bronze Age and before, but not until the Romans is there some record of events and places. Ancient geographers made reference to the Brigantinos, a branch of the Artabros, a Celtic people who lived along the coasts of La Coruña and who maintained commercial relations with Tartessos in Andalucía.

Baroña

Impressive remains of a Celtic village with round and rectangular houses and gateways. It is situated on a rocky promontory above the sea and is partially reconstructed. Its defences lie with the sea on one side and stout stone walls on the other. Across the peninsula from Baroña is the castro of Neixón, which is partially excavated and contains round houses.

La Coruña: Baroña. Celtic castro

Sights:

Castro de Baroña and Castro de Neixón.

Location:

Take the C 550 from Noia to just past Baroña. Site is signposted by restaurant "O Castro." Walk down to beach ca. 0.5 km. Neixón is near Reboredo on the C 500, almost directly across from Baroña on the peninsula.

Coruña, La

The lighthouse called the Tower of Hercules was constructed by Sevius Lupus from Aeminium (Coimbra). It stands 34 m high on a lonely bluff at the

La Coruña: Torre de Hercules

northern edge of the city. The present façade was built in the late eighteenth century, but it encloses most of its Roman predecessor, which was a three-storey central square block surrounded by a ramp which wound around it and which, in turn, was enclosed by an outer wall. Nothing remains of the great lantern. The lighthouse appears to have been modeled on the one at Alexandria and is now a unique monument.

Immediately S of the city is the partially excavated site of the Castro de Elvina, with remains of dwellings, which was occupied until the second century.

Sights:
Roman lighthouse and Celtic castro.

Location:
The lighthouse is in the northern sector of the city, while the castro is on the road to Feans, SW of the city.

Laxe
Partially excavated dolmen. A good specimen, but the viewer is disappointingly kept at a distance by the surrounding fence.

Sight:
Dolmen.

Location:
From Santiago de Compostela, proceed NW on the C 545 to Borneiro (just before Laxe), pass through town to crossroads and turn W (left)1 km, signposted.

Ribeira
The immediate approach to the dolmen de Axeitus is marked by upright stones on either side of the short trail, but pathway is currently somewhat overgrown. Dolmen is a good example and stands in a small clearing in the woods.

Sight:
Dolmen.

Location:
Take the C 550 from Ribeira toward Noia. At Oleiros dolmen is signposted. Go 1.4 km and turn right, 800 m on unpaved road.

Toques
Tenth-century church of San Antolín de Toques and remains of a monastery lie nearby in peaceful spot on wooded hillside, with Medieval painted walls in church. Key may be obtained from priest in village. Not far away and currently under excavation is the hilltop Celtic settlement or Castro de A Graña with remains of dwellings. In the vicinity also are the remnants of a dolmen, but difficult to find in the rocky hills. Guide recommended.

Sights:
Tenth-century church and monastery, castro and dolmen.

Location:

Turn off the C 547, Santiago to Lugo road at Melide. Toques is signposted. To reach castro, pass through town and turn left at sign which reads A Graña. The castro is on the hill requiring only a short walk of ca. 100 m up slight incline.

Tordoia

The dolmen here, abeit somewhat overgrown, is reputed to be one of the best in Galicia, and is located next to the road with no difficulty of access.

Sight:

Dolmen.

Location:

Take the N 550 N of Santiago to Ordes and go W to Tordoia. Signposted.

Vimianzo

The Celtic site, Castro de Barreiras, lies on the floor of the valley at the far edge of town. Its defensive earthen and stone walls, all that is left, are partially intact but neglected and overgrown. Disappointing site.

Sight:

Celtic castro.

Location:

Follow the C 545 from Santiago to Baio, then head SW on C 552 to village.

Other sites in the province are located at **Betanzos**, the Roman bridge here served the road from Lugo to La Coruña and is at the head of the estuary Ría de Betanzos which is fed by the river Minatos, 23 km SE of La Coruña on N VI in direction of Lugo. **El Ferrols**, NW across the bay from La Coruña, the church of Chamorra, 2 km NW of city, is said to have megalithic remains around it. **Santiago de Compostela**, a Roman and Swabian necropolis is situated beneath the cathedral.

LUGO

There are an estimated fourteen hundred or more archaeological sites in the province, excavated, partially so, or waiting to be excavated. These include ten Paleolithic or Mesolithic rock shelters, dating back before 4000 B.C., mostly in the E and central areas of the province, and around 275 Megalithic necropoli, constructed between 3000 and 1800 B.C. In areas of extensive granite outcroppings about twenty-five complexes of petroglyphs from the Bronze Age have been inventoried, each with numerous drawings, and from the Iron Age 720 castros have been identified, with another 150 relating to the Roman period, that is, the first to fifth centuries A.D. Apart from these sites there are also Roman towns, e.g., Lugo, villas—many still unexcavated—and Roman mines. Early Medieval sites from the seventh to twelfth centuries are still somewhat poorly defined, but include anthropomorphic tombs hewn from the rock, usually in areas of granite formations, such as those near Chantada, and totalling so far about one hundred fifty.

The following are necessarily only a sampling of the better-known and easily accessible places of interest.

Bóveda

Discovered in 1926, the church of Santa Eulalia contains an important archaeological treasure. The building consists of two levels but the bottom part is the best preserved. Here, partly below ground level and beyond the portals whose stones contain reliefs of dancers with garlands, birds, and a scene of two people that seems to show deformities of their extremeties, one enters a rectangular barrel-vaulted room through a horseshoe arch in which there is a natural spring and murals with geometric and zoomorphic themes of vegetables and animals (mostly birds) in red, blue, green and black. These decorative motifs are characteristic of Late Roman art in pictures and mosaics and inspired mural paintings of the Middle Ages.

There seem to have been two main phases of the sanctuary: Late Roman of the fourth to fifth centuries, and seventh to eleventh centuries corresponding to a pagan temple later converted to a Christian one. The monument is unique in all of western Europe, and can be visited any time by advising the custodian in the Casa de Correos almost opposite the site.

Sight:
Roman nymphaeum to Early Christian sanctuary.

Location:
Bóveda is ca. 12 km W of Lugo. Take road to Santiago de Compostela out of Lugo and follow LU 232 in direction of Friol. Signposted.

Cebreiro

✔ The village was known to the pilgims en route to Santiago de Compostela, for here was the famous Mesón-Hospital which, according to some estimates, dates back to 836 when the Benedictine monks built and maintained the church. The pre-Romanesque, ninth-century church, or sanctuary, nearly destroyed by neglect and fire, is now undergoing restoration begun in 1962. The

Lugo: Cebreiro. Palloza

baptistry has a basin for total immersion, which was the usual method up to the thirteenth century. Typical of the village are the Celtic pallozas which have endured with some restoration down to present times. The circular or semi-circular straw-covered houses remain much as they were in former times and one, lived in until recently, is now a museum. The oldest is thought to date back to the seventh century. A curious Iron Age stone plaque, depicting two horses and riders, hangs in the pilgrims' restaurant. (Some scholars have considered the plaque to be from the Bronze Age.)

Sights:
Pallozas, ninth-century church and baptismal font, Iron Age plaque.

Location:
The town of Pedrafita is situated on the border of Lugo and León on the N VI. From here take LU 634 W ca. 4 km to Cebreiro.

Chantada
An early double grave carved out of the flat rock and designed to the contours of the body (anthropomorphic tomb), known locally as the Sepulturas de Fornas.

Sight:
Early Christian double rock-cut tomb.

Location:
18 km SW of Lugo on the N 640 then 39 km S (left) on the N 540. Follow road out of town toward Antas de Ulla. Go exactly 2.6 km from road sign in town. Stop at large rock by right of road and climb bank. Tomb on top of rock.

Fazouro
The Celtic Castro de Fazouro, partially excavated, shows remains of dwellings, walls and steps. The site has been neglected for years and its state of preservation is somewhat precarious.

Sights:
Castro.

Location:
Take the N 640 NW of Lugo to Ribadeo then, W past Foz to Fazouro. Ask for directions in town.

Foz
Constructed in the eighth century, the monastery of San Martíño de Mondoñedo is one of the oldest in the country. The church was the episcopal see from 870 to 1113 but there is little left of the original building, its having undergone numerous restorations. The site has been identified as the Monasterio Máximo of the Swabian epoch (sixth century) but the present Romanesque church primarily dates back to the tenth century. Inside are two seventh-century columns with Visigothic capitals. The first Bishop of San Martíño— from 866 to 877—was Sabarico I, who established the episcopal see. The last was Nuño Alfonso during the years 1112–1136.

Sights:
Early Christian church and monastery.

Location
Follow the N 634 from Mondoñedo toward Foz and turn left to Foz on C 642 and left again at sign for San Martíño. Follow road for ca. 4 km.

Lorenzana

Rebuilt Benedictine convent with the tenth-century tomb of the founder, Osario Gutierrez, and a Paleo-Christian tomb.

Sights:
Benedictine convent and early tomb.

Location:
N of Lugo on N VI to Rábade and take the C 641 ca. 22 km to Villalba; here take the N 634 N ca. 43 km.

Lugo

The city was once a Celtic settlement but gained importance under the Romans, who called it Lucus Augusti. Excavations show the existence of a forum, temple and aqueduct. The well-preserved walls (maintained here and there by supports) were erected in the second century and, unlike many other places, were not destroyed by the Arabs. They are 2,130 m long, 10 m to 15 m high and 4.5 m thick. There were fifty defensive towers and ten portals. Other gates into the city were constructed in later times.

On the ground floor of the Balneario, located beside the river Miño below the walls, the ancient Roman baths with their pools of hot mineral water and vaulted ceilings can be seen. They are behind the first door on the left after entering the building from the parking lot, although alterations over the centuries, poor lighting, and neglected conditions make them somewhat of a disappointment. Under the main staircase of the building are the remains of another room entered through a rounded arch. To the rear of the room is another arch embedded in the wall with faint remnants of paintings. This room was probably the frigidarium or cold baths, which appear to have been converted in a later day to a chapel. A seventeenth-century text cites a chapel or place of prayer in the thermal installations.

Lugo: Roman wall

A few hundred metres away stands an ancient bridge supported by Roman foundations, but much rebuilt.

Sights:
Roman walls, thermal baths, bridge (and some small excavations in town).

Location:
In the city.

Montefurado

On the outskirts of the village, on the left as one enters it, are the remains of an extensive Roman gold-mining operation. Not unlike Las Médulas, the gold was washed out of the ground by water surging through dug-out tunnels.

Sight:
Roman gold-mining operation.

Location:
From the N 120 (Quiroga to Ponferrada), take road off at Montefurado.

Piornedo

Tucked away in the mountainous Ancares National Park near the Leónese provincial boundary, Piornedo can be reached only by high, winding, narrow secondary roads through rustic and wild country. The pallozas, that is, the primitive, round, thatched houses here with their typical hórreos, are considered to be living examples of Celtic times, and indeed they need only be compared with the remains of ancient castros elsewhere to see the similarities in construction.

Near Liber is a one-span Roman bridge—which, according to local legend, was built by the devil—over the river Navia on the LU 723.

Sights:
Pallozas, Roman bridge.

Location
SE of Lugo on the N VI to Becerreá. Take the LU 722 to Liber ca. 9 km, then go S on the LU 723 to Doiras, then N to Piornedo.

Quiroga

Nearby partially excavated Celtic Castro de Vilar with remains of walls and houses. Site eroded and overgown, not a lot to see.

Sight:
Castro.

Location:
S of Lugo 7 km on the N VI to Nadela, then take the C 546 ca. 65 km to Monforte, then E on the N 120 31 km to Quiroga and proceed N on the LU 651 ca. 12 km. Inquire in Quiroga at the Ayuntamiento for specific directions. Guide recommended.

Viladonga

Excellent Celtic Castro de Viladonga with defensive rings of earth and stone, remains of round and rectangular houses, well-preserved or restored. The site is about 100 m in diameter, but was once larger as it spilled out to the west and south. The main earthen wall had an average height of 12 m and a deep moat followed the contours of the wall. Excavation began in 1972. The interior of the wall was built up with slate and the agricultural community that lived here was familiar with metallurgy. Museum in situ.

Sight:
Celtic castro.

Location:
Take the N 640 NE from Lugo to Viladonga. Go through village and site is indicated to left ca. 1 km off the road.

Other sites of interest in the province are located at **Antas de Ulla**, N of Chantada on the N 640, stone engravings, i.e., Grabados Rupestres de Monte de Chaos. **Begonte**, NW of Lugo on the N IV ca. 20 km, nearby Dolmen de Chao de Mazós, little left save a ring of upright stones, overgrown and neglected. **Candaira**, S of Lugo and NW of Monforte de Lemos, reputedly pre-Roman fortress nearby. **Castroverde**, E of Lugo ca. 23 km on the C 630, current excavation of the Cova da Valiña a Paleolithic cave site. **Fonsagrada**, on the C 630 NE of Lugo ca. 64 km, Castro de Xegunde and Castro de Moreira, at this time unexcavated. **Pantón**, W of Monforte de Lemos on the C 546 ca. 10 km, Roman villa (Vila Romana de Castillós) with Paleo-Christian remains, partially excavated. **Penarrubia**, site name, ca. 6 km NW of Lugo on the secondary LU 234 above the river Miño, excavated castro dating back to the sixth century B.C. **Xermade**, N of Lugo off the C 641, nearby, partially excavated Roman villa of Vilar da Graña.

ORENSE (OURENSE)

Generally mountainous, watered by the Miño river and a host of other streams, and bordering Portugal to the south, this is the only landlocked province in Galicia. Like the rest of the region, it is a land of Celtic castros, Roman remains and Medieval Christian churches and monasteries, but it is not without prehistoric sites such as dolmens.

The oldest Christian remains in the province are said to be at Esgos. Mozarabic influence is seen in a number of early churches as this area, free from Arabic domination, attracted Christians from the south who brought their decorative skills with them.

Allariz
The Mozarabe church of San Martiño de Pazo at the entrance to this Galician Medieval village was constructed supposedly on an earlier Visigothic site.

Sight:
Ninth-century Mozarabe church.

Location:
Turn off W on OR 300 at Allariz and follow signs for San Martiño de Pazo. Key to church with priest in next village along.

Bande
Seventh-century Visigothic church of Santa Comba de Bande built in the form of a Greek cross and with horseshoe arches supported on Corinthian columns. Here also is a Visigothic sarcophagus, baptismal font and various

designs including a fresco. The building was somewhat restored in the tenth century.

Sights:
Visigothic church, sarcophagus and baptismal font.

Location:
Take the N 540 S of Orense. Site signposted ca. 15 km beyond Celanova.

Celanova

Small, well-preserved Mozarabe church, Capilla de San Miguel, with one nave and rectangular apse from the tenth century. The interior of the structure is reminiscent of the Great Mosque of Córdoba. It is situated in the main square behind the Casa Consistorial.

A little out of town lies Castromào, the ruins of a partially excavated Celtic village on the top of a hill requiring ca. 150 m hike upward over steep and rough ground. Most of the site is on the far side of the hill, hidden from the road, and contains round and rectangular foundations of houses and a defensive (overly restored) wall. The area is neglected, heavily overgrown and difficult to get around.

Sights:
Mozarabe chapel and nearby castro.

Location:
SW of Orense ca. 26 km on the N 540. Castromào is reached by taking road from Celanova toward A Cañiga 1.3 km. At sign for Quintela de Leirdo, turn left up hill. Signposted.

Esgos

A serene and meditative spot amidst forest and rocky outcroppings and originally a hermit's cave dating back to the fourth century. The church of San Pedro de Rocas, excavated from the rock, has been enlarged and reconstructed many times, and now consists of three naves. There are about forty Early Christian rock-hewn tombs in and around it. Considered to be the oldest Christian site in the province, it is presently under excavation by Benposta—an evangelical group.

Sights:
Early Christian monastery and tombs.

Location:
Approx. 19 km E of Orense on the N 120. Signposted on left just after Pinto.

Orense: Esgos. San Pedro de Rocas. Tombs

Francelos

Visigothic church of San Ginés (San Xinés) from the ninth or tenth century, with Asturian and Mozarabic influences. It is richly decorated with carved stone, especially the windows, and similar to those in Asturian buildings of the same epoch.

Sight:
Visigothic church.

Location:
S of Orense on the N 120 and SW of Ribadavia (toward Melón). Signposted.

Macedo

Pre-Romanesque ninth-century church, Santa Eufemia de Ambia, consisting of one rectangular room with wooden roof, was originally constructed as a defensive stronghold for the inhabitants of the hamlet.

Sight:
Ninth-century church.

Location:
Follow the N 120 E from Orense and at Alto del Couso continue on the OR 104 toward Macedo. Signposted.

Orense: Francelos. San Ginés

Muiños

Two dolmens are situated near this Medieval village, one large and one small.

Orense: Muiños. Dolmen

Sights:
Dolmens.

Location:
Follow the N 540 S of Orense and 1.5 km beyond Bande is a sign for prehistoric site ("Ruinas Prehistóricas"). Continue on this secondary road to Maus de Salas, pass through village 1.1 km and turn left toward lake. Dolmens just before bridge.

Orense

The city takes its name from the Roman Aquae Urentes and in the sixth to seventh centuries it was the capital of the Swabians, but contested by the Vandals and later the Visigoths. The city was destroyed by the Arabs and later rebuilt during the reign of Alfonso II. The large bridge of seven arches over the river Miño appears to have been Roman in origin, but was rebuilt in 1230 and again in 1449. Of the Roman hot springs and town of Aquae Urentes little remains except the springs themselves.

Sight:
Roman bridge.

Location:
In town, signposted.

San Cibrán de Las

A large impressive, partially-excavated hilltop Iron Age Celtic castro of San Cibrán de Lás. Seen here are inner and outer defensive walls, portals, a well with steps leading into it and remains of mostly rectangular houses. The site sits above the Miño valley and has extensive views.

Sight:
Celtic castro.

Location:
From the N 120 W of Orense ca. 19 km take secondary road N (right)to Eirás, pass through village and continue 2 km to site.

Trives

Spanning the river Bibey (Bibei) is a well-preserved, austere Roman bridge of three arches. It was built during the time of Trajan and was an important structure on the Roman road from Orense to Astorga. Beside the bridge are two Roman columns with commemorative plaque, a milestone and traces of the Roman road.

Sights:
Roman bridge, milliarium and remnant of road.

Location:
Take the N 120 from Orense E toward Ponferrada, between km 78 and 79 the road passes over the Bibey river on the Roman bridge.

Verín

Hilltop site of El Castillo occupied by Medieval castle with triple bulwarks. The site was originally the Celtic castro of Baronceli and there are some scant remains of a Roman fortification, but the earlier construction has been all but obliterated by Medieval building. The village, clustered around the castle and continuously occupied since the Iron Age, has been built over many times. There remains a Medieval cemetery.

At Mixós ca. 4 km NE of Verín is a ninth-century church, Santa María de Mixós, showing Asturian and Mozarabic influences and containing murals.

Sights:
Some earthworks and walls from Celtic or Roman times, Medieval sarcophagi and castle and nearby ninth-century church.

Location:
Verín is on the N 525 S of Orense.

Other sites in the province include **Baños de Mogas**, SE of Orense ca. 30 km, pre-Romanesque church of Santa Eufemia de Ambia. **Petín** on the N 120 E of Orense and just before A Rua with a bridge, Ponte Cigarrosa, on Roman foundations over the river Sil, signposted. **Readegos**, there is no well-defined pathway through the brush and up the hill to the nearby Celtic castro of San Aqueda. Nor is there much to see upon reaching the heavily overgrown and neglected site except some remains of dwellings and remnants of a wall. On the N 540 out of Orense N toward Chantada, between km 77 and 78, castro is signposted on the right and lies 0.5 km off highway (not including the hike up the hill). **Ribadavia**, on the hill in the town is a fair-sized and still well-defined Jewish quarter (with commemorative plaque) of the fourteenth century. The community overlooked the river below and was protected by a wall, still intact. On the N 120 SW of Orense.

PONTEVEDRA

Hilly and lushly vegetated province with fertile valleys, it borders Portugal to the south, has mountains in the east and the Atlantic ocean on the west. The principal river is the Miño forming the southern boundary, and to the north is the river Ulla. The most interesting historical sights in the province of the period covered here are perhaps those of the prehistoric rock engravings or petroglyphs found near the capital, Pontevedra, and north, in the area of Campo Lameiro, and the Iron Age castro at La Guarda, which is one of the largest and best-preserved in the region. There are also a number of Roman bridges which may be seen in various places along the ancient roads.

Campo Lameiro

In the vicinity of the village are at least six clusters of engravings in the living stone dating back to the Neolithic and Bronze Ages. Several such engravings are found on the hillside practically in the village itself. Most can be reached by easy walks of from 100 m to several kilometres off the roads. While the general network of sites is shown on a roadside map upon entry to the town, they are not signposted at the individual hamlets and villages around Campo Lameiro near which they are found. It is best to ask for directions at each place or find a local guide. The children usually know how to find the sites. The engravings are mainly concentric circles or other geometrical shapes and, less often, animals.

There is also a castro nearby at the Hermitage of San Antoñín. It has scarcely been excavated, but the floor plans of a few dwellings can be seen along with a stone engraving.

Sights:

Six complexes of pre-historic rock engravings each with several or more rock-cut figures, castro.

Location:

NE of Pontevedra 20 km, turn N (left) off the N 541 at Sacos for 7 km.

Grove, El

The peninsula of El Grove on the north side of the Ría de Pontevedra has been rich in archaeological finds. In the Ciudadela is a Celtic castro under excavation and at Adro Vello, near the beach of Carreiro are the remains of a Roman villa.

Pontevedra: Campo Lameiro. Rupestrian engravings

Sights:

Castro with remains of houses and Roman villa.

Location:

The peninsula lies ca. 18 km W of Pontevedra. Take the C 550.

Guarda, La

On nearby Monte Tecla with splendid panoramic views of the Atlantic coast, hinterland and the mouth of the Miño river, are the remains of a large Celtic village of an estimated one thousand dwellings dating back to ca. 500 B.C. Some of the houses have been reconstructed including thatched roofings. They were built close together and, like many other castros, without intervening streets. This is an excellent example of a Celtic village with museum in situ.

Sights:

Large Celtic castro. Museum.

Location:

Well S of Pontevedra at the mouth of the river Miño. Follow the C 550 SW from Tuy on the Portuguese border to La Guarda. Monte Tecla signposted in town.

Mogor

There is a complex of three separate petroglyphs on three different outcroppings of rock near the beach. Two of them are clear, but the other is weather-beaten and obscure.

Sights:
Petroglyphs.

Location:
Take road from Pontevedra SW just past Marín and follow sign for the beach Praia de Mogor. Above the second beach is the site.

Mondariz

Nearby five-span Medieval bridge, Puente de Cernadela, over the river Tea built on Roman foundations. The two main central arches were rebuilt and the bridge is still used for farm traffic. At the S end of the bridge is about 100 m of the ancient road.

Situated on the hill known as A Cidade de Caneiro, about 5 km from Mondariz, is the Castro de Fozara. Some of the site has been destroyed by a stone quarry and only part of the defensive wall remains, along with moat and parapets.

Sights:
Roman bridge (rebuilt), road and castro.

Location:
SE of Pontevedra and N of Ponteareas off the N 120 ca. 10 km. Site is just beyond town. Ask in town for the Puente Romano.

Pontevedra

Roman bridge, Puente Sampayo, a little S of the city, served the ancient road from Vigo to Pontevedra.

Sight:
Roman bridge.

Location:
S of Pontevedra on the N 550 11 km, cross the river Verdugo, the Roman bridge is to the E (left).

Troña

Small hilltop Celtic village called Castro de Troña measuring about 200 m by 150 m, with remains of round and circular dwellings, partially excavated, the last time in 1983, and reconstructed along with a stone wall. The hill is referred to as Dulce Nombre de Jesús due to the hermitage on the summit. It was defended by a moat nearly 18 m deep and 10 m across dug from the granite rock, and by two walls. The site appears to have beeen occupied from the second to first centuries B.C. It is now somewhat neglected.

Sight:
Castro.

Location:

S of Vigo on the N 120 toward Orense, turn N at Ponteareas on road to Mondariz. Approx. 2 km after Prado, turn E (right) uphill. Signposted near site.

Vigo

On the hill overlooking the town are two castles, Castillo de Castro and Castillo de San Sebastián constructed in the tenth century but many times rebuilt. Nearby are the remains of a castro where excavations were begun in 1952 and continued into the 1980s, revealing walls and dwellings. Not unlike many other Castros, the site was occupied by the Romans.

Sights:

Castro and early castles.

Location:

In town.

Other sites in the province include: **Cotobad**, NE of Pontevedra ca. 15 km and a little S of Campo Lameiro, nearby rock paintings, reputedly slight remains of Castros and vestiges of a Roman road, inquire at Ayuntamiento. **Cuntis**, N of Pontevedra on the E 50 turning E (right) at Caldas de Reyes on to the N 640, several dolmens reputed to be in the area and a castro. **Moraña**, N of Pontevedra, to Caldas de Reyes then SE (right) 6 km on secondary road to Moraña, reputed menhir in the vicinity, petroglyphs and a castro. **Pontecesures**, N of Pontevedra, reached by the N 550 ca. 35 km, on the south side of the river Ulla from Padrón are the partially excavated remains of the Castro Cessuris. **Ramallosa**, S of Pontevedra to Vigo, continue S on the C 550 17.5 km. Roman bridge.

MADRID, COMUNIDAD DE

Situated in the centre of the country, the region is high and generally dry, and consists in large part of a bare, exposed plateau with few major landmarks. An exception is the Sierra de Guadarrama in the north.

The capital, on the river Manzanares, while mentioned in the tenth century as an Arabic outpost of Toledo, did not develop much as a city until the sixteenth century, when Felipe II established the court here.

There are Paleolithic remains in the region, particularly along the banks of the Manzanares and Jarama rivers, including cave paintings. The area is conspicuously lacking in dolmens but at Ciempozuelos, a little south of the capital, there is a well-known necropolis associated with Bell Beaker finds from the Neolithic or Chalcolithic periods. There are also about forty known Roman sites in the province.

Compared to many other peninsular regions, Madrid seems to have been somewhat sparsely populated in the past and, with a few exceptions, there remains little in situ of archaeological interest for the non-expert. Many sites that were there have been covered over or have vanished.

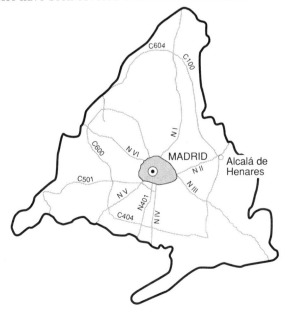

Alcalá de Henares

Remains of the Roman city of Complutum, which appears to have covered an area of 1 km by 2 km and was situated at the confluence of the Henares river and a small tributary, and was the Roman centre for the region. A small portion is under excavation. Some areas of the ancient city are under modern apartment blocks. Around it were a number of small villas scattered throughout the countryside but most of these have disappeared.

An Arabic castle stands on the hill behind the town but is difficult of access through private property.

Sights:
Remains of Roman city, some dwellings and part of water system so far unearthed. Museum in situ.

Location:
E of Madrid on the N II ca. 31 km. Site on W side of town.

Madrid: Alcalá de Henares. Roman Complutum

Reguerillos, Cueva de

Discovered in 1864 and sometimes known as the Altamira of Madrid, the 300 m cave contains prehistoric engravings which include fish, monkeys, a deer, a mammoth and two human figures. The open access site is not commercialized and lanterns and warm clothes are needed in the cold and totally dark cave. The small entrance measures about 1 m high.

Sight:
Rupestrian art.

Location:
From Madrid follow the N I to Venturada ca. 50 km turn E (right) to Torrelaguna on the M 103 and follow signs for Patones. Pass through town and continue 6 km straight ahead. Wind around mountain to two large water pipes coming down hill and passing under road. Almost immediately turn right on dirt road that doubles back toward pipeline. A sign says "Do not enter. Camino de Servicio, Canal de Isabel II." Proceed to just before the pipeline (ca. 0.3 km on the dirt road) and cave is on the left about 12 m up a steep path. Sign at mouth of cave.

Talamanca de la Jarama

The Roman bridge, concealed in the trees on the edge of town, is a fairly well preserved five-span bridge over the Jarama river, although one end is partially in ruins.

Here also are walls built by Romans and successively rebuilt by Visigoths, Arabs and Christians. There are said to be Visigothic motifs in parts of the wall.

Church of San Juan Bautista has an apse built on what was a Jewish synagogue. There is a Visigothic inscription in the portico.

Sights:
Roman bridge, section of ancient road, walls, Visigothic inscription.

Location:
Leaving Madrid take the N I, N toward Burgos, turn E (right) for Algete and after 7 km turn N (left) 17 km to Talamanca.

Valdetorres de Jarama
Small, somewhat isolated Roman villa, excavated but neglected and in poor state. There is a central building encircled by a roadway which in turn is encircled by peripheral buildings. Site enclosed by fence.

Sight:
Roman villa complex.

Location:
Ca. 5 km S of Talamanca on the C 100. Site is W of town 1 km on right of unpaved road.

Some other sites around Madrid include Neolithic burial grounds at **Ciempozuelos**, S of Madrid off the N VI on the C 404 ca. 5 km, but no longer anything special to see. **Puerto de Fuenfría**, in the Sierra de Guadarrama on the provincial boundary with Segovia, NW of Madrid, stretch of Roman road. **Villaverde Bajo**, a few km S of Madrid on the N 401, necropoli of fossae, but little to see as all material has been removed.

MURCIA

The province, conterminous with the region of Murcia, is generally mountainous and semi-arid. The principal river is the Segura. Archaeological finds, mostly in cave sites, demonstrate the presence of human communities in the area dating back to the Lower Paleolithic.

Settlements relating to the important Bronze Age Argar Culture, with twenty-two known sites around Jumilla and many more in the vicinity of Lorca and Cartagena, are still being discovered. In the fourth to fifth centuries B.C. a thriving trade was established between the Cástulo mines near Linares in Jaén and the Ports of Alicante and Cartagena (ancient Mastia), outposts of Phoenician and Greek colonies interested in the metal. The traders left their imprint in the region in the form of sculptures and pottery and, even more important, they left the legacy of a writing system which spread throughout the Iberian world from southern France to Andalucía.

Carthaginian occupation of the area transformed Mastia into a major city with the Latinized name of Cartago Novo (New Carthage) and the exploitation

of the mines helped the anti-Roman military objectives of Hannibal and Hasdrubal. According to Pliny, the shafts provided the Carthaginians with three hundred pounds of silver per day which, no doubt, aided Hannibal in paying his mercenaries fighting in Italy. The mines peaked during Roman times when there were some forty thousand men slaving in the pits.

In the province of Murcia are a number of spa towns whose origins date back to Roman times and whose "baños" were appreciated by the Arabs; for example, those at Alhama de Murcia, Fortuna, Puebla de Mula, Archena and Los Alcázares. Prehistoric artifacts found around some of them, for instance at the Balneario de Fortuna, suggest that the hot springs were known and enjoyed in even more remote times.

The regulation and distribution of water in this dry land has been a prime consideration for many centuries and, as may be seen in several places—for example, Alcantarilla and La Nora—the Arabs planned irrigation projects with care.

Alcantarilla

An Arabic wooden water wheel of large proportion is situated in the town and another, also very large, is nearby beside the Jesuit monastery of La Nora, whose name is derived from the Arabic term for the wheel. The site is referred to as La Noria de la Nora.

Sights:
Arabic water wheels.

Location:
W of Murcia ca. 9 km on the N 340, then, for the other, 2 km NE on the far bank of the river Segura.

Murcia: La Noria de Alcantarilla.
Arabic waterwheel

Caravaca de la Cruz

In the vicinity of the town is an Iberian necropolis, Llano de la Consolación, and a hermitage, Ermita de la Encarnación, built on the site of a Roman temple and currently in a state of reconstruction. Some of the ancient pillars are still visible. The adjacent pre-Roman settlements of Los Villares and Villaricos preserve some bits of walls and dwellings, but not a great deal to see. Sites on cliff overlooking river Quipar, where some Bronze Age artifacts have been found. Near the town also is the Roman bridge of El Piscalejo from the first century A.D. and still in use.

Sights:
Roman and Iberian remains, Roman pillars, and Iberian remnants of walls, dwellings and cemetery. Rebuilt Roman bridge.

Location:
W of Murcia on the C 415/C 330 63 km. For Roman bridge going E on C 415 ca. 5 km, turn on road to El Canal. Bridge currently in use. For other sites, go off the C 330 at Prados just S of Caravaca and N of Lorca. Signposted. Go 1.5 km to village. Turn left and follow road 1.4 km, then turn right up gravel road to pine trees 1 km to Ermita.

Cartagena
The city, an ancient naval base, was founded or enlarged by the Punic general Hasdrubal and became the centre of Carthaginian influence in Spain. Its gold and silver mines were a source of much wealth. Scipio Africanus the Elder besieged and conquered it in 209 B.C. during the second Punic War. Visigoths, and later Arabs, occupied the city, but it was reconquered by Christian forces in the thirteenth century. Its antiquity can be judged from the recent discovery of a Roman theatre which also yielded not only Visigothic but Iberian artifacts.

Sights:
Various archaeological sites are situated around the city. These include a Roman road in the basement of a savings bank (Calle de Duque 28), Torre Ciega; a Roman monument; part of a Roman amphitheatre; a theatre, under excavation at Cerro de la Concepción near the Cathedral; Paleo-Christian cemetery of San Antón, fourth to fifth centuries; Byzantine ramparts of the sixth century and remains of an Arabic lighthouse.

Location:
In and around the city inquire at Archaeological Museum for specific sites, locations and permission to visit.

Cieza
At the Barranco de los Grajos are rupestrian paintings, involving women in a phallic dance with some kind of quadrupeds. The paintings are in poor condition.
On the hill above the town are the ruins of an Arabic fortress, walls restored but little to see.

Sights:
Rupestrian paintings, slight remains of Alcázar.

Location:
NW of Murcía on the N 301 ca. 30 km. Alcázar, signposted on the C 330 to Mula. For cave paintings—difficult to find—inquire at Ayuntamiento for guide.

Fortuna
Cueva Negra, a hot springs grotto near the town and site of prehistoric artifacts, contains Latin inscriptions in a a reddish dye on overhang at the

mouth of the cave. They are faded and very difficult to make out. The site may have been equivalent to a kind of temple for the Romans.

Sights:
Latin rock inscriptions

Location:
A little N of Murcia on the C 3223. Cave, signposted, is 4 km out of town.

Jumilla
Nearby are rupestrian paintings in the Cueva del Peliciego, and near here are also the remains of a Roman villa whose mosaics have been removed to the museum in town. There is little left to see. At Coimbra del Barranco was an Iberian settlement, excavated, with remnants of walls and dwellings. In each case a guide is recommended.

In town is a Paleo-Christian funerary monument of the fourth century, signposted, and an Arabic Alcázar much reconstructed and built on an Iberian and Roman site.

Sights:
Rupestrian paintings, Iberian settlement, Roman villa, Paleo-Christian tomb, Alcázar.

Location:
NW of Murcia on the N 301 ca. 54 km, then NE on the C 3314 ca. 23 km.

Monteagudo
Village and once-Roman town at the foot of a large steep rocky hill on which are the remains of a Roman fortress, enlarged by the Arabs in the twelfth century, and conquered by the Christians in 1234. On the highest point is a statue of Christ.

Sight:
Roman and later Arabic fortress.

Location:
NE of Murcia on the N 340 ca. 5 km.

Mula
There are a number of ancient sites in the vicinity of Mula; the Ibero-Roman settlement of Fuente Caputa with scant remnants of buildings, a fifth- to first-century B.C. necropolis of el Cigarralejo, site of an important Iberian inscription, the Cigarralejo Lead Plaque, but site is neglected and overgrown with little to see except some remnants of wall and small excavations. Rupestrian art is found in the Cueva del Milano. The paintings are in very poor condition and scarcely discernible. All sites are difficult to locate and guide is recommended.

Sights:
Rupestrian paintings, Iberian necropolis and Ibero-Roman settlement.

Location:
Mula is W of Murcia on the C 415 ca. 35.5 km. Sites are in the surrounding hills. Inquire at Casa de la Cultura for guide.

Sabinar, El
The village lies on the river Benamor in mountainous country. Rupestrian art is found at nearby Cañaíca del Calar and Fuente del Sabuco and includes various signs, dots, suns and schematized human and animal figures. Paintings in fair condition.

Sights:
Rupestrian paintings.

Location:
W of Murcia ca. 77 km to Moratella on the C 415, then W on the MU 703 ca. 30 km. Inquire at Ayuntamiento for guide.

Yecla
On Monte Arabí some 15 km from the town are situated rupestrian paintings, but grotto is closed except for guided tours. The central frieze contains numerous paintings of humans, animals and various signs. Reputed petroglyphs in the area.

North of the town are the remains of Cerro de los Santos, an Iberian sanctuary on a small knoll where numerous votive offerings in stone and bronze have been found, as well as much ceramic material of Greek and Roman origin, and an Iberian lead plaque inscription. There are some slight excavations revealing foundations of structures.

Sights:
Rupestrian paintings, Iberian sanctuary.

Location:
In the extreme NE of the province and N of Murcia ca. 92 km on the C 3223. Inquire at Ayuntamiento for guide. The Iberian site lies a little NW of Yecla about 200 m off the secondary road toward Montealegre del Castillo in Albacete. Signposted on the left.

Other sites in the province of Murcia include: **Los Alcázares**, SE of Murcia on the coast. Some artifacts of Greek origin found here, but the town appears to derive mostly from Roman times. There were Roman and Arabic baths but the process of building the present spa in 1904 destroyed the last vestiges of the ancient baths. On the N 332, Torre de Rami, tower of Arabic origins, just to right of highway a little south of town. **Algezares**, S of Murcia ca. 4 km, reputedly seventh-century Visigothic church in outskirts of town. **Alhama de Murcia**, SW of Murcia on the N 340, ca. 32 km, Alcázar with restored tower. **Archena**, NW of Murcia ca. 22 km then W (left) on the MU 411 ca. 4 km., Iberian settlement on Cabezo del Tío Pío, many important finds but little to see in situ. **Lorca**, SE of the capital on the N 340 ca. 64 km, Alcázar and rebuilt walls. **Moratalla**, W of Murcia ca. 77 km and just N of Caravaca ca. 14 km on the C 415, rupestrian paintings in the vicinity, inquire at Ayuntamiento. **Puerto de Mazarrón**, on the coast S of Murcia and W of Cartagena on the N 332, reputedly Roman villa at Loma de las Herrerías. **Puerto Lumbreras**, SW of Murcia ca. 82 km on the N 340, Arabic tower.

NAVARRA, COMUNIDAD DE

About two hundred fifty dolmens in the region attest to the prehistorical presence of man, but of the hundreds known few remain in good condition and most have been reduced to a pile of stones, difficult to find in the forested mountains of the province. Some of the oldest Iron Age remains in the country (cromlechs, menhirs and tumuli) are here, as might be expected since Navarra would have been one of the first regions penetrated by Celtic peoples crossing the Pyrenees from Gaul.

At Los Arcos, at the intersection of the N 111 and the C 121 SW of Pamplona, were two menhirs known as Las Normas as reported in some guide books. The legend relates the story of two young girls turned to stone for not attending mass. They no longer exist, however, having been broken up and discarded by the farmer in whose field they once stood.

Much of the region was inhabited by the Vascons, a Basque people, at the time the Romans arrived in the second century B.C. Roman influence spread

throughout the middle and southern zones but had little impact in the mountainous regions of the north and east where the traditional way of life persisted. Pamplona was situated near the edge of Roman domination and features of Roman civilization are still present in the vicinity in the form of towns, roads and bridges. The Visigoths made no impact in this once entirely Basque province of northern Spain, and Arab remains are pretty well confined to the southern parts of the province where their influence was fairly intense for about four hundred years.

In August of the year 778, while crossing the Pyrenees after a failed attempt to defeat the Moslems at Zaragoza, the rear guard of Charlemagne's troops commanded by Roland was annihilated by the still-independent Vascons in the valley of Roncesvalles.

Artejona

Copper or Bronze Age tomb, Dolmen del Portillo, most stones are still standing, including those of the well-defined entrance passage, but cap stone missing. There are other, somewhat poorer tombs in the area about which information may be obtained at the monastery.

Sight:
Dolmen.

Location:
S of Pamplona and 13 km SE of Puente la Reina on NA 603. Pass through town and at first crossroad beyond monastery turn left and then right at cemetery. Continue 3.4 km to end of paved road and dolmen is just beyond parking area.

Cintruénigo

Simple but effective water distribution system, Partidero los Fieles, devised by the Arabs and currently in use, although reinforced with pipes and water somewhat redirected. Mountain water flowed along a canal to the *partidero* or stone divider which, when adjusted, would send the water coursing along connecting canals to the adjacent towns of Corella, Cintruénigo and Tudela, ensuring that each received its fair share. Water assigned to Tudela passed through a long underground tunnel and emerged at the bottom of a hill (at the *boquerón*) to resume its flow along the canal.

Sights:
Arab irrigation system, canals, tunnel and water divider.

Location:
S of Pamplona and a little E of Tudela on the C 101. Travelling S take gravel road between km 91 and 92 left (petrol station on right), pass stop sign at crossroads and continue ca. 0.5 km. Site is on the right by a small concrete hut. *Boquerón* is just over 1 km further along same road on right.

Cirauqui

Near the town are the ruins of a small Roman bridge over a tributary of the river Arga, along with the ancient road wending down the hill from the village, crossing the bridge and leading up the other side of the defile to disappear under the modern highway. Some of the contours of the road may also be seen on the other side of the highway.

Sights:

Remains of Roman bridge and road.

Location:

On the N 111 SW of Pamplona ca. 30 km. The bridge stands ca. 1 km S of the entrance to the village on the left.

Cortes de Navarra

At the nearby Iron Age site, El Alto de la Cruz, in the valley of the river Ebro, excavations were begun in 1947 revealing various strata of habitation, the oldest dating back to about 800 to 725 B.C., at the end of which time the agricultural settlement shows signs of having been burned before the next building phase. The best known level contains remains of three-room rectangular adobe houses similar to those across the Pyrenees, and dating from about 725 to 500 B.C. Four infant graves were discovered under the paving stones, one containing three bronze rings. Moulds for smelting demonstrate the use of metallurgy. The nearby urnfield necropolis (called La Atalaya) corresponds to the last phase of the settlement ,and is across the highway on the side of the hill. Some of the hand-made pottery excavated from the site along with agricultural implements and jewellery may be seen in the Ayuntamiento at Cortes; the remainder of the artifacts are in the Provincial Museum in Pamplona.

Sights:

Iron Age settlement with remains of dwellings, walls and remnants of the necropolis.

Location:

S of Pamplona and SE of Tudela (toward Zaragoza) off route N 232 at Vitrometal Factory. Turn left on unpaved road between km 114 and 115. Site on hillock ca. 0.5 km on right.

Lesaca

Once seemingly an important Iron Age cult site, the mountain ridge near the village contains a small dolmen from the Bronze Age, but with few standing stones, seven cromlechs or stone circles from about 800 to 300 B.C., some supposedly Iron Age sepulchres and a covered-over tumulus. On the highest point of the ridge are two Iron Age stone rings which were probably the focal point of local activity but over which there is now a modern shrine. These isolated and eerie remnants of a remote past, with their commanding views of the valleys around, are most interesting with a little imagination.

Sights:

Dolmen in ruinous condition, cromlechs in fair to poor state and tumulus marked only with a plaque.

Location:
N of Pamplona off the N 121 turn W (left) on the NA 400 toward Oyarzun; site is signposted next to highway and is situated along a ridge adjacent to an unpaved road.

Leyre
Hermits are supposed to have lived here in mountain caves in the seventh century, but the monastery was first mentioned in documents in 848. During

the Moslem domination of the region in the ninth and tenth centuries it served as a refuge for bishops and gentry of Pamplona and as a seat of government. The monastery was rebuilt in 1022 after its destruction by the Arab al-Mansur. Of special interest is the simple, unadorned ninth-century crypt, burial place of the first kings of Navarra. The monastery reached its highest period of splendour under Sancho the Great of Navarra.

Navarra: Leyre. Monastery. Royal crypt

Sights:
Monastery and royal crypt.

Location:
On the N 240 ca. 52 km SE of Pamplona. Signposted.

Liédena
Large Roman villa of the first to fourth centuries. Practically everything has been removed to the museum in Pamplona, and the site is neglected and heavily overgrown.

Sights:
Roman villa, remains of dwellings, rooms, wells, walls, and baths.

Location:
On the N 240 SE of Pamplona and a little W of Liédena at km 38 opposite the Hoz (gorge) de Lumbier. Signposted.

Mendigorria
Nearby remains of a large Roman town dating from the first to fourth centuries A.D. with extensive and on-going excavations and a large well-preserved water deposit (*Castellum aquae*) of the first century above the town. Water was brought to the city by a channel of ca. 300 m. The hilltop site is easily

reached by automobile, but is not well known and seldom appears in tourist information brochures and guide books.

Sights:

Roman city, remains of reservoir, water canal, walls, wells, roads, houses and columns.

Location:

Take the N 111 SW of Pamplona to Puente la Reina and turn S (left) on the NA 603 ca. 5 km. Continue through town and

Navarra: Mendigorria. Roman water deposit

take right fork over the river Arga on road signposted for Muruzábal. Proceed for 3.2 km to excavations on left of road in vicinity of a church. Roman reservoir on right of road.

Pamplona (Irunea)

The Spanish name of the city derives from the Roman colony established by Pompey in about 77 B.C. on the site of a Basque settlement. The defensive walls date back to Roman times, but only a few traces of the original are preserved. Most of it is from the sixteenth century. Also considered to be of Roman origin is the bridge of La Trinidad.

Sights:

Traces of Roman wall and rebuilt Roman bridge.

Location:

In the city.

Tudela

There is little remaining from the Romans in this city, with perhaps the exception of some spans of the bridge over the river Ebro. The villa "Soto de Ramalete" reported in some guide books is covered over, and although it is said that the Roman fortress lies under the Arabic castle,

Navarra: Tudela. Torre Monreal

there is nothing evident. Nevertheless, this southern Navarrese city contains many interesting sights, mostly from later periods. Beside the Castillo de Sancho el Fuerte, situated on a hill overlooking the city and river, are the slightly excavated remains of a Celtiberian settlement and the remnants of a Jewish cemetery. The city had two Jewish quarters, the old judería behind the cathedral, occupied up to the twelfth century, and a more recent one between the cathedral and the castle, which was occupied from the twelfth to the fifteenth centuries, that is, until the Jewish expulsion from Spain in 1492. In the cloisters of the twelfth-century Romanesque cathedral are the remains of a synagogue. There is also a Jewish plaque at no. 2, Calle de Benjamín de Tudela.

The Moslems left an indelible mark on the city with the magnificent Torre Monreal of the eighth century and remains of walls in various places near the Alcázar. Arab architectural remains are also found in the cathedral cloisters opposite the synagogue (now a museum), while the church itself displays Mudéjar architectural decoration.

Sights:
Some small excavations on the castle hill of a Celtiberian settlement. Two Jewish quarters, slight remains of cemetery and synagogue, plaque. Alcázar, walls, Torre Monreal.

Location:
S of Pamplona on the N 121.

Valtierra
Ancient ruined tower called La Torraza approx. 16 m high and about 8 m in diameter. Thought to have been a Celtiberian structure, its age is unknown.

Sight:
Ancient tower.

Location:
S of Pamplona, but a little N of Tudela on the N 121. Site in town across road from school.

Zubiri
Small Roman bridge over the river Arga known as the Puente Rabia. It has two spans and is still used for pedestrian traffic.

Sight:
Roman bridge.

Location:
On the C 135 NE of Pamplona, ca. 20 km.

Other sites of interest in the province may be found at **Arguedas** on the N 121 S of Pamplona ca. 88 km, where there is a reputed Roman town E of the city, but site has been covered over and there is at present little to see. **Baños de Fitero**, S of Pamplona and W of Tudela on the NA 693, some slight remains of Roman thermal baths. **Estella**, SW of Pamplona on the N 111 ca. 43 km, Jewish quarter on the other side of the steep pedestrian bridge on left after entering town (off Calle de Espoz y Mina) but rather unattractive and no important monuments. The synagogue was replaced by the church of Santa María. It is believed that Estella had a synagogue for women, the only case known in

Medieval Spain. **Milagro**, S from Pamplona on the N 121 go W at Cadreita on the NA 664, ruined Alcázar on a cliff overlooking the river Aragón with only two sections of crumbling walls standing. Can be seen from town. **Noain**, on the N 121 S of Pamplona, go through town and eighteenth-century aqueduct built on foundations of a Roman bridge over the river Elorz is a little S on same road. Little to see. **Olite**, S of Pamplona on the N 121 32 km, some traces of Roman walls. **Santacara**, S of Olite take the C 124 E, ruined tower overlooking town reputed to be of Roman origin. Access requires a short, uphill walk. Plainly visible some distance away.

PAIS VASCO

The Basque provinces consist of Alava, Guipúzcoa and Viscaya, and are well represented by prehistoric sites from Paleolithic and Neolithic times. Human cultural remains date back about one hundred fifty thousand years to the Lower Paleolithic. Sanctuaries in the earliest caves, with their painted or engraved animals and signs, are often near the entrance in the light of day. In later times, the drawings were generally set back further inside the cave, where the artist must have worked by firelight.

In the Cantabrian and Pyrenees valleys, during the final phases of the last Ice Age, the physical, cultural and linguistic characteristics of the Basque people seem to have commenced their development.

While the mountainous north remained impervious to much change, two major influences are in evidence in the southern areas of the Basque territory: Mediterranean peoples penetrated the Basque habitat, modifying the cultural and racial features of the autochthonous populations as well as agricultural development, and a later influx of Celts and Romans continued to shape the ethnicity and culture of this zone. Tumuli and dolmens relate to the Chalcolithic and Bronze Age, while cist graves, menhirs and cromlechs are from the Iron Age. For the megalithic-minded traveller, especially the hiker, the Basque provinces offer a wealth of sites, but most are difficult to find (except in Alava),

hidden away in heavily wooded, mountainous terrain and are far from roads. Many also have been reduced to a pile of rubble by treasure seekers, despoilers and the elements.

Basque is the only living western European language that is not of Indo-European provenance and which has no apparent established relationships with any other language. In linguistic terms it may be referred to as a language isolate. On the Spanish side of the Pyrenees, Basque people occupy most of the province of Viscaya, a small bit of Alava, all of Guipúzcoa and the northern quarter or so of Navarra.

The number of Basque speakers is estimated at about half a million in Spain and about a fifth of that number in France. Under pressure from Spanish and French, the Basque language has gradually lost ground. In the Middle Ages it was spoken in most of Alava and in over half of Navarra. Prior to that, Basque toponyms suggest an even more extensive distribution of speakers.

Nor has the origin of the Basque people been determined with any degree of finality. It may be best to treat them as an in situ development of local cultures that date back through the Bronze Age and Neolithic times to an even more remote past. This at least until some other theory can be proved beyond a reasonable doubt.

There is not a great deal from ancient times that can be directly associated with Basque culture, but their ancestors may have been responsible for the Paleolithic cave paintings found throughout the Cantabrian and Pyrenean mountains.

Basques have remained relatively isolated in their mountain valleys until recent times, and have zealously guarded their ancient customs and traditions. Primarily free peasants, shepherds, fishermen and more recently navigators, miners and metalworkers, they have also produced outstanding figures such as Saint Ignatius of Loyola and Saint Francis Xavier. The Basques were only nominally subjected to Roman rule and withstood domination by the Visigoths and Franks. Once converted to Christianity, they have remained fervent Catholics.

ALAVA (ARABA)

The province is well-endowed with good specimens of megalithic structures, Bronze and Iron Age sites, Roman remains and Early Christian complexes in the form of cave sanctuaries and cemeteries. The capital city is Vitoria-Gasteiz.

Alava is one of the best provinces in which to see dolmens, as many are in good condition and of easy access. All of the megalithic tombs are similar in size and construction, with burial chambers connected to the outside by a corridor, and are considered by some experts to be the oldest in the country. They are found along a route running W to E from the Balcón de la Rioja and Elvillar a little N of the Ebro river valley and S of the Cordillera de Cantabria.

Besides Iron Age and Roman sites in the province, Alava has over one hundred known rock-hewn caves in two major areas, one east of Vitoria and the other south of the capital. Most are off the tourist routes but of easy access. Some were religious sanctuaries and are considered to be the oldest churches in the province. Some of them still retain the stone altars and others have Latin inscriptions written in Visigothic lettering. Still others contain tombs and remains of paintings or engravings on the walls. These generally consist of human figures, animals, crosses and geometric designs. Some, of course, date back to prehistoric times, but those that were constructed as Christian hermitages seem usually to correspond to the eighth and ninth centuries, the period of the Moslem conquest.

Anda-Catadiano

Situated between these two villages is a group of four dolmens known as Cuartango in various states of preservation from poor (a few standing stones) to good. They differ in size and all are without cap stones. Some are heavily overgrown.

Sights: Dolmens.

Location:

NW of Vitoria on the L 624. Dolmens signposted in Catadiano.

Arcaya

Excavations in 1976 uncovered baths and related rooms of a smallish Roman villa. There is a hypocaustum with little circular columns of brick along the under-floor heat ducts, a caldarium, a tepidarium and a frigidarium. There are also several patios and water conduits. The discovery of the villa adds to the increasing evidence that Roman presence in the Basque country was more significant than previously thought.

There is another Roman villa and necropolis discovered at Cabriana not far away, but the site was excavated and re-covered, although some guide books suggest there is something to see there.

Sights:

Roman villa. Remains of baths, water system and rooms.

Location:

Take the N 1, E of Vitoria and SE (right) on C 132 for 1 km. Site is located at entrance to town on left just after small cemetery.

Arrizala

There is a dolmen here in the middle of a field and in plain view from some distance away. It is considered one of the oldest in the area, in excellent condition with cap stone, and noted for its stature and beauty. It is signposted at the entrance to the town as the Dolmen de Sorginetxe.

Alava: Arrizala. Dolmen of Sorginetxe

Sight:
Dolmen.

Location:
E of Vitoria on the N I, at Salvatierra take the L 128 S to Opacua. Between km 44/28 and 45/27 is the entry to the village.

Assa
Of the Puente Mantible, a once large and splendid Roman bridge over the river Ebro, with five spans and 164 m in length, only two arches remain standing. It is considered one of the great works of Roman architecture.

Sight:
Remains of Roman bridge.

Location:
S of Vitoria and a little NW of Logroño on the N 232. Bridge, signposted. Can also be seen from the road.

Corro
Almost within sight of the Cuevas de Santiago at Pineda is the Cueva de los Moros de Corro. There are actually two caves. The one lying a little to the north is rectangular with an arched roof, and contains two windows cut through the rock, a small oven, and six graves hewn from the rock. (there were more). The other has two entrances, two rooms, and a water drainage trench outside, a nearly triangular window, and a cross engraved on the door jamb. Inside are the outlines of a single grave where once there were more, but occording to local people an itinerant salesman occupied the cave some years ago and destroyed the graves while re-modelling his rent-free abode.

Sights:
Early Christian rock-hewn sanctuaries.

Location:
SW of Vitoria on the A 68 to exit no. 5 then take the C 122 ca. 10 km to where it joins the N 625, then N ca. 1 km and proceed W (left) on L 622 beyond San Millán toward Bóveda. Just before Corro take road N (right) which leads to the rock outcropping. Follow footpath around to the left and continue upward to cave sites.

Cripán
Remote village against the backdrop of high rocky cliffs and mountains. An ancient road, thought to have been Roman in origin,

Alava: Corro. Cueva de los Moros. Artificial cave

passed through the hamlet, but most of the paving stones have been removed to build retaining walls. Only the outlines of the road, obscured by debris from fields, are still visible rising from the nearby valley where a small bridge, also thought to have been Roman, spans the stream. The bridge, nearly completely overgrown, is almost lost to view.

Sights:
Ancient road and bridge.

Location:
SE of Vitoria near Logroño. Take the A 68 to Logroño and then the N 232 to Laguardia, 16 km, turn E (right) on road marked for El Villar, ca. 4 km and continue to Cripán. Proceed through village and follow unpaved road (right) into valley below.

Eguilaz
The dolmen of Aizkomendi, with a litle help from modern man, is one of the best examples in the country. Once completely covered over, the tomb was accidentally discovered in 1830. In its cavity, nearly 2 m deep, were human skulls and bones of Copper and Bronze Age burials. The last excavation was carried out in 1965, when part of the surrounding field was cleared in order to make the dolmen visible from the highway. The site once consisted of two parts: the dolmen chamber—of which the entrance or corridor has disappeared, but whose ten standing stones are impressive with a cap stone estimated to weigh nearly 11,000 kg—and an adjacent tumulus, which has now vanished, where Iron Age inhumations took place.

Sight:
Dolmen.

Location:
On the N 1 at km 381 E of Vitoria.

Elvillar
Discovered in 1935 the dolmen, Chabola de la Hechicera, with cap stone in place (if somewhat precariously) also has the corridor partially preserved. The structure appears to have been used up until Roman times, judging from the ceramic material excavated at the site.

Another dolmen in the vicinity, El Encinal, was rediscovered in 1943 and excavated in 1953. It was and is in poor condition, although a number of artifacts were found including human bones, a bone knife and ceramic fragments. Most of the stones have been displaced.

Sights:
Dolmens.

Location
S of Vitoria near Laguardia. Take the CV 140 toward Elvillar and after passing km stone 68 and in sight of the town, turn off on unpaved road where the signposting for the dolmen begins. For El Encinal, follow the highway from Elvillar toward Ciprán and turn off right at the second farm road and at the next crossroad, where the site is signposted, turn right again.

Iruña

The town of the ancient Caristios, a Basque clan, was called Beleia, but the indigenous population was supplanted by the Romans in the first and second centuries. In the third century the site was fortified with stout walls and became a military bastion. One side of the town was naturally protected by a steep escarpment and the river below. Over the river Zadorra a bridge of thirteen spans, still preserved in good condition, was constructed.

Alava: Iruña. Section of Roman wall

On-going excavations at the site are dotted over an extensive area and so far give little idea of the layout of the town. A walk or drive on the dirt road around the fenced-off site reveals that part of the defensive wall, perhaps constructed in haste, contains round stone pieces from pillars. Aerial photographs of the cultivated fields surrounding the town indicate the remains of sites still unexplored.

Sights:

Iron Age site but little to see, Roman town partially excavated showing defensive walls and tower and some remains of dwellings, Roman bridge over the river Zadorra (Trespuentes) somewhat rebuilt, and Roman bridge of Villodas, S of the town, much reconstructed. Museum in situ.

Location:

A little W of Vitoria on the N 1 ca. 10 km turn off NW (right) for Villodas and right again just before town to Trespuentes. Signposted as Oppidum de Iruña.

Labastida

Necropolis de Remelluri consisting of excavated rock-cut tombs. At the same spot is a wine or olive oil press from an earlier period, hewn from the rock. It is a cavity into which ran the oil or juice from an adjacent smooth crushing surface. A few

Alava: Labastida. Rock-cut tombs.

hundred metres away a Bronze Age settlement, of which nothing now remains, was discovered.

Sights:

Early Christian necropolis and oil press.

Location:

On private property but unrestricted. SW of Vitoria on the N 232 toward Haro ca. 75 km, at Briñas turn E (left) to Labastida. Go through town and take turning left toward Ribas. Continue to km 13/2, turn left into vineyard. Tombs ca. 0.5 km from road on low flat outcropping of rock on left.

Laguardia

The nearby site of La Hoya, lying on an ancient crossroads, was discovered in 1935 and shows layers of different epochs. The founding dates back to at least the fifteenth century B.C. by a people that appear to have crossed the Pyrenees to become neighbours to the megalithic people already in the area. The original population appears to have been enlarged by further newcomers from Europe, probably Celts, and formed part of the clan known as the Berones. Between the fifth and fourth centuries B.C. the arrival of Iberians from the Mediterranean coastal regions gave rise to a society referred to as Celtiberians. After this period the town reached its cultural apogee. The site was abandoned about four centuries later for unknown reasons.

Near the town stands the large Dolmen de San Martín, discovered in 1956 and excavated in 1964, with a 4 m long and 3 m wide corridor, but only one headstone remains in position. The dolmen was ravaged to build the stone shepherd's hut beside it and some nearby farm walls. It has been neglected and is heavily overgrown. Also not far from the town is the dolmen of El Sotillo discovered in 1955 and excavated in 1963. It has been somewhat restored and the stones set upright but remains barren of all head stones. The chamber contains nine stone slabs in a circle ca. 3 m in diameter. Artifacts indicate that it was constructed in the Neolithic period. Another dolmen, that of Alto de la Huesera—discovered in 1948 and excavated soon afterward—has no apparent corridor, and the cap stone is lying nearby; found here were numerous human remains. The burial chamber with six standing stones forms a pentagonal shape of some 3 m by 2.6 m in the interior.

Some tourist brochures mention a visit to the Old Jewish Quarter of Laguardia. It has virtually disappeared, replaced by new and renovated houses.

Sights:

La Hoya with necropolis, remains of dwellings and internal and external walls, and one zoomorphic sculpture. Museum in situ. Three nearby dolmens.

Location:

S of Vitoria and E of Haro on the N 232. Site signposted in town. Dolmen de San Martín lies beside the N 232 just N of town on the right in a vineyard. Signposted and parking. That of El Sotillo is also indicated on the N 232, 200 m beyond km stone 20/60 beside a farm road and, as the name suggests, in a small grove of trees. Alto de la Huesera may be found by turning off the N 232 to the left a short distance before entering Laguardia on the CV 140 toward Elvillar. Turn left again on a farm road ca. 0.9 km after km stone 65 and continue for ca. 0.7 km. The dolmen will be seen on a slight elevation to the right.

Layaza (Laiaza)

Discovered in 1952 and excavated in 1957, the dolmen was in poor condition with the cap stone and the overhead corridor stones missing. Human bones of only two individuals were found.

Sight:

Dolmen.

Location:

From Vitoria, take the L 122 S, on which the dolmen is signposted 60 m after km 37.

Marquínez

In and around this village are some sixteen artificial caves, some located in the face of the cliff directly behind the parochial church, such as that named Santo Leocadia. Many have been and still are used as stables, and most are in poor condition. In the greatly deteriorated cave of Santo Leocadia may be seen bas-reliefs in the stone (a feminine figure on a horse, and a standing male) which appear to have been once painted in red.

Beside the road on the left beyond the village are other caves, one of which near the Romanesque Hermitage of San Juan has two storeys and is referred to as Peña Castillo. The name derives from its appearance as a fortified cave (at least the upper part) and from what seems to be the remains of an ancient moat.

Sights:

Early Christian artificial caves.

Location:

At the same crossroads where the right turn is for Laño, turn left for Marquínez 6 km. Signposted.

Pinedo

Just before reaching the village are two caves in the cliff, Cuevas de Santiago, that can be seen from the road. The first has two entrances, a ceiling in the form of a cupola, benches in stone, a window, a niche for images and several rock-hewn graves. The second, much smaller, cave is less interesting with little to see. Both are much deteriorated around the entrances from falling rock.

Sights:

Early Christian sanctuaries.

Location:

From Vitoria take the N 1, SW and turn W on the L 622 at Nanclares toward Bóveda near the Burgos border. A little past San Millán go N (right) to Pinedo. Take road up to village and at last curve before village opposite km stone 49 (caves are now on cliff behind you) walk up farm road to right. Turn right again after ca. 1 km and continue on path to site.

Other sites in the province include **Molinilla**, SW of Vitoria off the C 122 beyond Salcedo, Dolmen La Mina, with apparently two burial chambers but many stones missing including cap stone and overhead passageway stones. Discovered in 1927 but not entirely excavated until 1956, the site revealed fragments of bones and teeth of six individuals and ceramics, a bronze knife and other artifacts. **Salcedo**, SW of Vitoria and N (right) off the C 122, go to the middle of the village and take road to left that leads into farm road. Dolmen La Lastra, discovered in 1942 and excavated in 1951, yielded human bones and ceramic fragments but only three of the stones remain today. **San Roman de San Millán**, E of Vitoria on the N 1, use of Roman stones, some with designs, in the composition of the Medieval church, a feature of other churches in the vicinity such as the parochial church of **Araya**, 3 km away, Nuestra Señora de Arzanequi at **Ilarduy**, 3.5 km distant, and in the Hermitage of Nuestra Señora de Elizmendi at **Contrasta**, S of San Roman.

In the province of Alava there are numerous dolmens besides those mentioned above, but many are difficult both to find and to reach. They are in various states of preservation, some existing only as piles of stones, and are situated mainly in several distinct zones as follows: in the vicinity of **Añes**, in the far NW of the province, three dolmens; **Guibijo** in the W of the province, over half a dozen dolmens; **Sierra de Encina** in the extreme E of the province, about a dozen dolmens or potential dolmens. Many sites await excavation. In the mountains along both sides of the Alava and Guipúzcoa border stand more dolmens, many of which require local guides to find.

GUIPUZCOA

Prehistoric investigations in the province, whose capital city is San Sebastián (Basque Donostia), began in 1871 in the cave of Aizkirri (Oñate) when a large quantity of bear bones were found. In 1879 the first dolmen in the province was investigated, and in 1892 a Paleolithic site was uncovered at Aitzbitarte (Rentería) and excavations started. Since then hundreds of sites have been found and examined, but many remain unexcavated.

Of the approxmately ninety-four caves reported in the archaeological maps of the region only two, Ekain and Altxerri, contain prehistoric paintings. That of Ekain contains about seventy animal figures, sixty-four painted and six engraved, while Altxerri has seven groups of animal figures, lines and zigzags. Most caves were inhabited from Paleolithic to Bronze Age times.

Megalithic constructions number about one hundred seventy-two, with about twenty-eight in good condition. Some of these have disappeared altogether, leaving only depressions in the ground. Of the twenty-eight or so good sites many are difficult to find, let alone reach. Most of those given here refer to the nearest town or hamlet where a guide may be found.

Iron Age Celts penetrated the Basque mountains and have left behind a number of monuments in the form of menhirs and cromlechs, but Roman remains in the province are few, with perhaps the most outstanding being the necropolis of Santa Elena in Irún. Visigoths and Moslems made no important inroads into the region and have left nothing significant behind.

Any sustained effort to locate and visit the ancient monuments of the province would require the *Carta Arqueológica de Guipúzcoa* by Jesus Altuna et al., published by the Sociedad de Ciencias Aranzadi, San Sebastián.

Albiztur

Some remains of Castro de Intxur, an Iron Age site excavated in 1957 and 1959 on mountain of the same name.

Sights:

Slight remains of Iron Age settlement, walls and dwellings.

Location:

S of San Sebastián on the N 1 to Tolosa, then SW and W on the C 6324. The site is situated between Albiztur and Bidania, further W.

Altxerri

The natural entrance to the cave is blocked by sediments, but beside it is another. The first engraved figures are found about 100 m inside. Further on into the twisting chamber of the cave are more figures, both engraved and painted, group II about 12 m along, III opposite and IV another 4 m. Many of the paintings have become very obscure or have disappeared altogether due to the humidity of the walls. The cave dips down about 10 m, giving access to more galleries in which two figures of bison are found. On the sides of the ramp leading downward are figures on the left seen by climbing up on a narrrow bridge of stone over the sloping chamber.

The cave was discovered in 1955 when an explosion in a quarry opened the passage to the cave a few metres from the natural (blocked) entrance. The sanctuary containing the engravings was found in 1963. There are numerous drawings of bison, goats, foxes, rabbits, fish, deer and bear.

Currently the cave, situated on private property, is closed to the public, but permission to enter may be given upon request to the Sociedad de Ciencias de Aranzadi.

Sights:

Rock engravings and paintings.

Location:

Take the A 1 W of San Sebastián to Exit 11, ca. 13 km and go S (left) to Orio beside the motorway. From Orio take the road to the Barrio de Ubegun and proceed to the Caserío Altxerri ca.1 km, behind which is the cave. The entrance is on the E side of the mountain called Beobategaña.

Ekain

The cave of this name on private property contains about seventy figures, sixty-four painted and six engraved. They are generally in good condition. The cave was discovered in 1969 and excavated over the following years, revealing various levels of occupation. The figures are of animals, fish and there are finger tracings.

There are several caves at this site but only one contains paintings, although most were inhabited by prehistoric man as attested by animal bones and stone tools. Most of the caves, including Ekain I, are currently closed to the public but this situation could change at any time. Inquire at the Ayuntamiento, San Telmo Museum or tourist office in San Sebastián.

Sights:
Rupestrian paintings.

Location:
Situated in the municipal district of Deba; take the A 1 W from San Sebastián to exit 12, turn S (left) toward Zestoa (Cestona) on the C 6317. Cross the river Urola and follow the road to Palacio Lilí. Continue to the hamlet of Sastarrain. About 200 m away at the foot of the hill is the cave.

Estela de Andrearriaga
The original stone, in the museum of San Telmo in San Sebastián, has been replaced with an exact replica where the original was found. The stone from Roman times (but seemingly produced by local people) has a rough engraving of a horseman and another human figure under which is a two-line inscription, VALBELTESO/NIS.

Sight:
Engraved stele from Roman period.

Location:
About 20 m from the local road Oiartzun (Spanish Oyarzun) to Irún between km 14 and 15, beside an old hermitage.

Irún
Discovered in 1971, the necropolis in the hermitage of Santa Elena, about 150 m², yielded numerous artifacts, some of which remain in the museum on the site. Found under the floor of the church, the cemetery of incineration dates back to the beginnings of the Christian era and earlier. On the site two Roman mausolea were also found. The large one was seemingly re-used as a Christian temple in the tenth century judging from the coins found in it—minted between 977 and 996.

Sights:
Roman mausolea and ancient cemetery.

Location:
E of San Sebastián on the French border.

Urnieta
In the vicinity there are numerous cromlechs, menhirs and dolmens, many discovered in 1978. The cromlechs may be found, with a little luck, about one hour's walk along the mountain path, but best to find a guide. Inquire at the restaurant. They are in good condition but unexcavated along both sides of the trail.

Sights:
Cromlechs.

Location:
A little S of San Sebastián on the SS 413. Approx. 1 km out of town turn left and proceed ca. 4 km to bar-restaurant Besabi near end of road. From here

take footpath opposite toward Mount Onyi. Take right branch of path after small white house.

Note: there are many more sights in the mountains—for example, E of **Andoain** and S of Urnieta and Hernani and N of the municipality of Elduain (Spanish Elduayen) in the area of Monte Onyi and Monte Adarra are dolmens, cromlechs, menhirs and cist graves. There is a maze of mountain trails and farm roads, presenting a formidable impediment to all but local guides.

VISCAYA

Dolmens and tumuli in Viscaya, whose capital city is Bilbao, have been catalogued so far at about one hundred, and are situated in mountainous areas where they have survived, although often in ruinous condition. They generally appear in groups of two or three, probably in relation to a particular community of the Copper or Bronze ages.

In the western section of the province a spur of mountains runs northward in the direction of the coast in the vicinity of Carranza (Karrantza). The area contains at least forty-four dolmens, cromlechs and tumuli. Also west of Bilbao in the region of the Galdmiz are another thirty or so sites, most of them in the higher parts of the mountains. Altogether there are about one hundred ninety-two Copper and Bronze Age sites in the province, but most in a very poor state of preservation and difficult to find.

Iron Age sites are few—about a dozen—and also generally in a poor state of preservation.

Romanization of the province was carried out against a background of changes already occurring as the Celtic peoples superimposed themselves on the indigenous Bronze Age cultures. It took place under the influence and activity generated from the colony of Flavióbriga (Castro Urdiales) and the city of Oeasso (Irún), and by maritime enterprises along the coasts. Villas and other agricultural centres were established in the interior of Viscaya according to Late Roman documents, but the sites are still unknown. Some small stretches of Roman road are still visible in some localities, and inscribed Roman milestones and tombstones have been found here and there.

For anyone contemplating a serious search through the mountains and valleys of the province for historical remains, it would be best to start off with the *Carta Arqueológica de Vizcaya* by Javier Gorrochategui and M. Jose Yarritu (University of Deusto, 1984) and a good compass.

Carranza (Karrantza)

In the prehistoric cave of Venta de la Perra are engravings of a bison, a bear and various astronomical signs, all near the entrance. They date back to about twenty-seven to eighteen thousand years ago. Nearby, in the cave of Cueva Negra, are some poorly preserved black paintings. There are other caves in the area, some with paintings.

In the vicinity are a number of megalithic sites, few of which have been excavated. Two that have been are the dolmens of El Fuerte and Cabaña IV. El Fuerte is situated on an elevated section of ground and, due to its large size, can be seen for some distance.

Sights:

Cave paintings and dolmens.

Location:

Carranza is due W of Bilbao on the C 6210. Inquire for sites and permission to visit at the Ayuntamiento.

Cortézubi

Situated nearby is the cave of Santimamiñe, with cave paintings from the Magdalenian period. The stratification shows inhabitation from the Aurignacian down to Roman times. One chamber, set off from the main gallery, contains charcoal drawings of bison mostly in excellent condition, along with horses, ibex, a stag and a brown bear, all about 60 cm to 90 cm in length. Human skeletons were also found in the cave, along with quantities of oyster shells—an inlet of the sea once came up to the foot of the hill where the parking lot is now. The drawings are about 50 m from the entrance, but there are three more kilometres of cave, not all of which is open to the public.

Sights:

Cave paintings.

Location:

E of Bilbao turn N (Left) on the C 6315 (exit 18 off motorway); site is 3 km N of Guernica. Signposted.

Elorrio

Medieval necropolis of Arguiñeta of the eighth to ninth centuries, with twenty-one heavy stone coffins arranged in rows and covered by stone slabs. All are above ground. Some have round tombstones common to later Basque cemeteries. Further up the hill, past the cemetery at the end of the road by a hermitage, are five more coffins of the same type, four of which are covered.

Sights:

Early Christian necropoli.

Location:

SW of Bilbao on the C 6322. Go off motorway S (right) at Durango, exit 17, and follow signs for Elorrio. Site next to hermitage on hill and signposted in town.

Viscaya: Elorrio. Necropolis of Arguiñeta

Meñaca (Meñaka)

Decorated ancient stone, probably Celtic, in the hermitage of Santa Elena in the Barrio de Emerando. The geometric designs appear to be in the Indo-European tradition and devoted to sun worship.

Sight:
Ancient stele.

Location:
N of Bilbao ca. 20 km just off the C 6313, the road to Bermeo.

Ondárroa

The bridge at Ondárroa is traditionally considered to have been Roman, although it has undergone some rebuilding.

Sight:
Roman bridge.

Location:
On the coast NE of Bilbao on the C 6212.

Further sites in the province are found at **Avellaneda**, W of Bilbao on the C 6318 ca. 30 km. and a little N of Ocharán. Stretch of Roman road of the Via Pisoraca to Flavióbriga can be seen here. In the chapel opposite the Casa de Juntas in Avellaneda is a Roman milestone. The inscribed stone cylinder of A.D. 238 is nearly identical to another at nearby **Erretola** and one found at **El Berrón** in Burgos. Other parts of the same ancient highway are visible in or near the following towns in the same vicinity. **Balmaseda**, the smaller arches of the Medieval bridge here appear to have been constructed by the Romans. The bridge formed part of the Via Pisoraca and lies SW of Bilbao on the C 6318 ca. 29.5 km and S of Avellaneda. **Sopuerta**, W of Bilbao at the junction of the B 1500 and the S 502; in the Barrio de la Baluga, the foundations of the bridge over the stream of Tresmoral are Roman. **Zalla**, also SW of Bilbao and a little E of Avellaneda where passing Otxaran, to the left of the road a little before the crossroad to Erretola is a *milliarium*, an inscribed cylindrical piece of sandstone of the same date as others in the area, Á.D. 238.

Roman stelae and other remains are also found in various places, such as **Forua**, in the northern outskirts of Guernica NE of Bilbao. In the parochial church of San Martín de Forua stands an inscribed Roman altar stone. To the right of the door of the Ermita de la Trinidad or San Gregorio is an inscribed Roman *cippus*, i.e. a large square block of marble, of the first or second century. At **Zarátamo**, a little SE of Bilbao on the Bi 511, embedded in the N corner of the parochial church of San Lorenzo, is a Late Roman stone with engraved Paleo-Christian markings, including a Latin cross.

RIOJA, LA

The region consists of one province, Logroño, which is also the name of the capital city, and receives its name from the river Oja, a tributary of the Ebro which forms the northern boundary of the province. The southern area encompases La Rioja Alta, and the Sierra de la Demanda and the Sierra de Cameros, rising toward the highland of Soria, while La Rioja Baja consists of flattish land descending toward the River Ebro. The region is watered by many streams and rivers flowing from the southern mountains north into the Ebro.

Few regions concentrate so much historical interest in so little space but much of it is Medieval history and beyond the scope of this book. There remains, however, a number of interesting ancient sites, ranging from Neolithic times to the Iron Age and the Roman period.

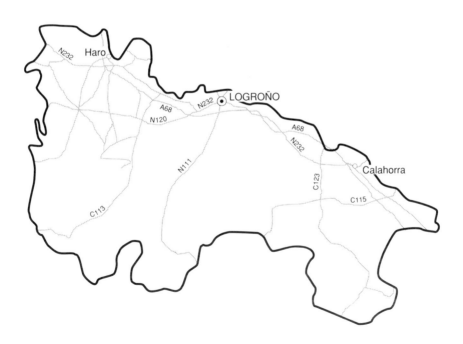

Agoncillo

Here are the remnants of what was once a large Late Roman bridge of six or seven spans—all of which have collapsed, leaving only the pillars as testimony to its grandeur. It is known locally, appropriately enough, as the Puente Caído (the Fallen Bridge) and served the Roman city of Egon, which has all but disappeared except for a few slight remains on the hill above the bridge.

Sights:
Slight remains of Roman bridge and city.

Location:
E of Logroño on the N 232. The bridge is situated ca. 0.5 km off main road on private land.

Alcanadre

On the N side of the river opposite Alcanadre stands a Roman aqueduct which has been cut in two by the modern highway. About 50 m have been rebuilt, but the remainder is in ruins.

Sight:
Roman aqueduct.

Location:
Take the NA 630 SE of Logroño almost to Todosa. Site is on right. Signposted.

Alfaro

On the banks of the river are the remains of a Roman fountain, consisting of an arch in the hillside through which the water issues from a natural spring. There are steps leading down to it. The site is neglected and well overgrown.

Sight:
Roman fountain.

Location:
SE of Logroño and Calahorra on the N 232. Crossing the bridge over the river Alhama out of town toward Logroño, site is immediately on the left.

Calahorra

Conquered by the Romans in 189 B.C. the town became the thriving city of Calagurria Nassica. Both Prudentius and Quintilian were born here. Unfortunately there is not much to see now; the modern town covers most of the ancient site. There are some Roman remains of pillars in town (just outside the parador), a small excavation on the edge of town next to the Colegio Angel Olivar revealing some bits of walls and foundations of some structures, very slight remnants of the circus NE of the city, a small bit of aqueduct, and the foundations of a rebuilt Roman bridge over the Ebro.

Sights:
Some Roman remains of the ancient city but disappointingly meagre.

Location:
SE of Logroño on the N 232 or the A 68 motorway.

Cervera del Río Alhama

Celtiberian city of Contrebia Leukade, under excavation. Site is very interesting, in a good defensive position, and includes remains of roads, a well with steep steps cut into the rock face and through an underground passage down to a natural spring, dwellings hewn from the rock, and a Celtic floor mosaic, perhaps inspired by Roman influence. A visit entails climbing about on sometimes rather precipitous rocky outcroppings.

Sights:
Iron Age hillside town with remains of dwellings, well, steps, roads and a mosaic.

La Rioja: Cervera del Rio Alhama. Contrebia Leukade. Celtiberian city

Location:
SE of Logroño. Take the LO 682 SW (right) at Alfaro to Grávalos and turn S (left) on the C 123 to junction with the LO 694 and follow right fork, remaining on the C 123 to Cervera. From town cross bridge, turn right immediately and proceed 4 km to site on the LO 693. Signposted on road, but actual site is several hundred metres across and down the valley and up the opposite hill.

La Rioja: Cervera del Rio Alhama. Contrebia Leukade. Celtiberian city

Peciña

Discovered in 1953 and excavated the same year, the nearby dolmen, called La Cascaja, yielded human remains of thirty-one individuals, eleven of whom were deposited in the corridor of the dolmen and the remainder in the burial chamber. Ceramic material was also found. Lamentably, the site has been severely damaged by agricultural activity on the farm where it is found.

Sight:
Dolmen.

Location:
NW of Logroño and a little NE of Haro, 3 km N off the N 232 between km 31/49 and 30/50. Follow the road N signposted for La Ermita de Nuestra Señora de la Piscina. Continue about 300 m past the hermitage to a modest bridge, from which the site can be seen on an unpretentious hill to the left.

Redal, El
Large Iron Age site, Parte de la Peña, on a low hill near the village, has so far yielded remnants of a road, fire sites and animal bones, numerous shards and some human graves near a stream (which were later washed away by a flood). There is not a good deal to see here, as most of the hill on which the village stood is unexcavated, neglected and somewhat overrun with sagebrush.

Sights:
Remains of Iron Age settlement.

Location:
SE of Logroño on the N 232 to Ausejo, then W (right) on the LO 633 ca. 2 km to village. Site is about 2 km out of village over very rough farm road. Directions and guide, if desired, can be otained at the Ayuntamiento.

San Millán de la Cogolla
The church of San Millán de Suso was constructed in the early tenth century, and Mozarabe influence is evident in the horseshoe arches within the church. It is built into the hillside and makes use of grottos in the rock for chapels. The site was one of the sanctuaries along the pilgrims' route to Santiago de Compostela (Camino de Santiago), and here are the tombs of the seven Infantes de Lara. From here came one of the earliest (tenth-century) manuscripts, the *Glossas Emilianenses*, in which the Spanish vernacular was written, glossing the Latin document.

Below the hill is the monastery of Yuso on the site of an earlier abbey which was later rebuilt. Here San Millán (Saint Emilian) is said to have appeared on a white horse to defend the Christians from the Moors. The building is currently undergoing restoration.

Sights:
Medieval monasteries.

Location:
SW of Logroño take the N 120 to Santo Domingo

La Rioja: San Millán de la Cogolla.
San Millán de Suso

de la Calzada, 17 km. San Millán is then signposted. Suso is on the upper road 1.7 km from village.

Other sites in the province include: **Cihuri**, W of Logroño and ca. 6 km SW of Haro, Roman bridge over the river Tirón. **Logroño**, Church of Santa María de Palacio, founded in the eleventh century, with a tower 45 m high. **Nájera**, historical capital of La Rioja 26 km SW of Logroño on the N 120, site of the monastery of Santa María la Real, founded in 1032, containing some tombs of the kings of Navarra, Castilla and León (Pantheon of the Kings) and beautiful cloisters.

VALENCIANA, COMUNIDAD

Valencia is the largest of the three provinces that make up the region, along with Alicante to the south and Castellón de la Plana to the north. All belong to the former kingdom of Valencia. Rupestrian paintings or, as they are often called, Pinturas Levantinas or Arte Levantino (as they were first discovered and examined in this area, called the Levante) abound here, but the more accessible ones are often in poor condition or have disappeared.

Similarly, Iberian sites, many unexcavated, are situated throughout the hills, but these also are too often in a poor state. Along the coastal plains Roman

villas, mostly unexcavated, lie in numbers under the orange groves, and that is where they will remain for some time to come. The villa at Nules is one of the few uncovered.

This is also the region where Greek settlements, now vanished, were reported—albeit somewhat obliquely—by ancient authors such as Avienus and (more concretely) by Strabo, who had never been to Spain. It is clear that Greeks and Iberians were in close enough contact in the region for the latter to write their language in the alphabet of the former—for example, on the Alcoy Lead Tablet—and to produce rich art work such as the Dama de Elche and various pottery designs that appear to have been somewhat influenced by Greek models. How much has been a matter of controversy for decades.

Carthaginian interest in the area came directly into conflict with Roman aspirations, and the Second Punic War, begun in 218 B.C., resulted in the complete Romanization of this desirable region.

While the Visigoths seem to have had no great desire to settle and work the fertile land of the Levante, the Arabs were not slow to establish towns and farms and devise an elaborate and still-working system of irrigation.

ALICANTE

From the Cova de l'Or near Beniarrés in the province of Alicante have come examples of domesticated wheat and barley that appear to have been cultivated together, and whose grains have been carbon-14 tested and date back to around 4500 B.C. This seems to demonstrate the establishment of Neolithic communities in the province. Paleolithic cave sites show the presence of even earlier cultures in Alicante, while the Cueva de Sarga containing cave art (now almost undecipherable) and other finds indicate Bronze Age settlements.

The ancient Iberian sanctuary near Alcoy, where an inscription was found in the Iberian language but written with Greek letters, suggests Iberian contact with the culturally more advanced Greeks, whose bases or trading posts in the province are yet to be discovered. One such Greek outpost could have been at Denia, where some authorities think the Greek site of Hemeroscopeion, mentioned in ancient texts, was situated. Another, Akra Leuce, is suspected to have been located in the area of the city of Alicante.

Some traces of the Carthaginians have been found in the province, and Roman, Visigoth and Arabic remains have been identified in various places, especially at Alcudia de Elche.

Alcoy

The Iberian site of La Serreta lies in the hills outside the city and is famous for the Plomo de Alcoy, an inscribed lead tablet. The inscription and votive offerings were found on the adjacent mountain-top sanctuary. (They are in the Archaeological Museum of Alcoy.) The site was occupied between the fourth and first centuries B.C., and excavations began in the 1920s, revealing some small areas of walls and foundations of dwellings which are now heavily overgrown with trees and bushes. Nearby, at Benilloba, surface finds indicate the existence of another Iberian settlement. The Iberian village of El Puig, built over a Bronze Age site, lies on the west rim of the Serra dels Plans, 5 km S of Alcoy, where excavations were carried out in 1964 uncovering remnants of an extensive wall and Iberian and Greek ceramics of the fourth to third centuries B.C.

Sights:
Iberian settlements, remains of walls and dwellings.

Location:
N of Alicante. Take the N 340 S of Alcoy toward Alicante and turn off on road to Benilloba (C 3313) just outside the city. A few metres along, just past the turn-off from the road that leads back to Alcoy, there is a dirt path on the right leading up the hill. Walk into site about 100 m and beyond. For directions to El Puig and guide, inquire at the Archaeologial Museum in Alcoy.

Alcudia de Elche
Ancient townsite under excavation. The well-known sculpture, Dama de Elche, was found here. The rather extensive ancient town lies in the lowlands of the river Vinalopó and is now mostly covered by palm trees and gardens, while the modern town developed 2 km away. The ancient site seems to have begun as a Chalcolithic settlement and was subsequently occupied by Iberians (three levels), Carthaginians, Romans (Colonia Julia Illici Augusta), and Visigoths. The town was first destroyed about the year 170 by the little-known Mauri, Berbers who invaded the peninsula. Excavations were begun in 1935, although the site has been known since the sixteenth century. It is fenced off and a small fee is charged to enter.

Sights:
Iberian settlement and later habitation periods, with remains of walls, dwellings and basilica. Museum in situ.

Location:
SW of Alicante on the N 340 ca. 24 km. Take road S of town toward Dolores 1.6 km. Signposted.

Alicante
A site on the hill above the city, where the castle of Santa Bárbara now stands, was chosen by the Carthaginian Hamilcar Barca as a fortress and focal point of the Spanish Punic Empire. The Romans established a town on an earlier Iberian settlement a short distance away and called it Lucentum. The later Arabs named it al-Lucant. The Iberian and Roman hilltop town at Albufereta, ca. 3 km from the centre of the city, is easily accessible but fenced off and a little overgrown. It is situated behind some highrise apartments. Site is closed to the public, but can be seen through the fence which has, of course, the usual hole in the wire.

Sights:
Ibero-Roman town with remains of walls, dwellings, streets, sewer system and water conduits.

Location:
Follow the road to the beach going N out of Alicante toward Playa Albuferete, which is signposted. Follow the road until it forks left toward

El Campello and take the first turning immediately left after the fork. Make a second left on to Calle Carrer de Dea Tanit. Site is just along the street on right.

Benidorm

Iberian settlement of El Tossal de la Cala, a small hilltop site perched above the sea surrounded by urban development, with some remains of walls and dwellings. The ceramic material unearthed here indicates habitation from the fourth to first centuries B.C.

Sight:
Iberian settlement.

Location:
NE of Alicante on the coastal road N 332, ca. 40 km.

Calpe

Once a Phoenician, and later a Roman, town, there are some remnants of fish-curing vats (probably for the manufacture of garum) and a Roman villa.

Sights:
Slight remains of Roman villa and fish-curing industry.

Location:
NE of Alicante on the coastal road N 332, ca. 60 km.

Alicante: El Campello. Roman villa

Campello, El

Roman villa situated on a promontory, Illeta dels Banyets, probably once an island, next to yacht harbour and behind a Medieval tower. The site is not signposted but easily accessible by a short walk across the beach. Some of the remaining interior walls are about a metre high. Artifacts and structures indicate three levels of occupation beginning with the Bronze Age, again in the third to fourth centuries B.C., and in Roman times. Excavations began in 1931. Iberian and Greek ceramics have been recovered from the site and inscriptions (graffiti) on pottery are written in the Iberian language, but with the Greek alphabet.

Sights:
Roman villa with remains of rooms, walls and cisterns. Traces of older settlements.

Location:

NE of Alicante on the N 332, ca. 15 km. Site is at N end of town.

Caserio la Sarga

Rock shelters, Cuevas de la Sarga; one with prehistoric paintings is fenced, the other open and full of modern graffiti. They sit high on the face of a cliff and can be seen from the main highway, but require a fairly strenuous climb up steeply inclined ground to reach. The paintings are in poor condition and not easily discernible, but depict parallel meanders and naturalistic animals painted over older geometric signs.

Sights:

Rupestrian paintings.

Location:

N of Alicante on the N 340 to ca. 10 km before Alcoy. The grottos are behind and above the hamlet, which consists of three or four farm houses, and can be reached by passing through La Sarga and up a steep, heavily-rutted dirt road. Less stressful (but more confusing): follow the N 340 further on and turn right just before km 788 onto gravel road, and proceed 3 km through a conglomeration of farms and urban development to site.

Javea

The national parador on the beach in Javea stands on the site of a Roman garum factory, whose scant remains and general outlines can still be seen.

Sights:

Remnants of Roman fish-curing industry.

Location:

NE of Alicante on the N 332, then E on the A 134 ca. 8 km.

Villajoyosa

Nearby remains of a Roman mausoleum in the middle of a campground with a few pieces of columns around it. The mausoleum now serves as part of a restaurant and living quarters.

Sights:

Remains of Roman mausoleum.

Alicante: Villajoyosa.
Roman mausoleum

Location:

NE of Alicante on the N 332 and 2 km NE of town at the Sertorium campsite.

Other sites in the province are sometimes difficult to find or have disappeared. There are also a number of Arabic structures scattered throughout, some of which are given below. While it has not been the usual practice in this book to report on the hundreds of caves in Spain that were inhabited by prehistoric man but no longer contain any visible relics of occupation, there are several in the province that are easily reached from major centres and are mentioned here. **Bañeres**, 21 km W of Alcoy on the C 1313, Alcázar. **Biar**, thirteenth-century Alcázar, E. of Villena 9.5 km on the A 210. **Cabezo de Mariola**, on the 1,000 m-high mountain in the Serra de Mariola running between Muro de Alcoy through Bocairente to Villena is an Iberian settlement not yet excavated. Much of it has been destroyed by agricultural work, but an inscribed lead plaque was found here. **Cueva de Canalobre**, ca. 24 km N from Alicante, take the N 340 and turn right at sign for caves 13 km off main road, forty minute guided tour inside. **Cueva de las Calaveras**, 95 km from Alicante, near Benidoleig, take the N 332 (W of Javea) to Gata and proceed SW through Pedreguer; signposted, cave occupied in Neanderthal and later times, evidence of ancient fires. **Denia**, N of Alicante on coast ca .124 km, slight remains of a Roman temple and remains of an Iberian town in the Serra de Montgo (a two-hour walk); inquire at Ayuntamiento. **Elda**, W of Alicante on the N 330, remains of Arabic castle overlooking town and remnants of an Iberian settlement 2 km N of the town by the river Vinalopó on a spur of the mountain. **Guadamar del Segura**, 37 km S of Alicante on the N 332, remains of reputedly Roman necropolis. **Monforte del Cid**, 23 km W of Alicante on the N 330, ruins of an Iberian settlement; obtain directions at the Ayuntamiento. **Monóvar**, W. of Alicante on the N 330 to Norelda, then 10 km on the C 3213, Alcázar. There are also remains of Arabic castles at **Orihuela**, SW of Alicante on the N 340, 24 km before Murcia, with walls and towers, and at **Petrel**, 40 km NW of Alicante on the N 330. **Santa Pola**, 20 km S of Alicante on N 332, sparse remains of Ibero-Roman necropolis of Ilici. Also, excavations carried out in 1987 to the west of the cemetery unearthed five assorted tanks for salting fish, about 1.39 m deep. Only a small section of the fish-curing site has been uncovered. **Villena**, NW of Alicante on the N 330, Alcázar modified in the fifteenth century and remains of a reputedly Bronze Age settlement 3 km NW of town.

CASTELLON DE LA PLANA

Somewhat misnamed Castellón (Catalán Castelló), the province is only partly *plana* or plains—much of it, especially the western part, is mountainous, with ridges running down to the Mediterranean sea. The hilly areas are well endowed with natural grottos and prehistoric rock paintings and remains of Iberian settlements. The Romans were more at home on the plains and coast with agricultural pursuits and fishing industries, but here, too, modern man has developed his urban settlements and holiday resorts, effectively effacing many of the ancient sites.

Albocácer

Grottos with prehistoric rock paintings are situated at nearby Valltoja. The grottos are situated in the cliffs near the confluence of the barrancos Matamoros and Valltorta. The paintings are few and mostly in a poor state of preservation. Many are undecipherable, but a few are clear enough to warrant a visit.

Sights:
Rupestrian paintings.

Location:
N of Castellón ca. 55 km, take the coastal N 340 to Alcalá de Chivert, then ca. 33 km W on the C 2310, N (right) on the C 238 a short distance and W (left) on the CS 801.

Almenara

Nearby at Casa Blanca is an excavation of a site dating back to the Lower Paleolithic and revealing animal bones and stone tools. The site lies in a strategic spot in the hills of Almenara on the flank of the pass that opens into the Huerta de Valencia. There are remains here also of a five-thousand-year-old, epi-Paleolithic culture, a Bronze Age settlement, and an Iberian village of the third century B.C. There is little to see, however. Of the Iberian settlement at Punto del Cid (Catalán, lloc de Cid), on the E side of the highway, there are the remains of some walls that extended for 1120 m, and a portal. In the fold of the hill below the Moslem castle are some more remnants of an Iberian population. There was reputedly a Roman camp in the area and a temple whose remains, E of the town, are now under water. The area seems to have much archaelogical potential. For recent developments inquire at the Ayuntamiento.

Sights
Iberian settlement, remains of walls and portal, and remains of Alcazaba with two towers.

Location:
S of Castellón on the N 340 near the Valencian boundary and ca. 9 km N of Sagunto.

Ares de Maestre

Hilltop village with numerous nearby rock shelters containing prehistoric paintings. Only a few are worth the effort to find, as many of the paintings are now nearly non-existent or have disappeared. One of the more interesting places is the imposing Barranco de La Gasula and several barrancos parallel to it such as Les Drogues, El Single and El Mas Blanch, which make up an exceptional focus of prehistoric art. In the barranco of La Casulla is the grotto or abrigo referred to as the Cueva Remigia, discovered, along with the others, in 1934. The paintings here are of hunters with bows and arrows and often with elaborate headdress, and animals (goats, deer, boar and bulls). Some are small, about 3 cm high.

Some 60 m to the E of the Cueva Remigia are ten other consecutive grottos, called Abrigos del Cingle de La Mola Remigia, containing about three hundred figures

Sights:
Rupestrian paintings.

Location:
NW of Castellón off the CS 802. The guide, Federico Barreda, may be found at the bar-restaurant Montalbana 8 km SE of town on the CS 802 toward Albocácer.

Bechí (Betxi)
The Iberian settlement of El Solaig on the spur of a mountain is 380 m long and between 32 m and 100 m wide. The village dates back to the first century B.C. and contains the remains of houses and defensive walls. Ceramic finds at the site also indicate an older Bronze Age settlement. On an isolated hill 2 km E of El Solaig was another Iberian settlement, unexcavated, where now stands the chapel of San Antonio de Bechí.

Sights:
Iberian settlements, walls and dwellings.

Location:
SW of Castellón on the N 340, then W on CS 223 for ca. 6 km. Then turn S (right) 2 km. Site is 2 km S of Bechí on a ridge. San Antonio de Bechí lies 3 km SE of the town.

Benasal
Rock paintings in the Racó de Nando; difficult of access but interesting pictures of hunting scenes and running animals. Guide recommended; inquire same as above. Near here are also the few remains of the Iberian settlement of El Mas Carbó de Dalt, 3 km W on the road from Benasal toward Villafranca del Cid and 18 km from Castellón.

Sights:
Rock paintings and Iberian settlement.

Location:
W off the CS 802 S of Ares de Maestre.

Benicarló
Excavated Iberian settlement, Puig de Benicarló, on a hill above the plain N of the town, mostly destroyed by dynamiting the side of the hill to quarry stone but still a good example of Iberian urban development showing well-preserved remains of walls of dwellings over 2 m high. Some of the houses appear to have had two storeys. This Iberian agricultural village seems to have flourished throughout the fifth and fourth centuries B.C., judging from artifacts such as Greek ceramics found at the site. It is not known why the town was abandoned, probably in the fourth century B.C. On neighbouring hills are the unexcavated remains of other Iberian settlements such as El Poblado de la Tossa.

Sights:
Poblado Ibérico del Puig with remains of defensive walls and a circular tower, dwellings, portals, steps (some hewn from the natural rock), and streets.

Location:

Benicarló is located on the coastal N 340 N of Castellón. Follow road out of N side of town crossing Avenida Magallanes, past cemetery and the Río Seco, and take the Camino Puig which passes over the motorway 6 km from town. Walk up hill to site.

Boriol

Rock paintings in the Abrigo de la Joquera, somewhat isolated from the other sites in the province. The most notable painted figure is that of a man with a twin-pointed hat, some kind of backpack, and a lance or arrow in hand, striding forward with great and seemingly determined steps.

Sights:

Rupestrian paintings.

Location

NW of Castellón on the C 238, 8.5 km.

Cabanes

Once a Roman town, of which few traces remain except the well-preserved triumphal arch through which ran the Via Augusta.

Sight:

Roman arch.

Location:

NW of Castellón 26 km on the C 238, site is ca. 3 km E of town centre. Signposted in town.

Castellón: Cabanes. Roman arch

Morella

Morella la Vella is a farmhouse situated 8 km NW of the city of Morella. Nearby are two grottos containing prehistoric rock art discovered in 1917. In the Galería Alta de la Masía, located about 100 m from the farm, are a number of very small figures, badly deteriorated, depicting hunting scenes. About 0.5 km away is the Galería del Roure, also containing small figures of archers in a dancing or battle scene, but they have nearly disappeared through deterioration.

Sights

Rupestrian paintings, mostly in poor condition.

Location:

Morella is N of Castellón on the N 232. From here take the road toward Chiva. After 4 km, where road forks go left on a dirt track to the *masía* of Morella la Vella. The proprietors of the farm who are the guardians of the sites will accompany the visitor to the grottos.

Nules

Partially excavated Roman villa of Benicato, discovered in 1954 deep in the orange groves near the town. The excavated site is fenced but viewable from all angles. The unexcavated part of the villa extends well out into the groves. The site has been despoiled several times in the immediate past by relic seekers.

Sights:

Roman villa, foundations of buildings, pool, part of column and street.

Location:

Nules is SW of Castellón on the N 340, ca. 19 km. Take road toward beach passing over railway. After 1 km turn right on Camino Camiñas, then left after one more kilometre on Camino Viciedo, a narrow track into the orange groves. At ca. 0.7 km villa can be seen on right, about 75 m down a dirt roadway.

Puebla de Benifasar (Pobla de Benifassar)

Nearby rock shelters beside the river Cenia, best approached from the village of La Cenia (La Senia). Beyond the village where the river forms a meander, and where the road turns sharply ninety degrees and crosses a bridge, is the abrigo or Cova del Polvorín, about 19 m across, 3 m high and 1.5 m deep. The shelter was discovered in 1947. Besides scenes of hunting, fighting and dancing there is a picture of a curious bird in flight and a noble-looking mountain goat.

Sights:

Rupestrian paintings.

Location:

N of Castellón, turn NW (left) off the coastal N 340 at Vinaroz onto the CS 332. Where road forks at motorway go left on secondary road ca. 17 km to La Cenia (in Tarragona). Continue following the river on a winding, narrow road for 7 km to site. (You are now back in the province of Castellón de la Plana.) The shelter is locked, but key may be obtained at the white house about 200 m away in direction of the nearby dam.

Tirig

Numerous grottos with prehistoric rock paintings in the area, such as the Cova del Civil showing a group of archers; Cova dels Tolls, few and badly preserved paintings; Cova del Rull, few and and again barely discernible figures; Cova dels Cavalls, hunting scene with archers shooting at animals; Abrigo del Arc, poorly preserved paintings; and Cova del Mas d'en Josep, few but well preserved representations of hunting scenes.

Sights:

Rupestrian paintings.

Location:

N of Castellón to Vinaroz on the N 340, then W (left) on the N 232 ca. 29 km, then S (left) on the C 238 5 km to San Mateo, then SW (right) on secondary road 11 km. Go to the Avenida Puig Roda 16 and ask for guide Miguel Segura.

Otherwise, leaving Tirig by the road toward Albocácer (take right fork where road splits 1 km from town), proceed 4 km where the road descends into the Barranco de la Balltorta and crosses it. Stop here. Continue on foot 400 m down the defile to the first three rock shelters (Cova del Civil) on the left of the gorge, about 15 m up from the bottom. Others are further along the barranco on the left. From the Cova del Civil to the Cova dels Cavalls and adjacent Abrigo del Arc is 2.5 km, but to get there it is best to travel along the top above the barranco. Take the road 1 km from Tirig where it splits toward Cuevas de Vinromá and travel 1 km along it to a road off to the right (camino del Povacho) that leads 2 km just about to the Cova dels Cavalls.

In the same area, near where the Barranco de Valltorta joins the Barranco de Matamoros, are the Cuevas de Vinromá, and nearby is the town of the same name. The guide is Manuel Centelles at Calle Calvarios Alto 26 in town. Here are the Cova Alta del Llidoné, with a single hunting scene of five archers pursuing two goats; Cova de la Saltadora, a group of abrigos with, among others, a painting of a wounded man pierced by arrows; Abrigos de les Calçaes del Matá, situated above Saltadora but with only traces of the paintings. There are also other shelters close by with barely discernible pictures. For a visit to these sites follow the road from Tarig to Cuevas de Vinromá and turn off after 4 km into the Masía del Matá on the right. From here a 1 km walk leads to the rock shelters.

Vall d'Uxó

Nearby is a hill referred to as La Punta d'Orleyl, on which is an Iberian settlement and necroplis (name unknown), source of important Iberian inscriptions written on lead plaques. Excavations began in 1962, and rich ceramic finds, including imported Greek pottery, indicate an occupation period from the sixth to first centuries B.C. This is one of many Iberian sites in the vicinity, but most are unexcavated. Another that has been excavated is the Iberian settlement of Sant Josep. Both sites—one on top, the other on the side of the hill—date from the Bronze Age to the first century B.C. Both are unattended, eroded and overgrown.

Sights:
Iberian settlements, remains of walls of various epochs, dwellings and two rectangular buildings that could have been temples.

Location:
S of Castellón ca. 27 km on the coastal N 340. Turn W (right) 4 km beyond Nules and continue 4 km to town, or take the C 225 SW from Nules. Town is signposted. The sites lie 3 km SE of the town and 1.5 km E of the road to Sagunto.

Vinaroz

Nearby hilltop Iberian settlement fenced but accessible. Site has stone quarries on three sides. Small but impressive ancient village, partially excavated and partially reconstructed. The walls of the houses are about 2 m high in some cases, built along narrow streets or pathways. There have been rich finds here in Iberian and Campanian ceramics and terra sigillata.

Some parts of the remains of the wall and towers of the town of Vinaroz are said to be Roman.

Sights:

Poblado Ibérico with narrow streets and dwellings.

Location:

N of Castellón on the coastal road N 340, then W toward Morella, 3 km. Go left on road to Caliz. Turn right immediately after road crosses motorway on to dirt track, ca. 100 m. From here walk up steep path to top of hill.

Castellón: Vinaroz. Iberian settlement

Other sites of interest in the province of Castellón are located at or near the following: **Alcora**, Iberian settlement on 439 m high mountain ledge of La Mormirá, above the left bank of the river Alcora. There remains very little to see of the ancient village, just a few piles of stones. W of Castellón on the C 232 19 km. The site lies 2.5 km NE of town. **Castelnovo**, SW of Castellón and a little NE of Segorbe on the CS 232, nearby third- to first-century B.C. Iberian settlement. **Jérica**, SW of Castellón on the N 234 W of Segorbe, ruins of Roman fortifications and an Alcázar. **Pobla Tornesa**, NW of Castellón on the C 238 19 km, Iberian settlement on Monte Balaguer; leave town on road to Albocácer, and immediately past Malpisa ceramic factory turn left on poor dirt track, continue to end and walk to other side of hill—site is just up the hill from farmhouse. About an hour's walk but little to see, Iberian dwellings reduced to piles of rubble. **Segorbe**, SW of Castellón, some slight remains of an Iberian fortification.   **Toro, El**, W of Castellón off the C 238 at Barracas on the CS 610, remains of Iberian settlement; inquire at Ayuntamiento. **Vila Real**, site of a Roman bridge. **Vivir**, SW of Castellón on the N 234 near Jérica, old tower incorporating some Roman inscriptions.

VALENCIA

The province consists of a coastal plain with foothills and inland mountains behind, a semi-circle of ridges and valleys. Only at the Cape of Cullera do the mountains reach down to the sea. The earliest vestiges of man date from the Paleolithic period. Traces of Neanderthal man have been found at Játiva and at Las Fuentes de Navarrés. In the lesser-known mountainous area are numerous prehistoric rock shelters and caves, many with ancient paintings; the earliest date from the Upper Paleolithic.

While few remnants of Greek and Phoenician colonizing sites have survived the centuries, the Iberians have left ample remains, from the fifth century B.C. down to the period of Romanization. The capital city of Valencia was founded by the Romans in ca. 139 B.C.

The area came under the suzerainty of the Visigoths in the sixth century A.D., only to fall prey to the Moslems in the eighth century, when Musa Ibn Nusayr conquered the capital. In the tenth century Valencia became a small Moslem kingdom, a Taifa, but it fell to the Cid in 1094. Retaken by the Almoravides, it finally succumbed to Christian rule in 1238 when Jaime I, king of Aragón, won it back.

For an excursion into the past, the following two sites stand out above most of the others and may be easily visited: Iberian settlement of Castellet de Bernabé (see under Liria), and the Ibero-Roman town of Sagunto.

Albalat

Grottos with prehistoric rock art are located in the vicinity of the town. To visit, inquire for permission at the Ayuntamiento.

Sights:
Rupestrian paintings.

Location:
N of Valencia and a little W of Sagunto, ca. 8 km off the N 234.

Alcudia (L')

Beside the highway in town stands a large Nuria or Arabic water wheel, framed by an unattractive modern brick structure. The wheel was once part of the local irrigation system of this fertile area.

Sight:
Arabic water wheel.

Location:
On the N 340, 33 km S of Valencia.

Ayora

Near the town are three small grottos with prehistoric rock paintings: Abrigo del Sordo, Cueva de Tortosillas and Abrigo de Pedro Mas. The Abrigo del Sordo, discovered in 1964, is reached over extremely poor farm and forestry roads (impassable at certain times of the year) and contains rather deteriorated paintings of hunters and deer. A guide is recommended. The Cueva de Tortosillas is located on a farm of the same name and has easy access off the road from Alpera to Carcelén. Paintings are in a poor state of preservation. The Abrigo de Pedro Mas, discovered in 1910, contains many paintings both schematic and natural, the most outstanding being the head of a goat. Most are not in good condition. The grotto is reached by a cow trail from the Casa del Heredero across the valley from the Cueva de Tortosillas.

Sights:
Rupestrian paintings.

Location:
SW of Valencia ca. 104 km and 22 km N of Almansa on the N 330.

Bicorp

In the vicinity are the rock shelters (with prehistoric paintings) of Cuevas de la Araña, El Buitre, Barranco Garrofero, Abrigo de las Sabinas, Abrigo del Barranco de los Gineses, Abrigo de la Madera, Abrigo de la Balso de Calicanto, Abrigo Gavidia, Abrigo del Zuro, et al. There are also prehistoric cave paintings at nearby Millares, ca. 22 km N of Bicorp, where the small Abrigo del Barranco de las Cañas, discovered in 1962, contains some fairly good representations of a deer, a goat, a horse and bull. Access is complicated; inquire at Ayuntamiento in Bicorp. More rock shelters and paintings are found near Quesa, 8 km E of Bicorp, and Navarrés, on same road 6 km SE of Quesa. Here are the Abrigos of Voro and Garrofero, discovered in 1972. The former contains paintings of a ritual dance performed by armed warriors, while the latter, nearby, contains fewer but interesting paintings of a woman in long skirt, three goats and two hunters. Both sites are protected by iron gratings. To reach them along forestry trails it is best to seek a guide in Navarrés.

Sights:
Rupestrian paintings.

Location:
SW of Valencia and near Quesa and Navarrés, where there are also prehistoric cave paintings. Approx. 55 km S of Valencia turn W (left) and then NW. There are various signposted roads.

Casinos

Iberian settlement La Monravana, partially excavated. A few remains of houses. The site has been damaged by ploughing and illegal diggings. Sporadic excavations have been in progress since 1932. Ceramic material indicates a date from the fourth to first centuries B.C.

Sights:
Iberian settlement, remains of dwellings and wall.

Location:
NW of Valencia on the C 234 ca. 42.5 km and NW of Liria. Take road toward Casinos and at 7 km turn right on unpaved road opposite restaurant La Granja. Continue past houses to monument on left and climb hill to site.

Caudete de los Fuentes

Iberian settlement of Los Villares, situated on a low hill on opposite side of highway from town above the banks of the river Madre. Medium-sized and fenced site, partially excavated, but nearly everything removed to museum in Valencia. Five levels of occupation have been found, dating from the Bronze Age to the first century B.C. Excavations began in 1956. The site has yielded important Attic and Campanian ceramics and painted Iberian vessels, as well as two treasures, one of gold and silver jewellery and third century B.C. coins, the other of silver vessels and ornaments and over one hundred coins from Sagunto, Saetabis and Segóbriga—that is, from Iberian and Celtic towns. The ancient village appears to have been an active trading station between the Valencian coast and the Celtic tribes of the hinterland.

Sights:
Iberian settlement with foundations of houses and remnants of walls.

Location:
W of Valencia, 9 km W of Utiel on the N 111, site lies ca. 1 km S of town on the opposite or right bank of the river Madre.

Chelva

NW of town ca. 8 km at Tuéjar is reputed to be an abrigo with some poorly preserved and hardly distinguishable prehistoric paintings. NW of Chelva stand the remains of the Roman aqueduct of Peña Cortada. In the E section of the old town are slight remains of a judería.

Sights:
Rupestrian paintings, Roman aqueduct and remains of judería.

Location:
NW of Valencia ca. 67 km on the C 234, ca. 74 km.

Dos Aguas

Nearby are the Abrigos de Ciervo, Pareja, Cinto de la Ventana and Cabras. The rock shelters are all found in the vicinity of one another, and contain paintings (generally in good condition, some large) of males and females, and of animals. The area is a labyrinth of rocky defiles and abrupt cliffs reached by a forestry trail and it is not easy to find the individual grottos. The Alguacil (Constable) of Dos Aguas doubles as a guide.

Sights:
Rupestrian paintings.

Location:
W of Valencia on the N 111 to Buñol, then S 28 km (branch left after 20 km) to Dos Aguas.

Játiva (Xátiva)

The Arabic fortress-castle on top of Mount Vernisa was constructed on Roman foundations and later renovated and enlarged. Near its walls stands the hermitage of Sant Feliú, a rebuilt Visigothic (some say Mozarabe) church. Nearby is the excavation of a prehistoric site at Cova Negra; inquire at Ayuntamiento if there is anything still to see in situ.

Sights:
Alcázar, walls and remains of Medieval church.

Location:
SE of Valencia 58 km on autoroute.

Liria (Lliria)

Iberian settlement of Edeta, on Cerro de San Miguel, situated below and behind monastery, destroyed in the Sertorian Wars ca. 78 B.C. There is now very little to see, except a few stones; site abandoned and overgrown. From here, however, were excavated a number of important pieces of pottery, some with Iberian inscriptions and many depicting cultural scenes of dancing, playing of musical instruments, battles and horsemanship. Another Iberian town nearby, Castellet de Bernabé, of the third to second century B.C., has been excavated and partially reconstructed.

Liria was also the   Roman town of Lauro, and on-going excavations in the city have revealed three mausolea of the first to fourth centuries at the same site; they are scheduled to be removed to the nearby Taller Arqueológico in the near

future. A few hundred metres away, also in town, is an on-going excavation of a section of the Roman city. On the right of the main road through town toward the Taller Arqueológico is the stub of a Roman triumphal arch, but only a very small section (one-fifth) remains.

Of Arabic vestiges there is only a small bit of wall, on the hill, with houses built into it.

Valencia: Liria. Section of Roman city of Lauro

Sights:

At Castellet de Bernabé are the remains of walls, dwellings, steps, hearths, street, niches in walls for objects, engraved floor decorations and a rebuilt stone oil or wine press.

In the city, excavations of Roman burial complex and dwellings. Two sites. A small piece of triumphal arch.

Location:

Liria lies 30 km NW of Valencia on the C 234. Castellet de Bernabé is on the left of highway VV 6092 NW of the city, running parallel with the road to Casinos. At 15. 5 km turn left onto dirt track for 0.6 km. Site can be seen from the road; it is fenced, with large hole in the wire at back of site. Inquire about key at the Taller in Liria.

Valencia: Liria. Castellet de Bernabé. Oil press

Mogente

Nearby lies La Bastida de les Alcuses, an extensive 800 m long Iberian settlement of the fifth to third centuries B.C. and an important site for Iberian ceramics and inscription. The site was excavated in 1928 and 1931, and then abandoned. It is currently well overgrown. Many of the two hundred fifty dwellings are now only piles of stone. It is fairly typical of Iberian settlements in which the houses consisted of three or sometimes four rooms, the walls were constructed of stone and adobe bricks made of clay mixed with straw, and the roofs were presumably of thatch, held up by posts fixed in the centre of the rooms. Greek influence is evident in the construction, as well as from the abundance of pottery found in the dwellings and mingled with native crafts. The site was contained within a double wall, and was abandoned at the time of the Roman conquest.

Another Iberian site, El Puntal de Meca, with very scant remains, is also in the area. Excavations were also carried out at El Corral de Saus, an Iberian cemetery 7 km up the valley from Mogente, where stepped pyramids were found, constructed with large blocks and dating back to the fifth century B.C. The site has been re-covered.

In the vicinity is a grotto with prehistoric paintings: Abrigo del Bosquet. The paintings are in poor condition and nearly impossible to distinguish.

Sights:

Iberian settlement, exterior walls and dwellings (mostly collapsed), and traces of streets.

Location:

SW of Valencia on the N 430 ca. 78 km. Follow signs in town for country road SW toward site. At km 10 turn left (unmarked here and signposted for Casa Bas, a farm). Follow dirt road 2 km to top of hill. Settlement is fenced (with large hole in it to right of gate): key and permission to visit the Iberian settlement and the prehistoric rock shelter can be obtained at the Ayuntamiento in Mogente. El Puntal lies 18 km NW, take the secondary road to the right off the N 430 opposite the turn-off for Mogente.

Sagunto

Ibero-Carthaginian, Roman and Arabic town site, the massive walls above the town surrounding the Alcazaba contain within them remnants of all epochs. The Iberian town, besieged by Hannibal but favourable to Rome, was instrumental in the pretext for the Second Punic War which brought the Romans to Spain. Seventeen stone inscriptions in

Valencia: Sagunto. Roman theatre

Iberian have been found in various areas of the city. The Roman theatre on the north slope of the town, on a base of natural rock, with thirty-three tiers and 90 m in diameter, held about eight thousand patrons and was constructed in the second century B.C. It is still used. The sites of the circus and hippodrome are mostly covered by modern structures, but there are some visible (albeit exiguous) remains of the temple to Diana and the forum.

Valencia: Sagunto. Roman theatre

The town was attacked and sacked by Vandals in the fifth century and fell into obscurity for a time. It succumbed to the Arabs in 713 and was later fought over by the Moslems and Christians until 1238, when it was definitively reconquered. Here also are remains of the old judería.

Sights:

Well-preserved defensive fortifications on the hill above town, with remains from all historical periods (Iberians to Arabs). Excellent, partially rebuilt theatre, along with various other sparse Roman remains below the hill. Museum in situ. Jewish quarter.

Location:

N of Valencia ca. 23 km (exit 5 on autoroute).

Valencia

The city was founded by the Romans on the site of a Greek colony as a place for some of the defeated followers of Viriathus as it was Roman policy to distribute such men far and wide to prevent a resurgence of their rebellious activity. The town was sacked by Pompey after his victory over Sertorius in 75 B.C., and was rebuilt as the Roman colony of Valentia Edetanorum. Visigoths conquered the town in 413, only to give it up to the Arabs three centuries later. It fell into Christian hands in 1094 under the banners of the Cid, but after his death it reverted to the Moslem hegemony. In 1238 the Christians again ruled under King Jaime el Conquistador. The walls and most of the gates to the city were demolished in 1865. The best-preserved remains of the Moslem period in the city are Abd-al-Malik's baths, popularly known as the Baños del Almirante.

Just E of the city, within the urbanization of **Valencia la Vella** (between Valencia and Ribarroja, but closer to the latter and 12 km W of Manises, now a suburb of Valencia), are some slight excavations of Roman remains which are both difficult to find and disappointingly meagre. At least one guide book mentions them as the extensive ruins of Roman Pallantia. Only a few stones are visible.

Sights:

Moslem baths, slight excavation of Roman remains in Valencia la Vella.

Location:

In and near the city.

Yátova

Iberian settlement of Picos de los Ajos, from which important Iberian inscriptions have appeared. The site has also been heavily plundered by fortune seekers, and many of the remains have been carried away.

Sights:

Iberian settlement with stone foundations of dwellings.

Location:

37 km W of Valencia and 4.5 km S of Buñol.

Other sites in the province include: **Albaida**, S of Valencia ca. 85 km on the road to Alcoy; in the vicinity are the sparse remains of the Iberian settlement of La Covalta, fifth to third centuries B.C., excavated between 1906 and 1919; ceramic finds suggest trade connections with Cabezo de Mariola and La Serrata (see Alcoy, Alicante). **Benavites**, fifteenth-century tower with inscribed Jewish tombstones, ca. 32 km N of Valencia and 1.7 km W of the N 340 on the VV 6002. **Benifaio**, S of Valencia on the N 340, ca. 28 km, two Arabic towers. **Bétera**, NW of Valencia, on the C 234 to San Antonio, then 5.5 km E to town, restored Alcázar replastered in pink, with Disneyland appearance. **Bugarra**, NW of Valencia 30 km on the C 234 to Liria, then SW ca. 16 km to town, nearby Iberian settlement of Los Villaricos. **Buñol**, W of Valencia on the N 111 39.5 km, large tower and curtain walls of an originally Arabic castle. **Chiva**, ca. 31 km W of Valencia on the N 111, ruins of Alcázar. **Domeño**, NW of Valencia on the C 234 ca. 63 km, remains of a Roman fort. **Gandia**, S of Valencia 58 km on autoroute, nearby Castillo de Bayren (on road to Valencia), twelfth-century Alcázar, and a little SW at **Rótova** another Alcázar. **Millares**, hamlet 22 km N of Bicorp over very bad road, two rock shelters nearby, one recently discovered but with extremely poor representations; the other, called Abrigo del Barranco de las Cañas, discovered in 1962, contains few but interesting paintings of a deer, a goat, a bull and a horse. Directions are very complicated—inquire in the village for guide. **Turis**, 31 km W of Valencia on the N 111 to Chiva then S on the C 3322 for 13 km. Iberian site, La Carencia; ceramic material indicates that the settlement began in the fourth century B.C. and was abandoned during Roman times.

SUGGESTED ROUTES

Artificial caves, Alava, Burgos   328

Asturian PreRomanesque Churches, Oviedo   328

Celtic, Roman and Visigothic remains, León, Lugo   329

Dolmens, Alava, Logroño   329

Greek, Iberian, Roman remains, Gerona   330

Iberian, Roman and Arabic remains, Jaén   330

Iberian settlements and cave paintings, Castellón, Tarragona   331

Megaliths, Roman and Jewish remains, Gerona   332

Phoenician and Roman remains, Málaga, Granada   332

Rock engravings, Pontevedra   333

Roman and Arabic remains, Cádiz   334

Roman and Arabic remains, Málaga   334

Roman, Arabic, Phoenician remains and cave paintings, Málaga   335

Roman and Visigothic remains, Guadalajara, Cuenca   336

Roman mausolea, Zaragoza   337

Roman villas with mosaics, Palencia   337

Rupestrian churches, Burgos, Palencia, Santander   338

Artificial Caves, Alava, Burgos

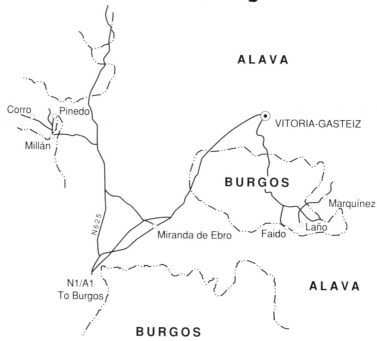

Asturian PreRomanesque Churches, Oviedo

Celtic, Roman and Visigothic remains León, Lugo

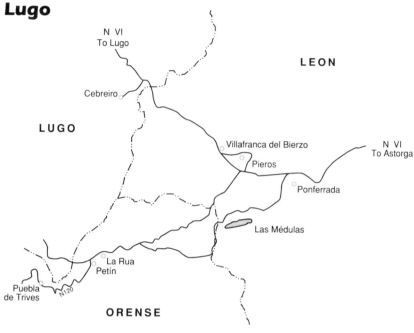

Dolmens, Alava, Logroño

Greek, Iberian, Roman remains, Gerona

Iberian, Roman and Arabic remains, Jaén

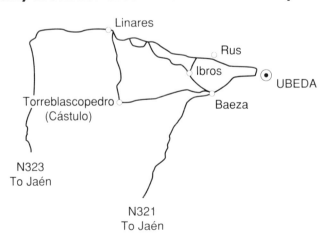

Iberian settlements and cave paintings, Castellón, Tarragona

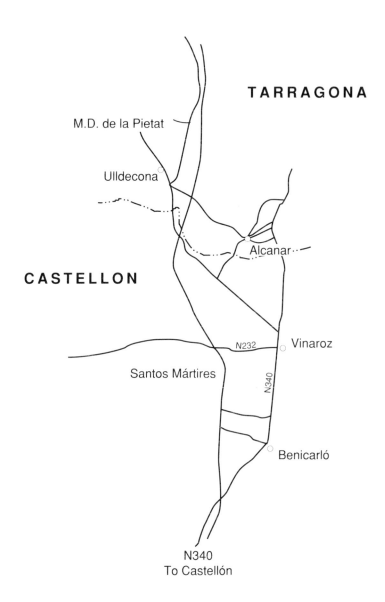

TARRAGONA

M.D. de la Pietat

Ulldecona

Alcanar

CASTELLON

N232   Vinaroz

Santos Mártires

N340

Benicarló

N340
To Castellón

Megaliths, Roman and Jewish remains, Gerona

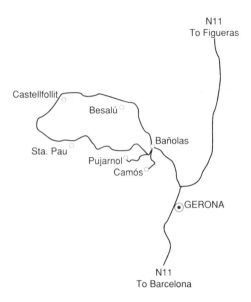

Phoenician and Roman remains, Málaga, Granada

Rock engravings, Pontevedra

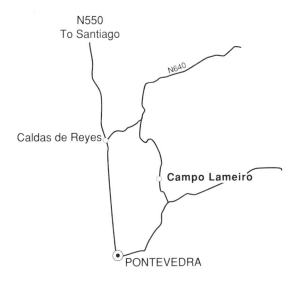

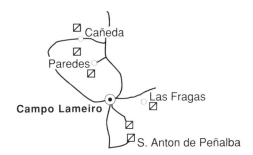

☑   Groups of rock engravings

Roman and Arabic remains, Cádiz

MALAGA

Estepona

CADIZ

Carteia

Algeciras

Gibraltar

Bolonia

N340

Tarifa

Roman and Arabic remains, Málaga

S. Pedro

Marbella

Estepona

N340

Río verde

Guadalina

Manilva

MALAGA

Puerta Duquesa

Marbella

Puente romano

Torreblanca

Fuengirola

N340

Roman, Arabic, Phoenician remains and cave paintings, Málaga

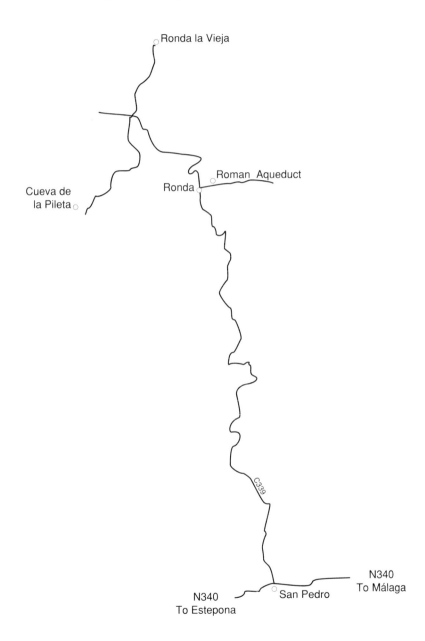

Ronda la Vieja

Roman Aqueduct

Ronda

Cueva de
la Pileta

C339

N340
To Málaga

San Pedro

N340
To Estepona

Roman and Visigothic remains, Guadalajara, Cuenca

Roman mausolea, Zaragoza

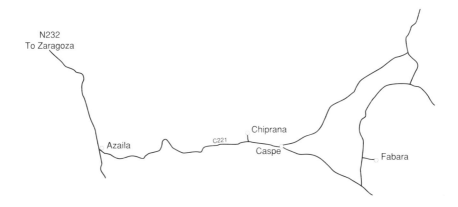

Roman villas with mosaics, Palencia

Rupestrian churches, Burgos, Palencia, Santander

SANTANDER

Las Presillas

Cadalso   Arroyuelas

S. Cristóbal

S. Martín
de Elines

Castrillo de
Valdelomar

Polientes

Sta. María
de Valverde

Olleros

N623
To Burgos

PALENCIA

N611
To Palencia

BURGOS

GLOSSARY

Useful terms for the traveller which may be found on highway signs designating historical places, or at the sites themselves labelling the different sections of interest. Information brochures acquired at tourist offices or at a given site may use terms given here to orient the visitor as to the various objects to see and their historical context. A few other miscellaneous terms are also given.

abrigo	rock shelter or grotto
acequias	irrigation channels (Arabic)
adobe	sun-dried brick
alcalde	mayor
alcazaba	Arabic fortified city
alcázar	Arabic castle or citadel
aljibe	Arabic cistern for rainwater
Almohade	North African Berber peoples
Almoravide	North African Berber peoples
amphora	ceramic receptacle, usually of large size
apodyterium	where clothing was placed before using the public baths in Roman times
arco de herradura	horseshoe arch
Arianism	Christian sect. Theological movement initiated by Arius that won strong support during the fourth century A.D. chiefly in the Eastern Churches
arroyo	small rivulet or spring
artesonado	wooden coffered ceiling
ashlar	hewn or squared stone
atalaya	watch tower
atrium	main living room of a Roman villa with an opening in the roof and usually a small fountain or pool below
Ayuntamiento (also **Casa Consistorial**)	town hall
azulejo	glazed tile
balneario	spa
baños	baths
barranco	ravine, dry river bed, gorge
barrio	suburb, quarter
basílica	Roman public building used as a meeting place for discussion (especially of economic and legal subjects). Became the architectural model for Late Roman Christian churches.

bodega	wine cellar
bóveda	vault
caldarium	hot room of Roman baths
calle	street, Catalán **carrer**
calzada romana	Roman road
cámara	chamber, room
campo	countryside, field
capilla	chapel
cantera	quarry
carretera	highway
carril	narrow road, farm track
cartuja	monastery of Carthusian monks
casco viejo or	
casco urbano	old section or centre of town
castillo	castle, Catalán **castell**
castro	camp, settlement
cavea	auditorium of a Roman theatre
cementario	cemetery
cerrado	closed, shut, Catalán **tancada**
cerro	hill
cippi	small pillars, often used as gravestones or landmarks
circumvallation	surrounded with a defensive fortification
ciudad	city, Catalán **ciutat**
claustrillas	small cloisters
claustro	cloister
claviform	shaped like a club
colegiata	collegiate church
columbarium	grave (Roman), usually built up above ground with niches for urns in the walls
columna	column
comarca	district, jurisdiction
conjunto	grouping, e.g., **conjunto arqueológico**, archaeological grouping
corbel	bracket of stone or brick
cortijo	farm (see also finca)
cryptoporticus	in Roman architecture a gallery, wholly or partially concealed with few openings, which served for private affairs
cuesta	slope or slight hill, ridge
cueva	cave, Catalán **cova**
dehesa	pasture or open land
desfiladero	gorge, defile
despoblado	uninhabited, depopulated
dolmen	Neolithic-Bronze Age burial site, consisting of megalithic stone slabs usually placed in upright position with capstone covering the top
double enceinte	double wall enclosing a defended area
edad	age, e.g., **Edad de Hierro**, Iron Age
embalse	reservoir, usually the backup water from a dam; see also **pantano**

epoca	epoch, era
ermita	hermitage, chapel
fachada	façade
ferrocarril	railway
finca	property (usually a farm in the countryside)
fons scenae	stage backdrop of a Roman theatre
forum	religious and civil centre of the Roman city
fossa	ditch, moat
frigidarium	cold baths
fuente	fountain, spring
funeraria	funerary
garganta	gorge; see also **hoz**
garum	kind of sauce made by the Romans with special liquids and fish parts
gitano	gypsy
grabado	engraved
hórreo	Celtic farm storehouse in Galicia or Asturias
hoz	gorge or defile
huerta	cultivated land
hypocaustum	heating system used by the Romans consisting of a space below the floor and or in the walls in which the hot steam could circulate
hypogeum	below ground section of an ancient building
iconostasis	partition on which icons are placed separating the sanctuary from the main part of the church
iglesia rupestre	church built in the rock
impluvium	pool to gather rain water, usually found in atrium of a Roman villa
in situ	at the same place, at the site
ithyphallic	sexually aroused male
judería	Jewish quarter, Catalán **call**, also Arabic **aljama**
labarum	military standard bearing a Christian monogram, used by Constantine the Great
lago	lake
lararium	the altar to domestic gods in a Roman villa.
Levantine	style of rock art
littoral	shore of a sea, lake or ocean
mamposteria	rubble masonry
mansion	stopping place
marisma	marsh
marmól	marble
masía	farm complex in Catalán
mausoleum	tomb
menhir	oblong stone placed in vertical position in ground
meseta	table land
mesón	inn
mezquita	mosque
microlith	small mesolithic flint tool
milliarium	stone marker indicating the distance of a mile

molino	mill
monasterio	monastery
monte	mountain
montilla	little hill, tell
morería	Moorish quarter
Morisco	Christianized Moor
Mozárabe	Christian under the Moors (used in reference to their architecture)
Mudéjar	Moslem under the Christians (used in reference to architecture)
Muladí	Christian converted to Islam
necrópolis	burial site
noria	water wheel (Arabic)
ogival	pointed arch or similar contour
oppidum	ancient fortified town
palaestra	public place for training of athletes
Paleo-	old, early
palloza	round, thatched house, said to date from Celtic times
pantano	reservoir
peña	large rock, or summit of hill
peristyle	a covered passageway around an open patio of a Roman villa.
pilastre	shallow, rectangular column attached to the face of a wall
pinturas rupestres	rock paintings
Plaza Mayor	main square of a town or village
poblado	settlement, village
posada	inn
pueblo	village, people
puente	bridge; Catalán **pont**
puerta	door, gate; Catalán **portal**
puig	hill (Catalán)
pulpitum	stage of a Roman theatre
puntiform	the form of dots often found in cave paintings
rambla	dry river bed
retablo	altar piece (usually sculpted, painted, carved)
ría	estuary (Galician)
río	river
romanica	Romanesque
romano	Roman
rúa	street (Galician)
rupestre	stone
salida	exit, way out
seo	cathedral; Catalán **seu**
Sephardim	Jews of Spain or Portugal
sierra	mountain range (or high hills)
sigillata	Roman ceramic pottery of reddish colour characterized by the sigillum or mark of the maker

stele	upright stone slab decorated with figures or inscriptions
tabernae	small Roman shops
tablinium	reception room or study in a Roman villa
taifa	small Moslem kingdom
taller arqueológico	archeological workshop
tapada	covered over (as in an archaeological excavation)
tectiform	abstract configurations in cave paintings assumed to represent dwellings
tepidarium	warm room in the Roman bath complex
termas	baths
tessera	small Celtic plaque of hospitality
tholoi	beehive shape (tombs)
torre	tower
tossal	hill (Catalán)
triclinium	eating area in a Roman villa (kitchen was often adjacent)
tumba	tomb
tumulus	mound covering tomb
vega	plain, meadow
verja	railing around a tomb
verraco	Celtic zoomorphical stone sculpture
villa	small town or Roman estate
vomitoria	exit or entrance of a Roman theatre behind top row of seats
yacimiento	archaeological site
zócalo	base, plinth

BIBLIOGRAPHY

Acosta Martínez, P. "Estado actual de la prehistoria andaluza: neolítico y calcolítico." *Habis* (1983).

Aguado Bleye, P. *Manual de historia de España.* Madrid (1971).

Aguillar, M. and Ian Robertson, ed. *Judía Guía.* Madrid (1986).

Allières, J. *Les Basques.* 2d ed. Presses Universitaires de France, Paris (1977).

Alonso i Tejada, A. *El conjunto rupestre de Solana de las covachas.* Nerpio Albacete. No. 6. (1980).

———— y Alex Mir i Llauradó. *El conjunt rupestre de la Vall de la Coma.* Barcelona (1986).

Almagro Basch, M. "El paleolítico español" in *Historia de España,* vol. I. R. Menéndez Pidal, ed. Madrid (1963), pp. 245–488.

———— et al. *Huelva, prehistoria y antigüedad.* Madrid (1975).

————. *Guía de Mérida.* Madrid (1983).

————. *Segóbriga, Museo Monográfico de Segóbriga* (1986).

Almagro Gorbea, M. *El bronze final y el período orientalizante en Extremadura.* Madrid (1975).

———— and Fernández-Miranda, M. eds. *C-14 y prehistoria de la península Ibérica.* Madrid (1978).

Altuna, J. et al. *Carta Arqueológica de Guipúzcoa.* San Sebastián (1982). (plus supplementary maps)

Américo Castro. *The Spaniards: an Introduction to their History.* Berkeley (1971).

Anderson, J. M. *Ancient Languages of the Hispanic Peninsula.* Lanham, Md. (1988).

Aparicio Perez, J. et al. *El primer arte valenciano II "el arte rupestre levantino."* Valencia (1982).

Argente Oliver, et al. *Diez años de arqueología Soriana (1978–1988).* Junta de Castilla y León (1989).

Arias Vilas, F. *Memorias de historia antigua.* Provincia de Oviedo (n.d.).

Arribas, A. *The Iberians.* London (1963).

Atrian Jordan, P. et al. *Carta arqueológica de España.* Teruel (1980).

Barandiarán, J. M. *El hombre prehistórico en el País Vasco.* Buenos Aires (1953).

Beltrán, A. *Rock Art of the Spanish Levant.* Trans. by M. Brown. Cambridge (1982).

Blagg, T.F.C. et al., eds. *Papers in Iberian Archaeology.* BAR International Series, Oxford 93 (i) (1984).

Blanco, A. *La ciudad antigua (de la prehistoria a los visigodos)*. Historia de Sevilla I. Sevilla (1979).
—— and J.M. Luzón. "Pre-Roman Silver Miners at Río Tinto" *Antiquity*. 43 (Oxford, 1970), pp. 124–32.
Blázquez, J. Ma. *Tartessos y los orígenes de la colonización fenicia en occidente*. Salamanca (1968)
——. "Orígines del cristianismo hispano" in *Historia de España*, vol. II. Madrid (1982), pp. 415–47.
Boardman, J. *The Greeks Overseas*. London (1980).
Bosch Gimpera, P. *El poblamiento antiguo y la formación de los pueblos de España*. Mexico (1944).
Breuil, H. *Peintures rupestres schématiques de la péninsule Ibérique I au nord du tage*. Paris (1933).
Broderick, A. H. *Paleolithic Painting*. London (1951).
Burckhardt, T. *Moorish Culture in Spain*. London (1972).
Burillo Mozota, F. et al. *Celtiberos*. Zaragoza (1988).
Cabello Janeiro, M. *Ubrique, encrucijada histórica*. Ubrique (1987).
Campo Lameiro. Guía de los itinerarios a los complejos inscultóricos rupestres. (1975).
Caro Baroja, J. *Los judíos en la España*. Madrid (1966).
——. *Los Vascos*. Madrid (1971).
Carpenter, R. *The Greeks in Spain*. Bryn Mawr (1925).
Castilla la Mancha historia, arte y etnología. (1985).
Cava, Ana "La industria lítica en los dólmenes del País Vasco meridional." *Veleia*, Vitoria (1984), pp. 51–146.
Cerillo Martín de Cáceres, E. *La basílica de epoca visigoda de Ibahernando*. Cáceres (1983).
César Morán, P. *Reseña histórico-artística de la provincia de Salamanca*. Salamanca (1946).
Chadwick, H. *Priscillian of Avila*. Oxford (1976).
Chadwick, N. *The Celts*. Harmondsworth (1981).
Childe, G. *The Prehistory of European Society*. Harmondsworth (1958).
Chevallier, R. *Roman Roads*. London (1976).
Clarke, G. A., ed. *Bronze and Iron Age Archaeology on the Meseta del Norte*. Arizona (1979)
——. *The Asturian of Cantabria*. Arizona (1983).
Collins, R. *Early Medieval Spain: Unity in Diversity, 400–1000*. London (1983).
Creswell, K. A. C. *Early Muslim Architecture*. Oxford (1969).
Dixon, P. *The Iberians of Spain*. Oxford (1940).
Enciclopedia Lingüística Hispánica. Madrid (1959).
Faust, M. "Die Kelten auf der Iberischen Halbinsel: Sprachliche Zeugnisse." *Madrider Mitteilungen* (1975).
Fernández Casado, C. *Acueductos romanos en España*. Madrid (1972).
——. *Historia del puente en España*. Madrid (1980).
Fernández Castro, Ma Cruz. *Las villas romanas en España*. Madrid (1982).
Fernández-Galiano, D. et al. *Arqueología en Castilla-La Mancha.*(n.d.).
——. *Complutum I Excavaciones, II Mosaicos*. Ministerio de Cultura, Madrid (1984).

Fernández Jurado, J. *La influencia fenicia en Huelva*. Aula Orientalis IV (1986).

Francisco Ondarra, P. *Nuevas monumentos megalíticos en Baztán y zonas colindantes*. Pamplona (1976).

———. "Los cromlechs y túmulos de la estación megalítica de Atxuri." *KOBIE* no. XV (1985–86).

Gallet de Santerre, H. *Ensérune, les silos de la terasse est*. Paris (1980).

García y Bellido, A. *Fenicios y Cartagineses en Occidente*. Madrid (1942).

———. *La arquitectura entre los Iberos*. Madrid (1945).

———. *Arte ibérico en España*. Madrid (1979).

———. Andalucía monumental, Itálica. Biblioteca de la Cultura Andaluza (1985).

García Moreno, L. *Historia de España visigoda, Ediciones Catedra*. Toledo (1989).

Garrido, J. P. y Orta, E. *Edad del Hierro: Huelva, prehistoria y antigüedad*. Madrid (1975).

Giner Sospedra, V. and V Meseguer Folch. *El poblado ibérico de "El Puig."* Benicarlo (1976).

Gomez-Moreno, M. *Iglesias mozárabes*. Madrid (1919), Barcelona (1945)

González Palencia, A. *Historia de la España musulmana*. Barcelona (1945)

Gorrochategui, J. y Ma. Jose Yarritu. *Carta arqueológica de Viscaya*. Deusto (1984).

Gran Enciclopedia de Andalucía. Tierras del Sur, Sevilla (1979).

Halperin, D. A. *The Ancient Synagogues of the Iberian Peninsula*. University of Florida Monographs, Social Sciences no. 38 (1969).

Harrison, R. J. *Spain at the Dawn of History*. London (l988).

———. *The Bell Beaker Cultures of Spain and Portugal*. Harvard (1977).

Herriaren, G. y L. Urratsak. *150 mil años de prehistoria Vasca*. Vitoria (1982).

Hubert, H. *Les celtes et l'expansion celtique*. Paris (1932, 1974).

James, E., ed. *Visigothic Spain*. Oxford (1980).

Jorda Cerda, F. et al.: "La cueva de Nerja." *Revista de Arqueología* no. 29, Madrid (1983).

Kaey, S. J. Roman Spain. Berkeley (1988).

Lauro, quaderns d'historia i societat. Liria (1984).

Lazaro Mengod, A. et al. *Materiales de la necrópolis Ibérica de Orleyl*. Castellón de la Plana (1981).

Leisner, G and V. *Die megalithgräber der Iberischen Halbinsel*. Berlin (1956).

Lévi-Provençal, E. *Histoire de l'Espagne musulmane* (3 vols.). Rev. ed. Paris (1953).

Lopez Plaza, S. *Aspectos arquitectónicos de los sepulcros megalíticos de las provincias de Salamanca y Zamora*. Salamanca (1982).

MacKendrick, P. *The Iberian Stones Speak*. New York (1967).

Maluquer de Motes, J. *Epigrafía prelatina de la península Ibérica*. (1968).

———. *Tartessos*. Barcelona (1970).

———. "Pueblos Celtas," in *Historia de España*, I. R. Menendez Pidal, ed. Madrid (1954).

Mañanes, T. *Arqueología Vallisoletana II*. Simancas (1983).
———— et al. *El mosaico de la villa romana de Santa Cruz*. Cabezón de la Pisuerga, Valladolid (1987).
Marcais, G. *L'Architecture musulmane d'occident*. Paris (1974).
Martín Ortega, M. A. *Ullastret: Guide to the Excavations and Museum*. Gerona (1980).
Mélida, J. *Monumentos romanos en España*. Madrid (1925).
Menéndez Pidal, R. *Historia de España*. Vol I. 2, *España protohistórica*, 2d ed. Madrid (1960); Vol I. 3, *España preromana*, 1st ed. Madrid (1954).
Mingarro, F. et al. *La Villa romana de Campo de Villavidel (León)*. Univ. Complutense de Madrid/Univ. de León (1986).
Minguez, C. and J. P. *Las cuevas de Puenteviesgo*. Madrid (1980).
Montenegro Duque, A. *Historia de España, Edad Antigua*. Madrid (1972).
Museo de Avila: Documentación gráfica. (1989).
Museo Numantino. *Diez años de arqueología Soriana*. (1989).
Narbaitz, P. *Le matin basque ou Histoire ancienne du peuple vascon*. Paris (1975).
Navarra, R. *The Durable Kingdom*. Reno (1982).
Neuman, A. *The Jews in Spain*. New York (1942).
Nicolini, G. *The Ancient Spaniards*. Trans. by Jean Stewart. Farnborough (1974).
Obermmaier, H. *El dolmen de Soto. (Trigueros, Huelva)*. Madrid (1924).
————. *Fossil Man in Spain*. New Haven (1924).
Oliva Prat, M. *Excavaciones arqueológicas en la ciudad ibérica de Ullastret (Gerona)*, vol. XIV. (1960).
Otero Pedrayo, R. *Guía de Galicia*. Vigo (1980).
Palol, P. de. *Arqueología cristiana de la España romana*. Siglos IV–VI. Madrid-Valladolid (1967).
———— and F. Wattenberg. *Carta arqueológica de España*. Valladolid (1974).
Pellicer, M. "Observaciones sobre el estado actual de la prehistoria hispaña," *Habis*, Sevilla (1981).
Percival, J. *The Roman Villa: An Historical Introduction*. London (1976).
Pericot García, L. *Los Sepulcros megalíticos catalanes y la cultura pirinaica*. Barcelona (1958).
————. *L'espagne avant la conquète romaine*. Paris (1952).
————. *El paleolítico y epipaleolítico en España*. Madrid (1954).
————. *La céramique Ibérique*. Paris (1980).
Phillips, P. *The Prehistory of Europe*. London (1980).
Piggott, S. *Ancient Europe from the beginnings of Agriculture to Classical Antiquity*. New York (1979).
Pilar Acosta. *La pintura rupestre esquemática en España*. Salamanca (1968).
Ponisch, M. y Tarradell, M. *Garum et industries antiques de salaison dans la Méditerranée occidentale*. Paris (1965).
Pulpillo Ruiz, A. J. *Historiografía de Rus y su entorno*. Córdoba (1989).
Read, J. *The Moors in Spain and Portugal*. London (1974).
Ripoll Perelló. *Ampurias*. Barcelona y Gerona (1976).
Robertson, I. ed. *Blue Guide to Spain*. 5th ed., A. and C. Black, London (1989).
Rollan Ortiz, J.F. *Iglesias Mozárabes Leonesas*. León (n.d.).

Sachar, A. L. *A History of the Jews.* New York (1960).

Savory, H. *Spain and Portugal: the prehistory of the Iberian Peninsula.* New York (1968).

Schlunk, H. and T. Hauschild. *Hispania antigua.* Mainz am Rhein (1978).

Service, A. and J. Bradbery. *A Guide to the Megaliths of Europe.* London (1981).

Sieveking, A. and G. *The Caves of France and Northern Spain: a guide.* London (1962).

Sturzebecker, R. L. *Athletic-Cultural Archaeological Sites in the Greco-Roman World.* Havertown, Pa. (1985).

Sutherland, C. *The Romans in Spain: 217 B.C.–A.D. 117.* London (1939).

Taracena, B. *Carta arqueológica de España: Soria.* Madrid (1941).

Tarradell, M. "Problemas del Neolítico." *Actas del 1 Symposium de Prehistoria de la Península Ibérica.* Pamplona (1960).

Thompson, E. *The Goths in Spain.* Oxford (1969).

Tovar, A. *The Ancient Languages of Spain and Portugal.* New York (1961).

Trump, D. H. *The Prehistory of the Mediterranean.* London (1980).

Tuñon de Lara, M. et al. *Historia de España I, II.* Barcelona (1980, 1984).

Untermann. J. *Monumenta Linguarium Hispanicarum,* vols 1 and 2. Wiesbaden (1975).

Van Doren Stern, P. *Prehistoric Europe from Stone Age Man to the Early Greeks.* New York (1969).

Veleia. Instituto de Ciencias de la Antigüedad, N.S. 1. Vitoria (1984).

Vicens Vives, J. *Approaches to the History of Spain.* Trans. by Joan Connelly Ullman. 2d ed. California (1970).

Watt, W. M. *A History of Islamic Spain.* Edinburgh (1967).

Wiseman, F. J. *Roman Spain.* London (1956)

Yuste Rosell, N. y F. Romero Giménez. *El mediterráneo España Almería.* Almería (1975).

INDEX OF TOWNS
AND VILLAGES

Adra 65
Ager 233
Agoncillo 302
Agramunt 233
Agreda 204
Aguilafuente 201
Aguilar de Anguita 163
Aguilar de Campóo 195
Aguilar de la Frontera 74
Alacón 125
Alamos, Los 95
Alange 240
Alba de Tormes 196
Albacete 154
Albaida 325
Albaladejo 155
Albalat 319
Albalete de las Noguera 158
Albarracín 118
Alberca, La 197
Albesa 233
Albiztur 296
Albocácer 313
Albolodúy 60
Albuquerque 244
Alcaine 125
Alcalá de Guadaira 105
Alcalá de Henares 270
Alcalá de los Gazules 66
Alcalá del Río 110
Alcalá la Real 85
Alcanadre 302
Alcanar 234
Alcañiz 119
Alcántara 245
Alcantarilla 274
Alcaracejos 70
Alcaraz 154

Alcaudete 94
Alcaudete de la Jara 172
Alcázar de San Juan 155
Alcázares, Los 277
Alcolea de las Peñas 166
Alcoleo del Río 105
Alconchal de la Estrella 158
Alcora 318
Alcoy 308
Alcudía, L' 319
Alcudía de Elche 309
Alcuneza 166
Aldealpozo 209
Aldeanueva del Camino 245
Aldeaquemada 85
Aldeavieja de Tormes 201
Alfajarín 130
Alfaro 302
Algeciras 70
Algezares 277
Alhama de Aragón 130
Alhama de Granada 75
Alhama de Murcia 277
Alhambra 155
Alicante 309
Allariz 260
Alloza 120
Almadén 157
Almagro 157
Almansa 154
Almarza 209
Almenar 233
Almenara 313
Almenara de Adaja 210
Almería 60
Almodóvar del Campo 155
Almodóvar del Río 74
Almohaja 125

Almonaster la Real 84
Almuñécar 75
Almunia de Doña Godina, La .. 130
Alora 104
Alpera 150
Alquézar 117
Altafulla 238
Altxerri 296
Ambrona 204
Anda-Catadiano 289
Andoain 298
Andorra 125
Andújar 94
Añes 295
Antas 61
Antas de Ulla 260
Antequera 95
Aracena 84
Araya 295
Arbolí 238
Arcaya 289
Arce 142
Archena 277
Archidona 104
Arcos de la Frontera 70
Arcos de las Salinas 125
Ardales 96
Arenillas de San Pelayo 196
Arenys del Mar 216
Ares de Maestre 313
Arévalo 181
Argamasilla de Alba 158
Arguedas 284
Arisgotas 172
Aroche 84
Arredondo 142
Arrizala 289
Arroyuelos 143
Artejona 280
Assa 290
Astorga 189
Atapuerca 182
Atarfe 76
Ateca 130
Atienza 166
Avellaneda 300
Avila 177
Ayamonte 84
Ayna 154

Ayora 319
Azaila 120
Aznalcázar 110
Azután 168
Badajoz 240
Badalona 217
Baena 71
Baeza 85
Balaguer 233
Balmaseda 300
Balouta 192
Bande 260
Bañeres 312
Bañolas 224
Baños de Cerrato 193
Baños de Fitero 284
Baños de la Encina 86
Baños de Mogas 264
Baños de Montemayor 246
Baños de Valdearados 182
Barcelona 217
Barchín del Hoya 162
Barranquete, El 61
Barros 143
Batea 238
Baza 77
Bechi 314
Bedmar 94
Begonte 260
Béjar 197
Belmez 74
Belmez de la Moraleda 94
Belvis de la Jara 172
Bembibre 192
Benadalid 104
Benalup de Sidonia 66
Benaoján 97
Benasal 314
Benavente 212
Benavites 325
Benicarló 314
Benidorm 310
Benifaio 325
Berja 65
Berlanga de Duero 204
Bernúy-Salinero 177
Besalú 224
Betanzos 255
Bétera 325

Bezas 121
Biar 312
Bicorp 319
Bochones 163
Boecillo 212
Bohonal de Ibor 249
Bollullos de la Mitación 110
Boñar 192
Bonete 150
Boriol 315
Bornos 67
Botorrita 126
Bóveda 256
Bugarra 325
Bujalance 71
Buñol 325
Burgo de Osma, El 205
Burgohonda 181
Burgos 188
Burguillos de Cerro 241
Busta, La 143
Cabanes 315
Cabezón de Pisuerga 210
Cabra 71
Cabra del Santo Cristo 94
Cabrera de Mar 218
Cáceres 246
Cadalso 144
Cádiz 67
Calaceite 121
Calaf 234
Calahorra 302
Calamocha 125
Calatayud 126
Calatorao 130
Caldas de Malavella 225
Caldas de Montbuy 218
Calera, La 148
Calomarde 122
Calpe 310
Cambil 94
Caminreal 125
Campello, El 310
Campillo 213
Campillo de Arenas 94
Campo de Villavidel 193
Campo Lameiro 264
Camprodón 229
Cañaveral 249

Cañaveruelas 159
Candaira 260
Candeleda 177
Cañete 159
Cangas de Onis 132
Carabias 167
Caracena 209
Caravaca de la Cruz 274
Cardeñosa 178
Carmona 106
Carpio 74
Carranque 168
Carranza 298
Carrión de la Calatrava 158
Cartagena 275
Cártama 104
Casalgordo 169
Casarabonela 104
Casares 104
Casas de Reina 241
Caseres 238
Caserio la Sarga 311
Casinos 320
Caspe 127
Castell de Ferro 80
Castellar de la Frontera 70
Castellar de Santisteban 87
Castellar, El 160
Castelldefels 219
Castellfollit de la Roca 229
Castelnovo 318
Castillo de Bayuela 172
Castilnovo 202
Castrocalbón 189
Castro del Río 71
Castrojeriz 182
Castroverde 260
Caudete de los Fuentes 320
Cazorla 94
Ceal 87
Cebreiro 256
Celanova 261
Cervera del Río Alhama 303
Chamartín de la Sierra 178
Chantada 257
Chelva 321
Chillón 158
Chinchilla de Monte Aragón ... 154
Chiprana 127

Chiva 325
Ciempozuelos 271
Cieza 275
Cihuri 305
Cintruénigo 280
Cirauqui 280
Ciudad Real 156
Ciudad Rodrigo 197
Clares 166
Coaña 133
Coca 203
Cogul 230
Cogulludo 166
Coin 104
Collbató 223
Coll de Nargo 234
Colungo 115
Comares 104
Compludo 189
Conil de la Frontera 70
Constantí 235
Constantina 111
Consuegra 169
Contrasta 295
Coral de Amaguer 172
Córdoba 72
Coria 247
Coria del Río 110
Corro 290
Cortegana 84
Cortes de la Frontera 104
Cortes de Navarra 281
Cortézubi 299
Coruña, La 253
Cotobad 267
Covarrubias 183
Cretas 122
Cripán 290
Cuellar 203
Cuevas de Almanzora 62
Cuevas de Soria 205
Cuntis 267
Dalias 62
Damiel 156
Dehesa, La 84
Denia 312
Diego Alvaro 181
Domeño 325
Dos Aguas 321

Duratón 202
Ecija 107
Eguilaz 291
Eirás 263
Elda 312
Elorrio 299
Elvillar 291
Embid 167
Encinasola 84
Erretola 300
Erustes 172
Escala,La 226
Escaló 233
Esgos 261
Espejo 74
Espinosa de Henares 163
Estany, L' 223
Estella 284
Estepa 111
Estepona 97
Estrella, La 173
Fabara 127
Faido 183
Fazouro 257
Felix 238
Fermoselle 213
Ferrols, El 255
Fonsagrada 260
Fontcaldes 235
Fortuna 275
Forua 300
Foz 257
Fraga 115
Francelos 262
Frías 183
Frías de Albarracín 123
Frómista 193
Fuencaliente 157
Fuendetodos 130
Fuengirola 98
Fuensaúco 209
Fuensaviñán 167
Fuente de Cantos 244
Fuenteguinaldo 198
Fuenteobejuna 74
Gabia la Grande 77
Gádor 63
Galera 77
Galisteo 249

Gandia 325
Gandul 108
Garray 209
Garriga, La 219
Gaucín 104
Gayangos 144
Gerona 226
Gibraleón 84
Gibraltar 111
Gijón 133
Gobiendes 133
Gor 77
Gormaz 206
Granada 78
Granátula de Calatrava 157
Grove, El 265
Guadalajara 164
Guadamar del Segura 312
Guadix 80
Guarda, La 265
Guardia de Jaén 88
Guernica 299
Guijosa 167
Guillena 110
Gumiel de Hizán 188
Hellín 151
Herguijuela 201
Hernani 298
Herrencias, Las 169
Herrera 108
Herrerías, Las 63
Hervás 248
Hijar 125
Hinojosa de Jarque 123
Hoya-Gonzalo 152
Huesca 116
Huéscar 80
Huete 160
Humanes 167
Ibahernando 249
Ibros 88
Ilarduy 295
Illescas 169
Illora 80
Infiesto 140
Irún 297
Isona 234
Isso 152
Iznáhar 74

Iznalloz 78
Iznatoraf 94
Jabalquinto 94
Jaca 117
Jaén 88
Játiva 321
Javea 311
Jerez de los Caballeros 242
Jérica 318
Jimena 89
Jimena de la Frontera 70
Jodar 94
Jonquera, La 226
Jumilla 276
Juslibol 130
Juzbado 201
Labastida 292
Laborcillas 80
Lago 134
Laguardia 293
Lanchar 80
Landete 162
Langa de Duero 209
Lanjarón 80
Laño 184
Lara de los Infantes 184
Laxe 254
Layana 127
Layaza 294
Layos 173
Lebeña 144
Lécera 130
Ledesma 198
Lena 134
Lences 184
León 189
Lérida 231
Lesaca 281
Leyre 282
Liédena 282
Linares 89
Liria 321
Llanera 234
Llanes 134
Lloret de Mar 226
Loarre 116
Logroño 305
Loja 80
Lora del Río 111

Lorca 277
Lorenzana 258
Luco de Jiloca 125
Lugo 258
Lumbrales 198
Lupión 94
Luzaga 164
Macedo 262
Madrona 203
Málaga 98
Malagón 158
Malpica del Tajo 170
Manilva 99
Manresa 219
Marbella 100
Marchena 111
Margalef 234
Marquínez 294
Martorell 220
Martos 90
Mataró 220
Mazaleón 123
Mazarete 164
Mazote 211
Medellín 242
Medinaceli 207
Medina de los Torres 244
Medina Sidonia 68
Medinilla 179
Medulas, Las 190
Mellanzos 190
Melque 170
Membrilla 158
Meñaca 300
Mendigorria 282
Menjíbar 90
Mequinenza 130
Mérida 242
Mijas 104
Milagro 285
Millares 325
Miravete 238
Moclín 80
Mogente 323
Mogor 266
Moià 223
Mojácar 63
Molar, El 238
Molinilla 294

Monachil 78
Mondariz 266
Monforte del Cid 312
Monóvar 312
Monreal de Ariza 128
Monteagudo 276
Montefrío 78
Montefurado 259
Montejo de Tiermes 210
Montemayor del Río 201
Montemolín 244
Moraña 267
Moratalla 277
Morella 315
Morera de Montsant 238
Morón de la Frontera 111
Motilla de Santa María
   del Retamar 158
Muel 130
Muiños 262
Mula 276
Munera 153
Mura 223
Muriel 165
Nájera 305
Navalmoralejo 170
Navas de la Concepcíon, Las ... 111
Nerja 100
Nerpio 153
Niebla 82
Niharra 181
Noain 285
Noalejo 94
Noia 253
Novales 145
Nules 316
Obarra 117
Obejo 74
Oix 229
Ojos Albos 179
Olérdola 220
Oliete 123
Olite 285
Olleros de Pisuerga 194
Olmos, Los 125
Oña 188
Ondárroa 300
Orce 79
Orense 263

Orgaz 173
Orihuela 312
Ossa de Montiel 154
Osuna 109
Oviedo 135
Palafrugell 229
Palamós 229
Palazuelos 167
Palencia 194
Pamplona 283
Panes 137
Pantón 260
Peal de Becerro 90
Pechina 64
Peciña 303
Pedraza 204
Pedret 223
Pedro 208
Pedroche 74
Pelegrina 167
Peñaflor 140
Peñalba 191
Penches 185
Perelló 235
Pereña 201
Petín 264
Petrel 312
Pieros 191
Pimiango 137
Piñar 80
Pinedo 294
Pinell de Brai 238
Pinos Puente 79
Piornedo 259
Plasencia 249
Pobla Tornesa 318
Pola de Allande 137
Pola de Siero 140
Ponferrada 191
Pontecesures 267
Pontevedra 266
Pontós 227
Porcuna 91
Pozuelo 83
Prádena 202
Prado 267
Prados Redondos 167
Pravia 138
Presillas de Bricia, Las 148

Priesca 138
Puebla de Benifasar 316
Puebla de Sanabria 213
Puentelarrá 185
Puente Viesgo 145
Puerta Duquesa 100
Puerto de Fuenfría 271
Puerto de Mazarrón 277
Puerto de Santa María 68
Puerto del Pico 179
Puerto Lumbreras 278
Puig Rodó 223
Purullena 80
Quesada 91
Quintanar de la Sierra 185
Quintanilla de la Cueza 194
Quintanilla de las Viñas 186
Quiroga 259
Ramales de la Victoria 146
Ramallosa 267
Readegos 264
Redal, El 304
Retortillo 146
Riba de Saelices 165
Ribadavia 264
Ribadesella 138
Ribeira 254
Rincón de la Victoria 100
Ripoll 229
Roda de Ter 221
Rojals 238
Ronda 101
Rosas 227
Rótova 325
Rueda de Jalón 130
Ruesta 117
Rute 74
Sabinar, El 277
Sabiote 92
Sádaba 128
Saelices 160
Sagunto 323
Salamanca 199
Salcedo 295
Saldaña 195
Saldeana 199
Sallent 223
Sallent de Gallego 117
Salobreña 80

San Bartolomé de la Torre 83
San Cugat del Valles 221
San Esteban de Gormaz 209
San Feliu de Guixoles 229
San Fernando 70
San Juan de la Nava 181
San Julia de Ramis 229
San Julián de Valmuza 200
San Just Desvern 218
San Martí d'Empúries 225
San Martín de Pusa 173
San Martín de Valdeiglesias 181
San Millán de la Cogolla 304
San Pedro de Alcántara 101
San Pedro de Latarce 211
San Pedro de Mérida 244
San Pere de Ribes 223
San Roman 139
San Roman de San Millán 295
Sanchorreja 181
Sanlúcar la Mayor 111
Sant Aniol 229
Sant Jaume dels Domenys 238
Sant Vicenç de Horta 218
Santa Coloma de Gramanet 221
Santa Cruz 73
Santa Cruz de la Serós 116
Santa Cruz de la Zarza 173
Santa María de Trassierra 74
Santa María de Valverde 195
Santa María del Hito 148
Santa Olalla del Cala 111
Santa Pau 227
Santa Pola 312
Santacara 285
Santiago de Compostela 255
Santibáñez del Val 187
Santillana del Mar 146
Santiponce 109
Santo Domingo de Silos 187
Santos de Maimona, Los 244
Sardanyola del Valles 218
Sarroca 234
Sasamón 187
Sastarrain 297
Segorbe 318
Segovia 202
Seriña 228
Serós 231

Sésamo 192
Segura de la Sierra 94
Segura de Toro 248
Setefilla 109
Sevilla 109
Siero 188
Sigüenza 167
Simancas 212
Sofuentes 129
Solosancho 180
Solsona 232
Sopuerta 300
Sorbas 65
Soria 209
Sorpe 233
Soses 232
Sotiel Coronada 84
Soto de Medinilla 212
Suano 147
Tabernas 64
Talamanca de la Jarama 270
Talavera de la Reina 171
Tarifa 69
Tarragona 236
Tarriba 147
Terrassa 222
Terrer 130
Teruel 124
Tharsis 84
Tiana 223
Tiemblo, El 180
Tirig 316
Tivissa 237
Toledo 171
Toques 254
Tordesillas 212
Tordoia 255
Tordómar 188
Tormón 124
Torralba 205
Torre de l'Espanyol, La 238
Torre del Mar 102
Torreperogil 94
Torresaviñán 167
Toro 213
Toro, El 318
Torrox, Costa 103
Tortosa 237
Tosantos 188

Tossa de Mar 228
Tournabous 232
Tremp 234
Trillos 167
Trives 263
Trubia 140
Trujillo 248
Tudela 283
Tuñón 139
Turis 325
Ubeda 92
Ubrique 69
Ucero 210
Ullastret 229
Ulldecona 237
Unarre 233
Urnieta 297
Utrera 111
Valdediós 139
Valdelateja 188
Valdetorres de Jarama 271
Valencia 324
Valencia de Alcántara 249
Valencia de la Concepción 110
Valeria 161
Vall d'Uxó 317
Vallgorguina 222
Valtierra 284
Valles 147
Vandellos 238
Vegas de San Antonio, Las 172
Vejer de la Frontera 70
Vélez Blanco 64
Vélez de Benaudalla 80
Vélez Málaga 104
Velilla de Ebro 129
Venta de Baños 196
Ventosillo 203
Verín 263
Vich 222
Viella 234
Vigo 267
Vila Real 318
Viladonga 259
Vilanova de Sau 223
Vilarblareix 230
Vilarrodona 238

Vilches 94
Villa del Río 74
Villacadima 165
Villajoyosa 311
Villalba del Alcor 84
Villamayor 201
Villamoros de las Regueras 193
Villanueva de Algaidas 103
Villanueva de Santo Adriano .. 140
Villanueva del Río y Minas 110
Villanueva y Geltrú 223
Villar del Humo 161
Villaricos 65
Villas Viejas 162
Villasabariego 192
Villaseco 200
Villastar 124
Villaverde Bajo 271
Villena 312
Vimianzo 255
Vinaroz 317
Vinebre 238
Viñon 140
Vitigudino 201
Vivir 318
Wamba 211
Xermade 260
Yátova 325
Yecla 277
Yecla de Yeltes 200
Yeles 173
Yuncos 173
Yunta 167
Zafra 244
Zafrón 201
Zahara de la Sierra 104
Zalamea de la Serena 244
Zalamea la Real 84
Zalla 300
Zamora 213
Zaragoza 129
Zarátamo 300
Zorita de los Canes 166
Zubiri 284
Zuheros 74

7-1592